The
Climbing Essays

Praise for *The Villain*

Ultimately rather poignant. *Scotland on Sunday*

Wonderfully crafted ... One of the most gifted chroniclers of mountaineering ... Perrin records it all with a subtle sympathy, laying bare British mountaineering's most mythologized figure.
The Independent

An extraordinarily rich and unsentimental vision ... The genius of this exceptional biography is that it articulates both sides of Whillans' characer ... It is by turns funny and tragic ... This is a fine book. It was worth the wait. *Climb*

Compelling, beautifully written ... There could not have been a better writer qualified to tell it. Ed Douglas, *Climber*

A kind of modern tragedy ... Yet for all his failings, Whillans remains a legend. *Observer*

A packed and entertaining book. All the anecdotes are there ... These stories are described with the drollness, skill and attention to detail we expect from Perrin, who shines through his own text – acute, sly, human and affable – as concerned as ever that we view climbing as the morally complex metonym of our humanity ... Exhaustively researched and beautifully written. *The Guardian*

Travels with The Flea:

The pre-eminent writer on the British landscape.

Peter Beaumont, *Observer*

Jim Perrin is an alchemist. He takes the base metal of his own experience and, in retorts fuelled by the power of his observation and skill with language, transmutes it into prose that coruscates with spirit and meaning.

Jamie Jauncey, *Scotsman*

Perrin writes the kind of evocative, elegant prose, lyrical but not fussy, clear but not simple, that anyone who has ever aspired to write ... will look at in despair, knowing they will never be half as good ... A refreshing spring from which to drink.

Robert Dawson Scott, *Glasgow Herald*

The spirit of [William Hazlitt], along with a measure of his writing skills is alive and well in Jim Perrin.

Gavin Bell, *Daily Telegraph*

Praise for Jim Perrin's writing:

In the last hundred and twenty years, from the age of Whymper, mountaineering has attracted a unique array of writing talent. Of all those writers, famous, infamous and unknown, Jim Perrin is by far the best.

Climber

A remarkable writer ... a sort of rucksack Thoreau ... some of the finest travel writing ever.

Jan Morris, *Guardian*

He gets his joy, and expresses it like a poet, from solitude and nature.

Observer

On and Off the Rocks
These essays are as fine as anything that has been written about climbing. *Geographical Magazine*

A beautiful and important book ... powerfully convincing ... a triumph ... brilliant ... gives the extra dimension of a language richer, more generous and prolific than any other climber can produce. *Mountain*

A collection of moral essays in the tradition of Johnson and Hazlitt. This highly articulate and lyrical writer combines great powers of description and a deep, perceptive vision with a strong, quirky sense of humour. *Western Mail*

The range, quality and humane breadth of the book, with its beautifully integrated photographs, amount to a literary achievement ... as strong in its impassioned polemic ... and its pleas for conservation as in its memoirs of climbing rock. *Guardian*

Spirits of Place and Visions of Snowdonia
No-one else in contemporary Wales is capable of writing prose of this exceptional quality ... he deserves to be recognised as the most singular, and the most outstanding prose-writer of present-day Wales. Professor M Wynn Thomas in *New Welsh Review*

Yes, To Dance
Delight in the range of his prose and ideas if they suit you. Struggle with them if they infuriate you. Don't ignore them. They come from the best mountain writer we have left. *Climbers' Club Journal*

Menlove
The star of English climbing writing today ... writing as powerful as any I have ever read, light years ahead of the bulk of climbing literature. *Rock & Ice*

An exceptionally wise biography. *London Review of Books*

Perrin has greatly raised the status of mountain literature. *Climbing*

The
Climbing Essays

The In Pinn is an imprint of
Neil Wilson Publishing Ltd
The Pentagon Centre
Washington Street
GLASGOW
G3 8AZ

Tel: 0141-221-1117
Fax: 0141-221-5363

E-mail: info@nwp.co.uk
www.nwp.co.uk

A catalogue record for this book
is available from the British Library.
ISBN 1-903238-47-1
Typeset in Aldine

The minute I heard my first love story
I started looking for you, not knowing
how blind that was.

Lovers don't finally meet somewhere.
They're in each other all along.

Rumi

My dear, my dearest dust, I come, I come.

Lady Catherine Dyer

In his youth Jim Perrin was one of the most notable British rock-climbers, 'the best rock-climber in the world for about six weeks in the summer of 1972', according to *Observer* editor Roger Alton. Since those days Jim has committed his time and energy to the craft of mountain writing and has taken it to new heights.

His first book, Menlove (1985), was the first outright winner of the prestigious Boardman Tasker Award for mountain literature, which his most recent book, *The Villain* (2005), also won, along with the U.I.A.A. Mountaineering History Award at the Banff Mountain Book Festival 2005. As well as these, he has written four collections of essays, a best-selling book on Snowdonia, *Visions of Snowdonia* (1997), and *River Map* (2001), an essay on love and landscape.

Jim Perrin contributes regular travel essays to the *Daily Telegraph*, is the *Guardian*'s Country Diarist for Wales, and writes monthly columns in *The Great Outdoors* and *Climber* magazines.

CONTENTS

INTRODUCTION

Put an ear to this book, and what will you hear? You will hear the soft rasp of a chalked hand on a gritstone hold. You will hear the cow-bell clink of hex on granite. You will hear the skirl of wind over drifted snow. You will hear the cry of a falling man, and the silence in the seconds after his death. You will hear the chatter in the Llanberis Heights on a Saturday night. You will hear the jubilant shout of a climber mantling over the top of a big route, and into rich, quiet, sunset light. You will hear a Himalayan ice-fall noisily rearranging itself. You will hear voices raised in funeral song.

You will hear, that is, all the mingled joy and tragedy and action and beauty of a climbing life lived to the uttermost: a life lived as fully on the lateral as on the vertical. 'Contact! Contact!' wrote Henry David Thoreau after his climb of Mount Ktaadn in 1846, and Thoreau's imperative might stand as Jim's motto – if Jim could tolerate something so officious as a motto. For contact of every sort is everywhere in this extraordinary book. It is the memoir of a man in love with touch.

Nearly 40 years' worth of Jim's essays are collected here. But do not mistake this for a ragbag or *omnium gatherum*. For these essays are bound together by many things: by their energy, by the images which recur in them, by their openness to beauty. They are all, too, about 'weathering', in both senses of that word. 'Weathering' in terms of how the forces to which we are exposed shape us. And 'weathering' as endurance: as getting through the difficult times.

To read across all the essays here is to learn three stories. There is Jim's own story: his move from the slums of Manchester, out to the moors of the Pennines, and from there to the quarries, crags and peaks of Britain and the world. Certain scenes flash out. Jim sleeping in the sandy caves of Stanage Edge, so as to be on the rock as soon as light strikes it the next morning. Jim, jittery, wired on cocaine, soloing *Coronation Street* in Cheddar Gorge. Jim whooping for joy in The Cauldron, with the green sea echoing beneath him.

There is the story, too, of Jim's writing. His prose style has changed with his climbing style: from what he calls – speaking of his rock-work – 'a wild and prehensile freedom of attack', to a 'coolness and control'. The enormous tonal range of Jim is to be found here, a range gained in part from the writers he has studied and loved: Hazlitt, Johnson, and Menlove Edwards among them. Listen again now – listen to this:

And I, I wanted the heights and the naked edges and the steep plunge of rib and groove, the splintered rock, wind-whistled and myself upon it. So up I went on that shattered hillside in company with a certain fear. It was so beautiful, I was lost. There were pinnacles and great drops; there were moves to be made and lakes far below, mauve horizons and I was unutterably alone; and the mountain did not shake me off, for I am not hubristic.

How far we are here from the usual workaday prose of the outdoor journalist. How strongly the rhythms of the Old Testament beat through those lines – in those repetitions, those inversions – imparting a proper sense of ritual and ancientness to this act of ascent. How precisely placed, in the still centre of the paragraph, is that extraordinary sentence – 'It was so beautiful, I was lost' – with its careful refusal to ascribe cause: the beauty does not make the lostness, or vice-versa, but rather both states exist within and around one another. And how precisely arranged is the topography of that final sentence, with the 'lakes far below', the 'mauve horizons' stretching out, such that the figure of the climber seems to exist in another world altogether, an apart-world or beyond-world of wildness. To read such a paragraph is to find one proof among many of Jim's brilliance as a stylist, his awareness of how revelation can be as much a function of syntax as of event.

And finally, there is the story of British climbing over the past four decades, and more. For Jim has known them all: Longland and Murray, Tilman and Shipton, Whillans and Bonington, Dawes and Fawcett – all 'the sport's great regulators and mediators.' He has moved through this fractious, egotistical world of climbing, and what has distinguished him perhaps above all is his immense lack of ego. 'I am not hubristic,' Jim writes, and if anyone else wrote this we would not believe them, for to deny one's egotism is usually to demonstrate one's egotism. But with Jim it is true. To read the 'Climbers' section of this book is to know this, to witness his extraordinary generosity of spirit in action. Jim is ready always to dowse out the good in a person; to consider them from all angles, and so to see what is valuable in them, and to do this one must be willing to forget oneself.

Of the great climbing writers of the past, Jim is closest in temperament to WH Murray. Murray knew Jim, encouraged him, inspired him, and Murray, the old eagle, hovers over these pages. When Jim writes of Murray's 'impassioned wisdom, detachment, humility, and scrupulous self-honesty', he might as well be describing his own writerly qualities (though one cannot imagine Murray using the word 'fuck' with such obvious pleasure as Jim. On reflection, in fact, one cannot imagine Murray using the word 'fuck' at all.)

What both Murray and Jim share is a belief in climbing as an almost mystical experience, one through which the outer landscape comes – in ways which are impossible to articulate, but unmistakable to experience – to shape the inner. What both look at rather askance (though Murray saw less of it than Jim) is climbing as gymnastics; a purified exercise in dynamics and musculature, which might be expressed as an equation. For both men, the 'star systems' that really matter are not those in the guidebook, but the constellations beneath which climbing takes place. Jim, like Murray, climbs for joy. 'Good! Know that! Kiss the joy as it flies ... ' he writes – and that's Jim, there, in a phrase: transient, aerial, passionate. 'Kiss the joy as it flies!'

Joy, above all, is Jim's lodestar. In 'The Vision of Glory', the great essay which ends the 'Climbs' section, Jim describes going alone up Beinn a' Chaoruinn, the Hill of the Rowan, which arches above Loch Moy, on a winter day. The morning begins dully, but near the summit, suddenly 'the mist is scoured with speed from the face of the mountain' and he sees out over the surrounding peaks and corries, 'all glitter and coruscation, shapes of the Mamores beyond a phantasmal ivory gleam.' From this epiphany, the essay develops by way of Wordsworth and Simone Weil, into a meditation on the power of such visionary moments – 'the occasional goings-through into the white world, into the world of light' – to call out a goodness in us. 'Our essential life, the joy-life, is a sequence of these moments: how many of us could count even 60 such?' The deepening and lengthening of the joy-life: this, in Jim's secular theology, is the reward for those who climb.

The risk for those who climb, though, is death, and everywhere here there is 'blood on the rocks' as Jim puts it (Bobcat ever, grimly tipping his hat to Dylan). I have never read a book so full of life that is also so full of death. You will meet so many of them here, the dead. Killed by avalanche, by altitude sickness, by lightning strike, by broken holds, slipped belays. Primo Levi, the mountaineer who lived through the worst that the world has yet devised, only to leap, neck-breakingly, down a stairwell. Paul Williams dying at the foot of *Brown's Eliminate* on Froggatt Edge. Al Harris, with whom Jim jousted JCBs, drank, and fought, and who eventually 'crashed himself dead.' And then, finally, recently, Jim's own dear son Will, whose life and whose death is celebrated here. I say 'celebrated' and I mean it. For Jim does not regret things. It is, astonishingly, not in his nature. What occurs, occurs. 'It merely was so,' he writes more than once. So it is that, in this exceptional book, the two extremes of the world of climbing – death and joy – bend round and fuse into one another, becoming of the same bright alloy.

'We must love one another or die,' wrote WH Auden. Jim has it differently: 'We must love one another and die.' Both are imperatives. This is what Jim has learned, knows, tells us here: that we must love one another and die.

Robert Macfarlane

STREETS, OUTCROPS, SPACE

AUTOBIOGRAPHICAL SKETCHES

FRONT STEP

The flag doorstep of my grandparents' house is rough and granular to the touch; I feel it on the back of my knees as I sit there and look up and down the terraced street. My grandmother whitens it with a stone the rag-and-bone man gives her, from a bag that hangs by the front of his cart. His pony clops down the asphalt, harness creaking. When the step's been cleaned, there's a puddle in the hollow. I sit to one side then, and finger the cracks between shiny red bricks. Their edges are hard and sharp. A girl from up the street stands in front of me and asks if I want to see her bottom. She bends over and pulls down her knickers without waiting for a reply. I gaze in puzzlement at the mysterious, lipped simplicity of her vulva. Behind me the stairs thunder, front door bursts open, shouting; the girl runs away, a hand cracks across the side of my head, my ear throbs and buzzes. When I tell my sister, she says 'Mine's like that – I'll let you see if I can see yours.'

I don't like it when my mother's here. But it's not often. Sometimes there's a barrel-organ with a monkey on a chain up by the main road. Every morning with my grandfather I walk down to Platt Fields. When my dad's here, on Saturday mornings we go to the U.C.P. shop on Stretford Road. In the window it has white trays full of animal parts at which I don't look. There are marble tables inside, cruets with fat, stoppered bottles of malt vinegar, and a sour, steamy, milky reek. He eats tripe and onions, ladled out from steaming vats behind the counter. I don't want any. Afterwards he buys me a penny apple from the greengrocers next door. Slivers of paint stick to his cuticles. He smokes Senior Service, tapping the ends on the packet and flicking a chrome lighter that smells of petrol. 'Salubrious blast of the obnoxious weed,' he mouths, to no-one in particular, inhaling deeply. He has photographs in his pocket, of when he was a soldier in the war. In one set he's in Orkney: 'This is Skara Brae, this is the Old Man of Hoy.' I study them wonderingly. He tells of a waitress in the Kirkwall Café who would fry sausage meat and give him two eggs, even with rationing. He talks about her a lot, but not at home. I can picture her. It was only ten years before. Now he's a journeyman-decorator with a wife, two kids, bad chest, no home of his own. One set of photographs are of the extermination camp that he reached after D-Day: 'Fucking Germans,' he mutters, goes quiet and puts them hastily away. We get the bus to walk the streets where he lived before the war in Salford. He used to play rugby league for the team, was the hooker. And he boxed. Hard little fucker, slim, muscular, keeps his head up; and his guard. But I see in memory his eyes, and they are not those of someone who expects to win.

Some time later, on this excursion or another like it, we fetch up in Peel Park, from which the view reaches out to moors pressing in close against the ragged margins of the city. He tells me about going there once or twice in his teens, walking for miles, camping out; stories of a mate of his from the next street, Jimmy Miller, who'd been trespassing, nearly got himself arrested; others had gone to gaol; 'lefties' he snorts, scattering clues to the way through the maze. Years later, with a jolt of instant recognition, I come across the following passage from a haunting account of a Salford slum childhood by Robert Roberts, *A Ragged Schooling*. I use it in the introduction to my first collection of essays, and dedicate the book to my dad, by then more than 20 years dead:

'One sunny Wednesday afternoon [my mother] took me to Peel Park. We sat on a high esplanade and looked far over the countless chimneys of northern Manchester to the horizon. On the skyline, green and aloof, the Pennines rose like the ramparts of paradise. "There!" she said, pointing. "Mountains!" I stared, lost for words.'

GRANDPARENTS

She baked bread, charmed warts, told fortunes in tea leaves, couldn't read. Soft-bosomed in a faded brown dress, hair in a net, she was full of old stories, little rhymes, gossip from the last century. He had a ballerina tattooed on his arm, had fought in the Boer War: the veldt, the Siege of Mafeking, the Relief of Ladysmith. Gertrude and Arthur Sproson, born in the 1870s, died in their eighties, believed in fairies and magic and ghosts; and so, falteringly, do I retain a sense of the quirkiness and mystery of consciousness. He takes me through the park, where hummocks seemed like great hills and the seasons turned, to his allotment a mile away behind a redbrick wall across the Wilmslow Road, chestnut trees shading it; we amble hand-in-hand along all the little sylvan footpaths with which south Manchester abounded. When I began school, at Little Birch by the Platt Brook, just across Birchfields Park from Dickinson Road where Joe Brown was then living, he'd walk me there each day and work in his allotment until the bell rang for home. When I was three, he taught me to read – from the *Authorized Version*, and from *Pilgrim's Progress*. What chance of avoiding the metonymies of rock after that induction into the Word? Also, in the back yard, above the coal hole with its stink of cat, a fern grew from a corner – a chance small clump of fern that each spring sent out shoots from its brown and winter-dry hard clump of root, with the dead fronds that flaked to dust between your fingers. The shoots croziered and fanned out across the wall and he worshipped it. I would see him down there sometimes from my bedroom window, his gaunt body stooped, the head of wispy grey hair bent towards it as though in prayer, his arm with the ballerina on her points reaching out and fondling the leaves with all the reverence we can ever accord to the sense of the other world where the brightness shines. He was vulnerable for that plant. It was his point of connection. To have uprooted it would have destroyed him. And watching him taught me.

BLACKING FACTORY

My dad's sister Elsie has a corner shop on Erskine Street in Hulme, between the Stretford and the City Roads. The streets are cobbled and the soot-steeped brick, like the air itself, is fumey with sulphur that mingles with the malted, sickly vapour drifting down from the brewery chimney. Elsie's husband Sam has a pub just across the City Road, down by the Pomona Docks. She and her family live there. My parents, my sister and I make our home in the two rooms above the shop. I'm six. There's a yard at the back, an alleyway, an outside toilet. The close rows of houses have gaps in them, interior walls revealed to either side, with fireplaces, wallpaper shredding and fading, hooks from which ghost pictures hung. Paired timber baulks that root in piles of brick and thickets of rosebay willow herb shore up the survivors. When the hazy sun filters through the smoke, up and down the street women put chairs on the pavements outside the doors, and help to them husbands and grandfathers blinded and maimed from the Great War, in which my father's father died. But for these brief spaces in the sun, they have lived inside for more than 30 years. I pass by one sightless man with a kind of terror. Half his face is still a raw and weeping wound. (Children in Kabul, Basra and Baghdad today will witness the same spectacles). Fallowfield was neat, clean, orderly, safe. There were trees in the streets. Hulme is harsh, bare and rough. One afternoon coming home from school I see my cousin Glyn on an old flatbed lorry down on the croft (another bombed site, for this area

3

was close to the docks, factories and commercial centres, so it was torched in the Blitz). A bigger kid is beating him up, all the other kids around jeering him on. I jump up, hang on to the big kid's legs, get a boot in the mouth for my pains. We go back bloodied to Auntie Elsie's. My dad gets me down the gym behind Hulme church to start boxing: 'Bigger they come the harder they fall,' he says cheerily, waving me out to play on the streets. I learn: vamp up the aggro when it's encountered, be prepared to go right through with it, and they'll mostly leave you alone. Bad lessons. Repeated every playtime in that echoey, grimed school. Beyond the dread, I get to enjoy the cool frenzy of combat. The watchfulness, the quick levers, the explosive movement, the rage externalised. And beyond that, every daredevil thing. On the roof of the bakery, throwing stones at the policeman, trying to knock off his helmet, and clearing off fast over the walls before you get caught, disappearing into the alleys and backyards, laughing. Feral. I take to roving. This shattered city.

Between the hoardings I peer down into a hidden world, burnt, but now the fireweed and the elder grow, and the white-tiled basements open to the air gleam strangely, footings of broken walls and flagged floors demarcate lost meanings, subterranean with the roof taken off. I climb over to explore. Police, authority – just run, just fuck off out of it, their power impotent against the rage for play.

One autumn evening around bonfire night in 1954 I go down with my dad to Uncle Sam's pub. He tells my dad about the whale and we set off walking. It's on a bombed site somewhere at the end of Deansgate, canvas screens stretched around, acetylene arc lights hissing inside them, the thump of a generator. He pays copper pennies for us to walk through a blind into the enclosure. I can't take in the whole picture. Something huge and dark on the back of a low truck. It glistens in the lights' flicker; there are rents in its flesh, clots of dark blood and runnels of clear liquid streaming down black hide, hoses intruded, folded and billowy fat showing through, and a smell like when I went to hospital to get my head stitched after falling downstairs when I'd taken my mother a cup of tea. The small, dull eye seems to fix me with reproach, the great weight of the thing settled into hopeless admonition of all this undignified and elaborate show. I store the spectacle like a dream, come to believe it could not have been.

Decades later I'm lying in bed on a Saturday morning listening to John Peel's radio show. A man comes on and starts to talk about being taken by his dad to see a whale on a low loader in Barnsley in 1968. Peel is downbeat, sceptical. I prick up my ears and think '1968 ... ?' The man goes on: he thought it must have been a dream; it troubled him; he went along to the Department of Circus Studies (I haven't dared check this out) at Sheffield Hallam University, asks a researcher there, and she comes up with this: in 1954 a blue whale is beached in the Firth of Forth, some enterprising local business men have a low-loader specially made, lift the whale on board, and with arc lights, tanks of formalin, generators and screens they set off to tour Britain. The following spring the show crosses over to the Continent, and does not arrive back on these shores until 1968. It makes its way from Hull to Barnsley, where the radio correspondent's father takes him to see it. By then, after 14 years on the road, formalin or no formalin it's getting a bit niffy. Bits are falling off. Some decent citizen calls the public health department, the whale's confiscated, and sent to Barnsley public incinerator. The guardians of public nostrils load all 80 feet of it into the breeze-block structure and fire up the gas. After the subsequent explosion of formalin-soaked carcass, fragments of breeze-block and scraps of rancid blubber rain down over most of Barnsley.

Unreal city ...

MY DAD AT BIRK CRAG

He gets a job with a flat in Harrogate but it doesn't last long. By now I've gone wild, wander wherever I will: Crimple Beck, the pinewoods, Birk Crag.

'What would you do if you were lost?' the schoolmistress asked, knowing where I go.

'Work out the way home, miss, from the sun and what time it was.'

'No, fool – you'd ask a policeman.'

The class looked blank. I got the strap. Birk Crag is a little gritstone outcrop on the rim of a valley, I never saw a policeman there. Maybe it's three or four miles to walk to it from home. I go there a lot, to scrape around on the rocks and jump about. My dad comes one Sunday to see what I'm up to, forbids me to go again. But how would he know? I love the place, crystalline, tactile, aloof; the sandy runnels and the rounded bluffs, the bite of it, the danger. My first acquaintance with gritstone. Soon we're back in Manchester. I go to grammar school – not a good move, given where I live. Scrapping, there's an accident to my eye. Broken glass. Operations and stuff, and I'm getting the sight back. On the bus to school one wet day, a woman with a careless umbrella and the ferrule jabs in; hospital, the eye's taken out. Back at school weeks later my headmaster – a good man – says to the class, 'Here's Perrin, boys, back at school – his left eye's been removed, but which of you could tell the difference?' No more boxing, a sense of disfigurement that dogs me and is compounded by cruel or thoughtless people, of whom there are many for decades; when I have started climb-

5

ing, I – who wanted to shine as a sportsman for my father, and would have done – show him a photograph of Joe Brown on *Suicide Wall* from the Cwm Idwal guide-book. 'You'll never be able to do that,' he says, 'you've only got one eye.'

'Fuck you ... '

A34

My father had one of those old Bartholomew's half-inch maps, cloth-mounted with the frayed threads hanging from the margins, blue-card-covered, the heights of the hills depicted by deepening tints of umbers and ochres. He'd used it before the war. The blues and greens and browns of this map were a fascination to me as I studied them in the drab world of the city. They lured me into spaciousness. In the agricultural depression following the Great War, my grandparents had moved from the Welsh Borders to the area around Congleton in Cheshire. One March day as a kid I thought to walk there, and set off in the morning from Manchester's city centre to follow the 20 miles of the A34 marked on the map through Handforth and Wilmslow, Alderley Edge, Monks' Heath and Marton that would lead me to it. By Redesmere, a new experience: the waves lapping under a grey sky and everything inside stilling down in response. Until, watching, I scarcely breathed:

One midsummer I went out of the road into the fields, and sat down on the grass between the yellowing wheat and the green hawthorn bushes. The sun burned in the sky, the wheat was full of a luxuriant sense of growth, the grass high, the earth giving its vigour to tree and leaf, the heaven blue. The vigour and growth, the warmth and light, the beauty and richness of it entered into me; an ecstasy of soul accompanied the delicate excitement of the senses; the soul rose with the body. Rapt in the fullness of the moment, I prayed there with all that expansion of mind and frame; no words, no definition, inexpressible desire of soul-life, equal to and beyond the highest imaginings of my heart.

It didn't matter then that I was walking along a road in my school clothes and shoes. It was still a journey, and to attend to the detail all around was still to dream.

STRAVAIGING

Next place to which my dad moves us, the slums having been demolished, is a flat on top of an office block of which he is employed as caretaker in Albert Square in the centre of Manchester, where we stay until he dies. No point going out to play here, so I read voraciously and live for weekends and holidays. At the bottom of John Dalton Street, on the corner of Deansgate, is a second-hand bookshop. The man who runs it, chaotic among piles of volumes, befriends and advises. Two books among the many he pushes my way are by Patrick Monkhouse, northern editor of the *Manchester Guardian* and a friend of his. The books are called *On Foot in The Peak* and *On Foot in North Wales*. Years later I write Paddy Monkhouse's obituary for the *Guardian*. I have a lot for which to thank him. Also, in my school library, from which I can see the Derbyshire hills, there's a red, cloth-bound volume by a man called Colin Kirkus entitled *Let's Go Climbing*. At first I don't, much: a bit of scrambling up shorter and easier routes on the Derbyshire outcrops, some adventurous ascents on the Welsh hills, and from time to time with my friend Ricky Richardson, who is older and more timid and has a rope, I do a few real climbs, easy ones like the *Sloping Crack* at Wimberry Rocks, on the Chew Valley crags. Mostly, I want to cover the ground, am greedy for movement. I meet a strange companion on the train home from some weekend hill destination, start to keep company with him. He's the same age as my father, who can barely conceal his disgust when I bring him home, and who refers to him ever after as 'that tramp!' He's slight of frame, with hooded eyes, streaming white hair, a lantern jaw; dresses in rags; is queer, makes a pass at me on one occasion, but I slap him off and that's the end of that.

Len Chadwick always gave the impression of 'a man/ Flying from something he dreads, than one/ Who sought the thing he loved'. Restlessness, an inability to stay still and be at peace in any one place, an absolute necessity always to be moving on were at the core of his being, and manifested in every quirk of his extraordinary character. In those days, before the genesis of a specifically outdoor media, you came by your information from the outdoor columnists in local papers: Tom Waghorn in the *Manchester Evening News*, Harry Griffin in the *Lancashire Evening Post*, Frank Wilkinson in the *Yorkshire Post*. Len was the doyen of these. For years he wrote a column under the *nom-de-plume* of 'Fellwalker' for the *Oldham Evening Chronicle*, in which he recorded his eccentric and phenomenal journeyings. My own outdoor wanderings as a 12- or 13-year-old were launched to the accompaniment of their refrain. The Tan Hill-Cat & Fiddle, the Colne-Rowsley, the Double Marsden-Edale – these were the test-pieces that Len imposed on my raw youth – 50, 60 or 70-mile weekend slushings through day and night and mire and high Pennine moors. And there were the later marathon contrivances: the Lyke Wake Walk, the Pennine Way, North Wales and Lake District rounds – these were Len's delight, and my brutal hill-walking initiation rites, through which I came to know the moors and fells and mountains of the North. Len's particular favourites were the bog-trots – vast slogs

7

across, at that time, often trackless expanses of grough, mire and peat-hag. They have a distinctive flavour in my memory. I can smell the wet vegetation and the sour black peat, hear the grouse chirping away, feel the slip of surface beneath my feet and see the threading, compass-ruled linkage of the close-bound, cloud-enclosed routes to this day. I saw the Northern Lights from Bleaklow, and Edale filled with white mist below a blue morning sky, and all the rimming western outcrops of Kinder Scout illuminated red-gold in the sunset – all these before my 13th birthday, and am profoundly glad now of these things: 'I have owed to them,/ In hours of weariness, sensations sweet'. They come into my mind with so lovely a sense of hare-and-plover-haunted moorland miles unwinding; of the endless brown, of bilberry and heather changing colour season to season; of the sharp blades of russet autumn bracken at the southern margins of these journeyings; of nightfall and the smoke-bruised skies to the west; of torchlight map-consultations at some dark track junction with the silhouette of Stoodley Pike and its monument dimly visible away on the left against the scudding, illuminated cloud; of the sudden rain-lash that came scurrying in on a bluster of wind and soaked us, clad as we were in ragged cotton anoraks, in seconds; of the way in which the knotted intensity of pain in a calf-muscle could be eased, ignored, by concentration on externalia – heads of the bog-cotton impossibly delicate and white within the thick green of the morass, the bluebells along the descending track pulsing with colour's sun-detonated emanation; sweetness of rest in cafés with clothes steaming and the great pots of tea upon the table – Ponden Old Hall, The Nag's Head, The Eagle & Child, Ma Thomas'; of the snatched hours of chilled and shivery sleep, head on rucksack, clothes still wet, under this or that breezy gritstone neb along the Derwent edges; of the switchbacks across Howden, the mire of Black Hill, the groughs by the Grinah Stones, the sense of a mode of landscape's ending beyond Grains-in-the-Water; of Boxing Gloves and Salt Cellars and Eagle Stones and Ringing Roger; of the bone-weariness as we ached down into Macclesfield or Matlock or Keighley after 60, 70, 80 miles in a weekend. Those rigorous, blissful days ...

But if rest, contemplation, quiet came at all along them, it came in snatched moments before racing on for the next objective. Len could not be still. Even his speech, muttering, colloquial, heavily-accented, autodidactically informed and forever leaping from one secure fact to another as though they were the peat-hags of his beloved Kinder Scout, came out as a frenetic jabber from between toothless gums – his teeth had been smashed out by a Japanese rifle-butt. His white hair streamed out behind him, his boots – soles often as not held on with string – were perpetual-motion machines, and his mind raced. It was always planning, piecing together. He

8

knew the little local bus services of those days in the North of England and North Wales by heart, and walked as though it was his life that depended on connecting with them, instead of just the completion of yet another hopelessly optimistic and extravagant day's itinerary.

There was the time we left the youth hostel at Maeshafn near Mold one June morning, raced down Pothole Valley and over the Clwydian hills to descend into Rhuthun, jumped on to a departing bus to Cyfylliog, sweated over Mynydd Hiraethog and the moors beyond by way of the sinister and lonely Rhaeadr y Bedd – the waterfall of the grave – to descend by lanes made lovely by the flowering of the dog-rose into Llanrwst, where there was scarcely a pause to draw breath before we were away again over the suspension bridge to Trefriw and up into the foothills of the Carneddau to tease out a network of old ways that led us to the youth hostel above Roewen, the steep hill up to which sticks in my mind as a version of purgatory, weary beyond weariness as I was, in the long blue summer twilight of the eastern flank of these hills. Its 40 or more miles were, I think, in retrospect rather too long a day for a boy of 13, as I was then.

I understand better now Len's need always to be moving – 'like a man/ Flying from something that he dreads'. When I first met Len, on a Ramblers' Special excursion train returning to Manchester's Exchange Station, those fearful memories of his from the war in the Far East were only 14 years distant – a gap of time that to me now seems inconsequential as I approach the age where recollection of events from 30 or 40 years ago is often more vivid than of those which took place yesterday. I was fond of Len Chadwick, regard him now as one of the major educative, indeed formative, influences in my life – this tattered, uncouth man who worked at menial jobs, was virtually penniless but always shared what he had, whose mind was so much keener and more retentive than those who might look down on him for his status and appearance. But his cast of mind, his temperament, his need, were not as mine were, even then. At the long school holidays I'd go off by myself particularly to Wales, for the blood-association of that country with my father's family. I loved the idea of journeying. That sense, when you're walking, of landscape unfolding in front of you, revealing its further dimensions, its horizons ever widening, its margins fading 'for ever and for ever as we move' seemed to me one of the most rapturous and intense of all pleasures.

So I came to know Wales, and the literature and language of that country became another theme. The northern hills of Wales were a very different place 40 years ago – different to what they have become, vastly different to my own home environment. To a deracinated Manchester slum-kid of Welsh origin, from a tense and fractured home background, who made his way to a region where an essential connection still existed between landscape and population, between place, history and culture, what I found there was thrilling, absorbing and necessary to me. I was fortunate in a way that few of my then-age could be fortunate these days. The fact that I had little but interest and need, and that this was no doubt obvious, led to my being given much in the way of hospitality, information, instruction. If I saw a shepherd half-a-mile away I would chase across a hillside and pester him with callow questions in book-learnt, half-remembered, pidgin-Welsh about name and legend and hill, and often as not be allowed to stay thereafter in hay-barns or even houses from Bugeilyn to Soar y Mynydd to Pennant Lliw in the course of endless wanderings at every available opportunity through this land. But that's matter for another book ...

Rock

Tired of my limpet-like fixation with the moorland edges we should, in his view, be hurrying by, when I'm 14 Len takes me along to an evening gathering of the Étrier Club in a derelict gritstone weaver's cottage at Grotton on the Greenfield side of Oldham. I spend the next months in the company of two young men who are still among the best climbers I've ever seen – Brian Ripley and Paul Fletcher. Every weekend, in the back of the grey Fordson pickup belonging to Brian, his brother Alan, and his father's building firm, we head out to the gritstone outcrops. 'You won't last long in this outfit if you mess about,' Paul warns me. Every night in the dark I climb up and down the underside of the fire escape in Albert Square, building up the muscles for steep rock. One night I look down and see my dad watching from the other side of a window. Our eyes meet. Nothing's said. I meet guys my own age (few girls of any age climbing then), and start to go out at weekends and in the holidays with them. Joe Brown and Don Whillans are my heroes – Joe particularly. I see him out on the crags, instructing, sidle near and listen, mostly watch. He chaffs me, casts a sideways glance to see how I do when I climb. He's tatterdemalion, vernacular-speaking, friendly, and from my own streets. His routes are all my ambition. I work through them. His are the ones I enjoy. The feel of rock is a kind of ecstasy – not just its texture, but the way it dances your body to its ancient, lithe configurations. On *Agony Crack* my body's like a flag of silk, streaming round the jut of that neb. No such feeling ever before. In time, at times, the dancing god deigns to accompany. High up in the dark, I climb rooftops, pinnacles, towers in the heart of the city with pavement beneath, for the sheer fear of it all, and the joy. One summer evening Arthur Williams turns up on his Enfield and we roar down to Helsby. He's seen I can't do hand-jams, so takes me up *Flake Crack* to teach me. 'Perfect,' he tells me. They are, and are the key.

Arthur's in the Alpha Club, the members of which – Pete Crew, Baz Ingle, Martin Boysen, Paul Nunn, Al Parker, Richard McHardy – are doing all the good things at the time in Wales and on grit. I get inducted into that group and the Wednesday night gatherings at Martin and his wife Maggie's flat at Keppel Road in Chorlton or later on Alexandra Road in Whalley Range: Eddie Birch, Dave Little and Brian Sullivan from the Black & Tans are usually there as well, the circle ever widening. There's talk and slides and plans and music, endless brews. But really, Manchester climbing in the early 1960s is one big community, and its component parts and gathering-places – the Manchester Gritstone Club in the Wheatsheaf on Shudehill, the Black & Tans out in Glossop, the Cromlech Club in some pub at the bottom of Deansgate, the Friday-night Wales-bound melee in the Manchester Sports Guild at the back of the cathedral – are amorphous rather than distinct. We all know each other. Still do, those of us who survive ...

CULTURAL

School for the most part's some kind of a dumb fuck and I don't like it. Trouble all my days. There are compensations. The girls' high school across the road and the leafy lunchtime lanes round about are a whole new province of discovery. English is just reading, which is what I've always done, and learning new languages – French, German, Latin – adds in more, more voices: Camus, Molière, Catullus, Goethe. Old Len Chadwick keeps in touch and takes me to Esperanto evenings in a coffee bar on Deansgate, where he and his friends talk left-wing politics in a daft and idealistic universal pseudo-language where every other word ends in 'anto', and which sounds to me more like one of those loathsome childhood codes where you slip additional syllables into every word to confound and exclude listeners. But on the way there I stumble on the Left-wing Coffee Bar, newly opened down in some whitewashed catacombs on Brazenose Street, and encounter bad coffee and intellectual ferment. It's 1963. Laurence Ferlinghetti's in town for a reading; the *Freewheeling Bob Dylan*'s coming through the loudspeakers. In an upstairs room at the Waggon & Horses on Quay Street, Harry Boardman's singing Lancashire industrial ballads and preaching the lot of the working man and the role of the bosses; Michael Foot's oratory, report-

11

ed in the *Manchester Guardian*, is knifing in to the last days of Macmillan and the brief tenure of Alec Douglas Home. In the Free Trade Hall, Pete Seeger's all limpid sincerity, civil rights songs and thunderous 12-string guitar, and on Sunday nights in the same venue it's John Lee Hooker, Muddy Waters, Howlin' Wolf, Sonny Boy Williamson, Brownie MacGhee. In the Sports Guild on Fridays, the Welsh singer Meic Stephens, who ten years later is hanging out at Bryn Bigil with Al Harris and myself, is acting as warm-up to Jesse Fuller's San Francisco Bay Blues. The Stones and the Beatles are the soundtrack to every party, Sylvia Plath kills herself, poetry's cool, the word is alive and in town and I drink it in on every street corner. If you could choose one time to be young, would it not be this?

CANCER

My dad dies. He fell badly changing a light bulb in the bathroom, broke the wash-basin. After that, something was wrong, the vitality draining away. He lost weight, took to his bed. I'd carry him in his pyjamas, put him down on the settee in front of the television. He was so light, proud that I could lift him and yet he weighed no more than pounds, bones protruding through the emaciated flesh. There were lumps on his back. Eventually the doctors noticed. Secondaries. They took him in to Salford Royal Infirmary. I was in the express stream at school, doing my A levels a year early, went in to see him each evening. I knew – same as I did when Jacquetta was dying. When you're that intimate, there are signs you notice, tacit communications that pass between you, that are not available to those who are not so close. Maintaining the lie of hope is part of giving the truth of your love. That you're there is what matters. After a time the secondaries blocked off the circulation to his legs and they became gangrenous. The doctors debated whether to amputate, but there was no point. Soon he was comatose. The stink of his rotting legs made me gag as I sat by his bed. It was a relief when he died. Pretty soon after, I fucked off out of Manchester, went to work in the forestry in Wales as a labourer, living in a tent that winter. Next spring, rough edges abrading everyone with whom I came into contact, they took me on as a voluntary instructor at the National Mountaineering Centre. I got to climb every day, had enough to eat, there were always plenty of young women around, new ones every week.

What else could a young man want?

FRIENDSHIP

I walk into the bar of the old Padarn Lake Hotel in Llanberis and barge into Al Harris. He takes a step back, looks at who he's stumbled into, and says, 'They tell me you're a cunt.' 'Just what I heard about you,' I respond. We go out the door together and hammer each other round the car park till we get bored, walk back in, bloodied, arms round each other's shoulders, laughing. He buys me a pint of mild. After that we're accomplices in every bit of mischief going. We borrow JCBs that the council's left for the weekend and joust with them. We climb together sometimes. He's always trying to freak me out. He walks across the grass slope above the main cliff at Cilan and I follow, petrified. He's better than me – better than almost everyone, in fact – but for the most part couldn't give a fuck whether he does it or not.

One weekend we've been over in Sheffield, partying, three days without sleep on the usual cocktail of dope, coke, speed and booze. We end up at Ramshaw of those jutting, rough nebs on a cold Sunday – Al, Chris Boulton and myself. 'We'll do that,' he directs, pointing at *Brown's Crack*. Ropes are not part of the deal. I'm told to go first, get the fist-jam for which you reach at full stretch under the roof, crank up and swivel round to mantel on it, skin ripping. 'Fuck that!' he laughs, and walks off. Caught again ... Sometimes we go over to Liverpool, work down the pubs – the *Bull* and the *Palatine* and the *A1 at Lloyd's* – on the Dock Road, winding up the stevedores and getting into scraps, getting comforted by the whores if we lose out too badly and are left on the pavement battered and tattered from the encounters. Other times we acquire cars, race them down to Wales, build up a collection behind his house at Bigil, and then play the chicken game. The drivers' doors come off, we get into our bike leathers. A mile up the road is the quarry at Allt Ddu, 80 feet down to 200 feet of water. We've snipped through the chain-link fencing. Now we loop it back to give a six-foot gap at which you can get a 100-yard run. The doors get thrown in first. Then the game. Gun the engine, aim for the gap, at the very last second jump so that you hit the fence in mid-air, bounce off and the car continues on its trajectory into black and midnight water; the plume of spray, the bubbles hissing to the surface, the returning silence. If the lights and sirens come up the hill, we melt away down the paths into the dark. Years later, after Al's death, there is a European Community environmental reclamation initiative. It fills in the quarry – it's now called Bus Stop, a popular venue for climbers. Before that happened they sent the police divers down to check it out. They found a pyramid of cars reaching up to 20 feet below the surface, and had to crane them all back up and check them out. Al's memorial ...

13

LOVE

One woman above all others. I meet her in the Llanberis Pass when she's 17, I'm 18. Instant instinctual rapport, she and I the same species. She's the girl of a friend of mine from Cumbria. Our hair mingles as we lean together over a wall. We can talk. She tells me much, with a hesitant, quiet wisdom, always looks for me when she comes to Wales, and I for her in Liverpool. After a few years she and the guy are breaking up. She's living by herself up some dark stairs in a Sefton Park flat and I'm there a lot. We do a lot of acid together. I remember listening to one track by the Grateful Dead – "Ripple" from the *American Beauty* album – and looking across at her on a note and in a moment that seems to hang throughout eternity. Her beauty imprints on my soul. She feels safe with me, I with her. One morning we watch the sun rise across the Sefton Park lake as we sit on a bench together, holding hands. The necessary deceits and concealments as she edges towards closure with her guy are getting oppressive. We have a weekend when she comes to Wales, insists on all the assurances – commitment, babies and the rest – and I, who want her and those things with her, give them.

She goes off to resolve matters, comes back without announcement to find me and is told I'm climbing up The Pass. At Pont Cromlech she asks a couple of guys if they've seen me. They point up at *Cenotaph Corner*. I'm soloing out of the top of it. She takes this – rightly, I suppose, and sensitised by her own history, her own back-story in which, at the age of 19, she was forced to give up a daughter for adoption – as not consonant with the promises I'd made, storms off, leaves the country. I don't see her again for 28-and-a-half years, in which time we've both made a comprehensive mess of our lives. Both of us are looking for the other, but we don't find. I go back to that bench in Sefton Park a hundred times in pilgrimage (when we finally go back there together, she says, 'that's not the one' and we have to return at dawn to check it out – she's right, of course). She looks for me too.

One day she sees a poster for a reading I'm to give, and turns up. 'You won't remember me,' she says. I laugh. Back at my house I play "Ripple". She leans back against me: 'I'm tired out. I'm spent. I'm going to have a nervous breakdown,' she sighs.

'Don't do that – come and lean on me.'

'I am doing,' she says, 'you're the only one who ever made any sense.'

'Did you really love me all those years?' she asks.

'All those years ... ' I answer.

After that we're never apart, scarcely need to speak, just holding hands and entwining in the night is enough: 'the utopia of love is completion to the point of stillness.'

So we live for a time what Matthew Arnold calls 'the ideal, cheerful, sensuous, pagan life.' We marry in a pagan ceremony down by the well in the cliffs at Braich y Pwll, with the raven, the seal and the chough as our witnesses. From my house, at Llanrhaeadr ym Mochnant in the Tanat valley, in May-time before the bracken was long and the blossomy black thorns confettied every hillside, we walk up to the pistyll four miles above the village, marvel at the water efflorescing across dark strata before climbing on into the long strath of the Afon Disgynfa above and seeking out a bed in the heather from which to watch the stars come out and the moon sail from behind the bounding, low ridges. We're not going anywhere. We're coming to rest. Cling close under whatever covering of blanket or coat we have with us as the dew falls and the last hovering kestrel scythes valley-wards. We watch the mottlings of shadow deepen and the rifflings of the breeze among the sedge, the jagged dartings of snipe, and we murmur minimally to each other of these things and snuggle a little closer and half-wakeful dream away the hours of the dark and doze in the sun of morning – this often and often, for the waincrat life was our joy and neither of us had found such sharing or such mutual joy before.

Many other such times in other places: one night on a Shropshire hillside, on a salient of sweet grass caverned into a thicket of gorse and facing west, from which we could see the sun's descent, rolling along a Welsh hill horizon before it finally was drawn down into the elastic earth and the liquid of its fire spilled across the sky. As response to which I cut and lifted squares of turf, gathered sticks from the copse beneath and soon the bright flames illuminated the beauty of her face as it turned attentive to the sounds of the night: the last creaking flight of the late raven across indigo sky, hush of an owl's wings, scurry of mouse and vole through dry leaf-litter, and the snuffle and scrape of a lumbering badger among the trees.

Light and colour were her metier. She created from glass designs of exquisite simplicity, drawn from the gentle attention she bestowed continually upon the world. To be in her company was to enter a kind of trance of the consciousness of beauty. One morning we awoke in a little, sandy cradle we had discovered in the falling cliffs by Hell's Mouth. We had lain there nightlong listening to the soft susurrus of small waves upon the sand. The grass of the overhanging dune that sheltered us caught at rays from the sun's rising, and its matter became light, a latticed and filigreed gleam of silver, cross-hatching the azure. Later the same day,

15

walking the beach at Porth Oer, stretched prisms before the crystal waves gave us gleaming, transfigured patterns in the sand under ultramarine water, momentarily, repeatedly. 'It's all in the stilling, in the moment, and the moment's eternal,' she breathed, turning to me and back to the water again, watching with her artist's eye this blessing of sight being obscured and renewed by each rolling wave.

In the stilling was where she found herself. I learned from her truly to come to rest within a landscape, open my eyes, and see. She had no interest in haste or achievement or distances, sought simply for the peace that comes when we are at one – with each other, with natural creation. I remember a day when I had been south to walk unfrequented hills, then drove back to meet with her again. We took bread and wine to a beautiful little river spilling down from the moors of longing, very quiet and unknown.

In its oakwood glen we sat on a shingle bank in the sunset, and I was communicating to her a picture from the morning's paper of an armless, burnt and bandaged child in Iraq – who had wanted to be a doctor, to help and heal, and who might now never master those skills, might never delight in the feel of his lover's skin or the cool lightness of spring flowers, who would never hold in his own arms his firstborn child or dangle his fingers in a stream like the one by which we sat – the flyers who dropped the bombs that had maimed him invulnerable; the press snapping away in a sort of exultation, capitalising on all his shock and loss ...

She heard me out, my hand in her strong one, and through her quietude, her still presence, over a space of hours these things we saw: a dipper working the stream feet in front of us; the sun setting as a great red and rolling orb; a sturdy horse with a white blaze that came to the far bank and communed; a little owl that alighted on a branch within arm's reach and peered, unperturbed. A bright half-moon shone down, a badger travelled across the field upstream in its gleam and two ducks scolded until it had passed; there was no human sound, no unnatural light; the stream pulsed on, the air very still, and a glimmer of frost settled across the moss and the bladed leaves from which more bluebells would soon rise. We felt the evil and the beauty of the world – no one kind and omniscient god, but an energy that splinters into these manifestations, and both perturbs and heals.

On a July day we drove down to the Radnorshire hills and by one of the mawn pools above Painscastle, remote from roads, on as calm and clear a night as I can remember we made a simple camp and built a fire. So windless was it that the flame of a candle we had placed by the trunk of a Scots Pine rose unflickering to map the seamed shadows of the bark. To her, these, and the green hachurings of the weed in the shallows of the pool, and the whiskery croziers of new bracken, and the streaked carmines and tangerines of the sky were the palette where her imagination mixed and dwelt so lovingly. I have known magic in my life, but no woman so magical as this.

When we returned to Llanrhaeadr after this night out on the Black Hill, late on a Sunday evening we poured a glass of wine and came out of the house to walk down into the old, circular churchyard of the village. She stepped on a rock in a low wall round the forecourt and it rolled away from her. A previous man in her life had beaten her savagely about the head, and her corrective balance was gone. Her feet flew in the air, she smashed down on the rock, and shattered two ribs. Six months later another fall, in which she cracked a lumbar vertebra. After that, her skin took on an ashen pallor. Our going into the outdoors was curtailed, but still, whenever we could, we would enter the margins of wilderness and come to rest there, to observe and to see: in the rainforest of La Gomera, on the wild western coast of Vancouver Island, or at bluebell and scurvy-grass time along the Pembrokeshire Coastal Path, the sea a shimmer beneath. With the death of my son, whom she dearly loved, last July, our joy was crowded out by grief. To be in each other's arms in the outdoors was our solace still, but she was forlorn and tired, physically and emotionally pained.

A fortnight after Will's passing she was diagnosed with cancer, began chemotherapy and bravely endured its discomforts and indignities and the loss of the glory of her long and auburn hair, which she, so womanly, took hard. The shrinking of our physical horizons focused her attention down ever more acutely into the splendour of detail, and its meditative power. Tint and pattern of a fallen beech-leaf of autumn consumed her for an hour and more, turning it this way and that, finally letting it fall. We went to the Caribbean, away from the rigours of home weather to give her warmth, and the towering cloudscapes and scintillating emeralds of humming birds and visitant presence of the blue-crowned mot-mot and a scampering, comical agouti and brilliant, fractured trajectories of fireflies absorbed her in glimpses of the joy of this jewelled world.

Always the prognosis was darkening. In March this year, she stood at the end of the bed and our eyes met as my face registered anguish:

'Why are you looking at me like that?' she asked.

'Because you are so very beautiful to me,' I replied, and the unspoken knowledge passed between us that she was dying. She had surgery and was told that the chances of recurrence were overwhelming, of survival beyond a very few years minimal. In the event, mercifully, it would only be weeks. On a Tuesday night, I supported her to a crystalline, mottled rock where we would often sit, water in front, west-facing across waves of tawny, cloud-shadowed moorland. Next day she went

17

into hospital for a regular cancer clinic, but was admitted immediately, put in a small room at the end of a ward on morphine and a drip with blackbirds singing in the cherry blossom outside. On her last night she ordered me peremptorily to stop messing about tidying things, get on the bed and cuddle her as we listened to the evening chorus. I held her, caressed her, told her how dearly I loved her as she slipped into sleep, and beyond that deep unconsciousness. Next day, peacefully, almost imperceptibly, she died.

That evening, sitting on the crystalline rock, the little lilac helium balloon that had floated above her bed was released. There was not a breath of wind, the curlews were calling from the marsh and courting redstarts flitted in and out of the leafless branches of the ash. The balloon rose straight up for 50 feet, and then at great speed and on an unwavering course, it took off westwards. At the exact point and moment of its disappearing from view, a star came out, blinked once, and was gone.

SYNTHESIS

On a river-bank in Sarawak, beyond the rain-forest and far up into the mountains that form the border with Kalimantan, I sit watching Merang, the headman of the village of Long Singut – 'the river-mouth of the honey-bees' – working on his boat, replacing with precision, minimal tools and infinite care a plank split by a boulder in the rapids above. Merang is a small, spare, sinewy man, grave in gesture, which is the only language we share, and given to laughter. His tribe, the Kenyh, had crossed those mountains 60 or more years before – no-one was quite sure when, but the old people as young children remembered it – to settle on this fertile and idyllic alp, grow their crops here, hunt for deer and wild boar in the forests below.

There was something about the way Merang worked that resonated in my memory. His every movement had a graceful and considered economy about it that put me in mind of hill-porters with whom I'd travelled in Garhwal. The way that, barefoot, they crossed glaciers and mud slopes, ascended the steep gravel of a lateral moraine with never a slip, never a hurried step, had made me look again when I witnessed it; at the whole art of walking through which we come to perceive the world of mountains.

Even the Garhwali porters' easeful adaptation to environment wasn't new to me. As a young Manchester rock-climber at the outset of the 1960s, time and again watching Joe Brown on rock I'd seen this identical quality of movement. Rock-climbing's not that different to walking. Its greater danger demands greater consideration be given to every move made, but the essential principle is the same – a step, and then another, and on you go in as smooth and unfussy a manner as the terrain allows. Not the distant object but the immediate act become your focus. You are immersed not in ambition but in movement, and in this all our human distinctions are rendered curiously irrelevant. With Joe's climbing, at times it was impossible to tell whether the route he moved up with such inexorable, studied grace was easy, or of the most extreme difficulty. I remember in my own heyday as a climber those times when concentration would be so acute that the rock became simply the matrix with which your own energy was perfectly attuned. The human and essentially egotistical gradations put upon these ways of ascent were irrelevant. All had become one, all climbs were of the same difficulty, unquantifiable. You moved, handled your materials, at those times with a universal rhythm that was the same as that by which Merang working on his boat, Joe Brown on a gritstone outcrop, or the Garhwali porters, whose names I can no longer recall, were possessed.

At the heart of all this is the notion of a respectful communion. Whether it be with nature or a loved one, this mutuality and consideration, this perfection of rhythm is its refined expression. That we should often consider those who most obviously possess it as primitive is one of our civilisation's many paradoxes. The modern mountaineer – 'conquistador of the useless' in Lionel Terray's grandiose phrase – often as not is rapist rather than lover; or if the latter at all, one clumsily and urgently bent on his or her own gratification, regardless of the cost, the mountains then 'so rudely forced.'

There is a 'how' as well as an enduring 'why' attached to our going into the mountains. A faction among the mountaineers themselves discuss endlessly the 'ethics' of what they see as their sport, but in general this is shallow, necessary, prescriptive stuff, promoting codes of practice – rules to ensure the continuance of some semblance of a primal environment, or a level playing field for adherents to the vertical realms – rather than contemplation of how our ways of being among mountains may otherwise inhabit our lives.

In terms of eliciting from us any coherent philosophical response, the mountains are problematical. All too often their heights and misty vapours set our thinking upon them towards the hieratic or the vapid. How many funeral addresses have I endured, for those of my friends who have died in climbing them, where the text, gesturally, unthinkingly, has been 'I will lift up mine eyes unto the hills, whence cometh my salvation'? What salvation was it for these friends, among whom down the years of my involvement with mountains there have been so many deaths? It is no use flourishing this verse emptily and providing no sense of its relevance, especially in situations like these – of young people passing so long before their time. What salvation do the hills bring? To us, who continue with our lives ... ?

'In the mountains, there you feel free,' wrote Eliot in 'The Burial of the Dead' – the first book of *The Waste Land*.

That sense first intruded on my consciousness when I came to notice the rimming hills of Derbyshire rising on clear days in the far distance above the bomb sites and slum terraces where I grew up:

'Look, mountains ... !'

Robert Roberts' response was to look – not just to glance with nodding assent but to look with his full attention, and to feel that they rose there 'like the ramparts of Paradise.'

To look, and to feel: as the hill-porter looks to his next step and feels the shifting balance of his body adjusting to it; as the hill-shepherds of Eryri with whom I lived and worked through some of the most intense and educative years of my life – they at the very end of their centuries-old way of life – looked across their mountain pastures and felt every nuance and affect of that landscape. It is through these patiently adapted modes of being that we climb on to the 'ramparts of paradise' – that might otherwise be just hills, recreational facilities, or mineral, sylvicultural and industrial resources. I was fortunate in that my childhood home environment of the city, with its smogs and slums and tight enclosure, was so dispossessed of that basic human right to interaction with nature that when, early, I made my fearful way out into the hills, all was new. I escaped from the city and, like a released prisoner, knew instinctively that 'In the mountains, there you feel free ... '

The guardedness and defendedness that not just the society of my upbringing but in some measure all societies require, was neither relevant nor necessary there. Memory takes me back to a bright morning in the harsh winter of 1963. I'd set off early from Greenfield. The Isle of Skye road was blocked by snow, and the gleaming drifts spread right across Wessenden Head Moor, where Ian Brady and Myra Hindley were burying the bodies of their victims. I kept to the rim of the gritstone edges – Dovestones and Ravenstones – making for Black Hill, and in front of me the arctic hares loped and scattered away, the crystal snow glittering as they ran, and there was a feeling in me for them that I had never before known and could not then name, compounded of love and wonderment.

Here is the essence of the 'why' of our going to the mountains. It is for the gifts they bring to our consciousness. The dark of a moonless night is thinning. I shift position in the crevice of rocks where I lie. My hair is pearled with mist. I climb from my sleeping bag, shivering in the damp air, busy myself about lighting the stove as the world grows bright around me. Suddenly, beyond Sgurr nan Gillean's black peak, the sun breaks though clouds, above which, islanded, are all the summits of the Highlands. It climbs free of its vaporous braidings and trailings and etches the ridge that stretches and switchbacks ahead into our day with vivid, golden light; and I know in that instant that it is the taking of the path happily, and not the acheing to be at its conclusion, that matters. And so it is: the small flowering plants among the rocks, gleaming from shadow; the texture and the grip of gabbro throwing my body upwards as I pad the slabs of Bidein Druim nan Ramh; that airy, fissile, basaltic crest of the Inaccessible Pinnacle – from each moment of perception that they bring comes a kind of joy that lures and thrills us on along the path. Maybe we will reach Gars Bheinn by sunset to greet the sun again as it circles down into the Hebridean Sea. If not, so what, for our store's laid in; of memories, dreams, reflections, delight.

For us to pick among, gain comfort from, and wisdom too, perhaps.

I sit on a snow shoulder at 20,000 feet in the Himalayas, the jagged rock ridge that led here dropping away beneath, hanging glaciers on either side. Out of the glare of the sun, its pinions hissing in the still, thin air, an alpine chough swoops down to land 20 feet away. I throw food to it, in gratitude and amused wonderment. It cocks its head, struts over like an old sailor, and gobbles it up, looks across to me for more. As I write this, remembering, I know that in my home hills of Eryri, in their nest on the back wall of the quarry high on Garnedd Elidir, already even among the snow the red mouths of the young ravens will be agape, and in a few short months, God willing, I shall thrill to the playful glories of their flight, smile as they harry the grey falcon who is their only peer.

These gifts that the hills bring, and the communion they share with us; seeing becomes being where we learn to bless and to love. And as they affect generously our states of being, so that we open to the world and are one with it, in that lies the value of the mountains to us.

PART ONE: CLIMBS

YOUNG CLIMBER

These are some of the earliest attempts – juvenilia, if you like – that I made to engage in writing with the experience of rock-climbing, and to convey as best as I was then able its atmosphere and motivation. I find it quite poignant, and historically interesting, to look back on their assurance, innocence and romantic enthusiasm after having witnessed the last four decades of intense development and change in the sport.

1: A NOTE ON COMMITMENT (1967)

Walk in to the Padarn Lake bar in Llanberis any Saturday night and look around among the motley congregation. Any preconceived notion you might have of the 'hard man' would surely go wildly amiss in picking out this sport's most polished performers. The boots and beards of the admiring cluster most thickly round certain shrines: a bandy-legged, close-cropped, short and sherpa-smiling man circulates in the central area, poking callous fun at all who come his way: close at hand is his chief member of crew, scoring with a quick inward laughter at any crass comment thrown to him. On the other edges, before delving into the brash wilderness before the bar (land of brag, boast and bombast), a long and stooping man smiles with a slow acceptance, aloof as the respect for his ability allows. Everywhere between them the crew's petty officer wanders in wild abandon, a fierce flurry of gesture, joke and endless enthusiasm signifying the nativity of each new half-commitment, each idea as yet, or ever, unresolved.

There seems a new attitude abroad for which all that is 'classical' or 'romantic' in mountaineering leaves us a little unprepared; an overt competition and mistrust of commitment in personal relationships which seems to stem directly from the nature of the sport's development; an attitude even or perhaps especially noticeable amongst its top performers. We sense a paradox: the more complete your qualities of commitment on rock, the less your degree of commitment in life. Even to those who know him best, Brown remains an enigma; Boysen is a man whom few know closely; Crew's motives are completely his own, unquestionable through being unknown.

What qualities have the new hard routes these men are engaging with? Is there a new isolation, a new degree of utter commitment to certain sets of crucial moves that climbs (with very few exceptions) had hitherto really lacked? Perhaps the best way to explore this attitude may be to analyse my personal reactions to three routes which seem to me to be classics of the new climbing. I could have chosen other routes: the continuous coolness required by a route like South Stack's *Red Wall*, or the short, sharp aggression of a hard gritstone climb; but the three I'd like to use here are *Vector*, *Nexus* and *Troach*, each of which could be claimed with some justification to be a classic of the last ten years.

With *Vector*, the crux moves begin at a large and very comforting runner (an aspect shared by *Nexus*) – a security which once left behind is unrecapturable. The first move off the pinnacle is one which I certainly couldn't reverse – a body lean and an awkward kick round into balance, followed by a layaway move up on to two small footholds; the next moves are the crux. To someone of my height, a delicate step up with a very rounded handhold gets you to a layaway hold; step up again, a breathless change of hand, bridge, layback and you're on the Ochre slab.

Having once left the pinnacle, you feel a commitment so complete that your only choice is to carry it through, a complete simplicity (within the framework of its particular technical complexity) of action, direction and situation.

Nexus is easier, but even more committing; the full-weight thread at your feet seems to possess a peculiarly rapid quality of diminution as you move away from it. Rounded layaway for the left hand, tiny fingerhold for the right, and for the feet nothing but friction flat against the wall.

A few feet above is a layback round a roof; tentatively you try the first half-move, winding up the mind, then it's made, a sudden coolness and control of physical action, at the roof a pause, thoughts of reversal quickly put aside; laybacking with a restful detachment, talking about your situation to the people beneath with intrigued objectivity, resting in the layback before making the next move up the thin groove. With a strange ease you have assumed an air of calm. Once committed, responsibility realised, there is an inevitability, no conscious effort, about carrying the action through.

On these two routes, an act of commitment to a complex technical problem is faced in a comparatively safe situation. *Troach* offers a similar, but slightly easier, set of moves in a completely different situation. You may not, to borrow Eliot's phrase, feel:

23

A fear like birth and death,
When we see birth and death alone,
In a void, apart.

But you will certainly be aware that your protection offers very little security in the event of a fall: you feel isolated, a small fly on a very large wall. To commit yourself to the crux moves is a lonely and responsible action (the appeal of which Bentham defines in the following note: 'Constantly actual end of action on the part of every individual at the moment of action; his greatest happiness according to his view of it at the moment'). In a situation like that below the crux of Troach, you are faced with this definition of happiness in close proximity to its ultimate form: the end of action is in view, its attainment demands for a few moments the total absorption in the problem of your mental and physical faculties – a totality of commitment, for should it falter, the outcome would most probably be fatal. In life that situation is a rare chance ...

2: HUBRIS (1971)

Boots, boots, boots; armies on the move; they will conquer these mountains. Marching, ever marching, trampling, scraping, clawing. My friend, I suspect you are insensitive. Hubris, my friend, with your bold laugh, your ambition, your avarice and your black beard bristling. I hear you loudly in this hollow cwm and I see the determination in your jaw jutting more fiercely than any crag. Hubris, my friend, I am down at heart yet I am envious of your strength, of your assurance. Beneath these cliffs my heart trembles and cries; stones, these stones; change me as they will, I will not nor could not change them. Yet they do not change you. How do you remain so, as immutable as the mountain? In what certainty did you grow, whence the armour of those bland, sure looks and easy laughter? Can you see this cliff, oh can you see it? Do you not see? What? That it does not reach the heavens. Flat. Not infinite.

There is a cliff above me and it is not black nor huge, as you would call it, I know. Nor will it uplift with voluntary power instinct. No: fixed and immutable, as you, my friends. It is not a black cliff. Let us not bandy words. Words that are brittle, that will snap the thread of meaning: it is a grey cliff, sometimes rose-red towards evening. And there are flowers here, so easily trampled down.

This carnival, these performers, walking up towards it: oh this I like, these people, so much diversity on a single track. Train with your metal lungs straining; effort is movement is vapour. Up and down. And here is Mrs Williams whose ministering smile never changes, though her lemonade comes in plastic cups and her tea is 'not now as it hath been of yore' you sentimentalists would say. From her hospitable bosom we go on to this grey cliff. I think I do not regret the passing of its well-fleshed ledges, for the bone structure is still fine. And here Hubris and I meet again; he shouts to me and his strong voice comes down from a dozen places disrespectful. And again the foreboding, not of the place, but of the event.

I don't know what I've come to do; one move is much like another, altered more or less by place or mood or time. And what's line against the tortuousness of a life? The Boldest – shall we do that? It has a long groove to start: the groove is no harder than it ought to be, as rock defines itself. Yes, it is good. The crux traverse is on comforting holds and not the crux: so far I have been in no doubt. But now a little wall and a long drop and little holds and little protection; I am aware now of certain factors: these little holds could break; indeed, will break if I pull a little too hard in the wrong direction. And these footholds, small, my boots ragged and near-rubberless: only by a great effort am I convinced of their sufficiency. You see I am not sure; the rock above me is grey mist that will become real only by touch. So few initiate, and their accounts secretive. I am really not too sure; about these feet and about these holds. The effort is one of will: yes, I want to; of my own volition I will commit myself; to this coming situation. No, I am not certain; I have only a startled faith in the outcome of the action; my certainties are in suspension and I scarcely know how these devotions came about. And you, Hubris, down there with your measured tread and your manner grand as oblivion and your covetous, uneasy stare, what assurances would you give me? I have chosen to be here; there are threads of assurance and hope. I do not believe that I am going to fall, no more than I know I shall get up. Pete Allison fell off and was not killed. Image of a body cartwheeling and freed from all restraint of will, the sound and the red flesh and the moment of utter silence ...

In movement is doubt's alternative – a calm and sudden panic, re-echoed through every sinew and nerve.

You must go so near to the edge really to know you are there. Hubris, your feet are on the ground and firm, but do you know how far you can go? What do you know, more than that your feet are on the ground? And give me no pretence, you would take the ground with you, so much for each foot, so much certainty. So you will know no more than that the ground of your belief has risen, and taken you up to the crest of this crag. Hubris, I cannot show you. Here on this tower, this whole kingdom which we cannot know. Walk along the edge: no, you can go no farther, unless the edge juts out a little farther from time to time; always that beyond which you cannot touch but towards which you yearn; always the quest for an ultimate, whether it be negation in that void or something gained towards an absolute never attained. But always promised, every movement along the edge a tenuous act of faith that it will not, though it could so easily, break and slide into the blackness that surrounds the narrowing, sharpest peak of consciousness. The action, and the meaning, and the meaning more than a derivative of the action. Perhaps ...

3: RIGHT UNCONQUERABLE: A GRITSTONE PAEAN (1971)

In retrospect, Stanage is for me the focal point in that Golden Age when we first came to the hills; a pastel-sketched mood of mellow remembrance, the eastern seaboard of the Peak, west-facing over wave upon wave of moorland edge. Brown peat and purple heather, the rock so softly red in evening sunlight filtered through the smoke-haze of distant, unseen industry. So much beauty in those smoke-bruised sunset skies: violets and purples and violent reds, sometimes the Northern Lights flickering columnar over Bleaklow and Kinder, flanked by the lume of vast cities below the moorland night.

A time past, when the rocks stood about unknown to us, and eager and lustful we explored their every intimacy, climbed until the failing light veiled the crags with shadow and widowed them into night; and tired we would gather bracken golden from the slopes to sleep in sandy caves, our hands lacerated by the crystals of many a crack savagely fought. Early days, early struggles, our blood on the rock as an inextricable bond of friendship about which we built the flesh of our climbing career. The smoke-blackened surface of the rough rock, grouse croaking away and the fresh smell of wet bracken on a June morning; these are the reality of the place. Great nebs worn by the wuthering wind into stern, harsh forms. Rough rock, wild wind, and the reality of the place. Gritstone has its own form of consciousness: quite simply, it possesses the finest and purest free-climbing ethic in the world. Every new wave in British climbing has gained its initial momentum from gritstone's wild and prehensile freedom of attack. The keynote of gritstone climbing is aggression: the climbs are short and steep; characteristically they deal out inordinately large quantities of pain and fear. Torn hands, scraped knees, strained arms and a dry throat are all in a gritstoner's day: the cracks in particular are armed with vicious teeth. They have about them a degree of static malignity which demands an equal display of controlled temper to overcome. It's not that climbing on gritstone is more difficult than climbing on other forms of rock, it's just that the defences are more systematically designed to disconcert: rounded holds, rough bulging cracks, and an overbearing angle; you just have to get used to them.

Stanage is the great crag; four miles long, and with over 500 climbs. It would be impossible to get a consensus of opinion on which one is typical, let alone best. There are probably 50 climbs as good in their own way as the *Right Unconquerable*. But this one exemplifies the gritstone approach, and historically it stands at the beginning of an era – the last of the great cracks of Stanage to be climbed, and the first of Joe Brown's classic gritstone climbs.

27

Brown and Stanage! Mohammed and Mecca and many subsequent prayer-mats. In 1947 the 17-year-old Brown came to the mountain long revered of his elders, and climbed it in unfaltering style, a rope attached to make the feat respectable. Since that time the climb has come to stand in much the same relationship to gritstone climbing as *Cenotaph Corner* is to climbing in Wales; it is not so much a test of technique as one of approach, an initiation into the attitude of the harder climbs.

Relatively short, 50 feet more or less, it takes an overhanging flake crack running up the face of an otherwise remarkably smooth buttress. Round to the left it has a sister, who leads you on gently but clams up at just the wrong moment. There is a common start, a short crack which most people fall off before they realise they're not going to run up it. A step right and it stretches out above you. The first straight section of the crack is easily climbed, before the way is sealed by the base of a jutting flake. Above lie step upon step of overhanging flake, 30 feet, and the crux at the top. There's a decision to be made, that's a long way to go on ever-weakening arms and what little courage is given to man; if you want it, you have to fight for it. Hunching your body beneath the flake, reaching high and out one-handed, suddenly you go, swinging right up on to the flake on huge layback holds, hooked hands, the crack sometimes closing, occasioning little shuffles rightwards, awkward hand-changes, anxious moments, racing up the flake to where the top layer juts disturbingly, and all the time on your arms, moving fast. If you do this climb at all, you do it quickly.

The top is rounded and frightening; you haul yourself over on flat hands in exultation. A race against failing strength and breath, fighting all the way, yet an absolute joy in movement. The gritstone essence, living it fully over a few feet of rock. Let them be never so short, for me there are no better climbs in the world.

CLOSING ON DARKNESS

The stepping aside from life's ordinary constraints, the modern version of what was I suppose the battle-frenzy, has been for me at times a crucial part of climbing's appeal. These three essays all evoke something of that. The first of them became very notorious, and has been referenced in publications as disparate as The Face *and the* Journal of Analytical Psychology. *It began life quite innocently as an honest account of a daft, semi-impulsive experience, embroidered on to which was a bit of coat-trailing intended to wind up an older generation who regarded such antics as beyond the pale. The po-faced footnote was insisted upon if it was to be published, and I went along with that in some glee, thinking its very po-facedness actually increased the piss-taking quotient. Am I now quietly appalled at what I used to get up to? Do I take responsibility for the example it might set others? No, I don't. Life is contingent. Responsibility for our actions is our own. And God preserve us from a world governed by Health & Safety decrees. If you want to climb, this is the core experience, and not the sad pastiche available from moulded resin bolted on to indoor plywood panels.*

4: STREET ILLEGAL (1977)

You would say I was not well. My life was in pieces and I was too shocked to recognise the case. But this is a broader perspective, and by-the-bye. I had been on Romney Marsh for a few days, trying (and failing) to get into the bed of a woman with large, sensual hands and a calm manner. We had smoked a lot of dope, touched once or twice without vibrancy, walked in greening fields, and little else.

Posthabui tamen illorum mea seria ludo.
    'For trifling sports I quitted grave affairs.' – [Virgil, Eclog. VII 17]

It was a willed thing. Very early on a March morning I left, drove fast along the South Coast, stopped briefly in Salisbury for tea near the Cathedral, and dreadful cheesecake, then drove on to Cheddar.

I parked at the upper end of the lay-by beneath *Coronation Street*. This I thought a wise precaution. In from the base of my ribs there was a certain thrilling tightness. As if the day for it had come. You have a thing suggested to you, perhaps even years before, and you know with a sense of terror that one day you have to put

29

yourself on those rails. In my case it had been seven, maybe eight, years ago, when I had first done the route with Frank Cannings. On top, he had said that it would be the great route to solo, and at the time he could have done it. I had just laughed, but really shuddered inwardly, really had been brought up sharp by the thought.

This day there was the momentum: inside somewhere quietly weeping, and all the while there was something inexorable going on. Firstly I put on my rock-boots, and fiddled with the laces several times to get the right balance between rigidity and comfort. Then I took two double tape slings and one shorter one, put them round my neck, checked my chalk bag, made sure the tapes were not tangled.

All this had been rather deliberately and slowly done, as if to wear down a bit of the momentum. I now sat in the car, took out the blanking plate where the radio would have been, reached in and brought out a tobacco tin. I cut myself two lines of coke on the lid – not too generous on this, I thought, take it easy – then snuffed them up, one for each nostril. Also, I unwrapped a piece of silver foil from a cigarette pack-et, which should have had some speed inside; but it had got damp and soaked into the backing paper, so I ate the paper.

I now sat back, shut my eyes, and breathed in and out, deeply, to relax. Part of me was subdued and very frightened, yet there was a sort of manic overdub on the basic rhythm of everything. I was zapping along and actually couldn't have given a fuck about anything; I was laughing. I set off and steamrollered it, pretty quietly up through the ivied bits, but then very powerful and determined, out over the two bulges of the first hard pitch.

On the bolt ledge I steadied my breathing, no more, just deeply in and out as I stood facing inwards, then up the crack, and out without hesitation round the jack-daw-polished hand-traverse of The Shield. It was easier than I'd remembered. Across The Shield I was so relieved I thought 'Good, take a blow,' clipped in two slings to the belay pegs, knotted, adjusted them, and sat there. It was not a wise thing to do. Up to this point I'd been motoring, moving fast and well. And now I broke the rhythm of the thing, sat down, and the subdued me broke back with a terrorised sense of the place I was in. I wept. Once in the slings, with the car park 300 feet below, I was so scared that I wept.

Leniter ex merito quicquid patiare ferendum est.
'Let pain deserv'd without complaint be borne.' [Ovid, Her. V 7]

It was something of a grey March afternoon with a suggestion of dampness about it and a little seepage from the crack in the bulge above. I was sitting there blubbering like a two-year-old, wanting my coke, my dog, horizontal earth under my feet, in just about reverse order.

The hysterics didn't last long, but once they had gone, I couldn't get back to being fast and loose. I was holding myself very tight, very hard, using a lot of control. I tried to focus out but there was nothing vital to focus on. The greyness – rock, sky, road – was everywhere. Even the grass had a wintergrey sheen. Not so much as a woodlouse faltering out of its crevice. If I just relaxed, I could relate to it, resign myself to it, and not give a fuck. I was letting myself down gently into being the objective correlative of a dead and inert world. Then some part of me rose on an inner scream, which modulated into a vicious controlling anger. Out of my slings and working myself on to the rock again, it was all wrong. I was absolutely tight. My moves were bad – jerky, hurried and imprecise. It was like watching a poor climber who might just make it. I saw a climber once on *Right Unconquerable* and it was the same sort of thing. His runners were coming out, he was right out at the edge of control, you were aching for him to make it, but the thing was so fine, so nearly not. Curiously, pathologically interesting, yet distasteful, as I would imagine a dung-beetle to be.

The groove and sidestep bulge of the crux were prolonged as something out of a nightmare. At the bulge my fingers felt to be slipping in the crack. I took the crack above very slowly, lumberingly, feeling almost safe. The last wall was damp and protracted. I was beginning to expect to make it, and holding back. At the top I crawled and bit grass, laughing.

Ridetque sui ludibria trunci.
'And soaring mocks the broken frame below.' [Lucan, IX, 14]

After a little while I got up and made my way down to the road. I now felt desolated. There was nothing cathartic in it. I felt worse than before. It seems odd to me that you, as readers, will evaluate it, say this or that about it, as though it mattered, which it did not. Just something, some sequence of psychic events combining with opportunity, produced it. Nothing changed by it. I doubt if I could ever do it again. Except that there are days when the rhythm builds up, the whole crazy edifice shifts, you cut loose, don't give a fuck, and you're away.

Dulce est disipere in loco.
'Wisdom at proper times is well forgot.' [Horace, Od. IV, xii 28]

Note: Even before publication the above article has been very heavily criticised, and the criticism may be justified. Three points seem to me salient: the drug references, the use of foul language, and the apparent intellectual snobbery of the Latin quotations.

On the first of these, my use of drugs, I can plead circumstantially that the time about which I write was one of emotional crisis. Some people find their outlets in drink or travel, work or suicide. My way out was, for a time, to become a habitual user of certain drugs. I don't now excuse it; it merely was so. With regard to the 'foul' language – not my phrase – the writer has a choice – to present a version of, or to represent, the peculiar idiom and rhythm of his own thoughts. I apologise to those to whom my representation gives offence. Lastly, the Latin quotations are not there to impress – I do not consider myself an erudite person and I do not wish to be considered as such. To me, these lines of Latin poetry have a currency; they comment, ironically, intuitively, humorously, upon situations in life of which their authors might not have dreamed. And by doing so, they affirm the ultimate community of Man. Contextualisation, not snobbery, is their purpose. The more learned of my critics will no doubt also have remembered their usage as epigraphs to the moral essays written by Dr Johnson under the pseudonym of 'The Rambler'.

5: ADVENTURING ON THE LLEYN (1991)

Hold your hand up to the white light above the dentist's chair and muscle fades to shadow, dark brittle sticks of bone show through. I noticed this the morning after our small Sunday afternoon adventure down on the Lleyn. Its intimation of mortality seemed more than usually apposite. My dentist is a climber. It's the way of things in North Wales. All the professional people are from the climbing ghetto: doctors, solicitors, accountants – even Ian Lowe, the climber's dentist:

'*Fantan B*, Ian – have you done it?'

'Yes – 23 years ago. It was quite popular at one time, wasn't it? Freda and I did it when she was six months pregnant. She found those top overhangs rather hard going. Dreadful descent to it, as I remember ... '

You can rely on Ian for an orderly account of things. I pressed him with another leading question:

'What is a *Fantan B*?'

'It's a drug. Pete Crew apparently found a discarded pharmaceutical container in the rubbish dump near where you start the route, and liked the name. I think it's an anti-depressant. Let's look it up.'

He picked up his formulary and thumbed through:

'Here we are – Fentan – that'll be it. Typical of Pete to get the spelling wrong. It's obsolete now, which would fit. When was the route done? About 1966 ... ?'

'Exactly then. He did it with MacNaught-Davies. I remember him raving about it. So everybody went down to do it and most of us ended up not being able to find it. Anyway, I did it yesterday. It was terrifying.'

Ian smiled his detached dentist's smile at this:

'Yes, I remember feeling a little apprehensive here and there ... '

I held up my hand to the light again, old mortality imaging forth, and comforted, relaxed back to await the drill.

Cold December morning on the streets of Llanberis. I skulk into The Newt's house on Goodman Street, let hot coffee and a fire take the chill from my fingers.

'Any bright ideas, Andy?'

'Have you done *Fantan B*?'

This stirred memories, but they were as vague and unsatisfying as December daylight, and all to do with horrid descents. In the course of the day they resolved themselves into having been to look for it once, and having gone to the wrong crag – Trwyn y Gorlech rather than Craig y Llam. This had given me a jaundiced view of climbing on the north coast of the Lleyn: 'Guano, shattered granite, vegetable decay – frightful to get at, worse to get off!'

'So you've done it?'

'Not sure – I remember doing something on Yr Eifl, but I've no idea what.'

'Paul's guide raves about it – let's give it a try. He also gives it a very long description, which usually means that he's had a gripper on it.'

'Show me ... '

One of many things that Paul Williams' guide *Rock Climbing in Snowdonia* is good for is getting you enthused. I read the Lleyn preamble: ' ... the Lleyn holds a certain fascination for a discerning clientele: the climber in search of adventure, the connoisseur of the esoteric, the seeker after solitude ... to see another party is a rarity.' So far so good – glimmerings of interest were aroused. But what did he have to say about the route?

'A thrilling sea-cliff expedition with impressive situations which has been compared with *A Dream of White Horses* as an experience, though *Fantan B* is much steeper and more isolated ... difficulties increase with height ... rock sometimes suspect ... belays and runners are often difficult to locate ... '

'All right – I'll go for that. HVS 4c – that means terror-terrain, doesn't it?'

'You get that impression from the rest of the description, don't you.'

We dawdled around, drank more coffee, and towards midday sauntered out of the house. This may have been a mistake. We were setting off on a miserable December day to drive for the best part of an hour to do a 700-ft route with a complex and frightening approach, difficult route-finding, seven or eight pitches, poor belays. All this, as you know intuitively at the time, adds up to the trap closing behind you. But you carry on because to commit yourself to it brings into play a primal reliance on your own resources that's close to the essence of why we climb.

Turning off the road beyond the grey-terraced chaos of Llithfaen, a track winds forever down plunging hillsides. Steep. Rough. Wet. Will the car get back up it? Already, questions-that-will-have-to-be-answered are being set. We park in a mouldering quarry. On its farther side a rusting hawser runs through a stone gap. We cross to it and look down on the sea, shockingly far beneath, the grey winter grass steepening out of view. We consider the matter, go back to the car, decide to carry a sack each and to descend in our trainers rather than rock shoes. Clearly we're not bound for some sunny, brief rock-outing.

When we return to the hawser, the sacks bulge more than might be expected if they contained only a pair of rock-shoes apiece. This leisurely approach and inspection has taken us beyond one o'clock. Barely three hours of daylight left! I

34

remember a December day at Cheddar 20 years ago when Sue Whaling and myself had started *Coronation Street* at three o'clock, finished the top pitch in darkness, been faced with finding the descent in pitch-black night. Looking around at the old quarry workings between the car and where the route must finish, it occurs to me that there may be similar excitement in store.

The hawser is knotted loosely round a granite block, the gap in the rock wall polished by passage of anxious bums. Andy heads off down. After 60 feet and a small rock step, the hawser ends. Damp grass heels over in convex plunge towards sullen water. We falter down, zig-zagging, fearful, questing for the route. A few sheep watch, then flounce purposefully away to gentler pastures:

'This is worse than the descent to Easter Island Gully!'

' ... And I always put a rope down for that!'

We don't have a spare rope, and if we did it wouldn't be long enough, so we carry on with our nervous crawl downwards. I remember Al Harris walking unconcernedly across the steep grass above Cilan, and think what wimps he would consider us. Eventually, matters ease. We reach rock terraces running out west 60 feet above the sea, and traverse across sluices and dripping slabs to ledges where the cliff rises vertically from the sea. Beyond them an arête rears at an 80-degree angle for several hundred feet. Above, fronds of grass like hanks of soiled and rotting fleece are caught in the mesh of this fractured granite. We belay on a Friend. Andy takes a bunch of pegs and a hammer from his sack.

'Psychological props,' he explains, placing a Leeper next to the Friend. Beneath us a seal the size of a small whale rolls and gawps.

Andy has left Paul's guide at the car – sensibly, since it weighs over a pound and our sacks already are mysteriously over-full. Instead, he has brought an old interim guide with an inexact description. The first feature is obvious – a pink ledge out on the arête. He ties on and leads across to it, belays, and I follow after hammering out the Leeper.

The climbing is easy enough but everything is covered in birdlime and the holds creak and shift as you use them. On the ledge I pick at his huge rack, adding to my own burden, reassure myself about Andy's belay and set off to traverse steeper rock to a further rib. Nothing is hard, but nothing reassures either. Cracks are all parallel-sided and poor for nuts, or behind detached blocks. Holds are latticed-about with fracture lines. Instead of simple, solid structures, the definition of the rock splinters, and with it ease of mind. Beyond a step up on to the rib that's given 4a in Paul's description but would be straightforward on sound rock, a scooped and blocky area leads up to overhangs. At a ledge beneath them I tie on to a rusted blade peg and drape a long sling carefully over a flat spike to back it up. There is no obvious way ahead.

My vote, when Andy joins me, goes to the left arête, which looks polished. But the guide gestures right. He traverses to an arête, disappears round it, the rope runs up, he reappears briefly on the edge, is gone from sight again, then stillness, silence. I wait. The rope snails out a foot or two more over the arête, then stills. It is very cold, the water very far beneath, Ireland somewhere over there in the haze, brighter in that quarter, reminding of time passing. I intone Buck Mulligan's address: 'Grey, sweet mother. The snotgreen sea. The scrotumtightening sea.' A seal wallows, a cormorant hustles past with a low, complaining croak. Lichens that would glow orange in the sun are muddy-hued. Tide withdraws in little, gasping sighs from a shingle strand across the headland. Our life and ambition are a presumption to the place. From somewhere above comes the 'ting, ting, ting' of a driven peg. I cannot recall when I last heard the sound. The halfway marker on our 180-ft ropes slips through my fingers. There is more movement, no sound. I shiver a little as a wind brushes the ledge where I sit. Minutes race as time crawls. The rope's taken in. I untie from the belays, stamp, shake warm blood into cold limbs, move stiffly to the arête.

The view is suddenly heart-stopping. The ropes run up and across into the centre of a huge, scooped face. Andy's perched, a tiny figure, on a ledge beneath tier upon tier of spiring, dark overhangs. Streaks of birdlime are the only light relief to the dark, gathered power of the place. I hurry to join him. The climbing is nowhere technical, just naggingly insecure. A hundred feet on fissile holds, and he's teased in three runners. I climb past him up an awkward ramp without daring to look at his belay, and in my turn tie on to two poor nuts, and a Friend in an expanding crack. The rock above is oppressively steep. When he arrives, we piece together the line from the description. The next stance, 60 feet away, is a jutting, ridiculous block between sets of overhangs, a falcon's perch, a wild trip. Simultaneously we look at my belay, then at each other. No words are spoken. I drag a jacket and scarf out of my sack:

'My psychological props,' I explain, and take a look at my watch. It is a quarter to four.

He climbs a wall for 30 feet without runners into the base of a groove, then places three of them with an audible sigh of relief. To his right are guano-streaked prows and roofs. He sidles across into them, flicks a chock up into a notch above him, launches out with the brief injunction to 'Watch me!' With a gasp he flops on to a ledge. Out of his sight a falcon flashes by. 'Out there!' he yelps, in fearful delight.

Paul's guide gives this pitch 4b, and technically it's no more than that. But the sea is hundreds of feet beneath, rock poor, protection scant. As you pull on to the ledge a nest of gorse-sticks, fur and bones greets you. You are in the fortress of the Roc.[1] There is no retreat.

Chance or bad management has given me the crux pitch. It climbs two overhangs. The first of them is straight above and the light's failing fast. I reach up for what look like holds and, fearful of delay, when they come to hand pull on them. They bring me to a ledge. I fiddle a nut insecurely into a fractured area of rock and heave up a smooth slab to the next roof. There is a flaking peg beneath it that I clip, fiddling the tape round a nubbin of rock alongside as I do. It looks like the last barrier. I step up on friction and grope for holds. There are none, so I layback an edge in strange exultation at its technicality, angle my right foot carefully into a poor nick, and grasp a flat block above in glad ferocity. A great sweep of slab soars black against the sky. I sidestep to a ledge, place a nut that might be good if I could see, and a worse one, and bring up Andy. He scrabbles round the top roof and surges past. Rope creeps out, darkness falls. He runs out the full length. Across the gloom of Caernarfon Bay, South Stack lighthouse flashes, the lights of Brynsiencyn and Newborough glimmer. I follow blindly, fingers an obscure, thin-muscled gleam, not knowing if he's belayed, climbing by touch. At the top, he fishes two headtorches out of his sack:

'More psychological props?' I ask.

'Alpine scale, alpine gear – I thought this might happen!'

We creep along quarry ledges, throw stones to gauge drops, reach the car; chastened laughter from prisoners on parole who know they must go back, are unsure which is captivity, which is release.

---

[1] Interestingly, there were recurrent reports of sea-eagles being sighted on this coast in the early 1990s, but no next was ever located. And this certainly wasn't a raven's or a peregrine's nest.

37

6: 'IN DREAMS BEGINS RESPONSIBILITY.' (1993)

Because of a certain anguish in my heart and mind I went out this evening with rock-shoes and a chalk bag to seek on the rock some clarity and peace. Not that I went far – just along the road to the Bus Stop quarries. I started by soloing the 5c pitch up the middle of the 50-ft slab on Blast Shelter crag, and did not feel good. Feet were shaky and the fingers felt weak, but there was a mental drive pushing me on. I forced myself up the slanting crack where fingers gouge into soft, repellent mud, then crossed the road into the Bus Stop itself.

There are times when you walk as if in a dream, drawn on. The Rippled Slab at the back of the quarry was gleaming, a glistening streak of damp here and there across its top from the morning's rain. As I flitted across the blocks jumbled beneath it, Stevie Haston's account of going up to identify Derek Hersey's body after his death-fall from the west face of Sentinel a few weeks before was running through my mind: 'All we could say was, "Yes, those were the clothes he was wearing." There's not much left of a body after it's hit rock from 600 feet.'

Normally an image so morbid and powerful would register, but when part of your mind is a dead zone your will drives on and the rest of you, hapless, does not much care. I found myself at the foot of *Massambula*, and though I'd not soloed anything of that grade, at that height, for years, knew that I was locked in – that from the emotional morass a fierce head had arisen, muttering its need for icy simplicity.

So I tightened my shoes, rubbed the edges until the rubber squeaked, bouldered the most difficult moves I could find to the first ledge, wandered up to the flared crack where, if leading, you can place a nut, moved past to the hand-traversing flake, stepped up and – for luck or in grim amusement – flicked the loose bolt-hanger so that it rattled dully round on its axis.

For some reason, I found myself wishing that I'd brought a sling with me. I was maybe 60 feet up by this time and the landing looked bad from that height – sharp boulders, wicked crevices, a steep slope. I think you might not survive a fall from here. But I remember too the time 15 years ago on *Coronation Street* when I'd had slings with me, had clipped into the pegs after The Shield, had sat there and become terrorised by the situation.

I began to feel at the moves above. Understand that I am not a particularly good climber these days. Ragged tendons and arthritic finger joints – legacy of 34 years at the sport – make the training without which there is no strength and stamina a purgatory to me now. So instead I just climb when the opportunity arises, which is not as often as I could wish, for the partners of your own generation when you reach this stage have mostly died or desisted. And what is it you see or seek anyway from these mirrors in the cliffs?

I look into my glass,
And view my wasting skin,
And say, 'Would God it came to pass
My heart had shrunk as thin!'

Isn't the heart, though, in all phases of our life, the last thing to shrink? As year mounts upon year and desire and illusion are stripped away, in the one direction, in the isolation of your warrior maleness maybe you're left only with the tragic exultancy of Byrhtwold's great rallying cry from The Battle of Maldon:
'Thought shall be the harder, heart the keener,
Courage the greater as our strength grows less.'
Not that my courage felt great by the bolt on *Massambula*, but in my mind I knew the crucial juncture. There is a sequence of moves – 5b going on 5c, with the rock above difficult to read and the climbing of a type that would be precarious to reverse. The rain had washed the chalk from the holds so I was unsure, even though I'd done the route on two or three occasions, which way to go. I ran my fingers up and felt holds at the extremity of reach, body spreadeagled on the slab. They are small. They take maybe a third of the first joint of three fingers. And they flex and are flat rather than incut. I can tell myself rationally in situations like this that they'll suffice, but still, as I splay my foot across to an awkwardly placed and equivalently sized edge, why should I believe what I assert? And the sun has gone in, the slab's white gleam has become a dull, cloud-shadowed ivory, and by that gate what dreams come in?

If I thought hard enough I would imagine the drops of rain, heavy and slow as the last moments after release, upon my cheek. So instead I feel intensely at these holds, hear from within my chest a strange swishing of blood against echo-chambered rock, move up, move down, move up and am decided through a convulsive arching of the back and a clenching of fingertips on these flat smooth nicks, and a breathless, precise angling of toes on to chalked rock edges. After which comes a trembling and a great fear, because now I am 70 feet up and the involuntary shake of a leg on holds like this will cause my foot to slip, so by effort of will I still the movement, relax, and then – what comes?

Oh, I'll tell you – a great deep breath and I am calm, fiercely happy and I climb slowly on in deliberate control, skitter back laughing down slatey scree and make my way over to the foot of *Scarlet Runner*, which is two grades harder all round at E4, 6a, and while the moment lasts – for all this takes place in a suspended moment – I climb calmly and delightedly up that and find it easier than the first. If I fell from here, I tell myself – well, I could jump into that tree. This is less difficult, I tell myself, its reputation rests only on the distance you must climb as a leader before clipping the first of its four bolts. Its supposedly ferocious move high up feels no such thing. Soon I'm clattering back down the scree again, to complete the trio of quality routes on the slab by taking in *Gnat Attack* – at E1, 5c supposedly the easiest of the three.

Except that it doesn't turn out that way.

Soloing is a quirky activity, with a psychology all its own. *Gnat Attack*, for example, is a relatively straightforward pitch to lead. Like the other two routes, it's about 100 feet long and bolt-protected. But as you start the crux sequence on *Gnat Attack* the bolt is at head level. Also, you cannot quite make the move statically – to the soloist an important consideration – and the edge you're making for dynamically is thin and fragile. Finally the landing, if you were to fall, is worse than that from *Massambula*, and from as great a height. To add to these mental problems, my son arrived beneath as I was feeling at the move and proceeded to chatter about television programmes. A frame of my dear friend Peter Biven's death – at an age younger than I am now – at his son's feet in the Avon Gorge flashed through my mind. I switched off both it and my son's chat, launched into the sequence before hard-won confidence ebbed away. It felt the hardest climbing of the afternoon, I had not expected it to be, and so was disappointed, needed something else, went over to *Fool's Gold* with its tenuous 6a move at 30 feet and thought to try that. Still William tagged along, talked away, exacerbated the feeling of guilt already present in this fool's game. So after exploring the moves and making up my mind that I could or should do them, I sent him home to feed the dog, and my sense of responsibility aside from action with him.

The thing I like about soloing is that you have to climb so cautiously and well. On *Fool's Gold* a thin crack runs down and divides. You move into it from an easy groove on the left. There is a good finger-lock, greasy with rain tonight, low down, from which you cannot quite span to the crucial objective of an incut hold above. The footholds are verging on non-existent – a polished pyrites excrescence for the right toe, a shallow vertical groove for the left. There is a higher but poorer finger-jam. To climb the route statically, you use the lower jam to position your feet, work the fingers of your left hand into the higher lock, straighten, transfer confidence and weight on to it, then breathlessly let go and reach for the hold.

If either foot slipped, the jam wouldn't hold but you'd get away with broken ankles. I made the move. The crack above was anti-climactic. I came down, took off my boots, ambled across the depths – filled in, grassed over now – where Al Harris and I played our youthful, fearsome games, and down to the road where young Jack Longland, grandson of the great, berated me for the performance and I just laughed and evaded. A woman walked past with a baby in a pram. The sun had slipped under the clouds to shine like a searchlight. It was the most beautiful evening, colours glowing and adrenaline-dyed to an aching splendour. I went and sat in a place in the fragrant heather where I often go, looking out west over the Irish Sea, and because I was relaxed and a tension had dissipated, I promptly fell asleep and dreamed a vivid dream.

You know the way it is with dreams – all the unpurged images of day in weird conjunction? I was sitting in the Sligachan Hotel with Menlove Edwards and Norman Collie, who were discussing incubus boulders and broken pipes whilst I talked with Sandro Delmastro, the enigmatist, who looked – in my dream as in Primo Levi's description – like Dermot Somers. It was after midday, raining beyond the windows. A sturdy, vigorous woman came in whom I felt I should know but perhaps, in the way of dreams, did not. She announced that it was clearing and sure enough, Sgurr nan Gillean resolved from the vapours. Menlove and the Professor continued their conversation. Sandro gave me a sly, encouraging look as the woman and I set off towards the hill.

How we raced across that bog and up the spur that curves sensually round past the tiny lochan to the foot of Pinnacle Ridge, where the rock at times was so rough to touch it seemed the magma still burned. Spires eased past as we mounted them in a sweet flow. We found ourselves beneath the abseil from the third by a traverse, and were soon slipping through the hole to emerge on the summit of the Young Men's Peak, where public schoolboys brayed of bloodied knees and lit mincing cigarettes whilst we pressed on down the West Ridge, swarming down the exposed chimney as a party from an outdoor centre were roped and belayed down a parallel line. We ourselves at the Bhasteir Tooth took out the rope, dismayed at the sight of Patey and Tiso beneath us, the former laughing at the latter up-ended by his own sack in the snow. There was a peg – no back-up to it, and it flexed, but still I threaded the rope through and lowered on to it, conscious of the weight of self and sack. The rope was too short. A leap into a gulley. When my companion came down she threw me her sack, then leapt too, the drop beneath immense.

All afternoon we pounded along, over Bidean Druim nan Ramh, over Sgurr a' Mhadaidh and Sgurr a'Ghreadaidh and Sgurr Thormaid, along the fissile half-world of this shattered ridge where the feeling and the symbolically feminine were unassimilated. And yet, in discreet crannies the saxifrage bushed and bloomed; from smoother clefts fleshy rose-root hung down its golden flowers and violets were everywhere, shades darker than the clear blue of her eyes. I remember reaching down and taking her strong hand in a wrist-lock, my other on a sharp spike, and hundreds of feet of space beneath us; I remember following her across a traverse on slimy basalt round to a gap in the ridge, both of us in our walking boots with heavy sacks, the consequences of a slip inevitably fatal.

St Kilda was a glistening fang beyond the Butt of Lewis and a great bank of cloud was welling up over the Outer Hebrides. A gibbous, yellow moon was sailing out across the Hebridean Sea. In our apartness, we had kept pace all day, neither knowing the other. The switchback ridge jagged on into a luminous distance but light and faith were ebbing away. Sgurr Dearg rose ahead. The spell broke. We chose to descend. Not by her preferred ridge route, but down the fierce draining gulley into Coire na Banachdich. The down-climbing was difficult. One swing round on a good hold maybe 100 feet above the gully bed led to a friction move across a gabbro slab. I waited at its farther side, watching, giving encouragement, but always she moved on, absorbed in her dangerous task, accepting the responsibilities the route and I had thrust upon her.

Who was she? Was she lover, friend, even the feminine side of my own nature? I cared for her, feared for her, yet always as I watched her head was bowed to the task. She kept on, elegant, engrossed, expressing no fear. Was she my responsibility? Was I hers? How had we come to be together in that place? The images flickered on: racing down through boulder scree; phosphorescence on the sea; an owl's call from the trees by Glenbrittle House; stretching ourselves out side by side on the gravelly sediments of Glenbrittle shore to the sucking waves and slow-dancing mist, above which cooled magma of rock and unconscious alike; the final benediction of her stooping, loving, forgiving kiss that awoke me with a start on my bank of heather to a chill draught of coming night.

I don't know what any of this means, or if it need mean anything at all. The man who sang praise of eating bear meat leapt to his death down a stair well. And I, who had soloed two 6a pitches on the Friday, fell on a 5c whilst leading the next Monday. Perhaps it is as well that in our dreams begins responsibility; or perhaps, if this is a man who desires to survive the concentration camp of his own nature, it is proper to ponder that, and also to disregard it – each in its proper place and time. Who knows ... ?

PERIPATETIC

Whether it's scoffing cream cakes among the sandstone towers of Rheinlandpfalz, hanging out at Tapovan surrounded by the sublime peaks of Garhwal or tripping over to Dublin for a day's climbing in Dalkey Quarry, the exuberant variety of climbing opportunity is one of the sport's lasting wonders.

7: SMALL CLIMBS IN GERMANY (1993)

Like civilisation itself, I got lost somewhere in the region of Dachau. Maybe it was the ordinariness – the grey skies, the flat plains, the traffic jams – but somehow, circumnavigating Munich, my attention wandered and instead of the autobahn to Stuttgart I found myself in deepest Swabia. We were retreating from a rain-sodden Kaisergebirge. The weather-map in the international edition of the *Guardian*, which we'd studied and debated the length of a wet and desultory afternoon in a Salzburg café, told us to head north. Andy Newton and Kath Griffiths had gone ahead and I was to meet them at the Bethof campsite in Rheinland Pfalz. But I was well lost. I went into a bright Greek café on a large square with lime trees and solid, careful sculptures in a modest, anonymous town. The waitress was dark and fine-featured. I'd anointed her with an olive complexion from the Sporiades, but when she began to talk she was a serious girl from downtown Stuttgart. I asked for the menu:

'We have bean soup,' she confided. Pre-empting further questions.

'Sounds like a fair synthesis,' I replied, in acceptance.

She grasped eagerly at the abstraction:

'So – you know Hegel was a Swabian, then?'

Two hours later my mind and slender stock of conversational German were exhausted. Customers waited in silent patience at the bar as she pressed on into an analysis of Kant's influence on Hegel. There were two empty bottles of Retsina on the table. I didn't remember drinking any. I paid and left:

'Why is it so urgent that you see your friend? Are you homosexual? Do you not want to talk philosophy?'

Beyond the Rhein I got lost again on the way to Landau, and stopped in the station bar in Bad Bergzabern to ask for the road to Vorderweidenthal and a glass of beer. The barman's name was Dietmar. He was from the Pfalz. Did I know the

Pfalz? No. Where was I from? Wales. He spoke back to me in perfect Welsh, held forth for the next hour-and-a-half on the origins of Celtic languages. Periodically a tumbler of schnapps materialised on the bar, in appearance harmless as water. Much later, I arrived happily in Bethof. I enjoy travel. Meetings like these don't happen every day in Lutterworth or Carshalton.

There's an interesting thing about schnapps. It appears not to produce hang-overs. Andy and Kath studied me carefully next morning for the tell-tale sounds and signs – the groans and sighs, the slumped posture. I didn't give them the satisfaction. Andy was anxious to do things and Kath, who is conscientious, was going to sun her-self in the campsite glade and – being a teacher – prepare what she termed 'all this National Curriculum bullshit.' So Andy and I consulted the guide. It's a thick red volume to the Sud Pfalz and opens with a 60-page essay on geology, complete with diagrams. The route descriptions are less expansive, and instead of stars there's a sys-tem of symbols. A flower denotes a three-star route, a cross something well worthy of your attention, and two fingers giving what looks like a well-known gesture means it's death. The other thing you notice in the guide is that almost every route was done by Hans Laub and Fred Frey in 1933, apart from those done by Fred Frey in 1943. We speculated endlessly on how he'd got the time off. After that, Wolfy Gullich added a few routes in 1980, then Hans took over again – he's apparently still doing new routes 60 years on. We wondered who he was and if we'd bump into him. The more of his and Fred's routes we did, the more impressed we became. The gritstone saga of Joe and Don pales into insignificance alongside their output.

My memory of this first morning in the Pfalz is hazy. Maybe I was over-whelmed by the beauty of the scene – round hills, red rock towers poking out of pine forests, small attractive villages with small attractive bars and large attractive waitress-es. Andy, who is a man who notices such things, hustled me past all these to a piece of rock called, if I caught the name accurately, the Piffelfels, where he'd recently seen a young woman clad entirely in Lycra ascend a route with ten bolts on it. I'm not sure which he enthused about most warmly, but the bolts at least were still there and he led up it with only a little whimpering and backsliding and I followed with a lot of both, and grievous complaints about how one's arms hurt. The route finished on top of a pinnacle, from which it was a 100-ft abseil to the ground. Back at the bot-tom, it was my turn to lead.

Since I was standing at the bottom of a pleasant little slab with two shiny bolts, I opted for that. He looked it up and it appeared to be something called the Kieselweg or Kieselwand. If my schoolboy German doesn't deceive me that means either the gravelly path or little pebbles' wall. I soon found out why. Also, he told me it was 7+, which was a couple of grades harder than the route I'd just been in desperate straits following, but my head was clearing and I had a new pair of sticky boots, so I thought to try it anyway, not having any idea of grades on the continent and liking the look of the thing.

I'll tell you something about the Pfalz. The rock is sublime – it's like Helsby in appearance and like Stanage in friction and reliability. But it has these pebbles that were rattled down some mountain stream and dumped on the gravelly bed of the ocean aeons ago and are slippery as glass. You have to stand on them, which is fine when they're the size of duck eggs but less so when they're that of mouse droppings. On this Kieselwand route you have to pull on them as well and they're the size of pigmy shrew droppings – British 6b moves to clip the first bolt, and I had to come down and change into my old boots, whose margins of friction I know, before I dared make the move and even then I did something wrong – clipped in the wrong karabiner because I didn't know, being incompetent, that these bent things were for ropes not for bolts. Andy, who is scrupulous, soon put me right. I sometimes wonder why he doesn't charge me for climbing with him, since he has to spend half his time on systematic eradication of errors in my technique.

After the second bolt the little pebbles wall definitely became the gravelly path. There was a smooth slab and the last bolt runner receded far beneath. I moaned terribly but Andy just laughed and told me not to fall off because the bolts only went in half an inch. This, added to the fact that every tree round about displayed notices about rabid foxes, disenamoured me of the place so we went for coffee to Dahn, and ate cakes until we felt sick. Dahn has the best cakeshops I've ever seen. There are chocolate-coated croissants filled with apple, and Matterhorn replicas made entirely of chocolate, and truffle-and-custard-dripping conch-shells. I could go on. Above the café was a 200-ft pinnacle with a crucifix on top called the Jungfernsprung, with a flowered route winding its way heavenwards. It was Andy's lead. He coasted up one side, then down and across the front to the other. I followed, cowering, to find him belayed to a bolt beneath a ten-ft roof cleft by a vile off-width crack. He was grinning and so was the crack, but I soon wasn't. These bolts in the Pfalz are massive affairs with welded rings through them. The crack had one on its left wall, the ring hanging out at a crazy angle.

'Should make it easier to clip if you're feeling bullish,' he told me. Afterwards he complained that it was the only overhanging crack he'd ever encountered that was more strenuous for the second than the leader, and that was before he'd even touched rock. I knew what he meant, but unfortunately there came a point where the runners were below and within and the crack had to be jammed. Imagine a wider version of *Brown's Crack* on Ramshaw and you'll have an idea what the fist jams were like. Also, getting at them demanded the most extraordinary contortions. It was grit-stone 6a and I could feel the muscle fibres in my left arm ripping apart as I lay horizontally beneath it. In situations like this you understand why Baron von Munchausen was German. There was a ledge above the roof that nobody had visit-ed or wiped for years, and the route book further on confirmed that impression. I draw a veil over our subsequent antics on this climb, except to add that they were very public. The whole town seemed to have a view on which way to go and a stance on how to do it. They were very friendly too. Imagine people who live above Lamorna or Wintour's Leap giving you amiable advice on how to do routes on their local crags, and you get an idea of how different is the atmosphere of the Pfalz.

Preliminaries over, Andy decided to placate me for his sadism in the matter of the crack by introducing me next day to Barenbrunnerhof. If you were to find your-self in a valley clearing with great towers of perfect, characterful rock rearing up from the woods all around, and a sunlit terrace café with friendly people, beer, gorgeous cakes, beautiful waitresses, might you not have to pinch yourself to find out whether you'd just died and gone to heaven? If, afterwards, you went into the woods, found yourself beneath a crack that sidled over a roof to run up 120 feet of perfect vertical red rock and finish at a line of bolt runners leading across a slabby, delicate wall; if you climbed it at a blissful grade of E3, 5c, what would you think then? When we got to the top we were ecstatic, and fortunately unable to write anything in the route book because someone had stolen the pen from the inside.

This route was called the *Jubilaumsriss* on the Nonnenfels – Barenbrunnerhof has a religious history, hence the Nuns' Rock and its neighbouring Cloister Rock on which we did a fine, wandering HVS called the *Klosterwand* later. We did some more things elsewhere too, but I'll leave those and tell you a couple of singular things to finish: of how, for example, we met a little fellow wearing a cloth cap on the Rodelstein one day. We listened carefully to hear if his wife called him Hans or Fred. He was five feet two, rather fat, in his sixties, at least, and cruised up the classic hard routes on the crag – 5c's, 6a's. One I liked the look of he told me how to do in two words and a mime:

'Untergriff ... loch ... ja?'

The undercling, then the hole. When I came to do it, I could grasp the holds but not the problem of how he, at his height, could reach between the two when I could not. Nor could I understand why the first bolt was beyond its ground-fall-potential crux. But it was a great little climb. And he, like every other climber we met on the crag or in the Barenbrunnerhof Café where we sat on the terrace drinking beer, eating our rye bread, bratwurst and sauerkraut and watching the glowing but-tresses merge down into dark pines each twilight, was as welcoming, outgoing and supportive as I remember the climbing communities of my youth to have been before commerce and competition spoiled them.

All this made the more sad something I saw on our last day there. We'd done a classic long 6+ on one of the buttresses around Barenbrunnerhof. Half way up there was a route book with the guidebook diagram and route descriptions carefully pasted into it, and some uplifting quotations too in Gothic script. There were respectful entries from maybe a dozen nationalities, and there was one from the Brits that read like this: 'Fuck the Krauts – pile of shite!'

All the names driving back – Mons and Lens and Le Cateau, Ypres and Poitiers and the Somme – and it still goes on. I coasted sadly through France, follow-ing an inclination to catch the Cork ferry and thence back to Holyhead and home, not wishing to encounter that version of civilisation I'd have met between Dover and Shrewsbury. Sometimes you just feel ashamed ...

8: DAY TRIP TO DALKEY (1993)

So why was I running through the security barrier at Holyhead in the early hours of an April morning, wearing three jackets with pockets bulging, and with my rock-boots in a camera-case? Here's the scam – Sealink do a day-return offer (their publicity people choose to call it a pleasure cruise) from Holyhead to Dun Laoghaire for £7. You can catch the boat at four in the morning from Holyhead, snatch a few hours sleep, disembark in Dun Laoghaire before eight, take the Dart from the station right by the harbour for three stops south to Dalkey, have breakfast in the Country Bake café on the main street, read Fintan O'Toole in the *Irish Times*, soak in the atmosphere of cosmopolitan Ireland whilst you're re-caffeinating, and then the quarry's half a mile away up the Ardbrugh Road. So you climb all day, get the Dart back into Dublin when you're knackered, take in the pubs, the films and the music and be back in Dun Laoghaire in time for the 11 o'clock boat. How's that sound?

Naturally, there's a problem. It's called 'Conditions of Special Offer', and it tells you unequivocally that no hand luggage is allowed beyond a 'small camera case for gentlemen and a small handbag for ladies.' 'Curious concepts at work here,' I thought, and plotted how to get round it. Hence three jackets (no restrictions on the amount of clothes you wear) with pockets bulging. As soon as I was on the boat and past all the checks, I took a rolled-up rucksack out of one pocket, filled it with the contents of the others, made a pillow with two of the jackets, a blanket from the third, and joined the rest of the ship's complement at that ungodly hour in billowy slumbers.

This is where the instructional bit ends. If you had a rope and a rack to carry, you'd have to devise your own means of bestowing them about your person, but from now on I cheat. A friend arrives as I walk down from passenger arrivals in Dun Laoghaire, whisks me off on a brisk constitutional to study the climbing potential of that most traditional of Irish Mountaineering Club stamping grounds, Bray Head. It appears to be either non-existent or to consist of a railway cutting. A man comes out of a shed in the latter with a shiny tin kettle and disappears. I mention this fact to my companion, who has not seen him, is pragmatic in these things, and would never have made the cast of *The Egg Man and the Fairies*.

'Nonsense!' comes the response. 'Where is he?'

'Down there,' I point.

We crane over the wall. No sound but the sea, and a faint rustling of thrift flowers in the breeze:

'Admit it – you made it up.'

'I did not – I'll bet you the money in my pocket.'

'Which pocket?' A sceptical eye is cast over the three jackets, and then more conclusively, having found one that jingles, 'You're on.'

We look back over the wall. A man disengages from shadow and walks to the door of the hut.

'There you are! I win!'

'What d'you mean?' I protest.

With all the aplomb of the scion of a betting nation, before she rifles through my pockets my companion points out that he has no kettle. We repair to the bakery café. A sulky-faced waitress of 16 or so slams cups of strong coffee down in front of us, spilling half the contents in the process. A teacherly woman in the queue at the counter asks one of her charges, 'Shall you be bold today, Ursula, or shall you be good?' We finish our croissants – Dalkey's that sort of town – and head up to the crag.

In *The Dalkey Archive*, which is by a good way Flann O'Brien's worst book, James Joyce is alive and well and experiencing a late vocation. I was feeling much the same way myself, but not for the Jesuits (of whom I had enough at school, for Christ's sake). It was the quarry that was calling. Here was a place of which I'd been aware for the whole of my climbing life, and the only time I'd set foot in it was on a day of tippling rain ten years before when my old climbing companion Emmett Goulding (who was, as a matter of historical interest, widely regarded during his sojourn in Britain in 1964-5 as being the most gifted technical climber of his time in Britain or Ireland) showed me round. He'd made a particular point of taking me to the top of a waterfall with a slab rippling beneath its surface before the stream flowing down it leapt over an undercut wall at its base.

'That,' he'd told me, 'is *The Ghost*, and it's one of the great outcrop routes.'

'Here?' I'd asked.

'Anywhere!'

This exchange I mentioned as we walked in from the car-park on Killiney Hill. I had no idea of its grade. It could have been anything from Diff to E6, but I wanted to do it.

'Sure, we'll do a route or two first to get you used to the place. You'll be grand.'

Dalkey's extensive, its ground plan resolved around two bays with a dividing ridge, a plateau area above, and beyond that the Upper Walls beneath the summit of Killiney Hill. The rock is granite, and was quarried from 1817 onwards for the building of Dun Laoghaire harbour. Apart from a brief re-opening during the Great

War, quarrying finished here in the 1850s, since when it's been going back to nature. Now it's a sunny, friendly belvedere above Dublin Bay: local people chat to you; ragged small eejits try to outdo the climbers and in the attempt frighten the latter more than themselves, especially on the higher walls, which reach 100 feet in places.

Mid-morning, the sun's shining, ropes uncoiled beneath a 40-ft wall of imposing steepness.

'What's this? Just looking at it makes my neck ache ... '

'Will you stop your complaining and hold these ropes.'

My leader sets foot purposefully on rock, climbs to a little roof, pulls over it – all eager confidence – places protection and adjusts gracefully and effortlessly up the ensuing wall and groove. I follow in due course. It's intricate VS climbing, the holds sharp and well-spaced, the moves not immediately obvious.

'What's that called?'

'*Jameson's Ten*. We'll do another route and when you've got the feel of the place, then you can look at *The Ghost*.'

Next choice is a thin crack, finger jams and friction, up a slab, and good VS. The leader skips up it, pony-tail bobbing assertively, and gives me a tight rope on the first moves. I don't quite catch the name, but it sounds like *Mahjongg*. When I ask for clarification I'm told to look it up in the guidebook. For several weeks now an extended discussion's gone on between us as to whether climbing has a better dimension when you dispense with the guide, so this wins points in the debate. My progress up the crack is considered and judgement deferred on whether I'm yet ready for *The Ghost*, but we wander across to the top of it anyway and peer over. A rope stretches down, with Calvin Torrans coming up it neatly, using a shunt. We hail him – you meet everyone on the Irish scene in Dalkey apparently. I haven't seen him for ten years. He comes over, exchanges friendly words, slopes off. We in our turn wander shamelessly off down to the pub for lunch.

When we get back, the slab of *The Ghost* is covered with abseilers – another joint Irish/British curse – so I'm dragged over to a sunlit wall in the East Valley and led up another of the quarry's classic VSs, *Street Fighter*. It's dispensed with in short order, and when I follow there are awkward steep moves to start, then strange crabbing movements up a slippery ramp before you pull out up a steep, fingery crack. At the top it's pointed out that I haven't done much leading so far, to which proposition I happily assent ... until the rider that it's about time I did is insisted upon. I've been eyeing up the neighbouring route – a flake crack to the right like a thinner and steeper *Right Unconquerable* that the guide I now avidly, and to my companion's great sarcastic glee, find myself consulting calls 'a classic battle', and 'probably the most fallen-off route in the quarry': *The Shield*, E2, 5c.

'But it's jamming – perhaps you don't like that?' I whimper, trying to off-load.

'That's alright – I'll manage.' (Attempt recognised and straight-batted.) I tie on. There are some intricate moves out of a niche, steep and on awkwardly placed finger jams, to gain a foothold on the right wall. Then comes the crucial sequence. It's not a simple crack – it overhangs, slants and cuts back in, and the jams are thin and awkwardly spaced. I use a poor left hand jam and move on to worse ones above. They start to slide.

'I'm jumping off on to this runner, but it's not very good.'

'Shall you be bold today, or shall you be good?' is the teasing response. The runner holds. I retreat to the niche for a rest. *The Shield* was living up to its reputation. When I went back up, I made a mess of the moves on to the foothold and the jams felt worse than before, so I grew a mite angry and frustrated, got a Friend at the ready, started the sequence with a higher left toe-jam than before, found better jams in consequence above, jabbed in the Friend and suddenly thought, 'I remember this feeling!' as I carried on in a state of elated absorption to the ramp above. My erstwhile leader, needless to say, climbed it meticulously, with only a trifling complaint about the difficulty of removing runners on which over-much reliance had been placed – and at the top emerged with hands that, unlike mine, were unmarked. *The Ghost* was still being abseiled and it began to rain. The boat sailed, I stayed: an Istvan Szabo film, cool Guinness, warm love in an unfamiliar bed – there are other boats in our lives.

It had become a point of honour to climb *The Ghost*. So I came back. I was led up a delectable HVS at Glendalough called *Scimitar Crack* to show that Ireland has other rock delights than Dalkey. It had two 150-ft pitches up a perfect line in the airiest situations on rough natural granite. The crag was covered in violets, heather still flourished on the ledges, and peregrines cried around us. But no other people. The valley below was as beautiful as any in Snowdonia. I wanted to stay for other routes, but *The Ghost* was now a voyage of necessity.

My first companion was working, so I recruited Paul Kiely, a friend from Wicklow with whom I'd climbed in Wales in the past. He drove at 100 miles an hour to Dalkey, rapping on about the attitude and its demise. Afterwards, we soloed a few routes: *Pilaster*, a reachy bold buttress on good grips; *Sham Gully*, with its boulder problem start. But we'd come to lay *The Ghost*.

It's an 80-ft slab, undercut at its foot. A thin, fractured flake slips between slab and lean. I tiptoe across, the ground falling away, and place an R.P. at foot-level. The ordinary path into the niche above is a lunge and scrabble at 5b on good hand-holds, but above on the slab is Dermot Somers' 5c variation – as bold (English meaning) and argumentative as its pioneer. So I take that instead, place an ill-fitting hex in a borehole at the niche, step up on slick granite and side-pulls and move out on friction that you must trust and that will support you to shimmy over to a good foothold. At knee-level there's a rocky Rock Three to be placed and – barely halfway up – that's your ration of runners for the entire pitch. I step far out right, unsure and awkward in consequence, to move up on dimples and rounded handholds – slate E4 but without the bolts – for distant holds. Two onlookers exchange cordialities from the side. I tell them, half-amused, how afraid I am, coming to terms meanwhile with cat-padding moves round a tiny overlap, nervous of what's to come, fearful of the fall, but knowing that to sight-lead this pitch is a fine adventure, is more than a climb, is a metaphor for the tentative spirit journey. At the top I look down on the boat that will soon be taking me away and know as Paul follows and I belay that this day-tripper will soon be back:

> *The dressed stone which rattled down the metals*
> *Is salt-bleached now in the quay of farewells,*
> *And gorse, nut-scented, brightens the shadows*
> *Above the harbour, where the quarry stows*
> *Its stock of migrant memory away,*
> *Turns its weathered face on our crass, light play.*
> *Schoolgirls judder breathless down fearful ropes*
> *Where quarrymen mined blocks to embark hopes*
> *On the passage to whatever new world –*
> *Toes on ripples supervene, fingers curled*
> *Round edges which support no other dream*
> *Than our ambiguous and escaping gleam*
> *That might, past all necessity, endure,*
> *Subsumed into the complete metaphor.*

9: BOGLES & BOG-TROTS (2004)

I was looking through the dictionary for a word this morning, blearily, and came across the two of this title, closely paired. 'Bogle – a phantom causing fright' read the definition of the first. 'Ah – so that's what it means!' I thought, and a whole texture of memory was back with me. Not initially of the route itself, for there is one called *Bogle*, but we'll be coming to that. What first registered – and with an odd sort of remembered pleasure and an equal mixture of delighted anticipation because the long days of summer are upon us – were long walks to crags. Which means Scotland, of course, or maybe Donegal if you're into the bog-trot bit, but perversely I was trying to figure out if there were any long crag approaches in Wales, and of course there aren't, because all Welsh crags are within a couple of miles of a road. The best I could come up with was the *Far Eastern Buttress* of Clogwyn Du'r Arddu, which as you'll all know, any of you who've ever been there (and if you haven't, then my advice is don't), is best approached from the top. In fact you can only approach it from the top unless you want to do one of those climbs on the Lower Far Eastern Buttress, in the case of which the previous advice is redoubled, because they're all on the kind of rock where the holds are like books on library shelves – fiddle them around and you can pull them out at will; chuck 'em over your shoulder and you strafe the people on the path. In my experience the same goes for the protection thereabouts, and also the rock has that peculiarly slick, non-grip texture that the base of Cloggy defaults to here and there and most unfairly, because when you don't have friction you might expect a bit of solidity. Of course that doesn't follow as you can see if you just look at slate, which dominates the view from wherever you are on Cloggy, and particularly the Far East, and seems to be laughing at you, saying, 'Whaddya want to flog all the way up there for? – plenty of snappy, smooth, slippy stuff down here that you can drive to.' Or as the train would say, 'Effort is movement is vapour.'

Anyway, to come back to the Far East, to get to it you have to walk virtually to the summit of Yr Wyddfa, which is what we should call Snowdon, just as that high mountain you can pay $50,000 to go and get killed on should be called Chomolungma, but who does? The same question applies to climbing on the Far East, to bring its title down to manageable proportions. Some advice here, which you will all naturally ignore because none of you, and wisely, have any intention of coming here anyway: the best way up is by the Snowdon Ranger Track, for three or four reasons: firstly, it is gradual in the ascent and quieter than the other side; secondly, there is one of the traditional Welsh boulders along the way, so if you're a boulderer you can see how you measure up against Oscar Eckenstein; thirdly, you get a really good view of Llechog along the way and will probably change your plans and divert there, because it's a better bet than the Far East and has one really very pleasant climb on it. I can tell you now, in a fit of paranoia, how I was twice robbed regarding this route, which I climbed some time way back in a wet summer at the beginning of the 1970s. Memory hold the door ... ! I did this route over two days when Mike Yates and I were writing the *Climbers' Club Guidebook to Cwm Silyn and Cwellyn* – thick little book, this, with a thin number of routes, but some of them were quite good as I remember, and this was one of them. Oh yeah – that bit about being robbed – we gave it this name, *Resurrection*, then four or five years later Rowland Edwards, bless him, went and pinched the name – no-one's copyright, of course, as the Climbers' Club might say – for that frigging route of his right of *Left Wall*. So everyone forgot about lonely old Llechog's original version until Paul Williams came along and put it into his bumper Welsh fun book, but by then it had changed, which is how I came to be robbed again, because Hugh Banner had come along, added a 20-ft long direct finish of which he stated that I'd failed on the first ascent, which was not true, and re-named the whole 400-ft route *Erection*, which I thought was a prick's trick.

Enough of paranoid whingeing! I've got these lovely memories of climbing it in that wet summer (I wonder if anyone's ever done a meteorological analysis of new-routing activity in Britain? In 1954, for example, when Brown and particularly Whillans were at the peak of their powers, it was one of the wettest years on record. Look in your guidebooks and see how many new routes were done in Wales that year!) *Resurrection* took two days – no blasphemies about being one better than someone else you know, please. The first time I went up there was with Nick Estcourt, who had just come back from Annapurna and spent all his time spitting and frothing about what a lazy (supply your own expletive – the editor will only delete if I do) Whillans was, and how cunning, and what bad sportsmanship and so on. Nick was brilliant to climb with, boundlessly enthusiastic and he chattered all the time, intelligently, and laughed, and we did a couple of pitches, pulling off the sods piecemeal and chucking them at each other, up this 'tall red slab' that Archer Thomson had drooled about way back. Then it rained and Llechog, which means 'slatey', is as bad a place as you can find to be in the rain so we abseiled off and were drenched but jokey and happy too. Next day, which was a Monday and Nick couldn't skive off work because he'd just been away for four months, I went back up there with Mike Yates and the crag was all seeping and 'slape' to use a Cumbrian word which is supposed to mean 'slippery', though my wife, who's from there, denies this, and we scampered up the pitches I'd done with Nick and added this top pitch up a crack in a wonderful slab, but the slab was holdless and the crack was a finger-crack completely choked with grass and in those days you didn't clean from above so what I did was tap a peg in lightly, tie it off, and rake out the crack with the spike of the hammer. I did this a couple of times to where things got a bit cleaner, then came back down, took out the pegs, and climbed it – all very protectionless and still totally 'slape', did a long foot-traverse left past a niche, out of which, for no reason apparent to me, rose Hughie's tiny later *Erection*, which was steeper than all that lay below, and grass-choked so I didn't even consider it because left again there was a big flake hold on which you could swing round a corner into the most perfect flake jamming crack and I thought this one of the best pitches I'd done in Wales at the time and so did Mike and it was only HVS, so we were well pleased, and years and years later I came back with Tom Leppert and we did a route up the left side of the slab and arrived at this same flake and it was as good as I remembered.

I didn't mean to write about Llechog. I was just going to give you four reasons for taking the Snowdon Ranger Track to the Far East. The fourth reason is that if it's a hot day you might as well just divert to Llyn Nadroedd, which means 'lake of the serpents' and is the best swimming place on Yr Wyddfa, and forget about climbing altogether. Or in winter and good snow when you'd neither be swimming nor heading for the Far East you might wend your way up that big, forgotten face above the lake that takes you right to the summit, and you'll see nobody else all day until you get there. This all brings me at last to the Far East, about which I had a thing at one time and kept inveigling people to go there with me. Once with Smiler Cuthbertson the clouds opened when we were high on *The Mostest* and we had to abseil off fast, which was freaky, and another time the same thing happened when I was leading the top pitch of *Woubits*, but that wasn't so bad because (whisper it soft!) contrary to myth the top pitch of *Woubits*, whilst very dramatic, is actually quite easy, and on the best rock on Clogwyn Du'r Arddu bar none. It's the texture of gritstone, or gabbro, and I don't understand how one cliff can contain such variations. Like on *Spillikin*, you teeter up all this fissile, rickety stuff, bury yourself in a bed of moss campion on a big ledge in despair, and then suddenly above you is this lovely, brown, pockety, sound wall you'd like to go on for ever. Anyway, I gave up on the Far East after I'd been rained off (yet again) trying what was then known as Woubits Arête, because it hadn't then been done, and I've never been back.

But I did go back several times to what I think is the best and most esoteric long-walk crag of them all – the Meadow Face of Beinn Tarsuinn on Arran. It's actually the only good crag, and the highest, on Arran (don't believe all that guff in *Hard Rock* about the Rosa Pinnacle being 1100 feet long – if it's 250 feet in vertical height I'd be surprised, and talk about a route wandering! It's the objective correlative of my prose style ...). The Meadow Face is quite different, and at the end of one of those Scottish walks, which are not as their Welsh counterparts are. This one's part bog-trot, part marathon odyssey, but it leads up to one of the most sweeping and beautifully architectonic cliffs you've ever seen, all curves and soaring slabs with three perfect, straight, 800-ft long crack-lines called *Brachistochrone* (wanna know? 'The curve in which a body descending to a given point under the action of gravity will reach it in the shortest time.' How lovely – think I'll steal it ...), which used a lot of aid but is free at mildish HVS; *Bogle*, which has the most sumptuous section of severely overhanging fist-jamming I've ever climbed on a mountain crag – used to be an aid pitch but that was an affront to anyone who's ever climbed at Brimham; and *The Bender*, a big corner groove of Bill Skidmore's on the left, about which superlatives fail me, and all three of them on Arran granite, which is gritstone-on-a-macro-scale and there are herds of red deer at the bottom, and solitude ...

All this, and I haven't yet been to Creag an Dubh Loch or Carnmore. Three more weeks on this accursed Whillans book and I'm getting my walking boots on, rain or no rain!

10: THE COW'S MOUTH (1998)

India both entrances and confuses me: the arrival by night in Delhi; the cacophonous manic jive of traffic on its main thoroughfares; the abject accepting plight of the dispossessed at every road margin; the weirdly circumlocutory process of train-booking and the frantic one of train-boarding; sticky heat and mingling odours of spice and ordure; methodical calm of attendants handing out patched and threadbare linen sheets in the second-class sleeper; earnest friendliness and proximity of fellow-travellers; sear of noon-heat, thrusting ferocity of auto-rickshaw drivers. Through all these I've just emerged into the cool peace and apartness of Shashank Singh's hotel on Asi Ghat at Varanasi, from the balcony of which in this night hour I look out across the great arc of the Ganga, mother-goddess river of all India, as it loops through the furnace plains of the north, watch the widows anointing the *shivalinga* with which the city abounds.

When the world was young and innocent, according to the myth, the Ganga rose here in Varanasi, but it retreated because of man's wickedness and retreats still. As I sit here in the stifling heat of the night, my thoughts and memories career a thousand kilometres upriver, to the ice-caves of its present birth in the snout of the Gangotri glacier, and to the ultimate *Shivalingam*, the mountain of Shivling itself.

I remember the sustained immediacy of sensation in trekking to Gaumukh: the cold boil of the river from grimy fissures of grey ice; the *babas* and *sadhus* with whom only the most minimal dialogue was possible; the lemon Indian dawns; the way an old man under a tree ceremoniously spread his dhoti for his wife to sit upon; the dotterels at Bhojbasa that were surely the same birds I see each spring on my Welsh home hills; the old woman with the Brahmin family, husband fat and self-important in front and her trailing nervously along the gorgeside path, a red bag balanced on her head as she sucked nervously on the corner of her plaid shawl; the evident devotion in which these pilgrims held the river; the sweet hay-smell of a parsley-like plant; the robin-like bird at Chulobas with a rich dark-chestnut back and a carmine breast; meadowsweet – that filmy-fragrant, creamy-laced summer rose of my own country of the summer stars; the faded blue Indian sky, the drifting flight of an alpine chough at 20,000 feet, the extra-human scale and indifference of a world in the sculpting stage of process of creation, the crystal glitter of Shivling's great ridges above Tapovan at dawn.

It was two years ago. In Delhi the last monsoon rain beat down. Moist, burnt air was like a slow, clinging slap across the face. This city breaks your heart, is first stage in a process by which you enter into the Himalayan mysteries. It's a point of disjunction, bears no relationship to your life *back there*. The insistent dry scrape of a beggar girl's thin fingers at your wrist, the gesture with her other hand towards her mouth, the lolling head of the infant whose mother – a shrivelled breast drooping from her sari – jabbers at you unceasingly outside the Mercedes showroom that 'this baby will die': these are not of your own country's mindscape. You reel from them into a maelstrom where all values are whirled from your grasp. *Here* is not a place you recognise. *Here* demands of you the readiness to see things, to look at them, entirely anew.

Delhi, however much of an interlude, an annoyance, a frustration it may seem to the unready, is the proper gateway to what the Himalayan traveller or climber must go through. Black kites circle lazily overhead; hoopoes flit eccentrically across the grass; pigs root in a dungheap; men and women shit in companionable groups below the walls of the Red Fort, then waddle duck-like to puddles to wash themselves. To fulfil the needs of India's Kafkaesque bureaucracy, I've come out to a decaying office in a tumbledown, filthy suburb. Above the official's head, streamside willows wave through a broken window as he talks of water from the Ganga, with a permit to visit the source of which he may soon issue me: 'At holy times we put a drop on the tongue; we bathe in it before marriage and before death. This water has the property that it never corrupts. There are no germs in it. It is always pure. The scientists have tested it, but have not found what this property is.' In Varanasi two years on, I remember these words as I watch the bathers in the dawn lift their brass cups to the rising sun and drink, ten yards downstream of a sewage outlet, five from a bloated corpse. Faith!

In the capital, restricted to the hotel in readiness for departure on the instant permits are granted, I watch translucent hippies waft by, nod to white-knuckled trekkers from the north of England whose eyes semaphore panic, exchange quick glances with mysterious long women whose Indian adornments and languid gestures glide across white pages on which they incessantly write. Then we leave – trains, buses, the terror of a night-ride from Uttarkashi up 100 kilometres of road with no surface, kerbed with blackness, a rage of water infinitely far beneath. Once the bus lost traction. Peering out I saw the edge of the road crumble into the abyss. We lurched forward, somehow. But Mother Ganga's song in Gangotri soothes ...

I sit on the temple steps from which the devout bathe and listen. The high surface note is all rush and hiss, beneath it a deeper, percussive rumbling of stones and boulders pounding along the river bed that seizes on your imagination. I feel the expansion of my own lungs, become absorbed into the rhythm of the place. Above the temple in slow, steep turns the path climbs into the Deodar woods. The deep breaths that impel you onwards are themselves an elation – that your breast could swell with so much of the living air, thin and sharp here at 10,000 feet, like cold springwater after too much of civilisation's fumey wine. I learn from those who are at home in this place. The Garhwali porters, sinewy and slight, trudge past as I sit drinking *chai* in the *dhaba*, at Chirbasa. They walk unconcerned, 50 pound loads secured by a twist of rope, across the log over the torrent where I balanced tentatively. I watch more closely. These distant-eyed men in sacking and flip-flops move as westerners do not move. The placing of each foot is deliberate, the transfer of weight on to it instinctive and assured. Their walking is an art that, once you have noticed, you begin to practise – too consciously and too late perhaps, and without their natural grace, but nonetheless, you have begun to learn to walk. Also, here you can begin to learn to speak, balance words, hear content and not talk merely for sound. You listen to the simplicity of porters, *sadhus*, cooks. Like that percussive rumbling deep in the river, you regain the gravity of your humanity.

For a few days, whilst the path's re-established post-monsoon and the brimming streams subside, I walk up and down to Chirbasa, first tea-shop on the way, acclimatising, returning each evening to sleep at the tourist bungalow in Gangotri. In a damp twilight Ed Douglas and myself sit on the terrace of the Hotel Ganga Niketan there. Four Korean climbers take a table by us, appraise our gear without approval, except for Ed's mountain cap, which they ask to see, examine thoroughly, ask for how many dollars he would sell it? Ed, irritated, firmly reclaims it as they list their peaks as though other items of merchandise. To get away, I move next to a monk in saffron robes who's smoking Capstan cigarettes. Where does he live? Upriver beneath a rock in the summer; Varanasi, where he studies Sanskrit and Ayurvedic medicine at Benares Hindu University, in the winter. And his object in being here? To teach meditation and sexual healing, for which many students come to him. He makes an expansive gesture with the Capstan cigarette. I catch the eye of Sylvia, the trekker from Dresden who has joined us. She transmits a delicate scepticism. The monk is very beautiful, aware of it too in the way he caresses his long, brown hair and practises expressions on us. He looks like the young Krishnamurti, and like Krishnamurti there is an element of mischief and showmanship about him, and just enough suspicion of charlatanry to free him from the taint of bland piety.

I visit the temple to make *Puja*. The priest views my awkwardness with patient amusement, goes to an ornate silver statue of the goddess Ganga in the dim interior to pray, returns with water in a tiny ladle which he pours into my hands to drink, and little balls of fine-ground sugar to eat, before marking my forehead first with red and then with yellow paints. Clouds drift among craggy spires above the village, accentuating towers, arêtes, great clefts. A Lammergeier glides across, its shadow traversing the rock face. Two helicopters fly up the gorge, minute against the peaks, their engine note absorbed into the river's roar, and we start for our base camp at Tapovan.

For the unacclimatised it's two or even three days' walk from Gangotri, but I wonder if there's a more enchanting walk anywhere in the world? It has excitement. The path's forever changing. Rockfalls sweep down. Cliff-traversing sections – crazy wooden stemple-supported constructions – decay and fall into the glacier torrent beneath. Its population changes too. Pilgrims constantly move up and down between Gangotri and Gaumukh, and trekkers, mountaineers, muleteers, sadhus clad in the orange of renunciation, soldiers and the quiet porters of the hills. There is an intensely dramatic and changing beauty, the great gorge arcing east then south, into the sun with the high Bhagirathi peaks bright beneath it.

Beyond Bhojbasa – a tented hamlet with a mouse-ridden tin hut of a tourist bungalow – you leave behind the birch scrub and enter a province of gleaming stone newly emergent from beneath the retreating glacier, the route vague, slipping between moraines and silt-margined turquoise pools, its line marked here and there by eccentric flat-slabbed cairns, painted Hindi ideograms. Until a few years ago, the path to Gaumukh and Tapovan crossed the river at Bhojbasa and held to the true left bank. Massive landslides scoured it away. Now it meanders up the right. By the Cow's Mouth – the great fissures in the glacier snout from which the river bursts out – are more dhabas, their canvas shelters weighted by low stone surrounds, the proprietors squatting on sack-covered sleeping platforms within, blowing up the wood fires, whose tang alerts you to their presence hundreds of yards away, and setting on blackened kettles at your approach. Ash-covered sadhus with matted hair immerse the devout in milky water so cold it burns. The path slants beneath cliffs thousands of feet high, down which stones whine and burst like shrapnel, then debouches into the glacier. I tack inland. Glaciers! Did you think they were white, gleaming places of snow riven by blue crevasses? This is a mile-wide highway construction site with towering hills of spoil 300 feet high. House-sized blocks rumble down them; rock-slides start at a touch; voids lipped with gravelly ice, the sound of rushing water deep within, block your path. The tributary ice-streams of Chaturangi and Kirti add to the fracture and chaos. At an altitude of 14,400 feet, 2000 feet above Gaumukh, and after a gravelly climb that leaves you gasping for breath, you reach peace and Tapovan.

I do not know in the abstract why some places are holy and others are not, but in its human and natural detail, Tapovan's distinction is palpable. You could, I suppose, question its three residents, Om Giri, Babaji and Mataji, and though just to meet the last – a small, dark and ageless south Indian woman – alerts you to the presence of holiness – their words won't provide any better evidence than that provided by your eyes. It's a high meadow; strange birds, the tracks of bear and snow leopard in the mud each night, and herds of *bharal*. Above you, always, is the great presence of Shivling, phantasmal by moonlight, glistening in the morning sun, by turns repellent and inviting, fulfilling in its atmospheres of warm rock and furious blast, its concealments and splendours, its crystalline apartness, the notion many have that this is the World's most beautiful peak.

Somehow, I do not have an overwhelming desire to reach its summit, and I have not anyhow come on this expedition as a climber. At times in base camp, looking up at its unworldly aspire, Menlove Edwards' words steal into my head: 'This climbing. Perhaps, really, one was never made for it. I have a conceit that I was even made for more than that: more than to satisfy extremely one's own pride.'

All of the expedition members, I suspect, have mixed emotions towards the peak, from aching, anxious desire to the psychological devastation of abject fear. Some look wisely at the serac barrier at 20,500 feet, below the final snow slope, and arrive at the detached conclusion that its threat is too great and unpredictable to put oneself beneath. Others accept the risk. There is an extraordinary degree of friction between some of the climbers, their egos and ambitions spikily conflicting, their attention on self rather than scene. Competition and the idea of conquest dominate, are at odds with the ideals of those who visit here without those fixations.

Sylvia, who is rather wise, and I, who am a little older, gravitate together and when the time comes for her to start her further journey to Madras, I go down with her to Gangotri, out of the stone world, its rawness and the savage attitudes engendering there. We find a room in a pilgrims' rest-house across the river from the temple. Warm water's brought to us and we wash. Hesitantly, we approach intimacy. In my poor German and her better English we explore the ellipses of communication. After the harshness of landscape and its human correlatives, there is softness and discovery. In the nights, with the rhythm of chanting and temple bells beyond the window, our bodies on the soft bed are glimmery, melding in a grace of nakedness.

A space of days passes, time which feels peculiarly blessed, and then she boards the bus for Uttarkashi. I come back to a room hollowed by her leaving, collect belongings, and return in a day, fitter now, to Tapovan. The expedition has fallen apart. I'm enlisted as a climber. Four times, by myself and with different partners, I'm drawn to Shivling's high camps and apartworld, load-carrying, feeling my way, becoming accustomed, nauseated by other expeditions' attitudes on the mountain, appalled by the sight of a Korean with cerebral oedema being dragged down, toes trailing, across the moraine of the Meru glacier in the twilight.

One morning in particular disturbs memory. Ed and I have spent a night of excruciating discomfort – my third sleepless one in a row – in the tiny tent at 19,000 feet, and set off exhausted at daybreak up the ridge above. In the blue shadow fingers and toes have no feeling. Avalanches and rock-falls are streaming down the sunlit face of Meru across the glacier. My usual reaction to our hill rations – puking and shitting, nauseous at the grease and meat that gluttony made me force down last night is in force. When everything's come up, the discomfort intensifies as fits of vomiting and coughing coincide to ram bile into every cavity of the head before it sprays out of mouth and nostrils to marble the snow around me green and yellow – all this to a gasping refrain of laboured breath. I'm encountering the pain of Himalayan climbing, the unfamiliar gear, the weakening resolve, the stumbling incompetence.

The rock steps on the arête ahead rear up. By effort of will I relax, determine upon rhythm and control, set to the climbing and become engrossed in its subtleties and technicality. There are two of these towers and the crux is on the second – a slim groove of red granite with festoons of fixed rope, frayed and abandoned, hanging down its sides and a ribbon of hard ice in its back. The drops to hanging glaciers on either side are immense, the risks as we solo up grave, but suddenly I'm captivated by the process of climbing, enraptured by surroundings, revelling in the certain delicacy of placing crampon prongs on tiny flakes and fractures, the smooth lean of the body in making for ease. In a half-hour's climbing I find out for myself what fascination is in this game, and it is enough. I understand.

I watch from the lateral ridge abutting the seracs as Ed – young, fit and acclimatised – climbs the short ice-wall which is the last technical barrier before the summit. He hesitates, his feet slip in places, chips of ice shower down. I cannot see the fixed rope up which he jumars, assume he's still soloing, watch him join the three Czechs who are ahead of us, look ruefully at my single walking axe and conclude that what's ahead isn't for me. It is ten o'clock on a bright, still morning, the summit 1000 feet above. I go down with only a tinge of regret.

Afterwards, by the stream through Tapovan, I rest. An avocet stalks past along the sand-flats on coppery-blue legs, upturned bill probing, pied plumage gleaming. RD Laing's acid illumination is my prayer to her:

'I have seen the bird of paradise. She has spread her wings before me and I shall never be the same again. There is nothing to be afraid of. Nothing. The Life I am trying to grasp is the me that is trying to grasp it.'

A week later, on an Agra hotel rooftop, the dome and minarets of the Taj Mahal glimmer above the haze under a bright full moon so that I ache with the evanescence of this most beautiful of human creations and finest of all monuments to human love. I have an intuition: that there are ways of approaching mountains; that properly, if your own character is to grow through contact with them, it must be by appreciation of their beauty, by respect and a concern to establish between you and your desire's object the perfection of mutual rhythm – that it must be to do with love and not the assertion of power, must be a marriage and not a rape.

Good! Know that! Kiss the joy as it flies ...

WAVE LENGTHS

The sea cliffs of the west of Britain have always been among my favourite climbing venues. Here are a few accounts of climbs on them – with my son on Anglesey and revisiting some of my old routes from the early 1970s; with Joe Brown in Pembroke on the loosest first ascent either of us had ever done; with the Edwards family in Cornwall, attempting to bring some objective witness to a fevered and personally abusive debate – sweet and scintillating memories, all of them.

11: VISIONS AND VIRIANS (1995)

The present condition of my son gives cause for concern. He's just turned 15, and until last summer he was as pleasant and interesting a kid as an adolescent can be, into mountain bikes and computers and building dens. All that's changed. He started hanging around the local climbing wall – I suspect initially because a girl at mention of whose name Will goes bright crimson and professes to hate was always down there. Then he caught the rock-climbing bug. Talk with him now is a delirious babble of crimps and slaps, dynos and French grades – all the *patois* of the modern rock-ape. He hangs off any excrescence around the house like a great sullen lemur, mopes on wet days and is off into the quarries at every permitted opportunity, 'clipping, working and top-roping' God-knows-what. When I tuck him into bed every night he's propped up reading the Slate guide. He wants a climbing wall for his birthday ...

Needless to say, all the members of the Llanberis climbing ghetto – The Crook and Radio Walton, Big G, The Creature, The Fugitive and the Lone Intoxicant – regard this as excellent sport whenever they call in or he sees them around, tease his incessant questioning into ever more ludicrously indefinable realms, so that his fingers there on the bullshit edge he and his mates so eagerly grasp loosen their grip and he falls into the subversive void where the rest of us, knowing the folly of taking climbing seriously, have long been content to play. Alas, poor Will, we know the state too well.

Me, I get parentally worried, remembering that inability to concentrate on anything as your mind runs over and over the moves of a climb. So what do I do? I insist he finishes his homework first, I don't let him go out too often on week-day evenings in case it affects his schooling (and sneakingly, I know that by not making it too easy for him, by giving him something to fret against, I help sustain the allure). I can't share his enthusiasm for the quarries where he climbs mostly – the burden of their industrial history hangs too heavy for me to feel easy among them, but he – without that knowledge to trammel his enjoyment, rejecting empathy with those who worked here – takes them on the uncomplicated planes of egocentric recreation. In which guise I can appreciate their appeal, envy him the simplicity of that response, and envy him also at times – mornings especially – his growing strength and ease of body, as my own creaks and aches its way into decrepitude.

Also, I try to bring in the other dimensions, to fill in the gaps our mockery tears in his value-systems. So on Sunday, though rain was forecast, the wind blustering around and thick grey cloud scudding in across Anglesey, we set off to climb on the sea cliffs near Holyhead. Our objective goes by the romantic name of *A Dream of White Horses*. It's a rising traverse of 400 feet across a steep grey slab of rock which forms one side of the deep inlet known as Wen Zawn, near the North Stack lighthouse. There is a famous photograph taken by Leo Dickinson of its first ascent in 1967 – embattled, tiny figures and the flung spray of a leaping wave – that Will has seen. So there is an element of apprehension in his mind, to which I add by telling him about hanging belays above the surging water, rock little better than dried mud and stances that collapse beneath you into the depths with a sulphorous roar, all of which exaggeration is the currency of those who climbed on these cliffs in the first phase of their exploration.

There is no one in Wen Zawn when we arrive. We creep down the descent route that crosses above its fearful void. I play mother hen, clucking over him, warning him about rock boots on wet grass, roping him to me where the path touches the cliff-edge by a 300-ft drop to the waves, explaining to him at the notch on the far edge of the slab from where the route begins that from now on we're *incommunicado*, and tugs on the rope are our language. On the slab the wind's less. I concentrate on placing protection that won't pull out when tension comes on the ropes' long parabola. The moves are not difficult by today's standards – even the smallest holds will take most of your fingertips, and the hardest thing is to identify footholds from the dappled cast of rock. I take the hanging stance in the crack of Wen, backing up the belays on each rope, checking his figures-of-eight and clove hitches when he's across with me, ensuring the ropes will run free.

So it goes on. Will relaxes, he's enjoying it, engaging with the differing demands of ropework, circumspect use of the rock, registering situation, relishing the huge drop beneath him from the security of big holds and an angle which puts little strain on his arms. For me, it is both pleasure and painful responsibility to see him habituating to this environment of deadly beauty in which so many of my friends have died. When we finish the sky's cleared, the hills of Wicklow are acid-etched on the horizon.

Back where we have left our rucksacks, ropes coiled, he asks to go down and look across at what he's done, where he's been. I look with him, see as if for the first time the slab's light, dusty grey, like new concrete, seamed and globuled as though some almighty artisan had applied a hasty scratch coat of rough render against the tide-roar; I see the patches of ochre and umber in the rock, the delicate pink tints that in summer pick up on the colour of tenuous clumps of thrift, I see the rough-cast, quartz-splashed back wall where the grand design is broken into pieces, fragments, where the rock is splintered, hard and veiny as old timber, with the wave-surge among black boulders below. The sea's running diagonals merge into opalescent sky and the choughs tumble with a call like rusty springs as we turn to head out on the white track, among sepulchral stones, in the last light.

12: THREE CORNISH CLIMBS (1992)

The Atlantic Ocean Wall (E5, 6a,6b,6a): I am 45 years old, unfit, overweight. I spend most of my time behind a desk. The rest gets divided out between too many responsibilities. Of time for climbing I get not nearly enough. Also, I am incompetent, my rock-gear palaeolithic, my body showing the strains of having climbed for too long from too young: arthritis, tennis elbow, tendons, shoulders. I last led a route of this grade in the year *Atlantic Ocean Wall* was first climbed. I'm apprehensive before I even see it, and when I do it looks huge. Patiently Rowland Edwards, who is to take photographs, explains the line. It's in the back of a square zawn, towers above as you view it from the top of Longships Wall. The angle of the section level with us is cruelly apparent – ten degrees over the vertical for perhaps 40 feet. Rowland's son Mark, who is to lead me up it, is entirely calm and composed. I ask if he has qualms about going on to it with an inept geriatric.

'None at all,' he replies, so I ask how often the route gets done.

'Five or six ascents to date, to our knowledge. Not that you can ever tell. Mick Fowler failed on it ... '

I look down at the incoming tide, study ominous black streaks of water at the wall's base, and then, farting with fear, launch on to the abseil down Longships Wall and scrabble across awkward moves to the stance at the wall's foot with waves slapping at my heels. Mark prepares to climb. I note the height to which the water's rising in the zawn corners, the lacey foam, the continous low-frequency roar, and hope he races up the first pitch. He's elected to start up *Astrodome*, which leads to the same stance beneath the second pitch of A.O.W. It's streaming with water, a black glisten of ooze down the initial wall. Mark despatches it in about five minutes, most of which is taken up in arranging protection for me. The ropes signal my reprieve from the encroaching tide. I start to climb. There's a difficult move on small, wet footholds to reach a bulging, diagonal crack. The jams in this are good but widely spaced, so you have to turn on the power to move up it, but that relaxes me and frees my stiff, fearful movements. I reach the arête and stand in balance, breathing hard. The groove ahead is easy but you have to leave it, balance across a steep wall with hands and toes on widely spaced breaks, then mantel on to the sloping stance. Mark clips me in, doles out extravagant praise, sorts out ropes and gear whilst I look around. There is a good peg crack at head height with a broken leeper in it weeping an ugly brown stain down the pale granite. To its left a crack takes a poor medium-sized nut. Beneath it, two bolts have been drilled into the rock – small bronze bolts without hangers, to which we're attached by wires from which the nuts have been pushed down.

'Why these, Mark?'

'We thought that, rather than have the crack battered apart by peg placements – and remember that ordinary steel pegs last no time here – the bolts would prevent degradation of the rock. But no-one wants to listen. They just rant on about bolts in Cornish granite – people who couldn't get to a place like this to save their lives dictating to us what to do ... '

He moves past me on to the rock. Fierce will and covert anger. Above is a roof giving into a diagonal, leaning crack. He crouches beneath it, makes the positional adjustments, then swings round to relax into jamming his way up the crack. The rope crawls and stutters out, I crane my neck to watch his unflurried progress, envy the lightness and stamina. Soon he's belayed. The swinging loops from beneath my ledge disappear upwards. It's my turn to climb. I make the crack, get insecure jams, place my feet carefully on a green vein intruded across the prow where I squat. The top surface of rock flakes away, leaving me dangling from a jam. I flail back in contact, grab for a runner. Blood trickles down the back of my hand. Panting, struggling to retrieve Friends from the crack, I wrestle to an area of crumbling holds and almost-balance. In front is a peg runner, above me an overlap. I rest haplessly on the peg, peering into illegible rock above. Mark decodes it for me – a side-pull, a better hold above and right, little footholds, the flake above. It overhangs gently, but somehow, in a failing rush, I make it to the latter, where all feels better. There are good jams, small footholds, the possibility of rest even in a layback, and the position is exhilarating. A little, easy traverse from the end of the flake and I'm at the stance. It's a good foothold in an overhanging groove. There are two small bronze bolts in the wall. Looking down at the sea 140 feet below, and then into the crumbling back of the groove, I don't feel like criticising them. Mark climbs the groove with finesse, tiptoeing and pirouetting. I just back-and-foot. After what's gone before it's a cinch. There are various bits of rotting iron driven into the mud at the back, sharp and flakey in their decay. A clump of Royal Fern sprouts sturdily. As I near the top, ledges are covered with rock sea-spurrey, star-petalled, long-sepalled, flowering from a thick, delicate succulence of tiny leaves. It brings me back to level earth. We scamper through a rock-arch into the strangeness of peopled land. The route is one of the best I've ever done. Like its flowers, it should be five-starred.

Demolition (E6,6a/b): Of an argument, perhaps? The route's at Sennen, takes a blank wall just left of Demo Route. Soon after its first ascent, a Cornish climber had written in to one of the domestic magazines complaining about a 'craftily erected foothold', about the route being a 'cunning example of the chipping art.' Well, I've seen chipping on routes in my time: the first ascent of *Linden* on Curbar, of *Downhill Racer* on Froggatt, of *Razzle Dazzle* and *The Gadfly* on Crystal Slabs. I've seen the effect of retro-chipping on classic gritstone problems like *Rusty Wall*, *Pedlar's Slab* and *Long John's Slab*. I don't think it admissible. I wondered what I'd find here. Mark led up the route. It was a gusty October evening with a spit of rain on the wind. He did it without faltering, took the rope in and I tied on. There's a hard, reachy move, like the crux of *Beatnik* on Helsby, for the first break and the last runners. Above is a 25-ft slab at an 80-degree angle with a thin flake at bottom right and a vague, incipient crack at top left. Between the two and level with the first are two scooped indentations, toe-sized. You step through into the second with your right toe and are faced with the crux. Above is a minute, rounded boss of crystals and just to its left a fingerhold. It's two centimetres long and two millimetres deep, slightly sloping, and the tips of two fingers can rest on it and gain enough purchase to keep your balance as you lash a foot way out left, not on to a hold, but on to a vague, rough rib. If you fell off from this position leading, you would hit the ground. If anything hereabouts has been chipped, it has weathered back into the appearance of naturalness. But there is nothing here anyway. A fingernail balance hold! 'The chipping art'? I cannot square the rhetoric with the reality. What's been said had its origins not in honest comment but in animus. The smallest example from any route listed above would appear far worse than anything that could conceivably be seen as having been chipped here. But then, as always, the factionalism of our sport ...

Rock Dancer (E1,5a): They decide to give me a route – or rather, I can choose the route to do before I set off home. In the morning we've been informally discussing a memorandum from the National Trust with the Chief Warden for Penwith. It states that 'climbing is damaging nature conservation interests in the area, and ... ways and means of allowing recovery and preventing any further damage need to be considered.' Afterwards we go to Kenidjack, where I want to ease my aching frame on something straightforward. They – Mark and Rowland – point me at *Rock Dancer*, a slab climb. Despite the low technical grade, it's sustained, the protection very widely spaced and the holds fragile. But it's also beautifully direct in its line, the climbing bold and intricate, and a much better route than *Saxon*, which I'd done before and which wanders around and across the face, seeking the easiest way up, its climbing undistinguished. I bring up an Edwards on each rope, which must be a unique experience, and then scan the new guide. *Rock Dancer* gets one star, is described as 'challenging and direct.' Saxon has three, 'one of West Penwith's great lines – classical and exhilarating.' It doesn't have a line and simply isn't as good. Odd how bias against climbers can extend even to their routes.

13: FOOLS RUSH IN (1981)

'You're not abseiling off that,' Brown said.

I didn't know whether it was a statement or a question, so I ignored him and threw the rope over. He watched. When I was ten feet down his face peered over the edge.

'Bollocks,' I grinned up at him.

'OK then,' he agreed, 'I'll tell Valerie to throw the rope down.'

We crouched together at high-tide level. Grotesque gargoyles of draining rock crunched under our feet. The rope swayed down and hissed into the water. 'Shit,' he said flatly, and scurried away, leaving me to coil it.

'I'll get you for this, you little bugger,' I yelled after him.

A glinting sherpa smile mocked around the corner. 'Ha, ha, ha!' it said. I slung the rope over my shoulder, salt water dripping down my neck, and followed him.

He was waiting. A wave slithered along the cliff and his ledge was awash. We leapt out of reach.

'You're not going through that fucking cave,' he yelled.

I carried on traversing, pausing on the corner to grin back down at him.

'Why not?' I asked.

His eyes narrowed, recognising the game. We got to the cave, five feet wide, ten feet high, devil's-heart black and the tide coming in. 'Pity about your legs,' I jibed.

'They're telescopic,' he replied.

A wave sluiced in before us, crashing and sucking, and another followed it. I moved before the qualms took over, bridging high up in the roof, stretching, going as fast as I could. Looking back, I could see him against the light, legs out at right angles, neatly plotting his way along. I was glad he couldn't see my scrabblings and lunges. After 50 yards of grazed shins and lurches in the dark, I was through, leaping across boulders to one that was well out of reach of the tide. He emerged, cat-cool and wreathed in smiles.

'Ha, ha, ha!' he cackled at me, hugely happy with himself. We raced across boulders to one which gleamed black and whale-like, ten feet from our line. He got there first and turned to laugh at me. We were only 30 yards out before a big wave was bearing down on us. I leapt past him for a little flat rock just awash, and thence to the marble-smooth base of the crack, thrusting a jam in, pulling hurriedly, swinging my body out horizontally as the wave careered by. When I was 20 feet higher, I bridged across the groove, dried the soles of my boots, and asked if he wanted a rope.

'You fucker,' he smiled.

'Better be quick, Joe,' I parried, spying another wave on its way. He waited. The little rock had remained obstinately submerged and the incoming wave splashed over the big one, dousing him. I roared with laughter.

'Get out of that, you little bastard,' I cackled at him, and climbed another 20 feet up the crack. The next wave got him fair and square, soaking him to the waist. He jumped in before another one came, and waded across. When we were 40 feet up the crack we had a wrestling match as I tried to stand on his head, then I sorted out the rope and belays as he fastidiously pulled wet cloth from cold flesh.

'You can lead,' he said slyly.

I set off, trying to impress, but got it all wrong at a bulge and had to come down, attempting to look unconcerned. 'Should've faced the other way,' I told him, then climbed 30 feet without stopping. At which point the crack finished and things became loose. There was a ledge 40 feet away. My last runner was 30 feet down. I put in half-a-dozen, tied them all together, and teetered onwards. 'Bit loose up here, Joe,' I shouted, prepared to call it quits.

'Ha, ha, ha,' drifted out from the crack below. I kicked a block off in that direction to shut him up. An hour to climb 40 feet, terror all the way. If I stand on it, will it move? If I press it this way, will it stay? What in God's name am I doing here? If you let me off this one, I swear I'll join the Lib Dems, subscribe to *Newsweek*, and grow fat in front of the telly ... Oh Lord ...

The ledge, realm of broken promises and the return of arrogance, arrives. I put in eight nuts, tie myself intricately and variously on to them, hope that the block I'm sitting on will remain here longer than I intend to, and tell Joe to come up carefully. He does. Above us, a little curving dièdre leads to the top.

'Up there,' I tell him.

'Fuck that,' he replies.

'Don't come on this ledge,' I say to him, 'or it'll collapse.'

That pre-empts his move to take over my belay.

'How many nuts have you got in?' he asks, with more than passing interest.

'Eight, and that's the best of them,' I answer, pointing to one jammed between a tuft of sea-pink and a fragile sliver of mud. I'm lying – a better one's behind me.

'Oh,' he says. 'Wouldn't you like to do this pitch?'

'No,' I reply.

'Then we'll get someone to rescue us.'

He puts two fingers in his mouth and lets out a most piercing whistle. Across the bay, Ben and Marion give no sign of a response.

'I don't think they can hear us,' he says.

'Better do your pitch, then,' I prompt. 'You're the experienced one ... '

He grins, trapped.

'I'll just have a look at it.' He gets a huge runner on, 20 feet up.

'Watch me here,' and swings across under the overhang.

'I've got you,' I reassure him, but he's already gone and the rope runs out, slowly at first, then rapidly. I follow and find him sitting in a hollow among the bugloss and the thrift, his feet down two rabbit holes. He drags me down and punches me. We roll over wrestling till he gets me in a headlock.

'You're fucking mad,' he says, grinning. Ben and Marion arrive.

'What were you whistling about?'

We join forces to curse them roundly.

At the top of the path down to Broad Haven I stop, watch them head over the river and out across the sand. A woman and two small, greying figures ambling along the beach, the tide ebbing away, colours pale in the twilight, the beam of a lighthouse winking across the sea. Before the stumbling, sandy rise to the car park, I catch up with them again. The engine fires, lights come on, we swing into the night.

14: THE GATE OF HORN (1980)

There are two gates of sleep; the one is made of horn they say, and affords the outlet for genuine apparitions.

Virgil, Aeneid VI, 893/4

There was an inauspicious feel to this day. It began badly. All the jollities of the previous night, all its jousting and shrieking and lechery had brought down on us the exceedingly polite wrath of the Vicar, in whose field we were camping. He requested that we leave. Even Mrs Weston in the Bosherston café was something less than her friendly self. The Sunday papers had no report on Boycott's century in the Roses match. It was a sunny morning and we all felt ill. Dicky Swinden and I had been climbing together all week, gradually getting so mellow that we'd almost ceased to move. Where the momentum came from to get us to the Cauldron I don't know, but that was where we went.

Of course, we'd had great ideas. There was this line right of the groove and we were going to put it together, wow them all, show them who was the pedigree team. But when we saw it in the clear light of morning all we could think was, 'What the hell ... ' Dicky and Kath lay in the sun. Ben, Ken and Dave threw ropes down here and there and ploughed down them. I fretted and mooched and eventually thought, 'Oh, well, I'll go down here.'

The Cauldron is a huge hole in the headland, something over 150 feet deep. At the bottom, the sea comes in through an archway on one side, and through a great cleft on the other. The pool at the bottom is at most 50 yards across. Today it was emerald and glinting with reflected sunlight. Until they started gardening, that is.

I tried to put in another belay stake for my abseil. It wouldn't go in. The other stakes sloped towards where I wanted to go. I tied them off and tried to make myself think, 'So what if they do fail?' Three bits of wood, two of them splintered broomhandle. I put a rope to the edge, tied the abseil rope to it, and threw it down the arête. By this time Ben, Ken and Dave were making the sea boil, whooping and cheering and crashing. Formation gardening. In this amphitheatre my head felt like a stricken submarine with depth charges being laid all around it.

The route lay down a groove just right of the arête of a tower on the landward face of the Cauldron. Within ten feet I knew it wasn't on; it was just too loose and too scrappy to be worth doing. I carried on down, kicking and prising off the odd block in a desultory sort of manner. My 150ft rope ended 20 or so feet above the sea and I'd forgotten to tie a knot in it, so after 100 feet I stopped and muttered across to Ben, 30 feet away on the far wall of the great cleft, that I wasn't going to bother, shit route, not worth doing, going back up, and got my prusikers on the rope. On impulse I looked round the corner into the cleft. I hadn't remotely considered the possibility of a route up this wall, which overhung at a constant five or ten degrees beyond the vertical for over 170 feet straight out of the sea:

'Jesus Christ!'

I was dumbstruck and juddered my way back up the rope as fast as I could to the top. I rearranged the belay, threw the rope down, and set off. Within a few feet I was hanging right out from the rock in the middle of the cleft gazing at a perfect, sound, straight crack. Not even a crack really; a plumb line of weakness with pockets and holds leading down to a cave and kittiwake ledge. Beneath that a crescent line of holds curved down and round to the sound lower section of the arête. I slid down and set myself swinging in the middle of the cleft until I could grab hold of the rock. Letting go, I almost hit the far wall, and this time made a total mess of getting from the Sticht plate into the prusikers. Back to the top I went, with the rope tangled in everything. I couldn't believe it. What would it be like? How would those holds feel when you were on them? Could you get to them from round the arête? I pulled the ropes up and ran round the top to Dicky.

He was somewhere between sleeping and waking.

'Well I'll go down if you want to go down, but I feel really sick.'

I said maybe we could do it tomorrow and that it was stupendous and that I just had to go for a shit, I was so frightened. And I was, so I ran off, leaving it at that, and ran and ran, and crouched behind a bank and shat. After that I felt better and ran along the track, and all the time I could imagine myself launching out across that wall, so I ran a bit more till my chest wasn't so tight and I was breathing easily and I ran over to Dicky.

'Let's go for it now.'

He came along. There was no sullenness or condescension about it. We both knew how each other felt. I knew he was feeling stale, tired, and a bit delicate, and that he'd rather lie in the sun with Kath, but that he'd come along and blast in there, supremely competent, and be happy to have done it. And he knew that I was on some sort of high and gripped out of my head and on to something big. So he brought round his gear and I was obsessive about big nuts and Friends and scrounged some of his chalk and he set up the rope and went down first whilst I fretted about how cold it would be down there and should I wear shorts or Polar pants. Then I followed him down. He was belayed beneath a little groove we'd seen in the base of the arête. I'd sort of bribed him on top by saying I'd go for the middle pitch and the rest would be easier, and though I was under a compulsion to go for that pitch, I was thinking what a good climber he is, and how much easier it would all be for him. But off he went up the first pitch, a 60ft slim crack, steep and solid. I was cold, belaying, and really worried, thinking I'd get stiff and tight and not be able to do it. But he wasn't long; he just drifted up it in his easy way and got belayed. I came up to join him on his pedestal:

'We must go round the arête somewhere about here.'

I bridged up past him, very awkward and intimate, hoping I didn't smell too badly after a week in a tent. Above his head I got a couple of nuts in a crack, and felt around for holds on the wall. Bridging wide, I could get some, smallish but good. The wall overhung as much as the one round the corner. I peered round:

'Oh, shit! Oh, Jesus!'

'What's up?'

'It's just incredibly beautiful.'

'What?'

'The colour of the water.'

He shrieked with laughter.

'What's up with you?' I asked, a bit peeved.

'There you are on a 6a move and all you can think about is the colour of the water.'

'It's not 6a. I just make it look that way. It's about 5b. Anyway, have a look.'

He did. Through the cleft you saw into the bay beyond, through dark green walls, and out in the daylight the water was an incandescent ultramarine glow, more emanation than substance, shockingly beautiful, an acid trip of sunlight.

Back bridging in my little corner, I was cowed and scared. The wall round there was unbelievably steep. I had another half-hearted sally out on to the arête. It was really tiring. I told Dicky to watch me and set off back. The top runner came out just as I was thinking of jumping off onto it. I was shaking:

'Oh fucking hell, Dicky.'

'Cold down here,' he said laconically, shivering in his vest. I had to make the moves. I put the runner back and another by it, moved back to the arête, groped across for a hold, shuffled, then swung down and round. The runner I tried to get in was the wrong size. There was a voice in my head saying, 'Go for it. Go for it.' Outside and over there I could hear Ben on his route talking to Dicky.

'He's powering up it. Christ! It looks fantastic. The holds must be incredible.'

They were! I stopped to put in a wire, and a Friend just above it. It was all so cool and good. I was so strong and concentrated, and the ledge came almost before I wanted it. 'I think he's OK now. He's at a ledge.'

'Oh Jesus, Dicky, this is so good.'

I sidled into the cave. It was flat, deep, and comforting. There was a big thread. I tied on and shouted down that I was safe. The place stank of birds. I kicked off a rotting, precarious nest, and underneath insects crawled and squirmed. The nest hit the water with a dull flack. Dicky's turn now. He was a bit apprehensive:

'Watch the ropes. I've just taken the runners off and I'm moving across.'

He was round on the wall, grinning and gurgling:

'Incredible ... unbelievable ... it makes Deep Space look pathetic ... This Friend's really good ... Oh, man! It's so bold ... '

He was up with me, clipped into the belay, and so happy. He could hardly wait to get on the top pitch. You could see it in him, he was hungry for it as he sorted out the gear and half-listened to what I'd seen about it. Then he was away:

'Oh God! God! I don't want it to stop. This is so good.' He was playing with the crack, delightedly. Ken peered over the top.

'What's it like, Dicky?'

He was climbing slowly to make it last, every move in exquisitely considered slow-motion:

'5a and fantastic,' he shouted to Ken. Then he was up and tied on and I followed up this soaring line out of the cleft with the wall dropping away green and shadowy beneath. At the top his eyes were shining. We were inarticulate. I believe we so far forgot ourselves as to hug each other and scream with laughter. And there it was, a supreme fiction, an experience lived through together which all the memorial words, all the splintered shards of definition we vainly tried to gather could never approach. Something quite beautiful, searing, and beyond. That evening Ken and I left to drive to Bangor. All the way he talked tawdry politics, but my head was singing:

... like a black globe
Viewed by sons of Eternity, standing
On the shore of the infinite ocean,
Like a human heart struggling and beating.
The vast world of Urizen appeared.

Before I slept I was hanging there again in that great cleft, watching the sun on the water as though, waking, I had passed through the Gate of Horn.

15: IN SEARCH OF TIMES PAST (2001)

Wasps. Ray was fascinated by them. He had his macro lens out and was focusing in. There were maybe half-a-dozen crawling up and down and over each other and around the rim of a pot of jam on the table, as we sat out over afternoon tea in the garden of Mrs Weston's *Olde Worlde Café* in Bosherston. Then Mrs Weston herself came bustling out – a little more stooped, but the sidelong observant smile and the immaculate make-up still as firmly in place as they were when I first sat drinking tea in her garden maybe three decades ago:

'Well, boys – Oh, hello there – now, how many years? – Oh, yes, it's been a few now, 'sn't it. 'Course, there's not so many of the climbers comes down these days. No! Not so many as there used to be. Well, you'll remember ... '

She gave Martin and myself a long, appraising glance, slotting us into place.

' ... full up inside for breakfast, it'd be, and 50 or 60 more waiting their turn outside ... No, we don't 'ave to work so 'ard these days. Not so many of the climbers. Plenty of the wasps, still, mind ... ' she added, flicking a teatowel amiably in their direction before drifting on to gossip the next table.

Some places feel like home, feel a part of the scheme of things, and South Pembroke for me is one of them. I'd not been for five or six years – that time too was with The Crook – and sometimes you get the urge just 'to see if everything is still the same.' There'd been periods in my life when the peace and isolation of this place had made it the focus of my climbing ambitions, other times when the mood had been more that of the wasps around the jam-pot – focused in, heedless, hustling and buzzing. I felt oddly grateful for Mrs Weston's imparted sense of reversion. Will, my eldest son who'd been recruited as care attendant for the weekend, was getting restless – you don't have the stamina for these long brewing sessions at his age. We were going to have to do something. It was early August, the showers were no more than drenchingly intermittent. We thought of heading for Mowing Word.

The thing I like about Mowing Word is that you can set off from the café and walk to it. Actually, that's only one of the things I like about Mowing Word. If I were stuck on a desert island, I'd hope this would be one of its headlands. The west face faces west, the south face faces south, and the Hidden Face is just that. These are all good characteristics, in my view. Also, it's a pleasing size for a crag. The higher bits reach 140 feet, there are plenty of little bits at around 80 to 100 feet, and the rock ... well, it has variety. The loosest route I've ever done is on the left-hand side of the west face. I wouldn't recommend it, and won't even tell you its name. You don't always like to remind yourself of a time when you sat on a delicately-perched 50-ton block belayed to a clump of thrift.[1] The hardest climb I've ever led is on the south face. It's not hard any more. But I'll get round to telling you about that. The best new route I've been responsible for, irrespective of grade, is here too, right in the middle of the west face. And that's what we'd decided on.

So we left the transport in the Vicarage Field where we were camping, just as we used to do years ago, and we took that walk, down past the lily ponds where once the water was clear and you could see huge trout, but that are scummy and stinking these days with algal growth, and managed by the National Trust. We cut over the headland where the small, sweet mushrooms grow, looked down into the Raming Hole with its terrifying descent path, every few yards dragged Will out of shakeholes where he was thinking he might find a tube to squirm down into some sea-washed and mysterious Xanadu, were too idle to go down to see if the old fishermen's rings on top of Gun Cliff were still there (Mortlock and I used to abseil off them in the 1960s, when we were first exploring around on these cliffs, but they don't have a UIAA mark so it wouldn't be allowed now), and arrived on *Mowing Word* just as a raucous crowd of young women intent on having a good time emerged from the top of *Diedre Sud*, which is quite possibly the best sea-cliff severe in Britain.

I sat in a little hollow sheltered from the wind and set memory into scanning mode whilst Martin and Will went to fix up an abseil: there was a time here, on top in a gale one winter in the 1960s, when the whole headland shook as the rollers from the Atlantic thudded into it and the spume was thrown 100 feet over our heads; another time I was setting off intending to do a new route, abseiled down with all the gear, was joined by my partner – I don't even remember who it was – and we'd both forgotten to bring the ropes. You'd have thought that would have been a lesson. Not a bit of it. When I joined Martin and Will (Ray had abseiled down to one side, because he was photographing) down at the base of the crag, what ropes did we have? Two ancient 9mms of indeterminate length ...

'I don't know if we should use that one, Dad. I had to cut a bit off it,' explained Will, enigmatically.

What we'd come to entertain ourselves on was a composite route – a combination of the initial pitch of *Heart of Darkness* and the top pitch of *New Morning*, the first ascents of which I'd done within a few days of each other with John Greenland almost exactly 30 years before, in August 1971. There was no anniversary intent about being here. It had just turned out that way. And nor was there anything proprietorial about it either. Comments about this combination being 'one of the finest

---

[1] Not quite the full truth – see 13 above.

sea-cliff HVSs anywhere,' and the three stars it gets, are pleasing. But once a route's done and written up, it's no longer yours (if indeed, in any real sense, it ever was), and it's an egotistical fallacy to assume it is. You just happened to have been first to have passed this way. You recorded some brief, coded and more or less authentic description (mine of *Heart of Darkness* was, I recall, pretty florid: ' ... the sea sucking at the black cave beneath, the great overhangs above and below, give the crucial pitch a tremendous sense of isolation and elemental conflict.' Something along those lines. They wouldn't use stuff like that in a modern guidebook. I was hanging around a lot with Peter Biven, and must have been into Wagner at the time). Then you had the privilege of variously imposing your ego and your fancy on this piece of innocent rock by according to it a grade and a name, either or both of which later generations might revise or discard. And then, you left it to its own conceptual existence, and others to their own versions of your experience. Good!

In my case, I'd revisited this experience on a few occasions. Once was in the winter of 1971, with John Kingston and Robin Ford. We'd driven across from London, slept in a derelict cottage at Stackpole Quay that's a National Trust holiday cottage now, and done this combination – basically because I'd remembered the rest of either route as being pretty unremarkable, and thought these two pitches would fit well together. I'd done it another time on a perfect summer's day at the end of the 1970s, with Roger Alton, who's the most amusing companion with whom I ever shared the pleasures of the rope. (You do well to raise an eyebrow. I've never known anyone so addicted to terror as Roger.) And I'd soloed it once, when I was down here by myself, because I was feeling fit and it's a safe, solid kind of climb.

All this was over 20 years ago. Here I was at the bottom again, watching the sea sluice in and out of the sculpted rock, remembering the boom of the rollers and the muffling sea-fret from the day I first did it as Martin paid out Will's rope. He padded up the slab, reached the horizontal band of strata, peered round the arête to the left and disappeared from view.

After this comes a space of time in which there is minimal communication, the rope edges out, Martin and I chatter and joke away about this and that, the rope's taken in, we have a discussion about who goes next, I pull rank as senior and least fit member of the party and he accedes because we're seconding this long traverse pitch on a rope each so there's no real advantage either way, and I start to climb. I scrabble up the slab, noticing the hard, smooth texture of the rock on this resistant band. I poke my head round the corner, remember the next few moves are the hardest on the climb, and feel mildly pissed off and panicky that the first runner on the traverse is all of 15 feet away. Then I climb it, in an inelegant, crab-like, scuttling and security-conscious fashion, by basing each move on a good jam. You can do this in the horizontal strata, and I have no wish to swing off and end up dangling from a single, frayed 9mm beneath those roofs. I revel anxiously in the pitch's atmosphere, remember the other routes I did hereabouts and trace their lines as I relax. I join Will on the small stance over on the far arête. He clips me in and sorts me out as I used to do him when he was just starting out on rock seven or eight years ago. I feel distinctly and paternally proud of his ease and competence. Martin joins us. Will leads off in a beautifully elegant and unhurried contemplative way up the immaculate top crack of *New Morning*. There's a brief shower of rain. When I follow I'm momentarily bemused by the line taken being to the right of the flake pinnacle, even more bemused by the continuing presence of the latter, and a little irritated by one of Gary Gibson's bolts in the fine wall between here and *The Flax of Dream*. I lurch up from jam to jam and recall that the first time I looked at this crack, with Colin Mortlock a couple of years before I climbed it, it had been completely choked with mud. I remember, too, noticing that the mud had disappeared – presumably washed out – when I did *Heart of Darkness*, but it was raining that day so we came back for it the next time the sun shone. I sit on top as Martin climbs and feel pretty happy, think what a good and varied and characterful route it was. But it's a long way from *New Morning* to 'Things have changed,' and that thought stays with me as we race back to the St Govan's Inn through the twilight, merry as youths, all four of us.

To pick up on a theme: I have a print in a file somewhere. It's a bit washed out, ghostly and over-exposed – not even Photoshop could do much with this one. John Greenland took it, looking up into the sun and the pale rock, with one of those cameras you had in those days where everything had to be set by hand. It's on the first ascent of *New Morning* and I'm setting off up the top crack – hippy hair, big forearms, and a Charlet peg hammer dangling from the belt of my tight jeans. There's a kind of museum ethos attaching to this hammer that complements the rest of the period detail. Charlet hammers, like Charlet ice-axes, were beautifully made, perfectly balanced. They had a metal sleeve round the top of the shaft to protect the wood. They didn't have a spike. In its day this was an ethical statement – spikes could be, and in some hands were, used to alter the rock. If you were on an unclimbed route at that time, you naturally carried pegs and a hammer. They weighed a ton. You might, very sparingly rationed, use them for runners. You could certainly use them on stances without good belays – that little arête stance on *Heart of Darkness* had a *leeper* that I'd put in as the belay for at least ten years. Some people would use them for aid. I was never happy with that, though I do recall one occasion at least when I tapped a peg in lightly, tied it off, stood in a sling, cleaned the rock above, then came down, removed the peg and did it without. That, in my view, was straining the limits of the acceptable, and I'd write it up in the first ascent description as 'peg used for aid whilst *gardening*' – lovely, archaic term that it is.

The wider context and code was that protection then was still rudimentary and first ascents were done ground-up without prior inspection. We all had our own ethical parameters. Those were mine as far as pegs and new routes were concerned, and the few occasions when I transgressed, I regarded as matter for self-reproach. It felt important because there was a sense that if these self-imposed strictures were not rigorously observed, the delicate regulatory balances of our absurd little game would be disturbed, and chaos would ensue. The heat that discussion in this area engendered was tremendous. There was a clear sense that our accepted codes were a brake on the garnering of those obvious lines of the future, but an equally sure acceptance that in time the next surge of genius would gather them into climbing's purlieu. In the event, the initial impetus to that process was not given by climbers of genius, but by those of vision who saw from their own necessity the wisdom of bending the rules. Chief among these were the strange, isolate and wayward Edwin Drummond and the cheekily iconoclastic, wholly endearing, tactically astute and sorely missed Peter Livesey. Neither of them climbers of any great or particular natural ability, by their questioning – or as the generation to whose values I subscribed would have had it, questionable – tactics they liberated a younger generation – Allen, Bancroft, Regan and Fawcett foremost among it – of consummate and extraordinary talent to lift climbing into the modern era.

So much for lectures on history, and we'll come back to the application of this later. Meanwhile, let's go climbing. There was a gap in the showers, the tides were right, so Will, Martin, Ray Wood and myself decided to go to Mother Carey's Kitchen at Lydstep. I've always been disproportionately proud at having sneaked this name, which sounds authentically local but is entirely spurious and invented, on to the maps and charts of the area. It came about because Colin Mortlock and myself, when we were sitting on the rocks at the bottom of an unnamed, impressive buttress one day in the 1960s, saw a couple of storm petrels – Mother Carey's Chickens – skimming the waves, and became so engrossed in watching them that we were cut off by the tide and had to climb a route to get out. Anyway, after that it became one of my favourite pieces of rock. *The Strait Gate*, which I climbed with Colin in the spring of 1970, developed a cult status in the mid-1970s among the few people who then went to Pembroke. On the first ascent, half-way up the top crack the rope-drag had been so bad because of my incompetence in placing runners at the back of the initial chimney that I'd made a tricky little traverse out left on pockets to a weird

Pete Crew on Great Wall, Clogwyn Du'r Arddu (John Cleare)

Top left: Jonny Dawes on first ascent of the Very Big and the Very Small - ultimate slate test-piece on the Rainbow Slab
Top right: Steve Bancroft on Strapadictomy, Froggatt Edge (Bernard Newman)
Below: Ron Fawcett on Cave Route Right Hand, Gordale Scar (John Beatty)

Gritstone Essence, 1972

Left: Suicide Wall, Cratcliffe Tor
Top right: Right Unconquerable, Stanage Edge
Bottom right: Valkyrie, Rfoggatt Edge (Ken Wilson/Baton Wicks)

These photographs were taken by Ken Wilson between showers on the same dank March day. He was laying out *Hard Rock* at the time, was short of pictures for these featured climbs, so we raced up from London, recruited Martin Jackson to hold my ropes, careered round the crags and Ken snapped happily away whilst I shivered up the routes. Note the white jumper – *de rigueur* with climbing photographers at the time. I've a feeling it was the same one that Pete's wearing in John's *Great Wall* picture. Things got passed around....

The Major! HW Tilman, with one of his dogs and the Raleigh bicycle on which he cycled across Africa, outside his Barmouth home in 1976.

Top left: Eric Shipton (Perrin collection)
Top right: HW Tilman
Below: Shipton (left) and Tilman (second from right) together

Top left: Fantan B – the fourth pitch
Top right: Peter Biven sea-cliff traversing at Long Quarry Point, Torbay (John Cleare)
Bottom left: Pete Crew – human dynamo, first of the pop star climbers (John Cleare)
Bottom right: Biven on the first ascent of *Magical Mystery Tour*, Berry Head, Devon
(John Cleare)
Opposite: Biven and Perrin retreating from the Elegug Tower during the first ascent
weekend in 1971 (John Cleare)

Bad Boys of Snowdonia
Top left: John Redhead – the Rasputin of Welsh climbing? (Ray Wood)
Top right: Al Harris – prankster, maniac, hero, saint and fool (Perrin collection)
Bottom left: Fachwen bouldering – the author on his own arete
Bottom right: Stevie checks on his credentials

stance in a tube, and finished up the loose groove above that. I did it this way again on a second ascent, with John Kingston in the winter of 1972, and had gone back to finish up the top crack direct with Dick Pierce, and to add another route of much the same grade to the right on the same wall in September of that year, when I was climbing particularly well. Nearly 30 years on, here was my son drifting up the easy 20-ft pitch into the cave, and then peering solicitously back down to ask if I needed a rope on it. I love the reversals that age brings. Next time I'll take him at his word and put him to the trouble of giving me one.

He'd laid out the ropes, I fixed a belay, and he set off. The Great Wall at Mother Carey's is about 150 feet high, plane-smooth and plumb vertical, and *The Strait Gate* ('strait is the gate and narrow the path that leadeth unto righteousness') takes the crack that rises out of a narrow chimney-cave and peters out near the top of the wall. The modern guidebooks tell you to climb the right arête of this cave on big holds, belay in a niche in the crack above, then do another pitch to the top, but that seems to rob the route of its 'big pitch' feel. Anyway, Will, who likes a degree of oddity in his climbing and gravitates enthusiastically towards any hole or dripping cleft that presents itself, ambled into the green depths of the cave, chimneyed and pirouetted up and out to its lip, and disappeared from view out on to the wall. I paid out the rope and watched an enormous crab with claws maybe two feet long sidle across the rock-pool below. After a while the rope was taken in and I followed.

Memory is a very odd and selective faculty. It generalises, loses so much of the detail and texture that is what delights or sears us in experience. I had a vague sense of the pleasure of being at the apex of this tall cave and swinging out on to the wall, but I'd lost the precise feeling of surprise at emerging from green, cool shadow on to this beautiful, white, rearing face. I'd forgotten how secure and satisfying the first 40 or 50 feet of the crack beyond were – the rough, solid rock, the perfect jamming, the scampering bursts of movement, the cunningly contrived arm-bar and knee-lock rests. I remembered a red tape on an aluminium chock that Mortlock hadn't retrieved on the first ascent. It was still there when Kingston and I had done it, but had bleached by then to white, the chock flaked and powdered almost entirely away. I remembered the taut, arm-taxing sequences of finger-and-toe precision – much sounder and better protected now than the run-out, creaky finale of 1972 – that leads to the top. I remembered the anxiety – the long, strenuous, probing reaches above diminishing gear, the looseness of the last few feet. I remembered the strength I had then, the timing, and contrasted it ruefully with the fading power left in my arms now, the hurried moves, the gratitude for the rope above.

Sitting there afterwards, I felt curiously pleased and proud: with Will, for being so unaffected and competent and funny and decent; with the route, for its presence and quality; with them both for being *sui generis*, of themselves entirely, owing nothing to me. A couple of people – a man and a woman – arrived. They didn't speak, and seemed not to like each other. They racked up swiftly and efficiently and roped down. I hope the experience, and not just its acquisition, held something for them. Martin joined us, and we scrambled round across razor rock to the foot of the White Sheet – an exquisite rock-feature on the next buttress east. There was an E5 there that Will wanted to look at, even though it was a cold, blustery day with showers scudding in. I was interested to see, because I'd not been round to the foot of it for 30 years.

What I saw when we got there I found curiously shocking. To explain why I'll start at a tangent. In passing, I mentioned that the hardest climb I'd ever led had been on the south face of *Mowing Word*, and that it wasn't hard any more. I did this route a day or so after the finish to *The Strait Gate* and *Wraith* (the route on its right), and called it *Charenton Crack*, after the lunatic asylum in which the Marquis de Sade was incarcerated. It's an 80-ft overhanging corner-crack that starts off finger-width and ends as wide jamming. It was filled with mud, the edge was fretted with lancet-like calcite that shredded my fingers, the gear was crap, and leading it on sight in that condition was sheer, balls-out desperation. A few people claimed it as a first ascent in the period between 1972 and the appearance of the first Climbers' Club guidebook in the 1980s, by which time the ground-up, respectful ethos that had held sway in the area was changing. I did the route again in about 1995. It was unrecognisable. It hadn't just been cleaned out. It had been hacked out ...

Back to the White Sheet. I'd looked at this in the early 1970s, and thought it unclimbable. There was an obvious crack to start that led to half-height on this extraordinary, glistening plane surface of pristine rock. But this crack was fretted across, filmed over and choked with the calcite that entirely covered the wall.

Not any more ...

In some ways I regret the way that climbing's gone. I think we had an innocence once, and a respect for the world we were given to play in, that regulated those driving egos which all young people should rightly possess. Where their necessity damages the world we all must live in, grain of sand though it may be, surely it's time to think again?

ASPECTS *OF THE* VERTICAL

From roadside bouldering to Scottish winter soloing, through climbing in the old slate quarries and 'Sliding Doors' sea-cliff first-ascent scenarios to the idiosyncratically troublesome, the breadth of context and appeal in climbing is extraordinary.

16: WELSH SLATE: ROCK & THE ART OF ABSTRACTION WITH WILL PERRIN (1997)

This next piece my son and I wrote together for a special slate issue of a climbing magazine. Though he started work on a few others, it was the only magazine article he ever had published – and this at the age of 17. I couldn't have approached the simple, evocative clarity he achieved at that age, or perhaps ever ...

Some 30 years ago the Dinorwig quarries were still working. I know climbers from the Llanberis ghetto of the 1960s who had jobs in the cutting sheds or as labourers. I remember too sitting in Pete Crew's house over a brew in 1969 and hearing the grating rumble of the rockfall that finally closed down quarrying operations at Dinorwig. It was huge, went on for three days, took out the roadways, hydraulics, electrics at the top of the quarry on the working levels at a time when debentures taken out by the operating company came due for payment. The place went bust.

So it slid overnight from working, if antiquated, industrial site to gigantic adventure playground. It was auctioned off, bought up by some big contractor for a piffling amount, sold on in months at a vast profit – there was a Tory government and insider dealing was a term that had no currency in those days – to the Central Electricity Generating Board as the site they were looking for to build a new pumped storage scheme. No-one bothered with the climbing here for years, except for Joe Brown's forays up the back wall of Twll Mawr, done to prove that you could, because everyone said slate was bad news, and because it was the biggest piece of unclimbed rock around. The quarries were for fun, for play, for looting and forays, for riding scrambles bikes up inclines and for bizarre sexual scenes on abandoned hospital operating tables with channels cut in them for workmen's blood to drain, and for exploring tunnels and climbing trashed ladders and trundling mighty blocks into cordite-scented holes as all the while the place went back and the trees grew and its industrial history faded into a memory.

I knew too much about it. The scarred old men with choked lungs who'd worked here had befriended me. I knew from them its long industrial history – the strikes and the lockouts and the theft of freehold land under the pretext of offering employment. The place hurt. I seldom went there. Then my son and I moved to Dinorwig and I started to look at the quarry again. I could still never see it with the freedom and facility of later generations, but still, I did some of the routes, and when Will started climbing in earnest, he was in there all the time, a slate-bred rock-urchin. To exorcise the feelings I had about history and context, I wrote the following piece for the essay I did each week on Welsh radio at the time. I give it you here as context for one of the most extraordinary landscapes in which I've ever climbed – man-made, derelict, moodily post-apocalyptic. It's called *Caban*:

'On the afternoon of a bright Sunday, as the *gweddill dewr* – the brave and age-ing remnant of a congregation were singing O *Fryniau Caersalem Ceir Gweled* in the vestry of Capel Sardis, I idled my way into the quarry. It's only just down the road from my house, but I don't go there that often. Even on a luminous day like this, I find it oppressive. In the gloom of a November afternoon it becomes unbearable. I think of the men whose brief, hard lives were spent wresting from the mountain the rock from which were carved rank upon rank of headstones in Deiniolen cemetery under which they now lie. And it saddens me. I think of the contrast between their harsh barracks, close housing, and the ostentation of Penrhyn, Vaynol, Glynllifon, and it sickens me.

'But that's to take an entirely negative view, and a sunny day's enough to put anyone in a good humour. It searches out the whole range of turquoise, umber, mauve and purple in a rock slandered by the description of being merely grey. It highlights fold and fracture, bodies them forth as abstract shapes that you realise with a sudden shock were the defining geometries of quarrymen's lives. Where one *bargen's* regular and true, another's splintered and bent – nature's accidents dictating even the sufficiency of a child's daily bread.

'It's all past, it's all finished now. Lacey brilliance of parsley fern colonises gaunt tips, the tiny stonecrop spreads bulbous and globular amongst razor litter of the terraces, rosettes of lichen encrust and emboss. A pair of choughs tumble and scream. Scratched initials from the last century hide shyly in the darkness of tunnels. There are trees rooting everywhere; a tenacious birch sapling trembles on a cliff-ledge, sycamores obscure the angles of an incline, by the old *caban* an ash tree grows.

'I know it was a *caban* because Rennell Pritchard, who worked here years ago, told me so before his death. Not that there's much left of it now. The slates from the roof, the table and the workmen's rough benches were taken long since. The lime render is flaking and loose, nettles grow in the hearth and the inevitable, ubiquitous spleenwort feathers the walls. I'm struck always by how small it is. Ten feet by 12 feet – no more than that. The small window looking out onto Snowdon and the lake is frameless, glassless now, and the door's gone. Yet the place still breathes or even whispers. If I stood here on a day when the mist muffles every sound and is so dull even the generator hum that now permeates this mountain is deadened, I think the old echoes would creep back warily to the place that gave them birth. There would be voices here again.

'What would they talk of? As I stand here now, a quarter-century beyond the quarry's closure, perhaps 100 years beyond the *caban*'s time, I see paragliders circling on thermals like garish raptors with their prey dangling; on rock slabs, climbers in vivid pastels pad and poise, delicate-footed where the facemen's hobnails sparked. This roofless room draws me away from that modern and modish world to the pre-occupations of another time. What would they have talked about?

'In the archives of the university college in Bangor, itself founded from quar-rymen's subscriptions, there is the minute-book of a turn-of-the-century *caban*. *Llyfr Cofnodion hen giniawdy Sinc y Mynydd, Llechwedd*, it's entitled, and it runs from St Valentine's Day 1902 to mid-April 1905. I don't imagine that the workers of Llechwedd were significantly more or less intelligent than their counterparts at Dinorwig. I suppose the topics raised in a single month – that of October, 1902 – are pretty much representative of the thoughts, the interests, the mind-set and the mind-play, of workmen in the slate industry at the time.

'There's singing – either serious solos, or more playfully the musical contor-tionism of setting the words of O Fryniau Caersalem – that hymn again! – to the tune of Crug-y-bar. There's recitation – of a poem, having only read it twice; of an abbreviated Dafydd Brenin Israel. There are competitions on grammatical themes – read a passage from which all the punctuation had been removed, spell difficult words, create new ones. There are discussions – should ministers of religion have a lifetime's or a defined term's appointment to office; should the measures of the 1902 Education Act as they affect Wales be opposed; is the taking of a wife a matter of choice, or a necessity?

'There are lectures too: 'How much greater is a man than a sheep' runs the title of one of them; in another, Owen Morris talks about his holidays. All this took place in dank tunnels, in crude huts 2000 feet up a mountain, in rain and wind, as the men slaked their thirst with bottles of cold tea and ate probably no more than dry bread. Yet, does that range of subjects, that desire to play and perform, that involvement with the issues of the day, that eagerness to live the life of the mind hold sway in Hotpoint's or Ferodo's works canteens today? Was the breadth, the awareness, the pride evinced through them an expression of their proud knowledge of difference, of cultural resistance, of intrinsic superiority to the vain, philistine and greedy pro-prietors who allowed them so meagre a living?

'I look across the abandoned terraces to where the rock-climber moves up his bald slab. Out of adversity he produces elegance and grace, moving with a purpose, reaching his goal. In the jumble of scree beneath him, pipework which drove the cutting machines is twisted as though cardboard tubing. The walls totter, inclines sag wearily, their work done. At their head, the wooden drums are scored deep by the hauling wire. One day, the buttresses that hold their axles will collapse and, freed, they will bound crashing down into the encroaching oakwoods, from which, on this bright day, rises the green woodpeckers' crazed laughter. And after that release, once again there will be silence, and the wind. As I walk home down worn steps, I see the congregation dispersing from Capel Sardis vestry, the few, leaning on each other. Behind them, the carpet-pedalled harmonium too has wheezed into silence. There will be no more O Fryniau Caersalem when these have "crossed the bar."'

It's a way of looking at the quarry, and to me an important one, but there's a new context to be celebrated, a new resourcefulness and invention and cast of folk-heroes. There are paintings in the tunnels and sculptures on the terraces, names that further names evoke, lines and intricacies for the toying with. The web of history in which I struggled has given way to a gossamer imagination drifting across blankness, adhering there, engraving action on abstraction: Stevie Haston knifing away the brit-tle of *Comes the Dervish* – maybe the newest-ever route to die of its own popularity; John Redhead's manic strain of straining, assertive life; Martin Crook – *homo ludens* of the Western crags – and his mentor the Space Captain, looning the tubes under visitants' eyes; Jonny Dawes, ineffably; Paul Pritchard like sprung, thin steel. These are the new echoes, intermingling with a chough's scream, a raven's guttural; cutting memories like the shadow of a peregrine's wing, like red berries against hued and cubist rock, brief and shedding. Maybe you'll like the climbing here, though the mood's unlike. You'll find your disturbances, your anomalies, and all expressed through the medium of small friction, razor exfoliant or perversities in the clip. Enjoy it! Here's my slate-reared son Will's annotated list of median names – confess-edly arbitrary, though maybe even comprehensively experiential. Or as Victor McClellan wrote on the stone he left us on the way to *Slippery People* last night:

'We were close, man – real close!'

Try it, then, if you want to know what's owed to what. To touch, after all, can be to find ...

Will's List:

Fool's Gold, Bus Stop Quarry (E1,6a – well, so they say!)
Know what I think about when this route's mentioned? Warm summer days, the bus
home from school taking forever, getting changed out of my uniform quickly and
racing through my homework if my dad was in – not bothering to do either if he was
out. Then I'd grab my sack, rush out of the house and head towards Bus Stop – all
of 200 yards! *Fool's Gold* is one of those routes we nearly always did and it never
seemed to lose its appeal. I first did it as a fat little kid with my dad – didn't enjoy it
much then – the object for me was just to get up. But since then I can remember on
so many different occasions: cowering beneath the overhang to brush the footholds,
that moment of insecurity as sweaty fingers begin to work loose from the hard-won
fingerlock, the coolness deep within the top crack on hot days. I've climbed it more
times than any other route – maybe I am a fool, but I think it priceless.

Launching Pad/Holy, Holy, Holy, Dali's Hole, (E1,5b/E2,5c)
I love lounging around beneath these two routes and gazing down into water like
green crystal with submerged buildings in its depths, and ghostly white trees that
wait to impale you after the mistimed dive. And the routes? Best described as user-
friendly. They flow like water. The layback on *Holy* ... those sharp crimps on
Launching Pad – and the sun's beating down and you're dreaming of the ice-cream
that Caradog doesn't sell from his van at Bus Stop on fine summer Saturdays and
that you maybe don't have the money to buy if you could be bothered walking down
to 'beris, which you can't anyway. That's what they're like.

Californian Arête, California (E1,4c)
As soon as you leave the tunnel the atmosphere overpowers you. Even on the bak-
inghottest days there's a chill that sends shivers down your spine and maybe it's not
temperature at all but mood exuded from black cliffs, jagged scree, and enclosed and
darkly magical place. When you stand beneath this route you begin to hear, even to
feel, a low distant vibration. It flows through your body from the power station hidden away in the mountain's heart. Maybe you tap into its power as you balance up
this grand quartz vein that the quarrymen left because it was useless to them – that
the quarrymen shaped into a great prow pushing out into the emptiness they'd left
behind. The climbing's indescribable, amazing, levitational, the protection imagi-

nary, the exit bizarre, the experience maybe the best the quarries have to offer.

Patellalectomy, Never Never Land area (E1,5c)
It's a route that's always intrigued me. You peer down on it from the track before Watford Gap. There's a weird sort of scaffolding cage on top that you could belay in if you were brave or crazy. At one point on the route a huge block's slipped out with precision like I've never seen before, leaving behind an alcove that's virtually feature-less and just the right size for back-and-footing. Well, maybe it's not the right size, because it's tricky back-and-footing and then you come to the bars. Long rusting bars sticking out of random shot-holes. Talk about arbitrary! Talk about cunning – aren't they just exactly where they're needed to climb the route and hey! it's brilliant despite the gloom, and somehow, those scattered clues from the forgotten time real-ly come home to you. Do it!

Seams the Same, Seamstress Slab (E2,5b)
Seamstress Slab's a strange feature. The outcrop of which it forms one side rises like an island from the Serengeti Plain, or like a shark's fin gliding through a purple ocean of slate. I was walking on the terrace above once in the pouring rain when the clouds parted and a shaft of sunlight moved across the slab. I was amazed at the way the light reflected off the vertically rippled and waved surface, refracting in just the same way that a climber on this route is nudged from balance by the off-vertical axis common to every ripple and hold. Occasionally I see someone climbing it and com-ing so close to the effortless glanced perfection that was that shaft of light.

Slippery People, Yellow Wall (E2,5c)
There are stacks of routes around in the quarries with pumpy, off-balance moves or anxious clips. This one has them both, and in the same place. All the holds slope the same way, and it's not in to balance. I try to keep my body in to the right (there's a door opening). I'm imagining broken ankles. I strain an arm up leftwards, tension in mind and body both. Clink goes fat krab-nose into thin bolt-hole. A huge blob of yellow lichen laughs at me, wills me to fall. My balance is going, I'm swinging slow-ly out ... there! The rope's clipped, the creaking door shut that wants to be wide open. A crozzly jug leads on into the room where you've found yourself, and more, so delicately, adjustment by adjustment, to the top.

Red & Yellow & Pink & Green, Orange & Purple & Blue, Rainbow Slab (E2,5a)
Rainbow Slab's an amazing piece of rock, with the best set of ripples around. On

light summer evenings as the sun's about to move off the slab, every minute detail stands out. I often hear people walking back to their cars chattering on about how beautiful it is. But if you were to ask these same people if they've climbed *Red & Yellow* ... the answer's invariably no, or some smart-arse might ask back 'Who'd want to?' I'll tell you why. In the adrenaline rush you get as you stand scared silly 80 feet up without a runner, you look across at the light glinting off dozens of different-coloured bands like prisms and it's perfect. I was here once getting the shadow of my outstretched arm to become part of the Rainbow. That's how you begin to understand.

Bela Lugosi is Dead, Rainbow Slab area (E1,5b)
This route differs from most slate crack-lines in that, instead of a straight, sharp crack that looks to have been cut scalpel-clean, this one's been sawn open with a blunt and rusty jagged knife. Hack, hack goes the edge, rough to smooth to ripped and razor-sharp and the rock, too, changing in texture so that you never quite know what to expect next as you cram toes and fingers in or dance them on the little edges that lie hidden within or are scattered all around on the slab itself. 'Surprise, surprise!' they say ...

Colossus, Rainbow Slab area (E3,5c)
I can't honestly remember the moves or the gear. The one thing that sticks in my mind is the burn I felt that first time. People talk about being pumped on something or other but this was beyond pumped. It just kept coming and coming, my arms on fire, skin barely strong enough to hold in the bulging veins, holds no longer had form – they were just there to be pulled on as a numbness began to spread through my whole body. I climbed straight past a bolt because I couldn't stop to clip it, climbed straight past a ledge because I couldn't stop full stop, reached the top and lay down for ages. When I finally came to, I couldn't even grip the rope to take it in. Steepest, longest, most sustained, of its grade – Yeah!

Journey to the Centre of the Earth, Lost World (E1, 5b)
Dreams – have you ever had one of those dreams where you're at the bottom of a deep, dark hole and there's no way out? Does everybody have them? They have a reality, too, you know – a physical expression. If you don't believe me, climb down into the Lost World. Maybe you don't *climb* there – maybe you're lured down into it by the mystery of the place, by its sequence of trashed and twisted ladders and its weird green pools among 300-ft walls of smooth dark slate. Hurt yourself down here

and you're lost. Only the crows will hear your cries for help. The waterfalls will muffle them, the crags set them forever re-echoing till they're just in your head and you can no longer scream, fading away, looking up at Paul Pritchard's journey out of, not to, the centre of the earth. Do it to escape, before the dream turns nightmare.

17: FICTIVE HEROES (1981)

He and I were very close: make of it what you will, but of all the myriad possibilities I can say no more than that. And on this day we kept company, in an odd sort of scenario. We set out, quite early in the morning, the tide well out, slack water and sea of no great roughness; a white crest here and there neatly counterpointed by a very few delicate riffs of white cloud. The path we took lay along flat cliff tops, across land used as a gunnery range. Shattered tanks from mock battles rusted down into the pitted earth. Twisted scraps of metal were scattered around, bright, powdery, or flaking and brown. We picked them up and thought it a great joke to toss them about, starting in mock fright at the imaginary boom.

Lest it should sound too desolate a landscape, let me say that the grass was short-cropped, dotted with bugloss and little round mushrooms, that skylarks sang and the sun shone. Also, in our minds we were happy. There was an expectancy there, and a longing too. We knew where we were going, for we had a couple of lines in mind. We had seen them, fleetingly and from a distance, had talked about them, enthused about them. We had even openly wondered about their probability, but had bolstered up each other's confidence. He had said, 'You do that crack, you're good at cracks, and I'll do the wall above.'

Each to his own abilities. What he said made me strut along the track, and if I got up my pitch then from our first stance and those hoped-for good belays, I would concentrate on him, pay out his ropes, ready myself for the urgency with which he would tug them through to clip each of his runners, play with him an infinitely caring game of watchfulness and consideration.

So we went along, sauntering, boasting, darting about after object or perspective, and soon enough arrived on the terrace above the cliff. There were other people there, some of whom I knew. A woman I'd met a time or two in a pub. Looking at her as she lay unconcernedly in the sunlight, I felt a certain desire for her, a wish that she and I might lie together, taken out of time and responsibility, under a gentle sun.

But he was busying himself about his equipment and I changed, reluctant to put aside this imagined interlude. We passed over to the abseil point. I belayed the rope on two long tape slings, and threw it down. Then there was the process of sliding over the edge, the cautious deposition of faith and bodily weight on to the belays, the relief of letting out rope and the lessening anxiety of the descent.

At the bottom I skipped across boulders, dodged waves and sat, in a beautiful calm of minutes, on a slab beneath the cliff waiting for him to join me. There was, for a time, no urgency about it. There were other climbers over to one side, on a more broken wall. There was the necessity for choice, but the tide had barely turned and would not be running over these sea-worn slabs for an hour or two yet.

So we sat and toyed with this line or that. What would they be like? What holds would there be on that little facet of slab which seemed to slip by the biggest of the overhangs? How wide was the crack in the corner by that rib, and what gear would it take? How steep was the wall? How sound was that block? You might say they were idle musings, but they were not. Into each situation, imaginatively, we could put ourselves, and our hands would sweat as though we were there. But imagination was not enough.

However happily we engaged in the creation of these fictions, their insufficiency was wormwood and gall to us. Our fictions became our rulers, compelled us to consider them in the forms of reality. What could we do, so long as we had the capacity, the energy, the active will, but resign ourselves to their realisation? What could we do but acquiesce?

'Let's do the one on the left,' he said.

So across we went to the foot of the crack. He uncoiled his rope, I mine. I tied them into my harness. He took them and put them in his Sticht plate, smiled, nodded.

The block above my head was rough and sharp. I pulled on to it awkwardly and squatted, untangling a clump of wires on my rack. To get it right, not to feel too heavy, not to be too accoutred, but to have the right thing for the right place; an ideal to which we seldom approximate. The crack slanted out left around a prow before straightening up and bulging a little underneath a ledge. I stretched up for a hold, pushing up from the knee, getting my body arrow-straight to curl my left hand around its edge. When it was there a quick exhalation of breath, a little should-I-shouldn't-I spasm over what was already decided, a swing out, hanging from one arm in a squat, a slight roll of the shoulder and foot-push to get the other hand on a hold. And a panicky sort of Oh-God-I'm-in-it-now giggle as the left arm went probing up again and felt, then flexed on to a hold. From which all the automatic adjustments of the body moved around a single point – the away movement of hips and shoulders, the up-kick of the leg, the turning out of the knee to get the toe just so on a squarish little block of limestone. The instant of hanging there, viewing what was above, sizing up, coiling, and then the long-timed move up and past and through, and the awkward half-secured tentativeness of a hand searching a crack for a jam. And relief when it eventually, however tenuously, slots in.

A runner, and by the ease with which the right rope comes through, you know he's with you, and you look at him, he smiles and your reply is a little snigger of complicity before you push air out of your lungs and immerse yourself in the rock again. It was not a hard crack, however it may have looked. I felt almost as if I had cheated. Overhanging, yes – seemingly difficult – but the holds were there, and I was fit enough. I didn't really even have any doubts, which is why it seemed like cheating, why I almost felt let down. I had known, even down there, that whatever abilities I possessed comprehended the problems of this crack, and so it was not enough, just a glib ending where I wanted an apocalypse. He was glad, though. He wanted to get on his track and this was just a thing in the way. He was glad that I was there and tied on, and that he could leapfrog over and beyond.

He was sitting on his ledge, well belayed, looking a little furtive in his squint-eyed avoidance of the sun. It was hot. There were no shadows on this south-facing cliff. He was sweating; he had climbed the crack with a heavy competence, not the climber he'd once been, the moves at their completion were jiggling and hurried now, where once they would have been ice-smooth and casually precise. But he'd done it and there'd never been any question but that he would. From time to time there'd been a ghostly memory of authority about his moves. And now he sat on his ledge in this curious avoidance of the sun, looking slightly diminished. The other took from him what gear he might need – put the bandolier over his shoulder and sorted out the rack, which was in a mess. The next pitch really worried him. He was edgy, uncommunicative. He found the attempted jokes irritating and the slight, high edge on the first man's voice made him nervous too. He stood at the bottom of the groove, one hand keeping balance and the other fumbling in his chalk bag. There was a small and awkward foothold at shoulder height; nothing much for the hands, a smallish layaway, a sloping fingerhold. He tried them, tried a little move on them. He could just hold on, but could he hold on enough, put in sufficient power to get his foot up there? He stepped back down to the belay ledge.

'What's it like?'

'A bit thin. I don't know what the holds are like above.'

'Ah, well. You can do it.'

He traversed left and spent a minute or so craning his neck about to get different angles on what he imagined was a hold over a bulge. From one angle it looked perfect, but from none of the others could he make it fit. He stepped back beneath the groove, shook out each arm in turn, then committed himself to it. It didn't even seem very hard, with all the impetus he'd built up. His feet edged perfectly on to little holds, or smeared across a particular rough area with complete precision. It was

95

all-in-control, well-back-from-the-edge stuff, and he stopped after 25 feet to fiddle in a couple of good wires. The bulge above came easily. There was an obviously good firm hold and he wound himself up for it, went, got it and carried right on through until he was standing on a slab – quite a large slab, stretching up for 25 or 30 feet to the next steep section. He looked around for a runner; nothing much came to hand, but he jammed a hex in a crack as a gesture and carried on. As he moved past, it lifted out of its crack and slid down the rope. There were some clouds moving in from the west and it was colder now. Beneath the wall above the slab was a good foothold but, sloping slightly from one end to the other, it made his calf ache. Looking up, he felt a spot of rain on his cheek.

He scanned the wall anxiously. Over to the left, 30 feet above, an easy groove with samphire growing led to the top. On the wall between there seemed to be very little. A few small fingerholds to start, a thin crack and what might be a good hold to reach the bottom of the groove. He looked to place a runner by his feet, and cursed for the hex that had slid down the rope. There was a slot which would surely have taken one of that size. The next size down waggled about, held in place only by fretted, thin edges of rock. He left it there as token, and chalked up. He dabbed chalk on the fingerholds too so that he'd be able to see them clearly when they were needed as footholds. Moving on to the wall, the lack of protection frightened him. He felt for the first moves, came back and tried to rest his leg on the awkward foothold.

It was definitely beginning to rain now. He let his mind run from thoughts of a fall to a grey, nervous, uncaring state. He sized up the thin crack and sorted out the wires on his rack. The first move up was dynamic, a long reach for two fingerholds, his body flattened on the rock and pointing like a ballet dancer on his toes to get an extra inch or two of height. A ripple of tension ran down through his body. He kicked his feet out and ran them up the wall to edge with his left foot on a tiny flaky hold. Locking off on his left arm, he reached for a pocketed finger-jam at the base of the crack, laying away off it, swivelling his left knee out and rolling his hips over the foothold so he could stay there and fumble a wire off its krab. He slipped it into the crack, clipped in a krab, tugged on it gently and clipped in the rope.

Whew! He felt safe. A runner above his head. Another reach for the hold and the route would be there. He straightened up on the foothold, still not quite able to reach. His right arm was pumped solid with the strain. The runner was at eye level. All his hopes centred on this one hold. He moved his right foot awkwardly on to a little flake near his left thigh, eased his left foot off and canted his

leg out to keep balance, leaning right out on the crack. Every scrap of timed awareness went lunging for the hold. His fingers snatched on to it. It was flat, but rough.
Not very big. Should he go on it? There was a foothold out left if he could change
hands ...

*(What should have happened here? He was strong; his momentum had carried him
thus far. He had one move to make and had already attained the holds which, for a few
moments of time, had been the focus of his aspirations. But just then, something entirely adventitious happened.)*

His right foothold snapped. He grabbed for the security of the runner. It
pulled; the one below likewise. His limbs cascaded down on to the fretted slab,
headlong. The lancet rock carved his flesh as its bulk crushed his skull and thrust
him raggedly outwards. He seemed to float in the air as he came within sight of his
companion, but he was bound inexorably beyond help, limp and silent in his
flight.

The tide was coming in fast. There must already have been six feet of water in the
channel below and each fresh set of waves brought it a little higher. I felt worried
for him up there and tried shouting, but he would not have heard me above the
sound of the water. When I looked up, rain dabbed at my face.

Some of the blue rope pulled through, so I guessed he had a runner on and
felt a bit easier. I was wishing we were back on the clifftop and running for the café.
Then the ropes went slack. I heard a thud and he was in the air above me,
grotesquely spreadeagled and the rope snaking down. I tried, hopelessly, to take in
the slack but he was past me and came on to the wires in the groove. The top one
pulled; I was jerked upwards. There was a splash as the bottom one held. A wave
sluiced gently up the slab where we'd been sitting. Everything went silent.

I didn't know what to do, hardly daring to look down. The rope was holding him on the surface of the water and there was blood coming from his head. I
knew he was dead.

I sat above, shocked, morose, and strangely uncaring. The tide hung about
the full, timelessly, and the rain spattered down. No one shouted or saw. As the
daylight faded, the tide came to ebb. The sky cleared; points of light glinted far
away on the other coast. A ship passed, out at sea. The channel grew shallow,
splashier, then drained and dried. I let him down, unfastened from the rope and
pulled it through his runner. I slid down, untied his corpse from the ropes and

97

pulled it up above the high water mark. Above us the cliff was patterned with shadow. Great areas were now impenetrable. All intimacy of detail was lost in its vast loom. I turned a corner and went away.

The abseil rope was still in place. I climbed a crack by it in the failing light. When I was 40 feet below the top, I pulled it up and tied on to it. A little groove led upwards. I climbed it, testing each hold, stiff and fearful. At the top I coiled the rope and went over to the sacks. It was all just method, memory, routine. Bone-weary, I sat down, stretched out my legs, put my head on a sack and slept.

I woke in the darkness. Its intensity, the strangeness of familiar forms, made things seem urgent. I sat up, hearing the sea, put a sack on, the rope across my shoulders, then the other sack, and thus burdened set off. On the range, lights were coming towards me. I blinked as they shone in my face.

'Where's your mate?'

'He's dead. I left him on the slab.'

'Are you sure he's dead?'

'What happened?'

'Does anyone know where they were?'

I couldn't think what to say. A case of unrealised aspirations? The cost of living like this? Over on the far coast a lighthouse winked. Mechanism or conspiracy, I wondered. Back there, a wave had already licked him from the slab, carried him through the channel, released him to current and fathom.

Somehow I thought it must be so, the lightness, the deftness, the pearls of his vision clammed down into fearful depths, clouded, rotting, devoured. Cost and contrast and a seeming grasp, all those witty rhymes, all our fictions, quiddities, and vapidities, all coming down to this. Out over the sea, clouds lumbered from the west. Perhaps we would evade them. The horizon was ill-defined, the water an oily presence, sucking, crashing and booming around the base of the cliffs. I lay down to rest among the withered flowers and my mind confounded the moon. After many days they visited me.

'What are you doing?' they asked.

'Climbing,' I replied. 'Climbing up the walls of my mind. Trying to get out.'

I could tell they were not happy with such a reply.

'This is all very well, but, you know, those walls do not exist,' they explained patiently. The clock chimed. I was ravenous.

'Let's do the one on the right,' he said.

18: A TRUE AND AUTHENTIC HISTORY AND DESCRIPTION OF FACHWEN (1989)

The acid test for determining whether or not a person is a true climber is his or her devotion to the subtle arts of bouldering. I was talking to Rob Collister recently, just before he set off for Makalu, and the main thing on his mind was whether or not, in order to lighten his load, he could get away with taking a pair of rock slippers for the bouldering around base camp. That's the sign of a man who's got his priorities right.

My old friend Peter Crew, on the other hand, who always gave the impression that climbing was just a phase in his life to be hurried through on the way to the next (phase, that is, not life, though his style of climbing made that a fair likelihood at times), was without doubt the worst boulderer I have ever known. It wasn't a function of lack of ability, it was simply lack of interest. Pete was someone who climbed on momentum. He just accelerated away up routes until the holds ran out and gravity, in time-honoured phrase, supervened. He was like a climbing version of a Rolls Royce – no acceleration, no good on bumpy, intricate, winding narrow roads, but give him the long straight and you were into the *gran turismo*. Whereas Al Harris, who was the great boulderer of his generation, was a sort of climbing Kawasaki Z-1300: standstill to 6b in half a second.

It was on the back of Harris' bike that I was first introduced to Fachwen. It wasn't a Kawasaki, it was a Greaves scrambler, and Al loved to do wheelies on it in the field in front of his house. One day he took me for a ride over the back of Bigil. By the time I eventually parted company with his pillion there was enough adrenaline coursing round my veins to have kept San Francisco tripping for the whole of 1967, which was the year in question. So I wandered off, nursing all sorts of bruises, Harris' words about there being some bouldering thereabouts murmuring solace in my ears, and found myself on a beautiful hillside, looking out over Llyn Padarn with Snowdon opposite shining in the sun and Cloggy hulking in its shadow.

There were stands of Scots Pine and I saw a red squirrel. All around were suggestions of white rock gleaming out of the heather. I went and touched them. They were steep and clean. The sharp, sound little holds bit into my finger-ends and the sunlight flowed over and illuminated the whole lovely landscape. It was coruscating visual and sensual delight to be there. I'd arrived in one of the primal places.

So this was 22 years ago and since then Fachwen has been one of my constant points of reference. I go there whenever I can. Things change. Holds snap off, companions disappear, groups make use and abuse but the lyrical nature of the place is unchanging. I don't know who first climbed at Fachwen. No true and authentic history attaches, just a matrix of anecdote and hearsay, memory and remembered desire. Some of the great problems have names bestowed, others retire shyly. The rowan branches grow across them over the years, they sink into a fading oral tradition and the moments of their discovery are all but forgotten, which is perhaps as it should be. But let me show you round, and gabble on a little about my own sense and recollections of the place as we go.

This is the how and why of getting there. You are sitting in Pete's Eats in Llanberis. It is late morning and late summer and you have worked your way through your sports plan for the year. Up the Pass, up on Cloggy, up on Cyrn Las, across on the slate, all the status routes are crawling with people busily ticking and collecting and adding to their personal lists. The whole scene gets you down (nothing new in this, it was always thus), for the moment you want no part in it, want something fresh. Someone mentions Fachwen, so off you go to look.

You drive a long mile up the Caernarfon road. If you're walking, there's a roadside boulder just beyond the Lake View Hotel to entertain you along the way – nothing too hard, but it stretches the muscles. At the end of the lake, where you get the famous view of Snowdon, turn right and right again. The old road goes straight ahead from here, closed off now, and above it is the Yellow Wall, which is extremely popular these days because you can drive virtually to its base. At one time, when the road beneath was in use, climbing here was deadly. Nowadays it's just deadly dull, quite the worst of the Fachwen buttresses. It's north-east facing, has been blasted, is smooth. The technical problems are on the left and involve cranking on tiny flat edges to reach a ledge system at 15ft, but the best problem is the tall, faint groove with the big jug on the right, where you get very high up very quickly, and are faced with some crucial and committing moves to finish 25ft above the tarmac.

I had a picture of young Andy Pollitt on this problem once. It was a beautiful picture – fine muscle definition, fascinating textures in the rock. A small gay painter from Bethesda, whom Andy and Johnny Redhead used to tease by going round to his studio in nothing but their floral Lycras with socks stuffed down the front, borrowed it from me to base a picture on once. I never saw it again. A young woman of my acquaintance moaned at me to get it back and have a print made for her for ages. The saga sums up Yellow Wall for me – good-looking, a bit of a tease, a bit of a disappointment. I don't go there much these days.

Electrocution Wall is quite different. You get to it by crossing the lake outflow, turning up the Fachwen road proper, and parking in the second lay-by. When Harris was alive, you'd risk your life climbing here. It's above the narrowest part of the road. He used to pass here at 60mph. Fall off and you'd have been wiped out. Nowadays no-one drives that fast down Fachwen[1], though it's always possible that one day Jonny Dawes will discover the place. *Electrocution Wall* has a bold easy classic at 5b – the mantelshelves. The crux comes right at the top, 20 feet up. Two feet behind your back as you grope insecurely upwards is the electricity cable which gives the wall its name. If you psyche out, it's grab for that or 20ft down to the tarmac – or a passing car bonnet.

There are three other problems worth mentioning. One is the traverse, which is good and balancy with the opportunity for some fancy footwork. There's a fine, steep wall problem going up from the resting place near the left end of the traverse to a notch. Pat Littlejohn did it first, in 1973. It used to depend on pinching a wobbly downward-pointing sliver. I've not been able to do it since that disappeared, but that's probably a reflection of my declining abilities rather than the route's increasing difficulty.

The problem to its right, going straight through the crux of the traverse, is the best on the wall. It involves tenuous layaways to a point where you can tip two fingers into a nick to keep balance, then slap for a flat jug out right, mantel, and finish with some bold, easier moves direct. I did this once in 1981 when Stevie Haston failed on it. He called me a strong old bastard. I glowed with pleasure. It was definitely the proudest moment of my climbing career. Then I tried it again to show how easy it was and fell off, rolled backwards across the road and cracked my head open on the wall opposite. I've got the scar on my bald patch to this day. He told me it served me right for being so old and feeble. The young are so fickle. I still haven't worked out whether it was hubris or karma. So much for *Electrocution Wall*.

Above the small lay-by beyond *Electrocution Wall* are three or four problems which are usually avoided as not being on the main itinerary. This is because they are serious and frightening. Any true Fachwener will insist on at least one of them. There is firstly Harris' *Mantelshelf*, which is an innocuous little prow low down on the right, by the roadside. Harris was good at mantelshelves. To its left, slightly higher, is a square-cut, rightfacing groove. It is hard to get into. Once you're in it, falling out of it does not appeal. By that time, however, holds have appeared. To its

---

[1]Not quite true! I was driving down Fachwen recently, when a beat-up Scirocco screamed round the bend in front of me, honked, skidded up on the bank, then gently toppled over on its roof onto my car. The passenger door prised open. Out of it, shrieking with laughter, burst Al's son Toby ...

left, a thin crack soars up a tower of rock. This is the *Lay-by Crack*. It is 25ft long, the ground below is very steep, and the crux is at the top. It looks fearsome. Paul Williams and myself spent weeks eyeing it up in 1981. Paul said it was too high to be a proper problem, and that he was going to look at it on a rope first. I did it a few times to half-height, where you can step off left, looked down it from the top, then eventually lurched out into it one evening and thugged up to the top. It's about 5b. It is very frightening. There are good little holds for the top moves. They're not obvious.

These lay-by walls are at the foot of a steep gully with a right wall where there are any number of easy problems. Local centres have been so kind as to put protection pegs in some of them. One of the delights of Fachwen is that the range of standards available is very wide. There are things for everyone, from the most inept beginner to John Gill clones. I've even seen Ken Wilson get off the ground on a problem here. It was on 'Brailsford's 6a', but we'll come to that. If you head on up through the gully, in 100 yards or so you come to Split Rocks, which is the best warm-up area. It's sheltered, attractive, interesting. There's a classic easy problem, stepping off a boulder into the obvious crack. This is *Split Rock Crack*. It rises out of a cave. If you sit in the cave with your feet off the ground, what confronts you is the *Fachwen Roof*. Be prepared to leave some skin behind. The crack flares and you have to jam hard. Some days it feels easy, on others desperate. It seems to depend on how much humidity is in the air. The arête on its right is about 5c, but very awkward and barndoorish at the start. I fell off it once from the top and landed between the boulders without a scratch. I don't know why I fell off it from there. It's easy by then. Anyway, they named it after me. Harris used to tell me that it was because it was two grades easier than his arête, which is a quarter-mile away, and that that was a fair reflection of our respective climbing abilities. I never saw him do my arête, though, but you could take an insult from Al. You had to – it was the substance of his conversation.

To the right of Split Rocks there's another cave roof. This is Shorter's Overhang. It's one of the great sitting problems. You start in the back of the cave, feet on the back wall, and crawl out horizontally. If you want to make Shorter's Overhang into a longer overhang, you can traverse along the lip. It's all quite exhausting. Nowadays the cave beneath is full of empty lager cans.

Round the back of the Split Rocks there are lots of little fingery things, all quite trivial and fun. One of them is a ten-foot wall on the north-west side, part of a great flake of rock. It used to have a blob of white paint marking it, because some misguided person had painted circuit-markings-a-la-Fontainebleau all around

Fachwen. I'm not saying who it was, but I know. White was the 6a circuit. My old mate Barney Brailsford was immensely pleased because he could get up one of the problems on it. 'I'm 50 years old,' he used to gloat, 'and I can still get up 6a!' It would be ungenerous of me to offer an opinion as to its real grade, so suffice to say that 'Brailsford's 6a' has passed into the book of great jokes, and as I said, I once saw Ken Wilson get off the ground on it. (In fact I think he finished it.)

After you leave Split Rocks, the serious stuff begins. Head north, cross a stile, descend round a corner and you come to the Swamp Walls, two of them, the *Altar Wall* and *Far Swamp Wall*. *Altar Wall* has two great problems, both on its right-hand section. *Ken Tom's Crack* is the slanting, energetic, difficult-to-start, often-wet little gem on the left at 5c. The wall on its right to the spiky little razor-jug in the middle and finishing either direct or out left is 6a. They're both 20-ft high, and bold, but the landings are quite good out of bracken-season. They've been very neglected in recent years, and are almost as lichenous now as when we first found them in 1972. *Far Swamp Wall* has four problems in a logical progression left-to-right of 5a to 6a. The left arête is sharp and spectacular, the crack – *Crew's Crack* – demands a confident approach, and is the only Fachwen problem Pete ever did; the groove right again is awkward and delicate to start, but leads to some enjoyable swinging moves up on exquisite finger holds; the only thing exquisite about the right arête is the pain of pulling on scalpel-sharp tinies.

So much for the preliminaries. If you've got through the tour so far, you're ready for the upper circuits. *Lion Rock*'s an obvious starting point from this end. It's the outcrop which looks down over the whole area. The slabs on the right are all easy and the habitual reserve of centre people, but the streaked wall of Gogarth-like quartzite on the left has a crack problem of Harris' where you'd leave the tips of your fingers behind in one place if your feet came off, and a ramp on the right which is indelicate and slippery. A fall from this could see you bouncing a long way down the hill.

Much safer are the conglomerate boulders. To reach these you wander off southwards through heather for what seems like miles until, quite close above the road and at the back of a boggy flat area, you find an incredible jumble of blocks with a strikingly beautiful little sharp arête on the left. This is Harris' Arête, it's 6b, and is reputed to date from the 1960s, though I have heard this disputed and I never saw it done then. It was Harris' party piece. You climb it direct, on pinches. Fall off and you'd only sprawl in a bog. I went there recently with Paul Trower. He floated up it. He's current King of Fachwen. I couldn't get off the ground. It's that sort of problem. Harris used to do it every time in a pair of floppy EBs wet from standing in the bog.

Well over to the left of here, over a little col and at the head of a small valley where there was once a dam is the *Witch's Crag*. I don't like the place at all. I saw a ghost here once, very angry, waving a stick at me. When I looked again she'd disappeared. It's a featureless place, the rock smooth, laminated and rather loose. Brian Molyneaux fell off one of the problems on the right and broke a leg. The two best routes are on the right, one by Rab Carrington, the other Henry Barber's. That gives you the measure of the place. You get more brownie points on the North Wales scene for having done a new problem on Fachwen than you would for a new route on Anglesey. And it's harder and more dangerous to do. But as I said, I don't like the *Witch's Crag*.

Quite a lot of the upper circuit is of this character as well – bad landings, suspect rock, hidden away. But there is one gem among the hosts I'll leave you to rediscover. It's miles up near the top of the hill below the mast, and the best way to reach it is from the Bigil track. It's called *Accommazzo's Wall*, after an Italian American from California who stayed with Harris for a time in the late 1970s and was taken out to do his stuff on the Fachwen circuit. He flashed everything in sight, so Al took him to this wall, which Paul Trower had been working on for months. Paul was in the Alps. If he'd known what Al was up to, he'd have been back faster than the speed of sound.

But it was too late. Ricky Accommazzo sniffed it, felt it, and powered up to place his name among the neon legends of Fachwen. I've never been able to do it. Al took me there once. It was in 1981, the last time I was climbing well. He and I were very competitive with each other. It was a golden autumn day, and I was as fit as I'd ever been. I looked at it, flexed my fingers on the holds. It felt good, straightforward. Al gave me that big-toothed grin of his. I did it in one surge of movement, was so exhilarated that I reached wrong-handed for the top. Arms crossed, I couldn't mantelshelf.

'I'm jumping off!' I shouted to Al.

'I'll spot you!' he said.

'No, leave it, I'm going for the grass.'

There was a small patch of grass. I leapt for it. Al caught me and dragged me on to a boulder. My foot turned sideways, every ankle ligament torn. I lay in the grass and wept with pain. Toby, Al's son, helped me down to Bigil. Ice-cubes and boiling water. I had a week's guiding starting the next day with that strange Llanberis institution Roger Alton. Al just grinned, told me between those tombstone teeth of his that I could do it, and when I'd been paid could I lend him 30 quid for half an ounce of black?

A month later he was dead and the place has never seemed the same since. I still go there sometimes, with friends, hoping they'll appreciate it too. It's the great Welsh bouldering area. Even devotees of Almscliff or The Kebs would be pleased by it. Ah well, how does the line go? 'In the dew of little things the heart finds its morning, and is refreshed.'

19: SMALL PERSONAL DIFFICULTIES (2003)

All right, so you can cruise or flash anything you set your hand to, but I'm not like that. I have some real bugbears, devil-routes I get to wishing I'd never set foot on every time I venture there, and maybe I'm not so unique in that either. The odd thing about it is that grade's not a factor. If I were to be really upfront, I could probably dredge up V.Diffs or even Diffs that have got me in this way in the past – you know, that sense of what on earth do you do here, how do you manoeuvre your unwilling and timorous body over the next ten feet of rock with some semblance, however remote, of elegance and control?

' ... it is stupid: what could you do if you did get ten feet higher up, the rocks have not yet started to become difficult, take yourself off from this cliff: oh, this climbing, that involves an effort, on every move the holds to be spotted and often there are none, then every limb placed, the body set into the one suitable position found but with trouble, then with the whole organism great force must be exerted, before anything happens, and this is to be done while the brain is occupied sick and stiff with its fears; and now you have been doing this for well over an hour and a half and the strain must be telling: get down therefore.'

Recognise the feeling? Remember when and where you last experienced it? All Menlove Edwards tells us in this passage is that approaching whatever climb it happened on 'involved walking along a stretch of road, then a slope up towards the cliff.' I've got my own versions: *Nameless* at Bosigran, *Bilberry Buttress* on Raven Crag, *The Black Chipper* at Brimham, *Grotto Wall* on Stanage. Wonder what grade the latter is these days? It's one of those routes I always used to think I should do because it was good for me, a bit like cod liver oil and similarly repeating on you. It used to be one of those lurking Stanage VSs that locals in general knew better than ever to engage with or be seen upon: right in the most popular area, completely tricky, devoid of protection, terrible landing and with insecure move following insecure move all the way to the top. I remember doing it when I was a good climber at the end of a long day in which I'd romped up all sorts of standard HVS and extreme classics – *Impossible Slab, Fern Groove, Millsom's Minion, Left Unconquerable, Congo Corner, Desperation, Cave Arête, The Asp* – and thinking it more formidable and frightening than any of them. I mentioned it to other people in that tentative way that you do, imagining you'll be rubbished and sneered at, and they cocked their heads and listened and then came over all disclosing about how they'd – wobbled: that upper wall, those undercuts, the way it bulges and pushes you out as you try to balance up ... ! I tried the same tack with Paul Nunn once after yet another bad experience on it. He just threw his head back, roared with laughter, leant in close with that manic grin of his and whispered confidingly, 'I know ... !' Which meant that all of us should know better, but don't tell anyone else because these esoteric little stoppers scattered about through the grades are a part of the sport's rites of passage – inductions, apprentice tests, terrorisers ...

Not just the esoterica either. Here's a really bad confession. I've soloed *White Slab* on Clogwyn Du'r Arddu a few times over the years – not as problematical as you might think as long as you take a rope for the lasso move, and you remember the technique for getting the spike first time every time (very simple – you just toss a few loose coils into the groove above the spike and let them trickle down and catch). Anyway, that's not the bad part or the confessional part. The thing is, you'd think *White* would be the ultimately enjoyable solo – wonderfully exposed, good rock, low technical difficulty, long pitches. And I can remember exquisite moments in the course of these ascents – the feel of those solid little fingertip-incuts on the first long slab, that strangely-textured grippy rock beneath your feet, the wheel of the apricot clouds above in a sky of robin's-egg blue, the darkness of the lake below – all those brief moments of awareness, glimpses into the real context, that you somehow manage to edit in even to the narrative of soloing a climb, where the focus generally is on maximum concentration and carrying it straight through, without distracting and unsettling digression, to the end. But I've never really relaxed into finding the experience of soloing on this route entirely pleasurable for one very simple reason: you finish *White Slab* up the top pitch of *Longlands* ...

Now I don't know why, but the top pitch of *Longlands* terrifies me. I can never get it right. No matter that *White Slab's* E1, with 5b in there somewhere too on that funny little flop-across bit right at the start, and that the top pitch of *Longlands*, done way back in 1928, is lowly VS 4c. To me it's the hardest pitch on the route, and apprehensiveness about it has spoilt my enjoyment of *White* every time. I get right up there on the Crevassed Stance, look up at the innocuous little final hanging rib, and for some reason it robs me of all composure and sets my limbs in to some strange uncoordinated version of St Vitus' Dance. I just can't ever do it neatly. I grab for things, my feet swing the wrong way, I barndoor, have to yank and heave, emerge out into the heatherlands all ruffled and panting and swearing about 'only VS ... !' Or if I'm soloing, thinking, 'My God! I might have died ... '

Yet it is only VS. I'm not arguing for grade re-appraisal. It's been as it is for three-quarters of a century and I'm sure it's right. I'm just wondering why it never seems quite to fit the configuration of my limbs or the set of my mind. Maybe its maker had something to do with it – the human one, I mean, not the divine, the lat-

107

ter's purposes being presumably forever unknowable. Old Jack Longland was distinctly formidable and adversarial, would establish a psychological advantage in argument with a few deft and telling blows before you ever really set to. Thus the man, thus the route I suppose. It's like the way that for my generation of climbers a Brown route or a Whillans route always had a certain cachet – the first ascensionists' names alone adding to the grade. You might go to Wimberry, for example, and find yourself beneath all these formidable-looking cracks and get totally psyched-out, even though in fact they were all technically quite straightforward compared to routes on Ramshaw, Black Rocks or Helsby. Take the old Brown classic from 1948 of *The Trident* – if you're confident in all the black (or green in this case!) gritstone arts of jamming, udging up, judicious knee usage and so on, *The Trident*'s actually a very restful, very easy classic, hovering around the VS/HVS borderline (another psychological ploy here – Wimberry was one of those crags where everything used to be VS). But I've seen people time and again getting it horribly wrong, struggling frantically, ripping their skin off – and all, I'm sure, at the behest of aura rather than actual technical demands. Which maybe proves that I'm not alone in experiencing these small local difficulties.

I've been pondering on which route is the worst bugbear for me, regardless of grade. Find your own parallels. I'd better lay down a few parameters here. It should be something of a grade you'd normally expect to cruise confidently in most conditions without experiencing any difficulty whatsoever – something you'd normally expect quite confidently to be able to solo, but instead find it assumes the status in your mind of something you'd do anything – including much harder routes on either side – in order to avoid. So a name comes immediately to mind and I feel really ly sheepish about admitting to it, as no doubt you will for your own versions. Mine's *Leg Slip* on Craig Bwlch y Moch. I don't know how many times I've done it but I never get it right. There's one section on it and I don't even think it's the crux, and I've never ever been able to do it with any suggestion of confidence or ease. It's that bit on the second pitch where you come up a gangway and find yourself in a brief, smooth V-groove. I get into the bottom of that groove, and even though I've done it countless times, I never have the faintest idea what to do. I try to bridge it, I try to back-and-foot, I stitch together every apparently feasible combination of holds in the hope of attaining neatness. I waste infinite hours, my seconds twitch and murmur, I drop down disconsolate every time to the ledge at its foot. I could describe what you end up doing right now – there's a weird hold high on the right wall and you sort of pinch and pull and mantel on to it. But when I get beneath it, I can never simply launch into the moves. It doesn't feel right, and it feels even less right when I start them, so I get all brutal and thuggish, lose any finesse or sense of my body and flail and sprawl and feel infinitely pissed off at what a crap climber I am and all that. Every time I've done it, I end up thinking I never knew I could climb so badly.

Last time I found a solution. You just step round on to the arête on the left and follow that right to the top. Perfect! You could even say it was a harder pitch, more tenuous, delicate, unprotected, exposed. But in your heart the threat of that little beast-groove would still lurk. Good job it doesn't matter ...

20: (BEINN A'CHAORUINN AND) THE VISION OF GLORY (1993)

Three dreary months round Christmas, sunless, short-dayed, my mood dull as the season. Trudging between dark squads of regimented conifers up the forestry track into Coire na h-Uamha, above Loch Moy, there was no expectation in my mind beyond that of dogged exercise. The northernmost of the mountain's trio of east ridges bulked sullen into dank cloud above. There was not even relief in the particular. Everything crystalline and light-reflecting was subdued, stilled. I shuffled through soft snow to the foot of the ridge's first buttress and embarked on the climb.

There is something to be said for creating interest in your choice of line for the ascent. Technicality puts an edge on the way the mind apprehends the immediate world. The focus closes down: to the ash-petalled lichen on the blocky face before you; to fronded heather moustaching the ledge into which you have swung the pick of your axe; to a fine balance in the configuration of your limbs across this airy crest. You are entering the dimension of approach; a lightness is beginning to hover in hitherto-leaden air. You're heading into the white world, cloud and the void beneath.

Which is how it was on Beinn a'Chaoruinn. I picked my way up the buttress – easy enough in summer but treacherous terrain now: powdery snow, rock greasy underfoot – and onto the snow slope above that curved up to the summit.

Let's introduce an element of misadventure. I took my crampons out of my sack at a ledge above the buttress, for the slope beyond was iron-hard *neve*, and steep. In my carelessness, my hurry to get out that morning from the chalet at Roy Bridge, I'd forgotten that they were adjustable, had last been worn by a friend with bigger feet. When I stood up, they rolled off my boots. In amused disgust, I pushed them back in the sack.

Amused? Oh yes – and you would be right to question by what token I found it thus. A few hundred feet of hard snow ahead, the potential for a fall of 1000 feet, bumping and sliding into the corrie below. But I still went at it, smashing the axe into the snow with murderous intent, belting at it with my boots so that three or four ferocious kicks would produce half an inch of precarious purchase, getting a rhythm into the work, resting after 100 feet or so with one leg down a little crevasse the melt-and-freeze had produced against a small outcrop of rock.

Then it came. I was slumped contortionate against the rock, panting from exertion, head lolling backwards over my left shoulder, when the hovering brightness intensified. Suddenly the mist was scoured with utmost speed from the face of the mountain, shreds of blue sky tore across, shafts of brilliant light pierced into the corrie. From the ridge opposite, diamond whirlwinds danced along the cornice edge, all glitter and coruscation, shapes of the Mamores beyond a phantasmal ivory gleam.

I do not know how you can adequately describe these moments and their effect on our lives. I write this eight months after the glance over my shoulder away from the dangerous world of the particular in which I had been engrossed. Yet what I saw in that moment is imprinted on my consciousness, is a part of the heart-life.

Our essential life, the joy-life, is a sequence of these moments. How many of us could count even 60 such? I recollect: the badger that passed three or four feet upwind of me one moonlit night, and I was so still it knew nothing of my presence there; the descent one evening after doing one of the difficult ice-gullies on Cyfrwy down the Foxes' Path on Cader Idris at sunset, and the sun caught ice-rimmed melt-holes where rocks pierced through, making each a flaring rosette sharp against the mauves and blues of gathering night; morning light in a room above the sea in West Cork, hair of spun gold on the shared pillow and her eyes a clearest blue flickering into wakefulness; or on Brandon Mountain, a glory round each of our spectral reflections on the mist ...

There is a common element in all this. It is beauty, and I am continually astonished how little is said about it in our modern world, and in our specific outdoor world where it is surely the prime and common factor in all our activity.

Once, years ago, I was out walking in Derbyshire. It was an October half-term, I was 12 or 13 and had caught the train from Manchester to Hayfield, intending to walk up on to Kinder Scout by way of Kinder Low and descend Grindsbrook to Edale. I knew next to nothing about mountains and to me this was a mountain. The day was fine, the bracken golden on the lower slopes. I dawdled along, started to climb the hill's shoulder towards a prominent group of rocks. In an instant the sky darkened. From the moor above streamers of mist poured down in front and behind. The gritstone outcrop ahead writhed, its nebs and boulders shape-shifting amongst the vapours. I was suddenly cut off from all the world of normality, nature animate all around me, and I was intensely scared. I fled. I ran terrified down out of the mist to the top of Jacob's Ladder, stopped there, chest heaving, watching all the frightful mystery down out of which I'd come. And it transfigured itself before my eyes. There and then it became not a thing of fear but a vision of vital and resonant loveliness.

The valley-greens flared with fierce intensity, bracken seemed on fire, mist was gilded with the sun. What had been terror was now beauty. As I sat and watched it there was a stillness within me beyond anything I'd known. I was annihilated, had no existence, simply looked out at the inconceivable beauty of the world that had detached me from any concept of self in order that I might *see*.

Does not everyone who comes to the mountains know something of this experience? It is at the root of a thousand hero-myths; it is Wordsworth's 'Fair seed-time had my soul/ Fostered alike by beauty and by fear'; it is Simone Weil's 'Everything has to pass through the fire. But those who have become flame are at home in the fire. But in order to become fire it is necessary to have passed through hell.'

The moments seem to come more easily in the mountains. Their literature – beyond the ego-fixated narratives of achievement – is permeated by accounts of them. Here's Eric Shipton – greatest mountaineer-explorer of the century – groping towards its definition as he falls asleep in the Karakoram: 'We settled down on a comfortable bed of sand, and watched the approach of night transform the wild desert mountains into phantoms of soft unreality. How satisfying it was to be travelling with such simplicity. I lay awaiting the approach of sleep, watching the constellations swing across the sky. Did I sleep that night – or was I caught up for a moment into the ceaseless rhythm of space.' (from *Blank on the Map*)

Once, on the High Street of a busy Welsh town, I stopped to talk to a good, resentful, careworn woman who told me this or that ugly thing about her husband, knowing he and I shared a passion for the hills. Behind her I saw light travelling across the cliffs and gullies of Ysgolion Duon, and wished her the moments that being there might bring, that her anger might be purged, affronts to her sense of self cleaned away by them. What you go through on the mountains is not the nagging, passive fear of abandonment and loss; it is not the burdening responsibility; it is the occasional going through into the white world, into the world of light.

Whatever our stated reasons for coming to them, it is the vague sense, the half-understood glimpse of this that draws us back time and again to go beyond fear, effort and discomfort into quietude and appreciation. We should not plan to conquer our hills, but rather to abandon ourselves to them. I remember so thinking as I pulled my foot from its crevasse on Beinn a'Chaoruinn and set back into the slope, into the sting of spindrift that obliterated the summit, my movements a joy, and imprinted in my mind the vision of glory harvested there.

PART TWO: THE CLIMBERS

I don't know of any other sport that can produce a cast-list of characters from among its performers quite as interesting and varied as that of climbing and mountaineering. Here are some of my favourites, from the years I've been involved or earlier.

1: PETER CREW
THE WAY YOU CLIMB IS THE WAY YOU ARE (2003)

Periodically life throws a crux at you, and you set to wondering how best to move on, what style might lead you past it? And once at the safe perspectives of stability again, maybe you start to consider that point of style in more detail, with more attention. I've always been intrigued by this curiously central issue of style – curiously central to me, that is, and to the way that I view climbing. I have a suspicion that there are increasing numbers entering the sport to whom it doesn't ever remotely register in the scheme of things: 'Style – what are the numbers, man? What matters is finishing, topping out ... ' Fair comment – if that's the level at which you want to keep it, then stay focused and enjoy! It's just that it never quite seems to me to have much to do with being, when your sights are always set on finishing.

There was a time way back in the 1960s when I used to climb a lot with Pete Crew. Maybe there'll not be so many who know Pete's name these days – he'd given up before most of the current generations of climbers were born – but he was the original and authentic media-star of British climbing. Al Alvarez wrote a wonderful, wildly over-the-top essay for the *Observer* magazine – the first of the Sunday supplements – in 1965. It was called 'The Edge of the Impossible', had a whole set of John Cleare black-and-white masterpieces to illustrate it, and it fastened on this amazing drive that Pete had. It did a very good job in turning him into climbing's first pop icon – a task Ken Wilson then took over and pursued with his characteristic zeal until the strange fire that Pete possessed burnt him and he retired huffy and hurt to promote more amiable causes: Gogarth, tick-lists, admission of women to membership of the senior clubs (you wouldn't believe now the amount of heat that generated then), chalk-free ascents, bolt-chopping – all that stuff we don't talk about now.

Anyway, to come back to Pete, he was already established as the *wunderkind* by the time Al's *Observer* piece appeared. He was this mop-haired blond kid with

Cybulski (Zbigniew of that ilk – pin-up for the generation before mine and star of the Wajda trilogy) specs, whose dad was a railwayman, who came from Elsecar, won an Oxford scholarship, left after a term because he couldn't take the snobbery, and then briefly became, I suppose, the first of the professional climbers (I'm not counting mountain guides here, whose main distinguishing characteristic over the years has been the distance at which they trail the top performers of the day). Most often in the company of Baz Ingle, he raced around picking off the plum lines, putting up routes that were thought the classics of their time: *Great Wall, Pinnacle Girdle* (who does that these days? My advice is, 'Don't!'), *Plexus, Hiraeth, Mousetrap* – all that stuff.

When I was a kid, I used to think Pete pretty amazing. He was loud, arrogant, confident, brash, dismissive – and that was just on the rock. He'd tie on the rope, psyche himself up behind those myopic specs, and blast off. It was kind of hurried, urgent, impatient – technical and physical resources applied with breathtaking efficiency to the task in hand, and stuff the loose ends, the skidding feet, the quick snatch of the fingers for the lurched-for holds, the occasional hurling backward flight and the twang of stretched nylon ...

Pete, in his climbing *achievement*, was way ahead of anyone else in his brief day. I remember when Ed Ward-Drummond (as he then was) came on the scene with these massive claims for mega-routes, complete with complex new gradings, in the Avon Gorge in the mid-1960s. Pete had to do a lecture down there to the university club and Drummond took him out on *The Equator* – his massive Main Wall girdle – to sandbag him. It'd taken something absurd – seven weeks, maybe – for Drummond to put this route up.[1] Hugh Banner had crawled along it in probably the best part of a summer – he was never a quick climber, Hugh, but he did a good line in the inexorable. Pete just curled his lip., focused the gaze, and blasted across in a couple of hours.

They arranged a return match on the Main Wall at Gogarth, competitive young men that they were. Pete pointed Drummond at the big second pitch, sat on the stance smoking, ropes draped loose, watching, smiling, jibing in that infuriating mutter of his. After an hour or two he gets pissed off, hauls Drummond down, grabs the gear off him, sizes up the situation, whacks in a few pegs, and motors on through – no style, pure performance. The result was *Mammoth* – still one of the five-star

---

[1] *A propos* of this, there's a quip of Joe Brown's that's worth preserving. Drummond, in the days before *Mountain* info and area reports in all the magazines, used to advertise what he'd done by the ruse of listing them with appropriate fees for guiding in the classified column of *Climber*. He'd taken three days to do *The Boldest*, which was in there at £6: 'Not bad value, two quid a day,' was Joe's summary comment.

classics in the Welsh repertoire. And okay it took a few generations of Free Willies to clean it of the ironmongery and tat (most of which still seems to be there), but it was Pete's blast that forged the way.

He didn't last. There was all that energy on tap – astonishing, free-revving dynamism in all spheres of his life – physical, intellectual, imaginative – so naturally, the hunter became the prey. There was canny old Joe Brown, for a start, who was always the wiliest of human-chess-players. He took Pete on – the old master making an alliance with the young hot-shot who had, in the general perception, burnt him off. And he watched, and bided his time, and made use of Pete's talents to his own pioneering ends. And when he'd picked and manoeuvred his way into a position of renewed confidence, because his talent for the activity, his particular practical genius, was huge, he simply turned it on when he'd learned it was safe to do so, and left Pete trailing and demoralised behind him. This is the hallmark of the survivor. Pete was already pretty demoralised anyway – messy, rancorous divorce, denied access to a replica-firstborn he adored, strange business of the Cerro Torre expedition with Dougal Haston, Mick Burke and Martin Boysen. They were man-eaters, that lot, and Pete was a fragile boy again by this stage. He had a bad trip, undermined, overawed, and his climbing never came back – not really. We all used to have a little mantra to console ourselves, which was that Pete was a crap climber because we could all out-boulder him. There was Al Harris' famous jibe that anything Pete could lead he could follow in winkle-pickers, and the ritual proving of that on *Zukator*. None of that meant anything, you know, because none of us out-performed him on the front end of the rope, which was where it mattered at a time when climbing was still a dangerous and pioneering sport. But the dancing god's only with you for a short time. It left Pete, and he left the sport – has nothing to do with it now – that dismissive curl of the lip, that impatience. The way you climb is the way you are ...

So you see, over the years I've seen so many, and it makes you wonder at times. You know our traditional biographical approach to climbing history? I've done a bit of that – this on Menlove Edwards, for example: ' ... *the events of his life ... turned him to a search for a correlative to his states of mind. The fissile, the dank, the rotten and the vegetatious drew him when his life seemed thus. When touched by love and happiness, his climbs too became lighter, more delicate, more airy.*' That's more a case of what you climb is how you are. To come back to the way you climb, I find myself thinking over what I've just written about Joe Brown. I've got enormous admiration and affection for Joe – he seems to me the most significant all-round genius in the history of British climbing. For the proof of that, simply look at what he's done and compare. No-one else comes close. But I always find myself at a bit of a loss around him. Basically, he's a tricky little fucker, playful, inventive, wiley and watchful as a cat. Try wrestling with him – physically, verbally. With people like Pete, or Brian Ripley or Martin Boysen, who were the style-heroes of my climbing youth – these last two languorous, elegant, flowing and precise, which was always the model to which I hoped my own climbing would aspire, but very seldom did because in my heyday I was too damned strong and always liked to use that – I could always understand with perfect clarity what they were about. They might make it look easy, I might not be able to emulate them in that, but I always knew how it was done. It was consummate, but straightforward. Not with Joe. The Rock & Ice had this strange word that they used to use, 'finurgling' – Longsight dialect, I think, and you won't find it in any dictionary. I have a suspicion it was one of those industrial words that tried to define an aspect of the craftsman's inventive genius being expressed around his material. Anyway, those good ole boys, when talking about The Master (they really did call him that), would usually have to resort to that word somewhere in their account, and it expressed the mystery. How did he do it? How does Jonny Dawes do it? Get along to one of the latter's master-classes and see if he can explain. And I'll bet you he can't, because what he does is what he is, and how do you communicate that other than through actions ... ? I want to hear the boulderers start talking about each other in these terms – it's all apparent and uncomplicated there, cuts right down to physical expression of mental approach.

Me, I'm slow and ponderous and reflective on the rock these days, focused down on to the minute and the moment and the intimate. Yeah – it's how it is when you get older. You change, it's to be hoped. Then that soft summer wind drifts across the outcrop, limb and sequence interlock and the touch has all its light magic again. Even if only in dreams.

2: JOHN HOYLAND – THE MISSING DATES (1985)

If things are as you fear, I can only say that I looked on John as potentially the best mountaineer of his generation. There is literally nobody of whom I hoped such great things, and to whose development I looked forward so intensely. I doubt if there has been any young English climber since George Mallory of whom it seemed safe to expect so much ...

These characteristically generous words were written by Jack Longland – himself outstandingly the best all-round mountaineer of his own generation – in mid-September, 1934. They were addressed to John Hoyland's father as the latter set out with Frank Smythe to instigate a search for his son, who, with his companion Paul Wand and with the intention of bivouacking on the Col Eccles before ascending the Innominata Ridge of Mont Blanc de Courmayeur, had left the Gamba Hut on 23 August of that year and had not been seen since.

Let me scatter on the floor a few more pieces of the mosaic. There arrived on my desk the other day a small, grey volume, limp-bound and 50-years-fragile, simply entitled John Doncaster Hoyland. There is no date on it, but it was probably printed in the autumn of 1934 and put together by John Hoyland senior, who was at the time Warden of Woodbrooke, the Quaker college in Selly Oak, Birmingham. I already knew a certain amount about its subject – knowledge accrued over the years, tabulated, silently stored away. Then came this memoir, and snatches of conversation, moments of experience, came drifting back to me. You know how a mood can attach to a name? Well John Hoyland for me was redolent, I suppose, of high, colourful summer. I first heard his name from an old Quaker friend, David Murray-Rust (the man, incidentally, who introduced Wilfrid Noyce to climbing) during the time that I spent at Woodbrooke. I knew that John Hoyland was related to the Doncasters who had made, in the 1920s, that exquisite little VS (one of my favourite ways up or down the crag on the glowing June evenings when Stanage is at its best) which now shares a start with Goliath's Groove. And that distantly, therefore, he was related to a friend with whom I'd shared many memorable, if often prickly, climbing days. I was aware, too, that his cousin was Howard Somervell, of those muted and haunting mountain paintings. And I also knew that his name was the opening bar in the litany, 'John Hoyland, David Cox, Robin Hodgkin', which, when chanted, brought back all the freshness, enthusiastic endeavour and bright optimism of mid-1930s mountaineering, when the balance between romance, risk and achievement was so perfectly held.

So I set out to discover a little more about the man. First stop, and one which is always a pleasure, was with David Cox in Oxford:

'John? Oh yes. I first met him on an OUMC meet at Helyg in March '34 – he must have come up in October '33, which was a year after me. Nobody'd ever heard of him and he turned up on about the second day. In those days the OUMC's level of performance wasn't very high – Idwal Slabs, North Buttress of Tryfan, Gashed Crag if you were lucky. There was quite a lot of snow down and we were loaded up with ice-axes, taking about six hours over Gashed Crag. To our surprise John Hoyland appeared that evening having done *Cheek Climb* on the Terrace Wall and also the *Direct* on Glyder Fach – in these conditions – which in those days was one of the hardest climbs in the Ogwen area.'

David inspected his pipe carefully, as though searching for a clue, smiled, and off he went again:

'He'd taken a boot off in order to do the final crack and he'd dropped it, couldn't find it, and he'd walked back to the hut through the snow with just a stocking on his foot. His foot was very cold but he didn't seem to be making much fuss, and we thought, really, this fellow seems to be upsetting the standards of the OUMC just a bit. However, it was interesting to talk to a chap who was obviously serious about his climbing ... '

The subject of Jack Longland cropped up at this point, and David remembered that John Hoyland knew Longland and had with him a description of his climb on Clogwyn Du'r Arddu: 'And he actually wanted to do it, which we thought absolutely barmy, particularly since it was March, with quite a lot of snow about.' After a day or two spent on Dinas Mot, where Hoyland led a party up the *Cracks*, attempted the *Direct* route in the rain (having to retreat from high up on the long second pitch), and 'mucked about over on the right-hand end, but didn't do a definite route – it was mucky and wet and raining', the OUMC group was inveiled into going over to Cloggy:

'There were four of us with the intention of climbing, and two or three other OUMC chaps came along just to muck about and walk, and it turned out to be a jolly good job they were there. We didn't start up the thing until about 12.40 – and then we did that fearful thing at the bottom which nobody does nowadays – the Middle Rock – it was an absolutely dotty thing to do, but you see Longland had done it and there: it was ...

'We got into the most frightful trouble higher up ... '

More smiles and musing on his pipe. I prompted him to continue.

'We got benighted on the cliff and had to leave the fourth man, Anthony Seraillier, below Faith and Friction. He was on the stance there for nine hours, had to rope down in the dark, and we hadn't known whether his rope was long enough to reach the bottom. Two of the walkers had to come round to the top and pull us out on a rope, so that was rather a shambles.

'We were all a bit surprised to find that the first slab was not all that difficult, nor even particularly exposed really. When we got to that little perch below Faith and Friction, it was very wet and cold, with a lot of snow up above. John took off his boots and dropped them at that point – yes, he did make rather a habit of doing that on this particular meet – and it took him a long time to get across Faith and Friction, which I gather is one of the pitches whose currency has greatly depreciated – I think they go further round these days. My recollection is that Jack, on the original climb, made a very delicate step across on to a rather nasty and sloping hold, whereas if he'd taken a slightly wider circle you could have gone round more easily.

'Well, we all found this jolly difficult. I took off one boot, I think, and the third man did it in nails. We were all terribly slow and very impressed by the exposure there, and by the time the third man was over it was getting dark – short days and all that. Anyway, that was all a bit of a shemozzle and we got home to Helyg about four in the morning, I suppose.'

In a letter to his father, John Hoyland reveals how much David Cox – who had never, it should be remembered, been on anything harder than a V.Diff before this holiday, is playing down his own part. He takes up the account above Faith and Friction:

' ... after climbing an easy pitch, there came another hard one, and I found I could not do it under the conditions, but Cox very gallantly undertook to lead it, and much to our relief just managed it before it got dark. It was a really magnificent effort, and ... has showed me more than anything else the worth of a good upbringing and education, as two people I was climbing with last Christmas who were physically just as sound, cracked up completely under far less trying conditions.'

Cox now finishes the story of this epic first encounter. A day of rain has intervened:

'We'd left stuff all over the place – John's boots and I think my boots as well were at the bottom of the cliff and the rope Anthony had used to get down was still in place, so two days later John and I went back. It was the last day of the meet and the others were all cleaning up Helyg. We were supposed to be collecting all this equipment but it was rather tempting to do the climb.'

Which is what they did:

'We took a long time, three or four hours, because we were loaded down with equipment – boots, ropes and so on – and there was still a good deal of snow around. But the way John climbed those two crucial pitches – Faith and Friction and the final overhang – was magnificent.'

This was on the 27th of March. Four days later Hoyland was again on Cloggy, this time working his way up Pigott's East Buttress Route ('harder but less exposed than the West' was his verdict on it). Jack Longland, Paul Sinker, a Professor Turnbull of St Andrews, and AB Hargreaves were climbing Longland's at the same time. Jack Longland tells the story:

'In those days we used to climb the open groove below Faith and Friction facing outwards, legs and arms splayed. OK provided you knew what your feet were doing. Turnbull was about two-thirds of the way up when he placed his right foot smartly on thin air beyond the edge and nose-dived over the overhang guarding the Black Cleft. Paul Sinker, anchored on my original piton, held on nobly. I had a poorish flake about 12 feet higher up, so that if his piton had gone – it bent through about 40 degrees – I think we should all have been over the edge.

'Turnbull was left swinging about 12 feet away from the crag, relatively help-less. I shouted across to John Hoyland to come and help. He must have abseiled down rapidly, as he was very soon at the start, had lassoed the wretched Professor, and drawn him in to safety. John asked him whether he took any precautions against such happenings, and he answered that he always carried a small flask of brandy. Challenged on whether he had used it now, he gave the splendid reply, "Oh no, I keep that for real emergencies!" Realistically, we were all very lucky to be alive, and ABH never forgave the tumbling Professor.'

Which latter offered the opinion about John that 'from the way he moved about on the cliff it was obvious that he was a wonderful climber and full of joyous adventure.' This particular adventure over, Hoyland went back to his East Buttress route to continue the ascent of Pigott's, in the course of which he made the first lead of the top crack – an awkward 5a off-width which still causes consternation to many leaders. At the end of the day's climbing he returned with Longland and com-pany to join Geoffrey Winthrop Young's annual Easter party at Pen y Pass, where he met 'all sorts of great men – two Everest men and the son and daughters of Mallory among others. It was very interesting and great fun ... '

Term-time in Oxford, far from the mountains, quietened his activity for a while. But David Cox remembers one outing from there:

'John Jenkins wrote – in the most ridiculously exaggerated way – about some piffling little crags in Shropshire called Pontesford Rocks. There was a thing called the Pontesbury Nose which he said hadn't yet been led and was harder than anything on Gable's *Eagle's Nest Direct* – which in those days was thought to be quite a climb. John, when we got there, led this thing without even a rope. That was where I fell off and that was very unfortunate because that was the last serious occasion on which I climbed with John. Except ... '

There appeared a broad, boyish grin, his eyes creased about with laughter lines: 'D'you know about the Indian Institute and the elephant? No? Well next to my college in Oxford was the Indian Institute, on the roof of which, on top of a little dome, was a handsome bronzed weathervane in the shape of an elephant, on a long spike. It really involved no climbing, because I had rooms on the top floor and you just got out of my window, walked along the roof and climbed the dome, which was about 20 feet high and rather smooth.

'Anyway, we roped up and while John was about halfway up this thing a trap-door opened in the roof and out came an Indian caretaker, looking very sinister in the dark. John got down as quickly as he could and we ran back along the roof into my rooms. I was the only man in the college who enjoyed climbing, and my rooms were rather adjacent, so I came under suspicion. But then I had this accident at Pontesford and later developed an abscess where my head had been cut, and had to go into hospital. So John and Paul Wand, knowing there was no risk of my being suspected, repeated this effort, with very much the same result, except it went a little further this time. He got the elephant off and slung it round his neck with some rope – it was surprisingly heavy, I remember, because I had dealings with it later on. Out at this point popped the caretaker, and by John's account got hold of the rope. Paul Wand roped down into the street somehow on another length of rope and John, with the Indian between him and his escape route, had to rope down into the college on yet another length of rope – why they should have had all these lengths of rope or whether they'd cut one in half I really don't know.

'This all left John prowling around in a strange college at about two in the morning. However, he found a way out over some rather awkward railings which landed him in the garden of the Warden of New College. He climbed over these, not knowing where he was going, and landed on top of the Warden's wife – a formidable lady called Mrs Fisher – who was asleep in a hammock, since it was a fine summer night. To her great credit, she didn't say "I'm going to call the police." John, who was a modest, quiet fellow, explained his predicament and she responded that if he went back the way he'd come, she'd say no more about it ... '

Hoyland's first year at Oxford, where he was reading medicine at St Peter's Hall, ended. He went to teach for a few weeks at his old prep school, The Downs at Malvern, and during that time snatched climbing visits at weekends to Wales, the

Lakes, gritstone, and the limestone pinnacles of Symond's Yat:

'John, armed with some fine rock-pitons which the local blacksmith had made to his directions, proceeded to explore Pear-tree Rock. He was some 20 to 30 minutes on the exposed 80-ft face of this pinnacle, hammering in pitons and arranging all sorts of rope slings for himself. He at last reached the top to our united cheers, and we all swarmed up after him. The locals below were amazed to see seven young men standing on the top of the hitherto "inaccessible" pinnacle.'

Other memories are of him attempting, and just failing, to make a free ascent of Scafell's Central Buttress on his first visit to the Lakes; of the way 'the mountains were always at the back of his mind'; of his exceptional genius for rock-climbing; of his 'sixth sense, which brought us direct to the foot of a climb in thick Welsh mist without any trouble at all.'

Nobody seems to know when he started climbing, nor how much he did before arriving at Oxford, except that his beginnings 'were on Stanage Edge and Almscliff, with the aid of an old piece of box-cord.'

He left very few writings behind him, but those that do survive show a sense of humour and proportion allied to a precise descriptive style in conveying his emotional responses to a landscape. His handling of effects, too, is at times remarkably assured for (as he was at the time of the following piece of writing) an 18-year-old:

'I was inexpressibly lonely, not with the loneliness of a lonely man in a great city, nor yet with the loneliness of one alone under a wide horizon. It was a kind of companionable loneliness, wistful, kindly and sympathetic, expressive of a great yearning. I felt as if I would go on, and on, and on for ever, lulled to a walking sleep by the moving mist. Still there was nothing but snow, snow and a pair of boots mechanically moving forwards. Then something black appeared. I had consciously to focus my eyes upon it. It was some rocks and a cairn ... '

Frank Smythe's influence lies a little heavily on this, but John would, on the evidence of his last letters, quickly have outgrown those mannerisms.

The only new pieces of climbing he recorded were all in Wales: the top, and hardest, pitch of *Pigott's*; the top crack of what is now *Hodgkin's Variation* on Glyder Fach; and a long, rambling Diff on Ysgolion Duon called *Hoyland's Route*, climbed at the end of July 1934, on his last visit to Wales. He went out to the Alps at the beginning of August, his first route being the Mer de Glace face of the Grepon, which was badly iced and up which he led a rope of four, including a complete novice. The Knubel Crack was in such poor condition that he elected to try it in socks, but fell off after ten feet and so donned his boots again and surged to the top. It was only the second British guideless ascent.

Bad weather came in. He and Wand retreated to Chamonix, then moved camp to near Montenvers. David Cox reminisces:

'I had an oldest brother who ran the old-fashioned reading parties that they used to have in those days, this privileged class at university. It was on a spur of Mont Blanc below the Gouter Hut. You were supposed to spend your time reading Cicero and people like that. It was absolute agony. But I got away on one day, hired a guide, and – it was my first excursion in the Alps – did the Pointe Albert and the Aiguille de I'M. Walking up to these, there was a tent visible at one point where John and Paul Wand had told me they intended to camp. I meant to go and call on them, but it looked rather a long way away. In fact, it must have been empty at that stage ... '

On the 22nd of August, Hoyland and Wand arrived at the Gamba Hut from Courmayeur at 10 pm. They were tired, and carrying extremely heavy loads. Next morning, the 23rd, at 9 am, they left the hut, informing the guardian that they would bivouac that night on the Col Eccles before climbing the Innominata Ridge. Again, they appeared tired, and were last seen moving very slowly up the Brouillard Glacier. The following day the weather broke. Nothing more was heard from them. Their camp was not reoccupied.

Almost a month later Wand's guardian and Hoyland's father arrived in Courmayeur with Frank Smythe, who engaged two guides and went up to the Gamba Hut. After spending the night in the hut, Smythe and his guides set out up the Brouillard Glacier and reached the Col du Fresnay. Just above the col, its pick protruding from fresh snow, one of the guides discovered an ice-axe. Looking down from this point on to the Fresnay Glacier, the party could see 'an object on [its] surface which did not possess the appearance of a stone.' They descended, on their way down coming across 'items of equipment ... which included full-size table forks and spoons, heavy skiing gloves, heavy woollen sweaters, guide-book and underclothing, a condensed milk tin, a bivouac tent weighing at least six pounds ... The bodies were lying some 50 yards beyond the bergschrund and it was obvious from the nature of their injuries that they had been killed instantly.'

They were wearing crampons, which would have been positively dangerous in the soft snow conditions which had prevailed. Their bivouac equipment had not been used, and a watch on one of the bodies had stopped at 3.52, which suggested that they had taken nearly seven hours from the Gamba Hut to the Col du Fresnay. At that pace, in bad conditions, and with the weather due to break the following afternoon, Smythe concluded that 'disaster must have overtaken them.'

Their bodies were brought down and buried side by side in the graveyard at

Courmayeur. Paul Wand was 23, John Hoyland six months off his 20th birthday. Jack Longland sadly recalled, 50 years later, that 'he might have done much – but for that silly accident, deriving from inexperience, overloading and under-acclimatisation.' David Cox, too, reflects that 'simply as a rock-climber and simply from the point of view of his absolute dedication to climbing, John was already terrific. To go on Cloggy in March with climbers who'd never done anything above V.Diff before was pretty ambitious. Similarly in the Alps, to go straight on to the Mer de Glace Face of the Grepon. The mystery to me is, how come he was as good as he was, and as ambitious ... ?'

A few more fragments of recollection tumble out: he rowed; he was 'just a very delightful man, very modest'; he was of average height, brown-eyed, broad-shouldered, strong-armed.

The span of his life was so very short, yet the memories endure with such clarity. The sage counsel is obvious – it was foolhardy, imprudent, fatal, to go where he went, to plan and dream as he did. No, you should not bolster up foolhardiness. But how can you not applaud courage? His sister states the case: 'I find myself almost immobilised with ambivalence – of course I thought he was wonderful, but I would he had not died so young. Maybe the war would have got him if he'd lived – like it got Denys [his brother]. Better by far to have died as he did.'

It is easy to look back judgementally or even wishfully – to imagine, for example, what might have been had he lived to team up with Robin Hodgkin, who came up to Oxford in the autumn of 1934. That, surely, would have been a partnership to have matched any in climbing history. But those are the missing dates. Instead, we have to accept that his ambition overreached itself, colluded with adverse circumstance, and brought about his death. Yet all that rich promise he possessed is not a mere *ignis fatuus* – it is the ore, the essence, the inspirational element of our humanity, which only hard-won experience – which must sometimes entail loss – can refine or distil into achievement and perhaps beyond that wisdom:

> *Somebody remarks*
> *Morello's outline there is wrongly traced,*
> *His hue mistaken; what of that? or else,*
> *Rightly traced and well ordered; what of that?*
> *Speak as they please, what does the mountain care?*
> *Ah, but a man's reach should exceed his grasp,*
> *Or what's a heaven for?*

3: Batso & The American Dream (2003)

One of the things that I'm really not sure I like about us – by which I mean climbers – is that on the whole these days we take ourselves very seriously. We give our rock-routes and our literary productions these echoey, portentous titles. We inflate our deeds, philosophise into our beards, sports bras or whatever, elevate self-preservation and invited catastrophe to noblest status, perfect the faraway gaze and the lifted pro-file, and intone to all who'll hear us our unwritten rules. To anyone from outside, we must come over as a pretty sanctimonious tribe. I put this not-entirely-recent devel-opment down not just to modern buzz-terms like 'focus' (an odd word that used to mean screwing your eyes up until you could see an object clearly, but nowadays has been annexed by the sports psychologists and means fixing your small brain on the quickest route to enlarging your rampant ego), but also on the demise of our soci-ety's great regulators. When Al Harris, Don Whillans, Mo Anthoine, T.I.M. Lewis, Paul Nunn died, a sense of proportion went with them, a society that had never lacked for robust (i.e. if you can't take it, don't hand it out) mockers, detractors and rebels suddenly found itself near-devoid of them. One of the greatest and most gim-let-eyed of the laughing tendency, the all-American anti-hero Warren Harding, has just departed this life from his home in Happy Valley – I kid you not! – California, at the unexpectedly ripe age of 77. So what I want to consider is whether the mod-ern sport can afford his passing ...

Actually, that's po-faced bullshit. I just wanted to get in on the act and cele-brate him a bit because when I met him I thought he was a good guy and sensed (not that you had to be very sensitive to pick this up) that he liked the same kind of things as me – shooting the breeze, taking the piss, causing trouble, shagging women, drinking wine and whisky, cunnilingus, hanging out with his mates, driving too fast, climbing now and then when you're up for it but not up to it – all that stuff I was brought up on and am reluctant to let go too easily despite advancing years, moral opprobrium, mutterings of peers, physical cost, emotional turmoil and all the rest of it that many believe we should take very seriously indeed despite the fact that, as Batso has just shown, we'll all be dead soon enough anyway.

I've a few things to tell you about Batso that the others who are writing about him might not cover or might misjudge from not having been around to feel the temper of those far-off times. OK – now here's the case for the defence, character-witness stuff, mitigating circumstances and all that. Because there are factions within our community who mistakenly believe that it is appropriate to put its dissenters on trial. Always have been. Whymper copped for it from the establishment of his time,

John Dunne from that of ours – 'everybody wants me to be just like them', and not fat and still able to climb better than his critics, or a tradesman in Whymper's case, God help us ... !

Firstly, you need to hear Chuck Pratt. When I was putting that big Diadem anthology, *Mirrors in the Cliffs*, together 20 years ago, there was a piece of Chuck Pratt's that by some crass oversight I missed out, that I've always regretted missing out, and the absence of which flaws the arrangement of the book for me. It was one of those cases where I had an idea this article had been creamed off for use in Ken's earlier pick-of-the-bunch set, *The Games Climbers Play* – but in fact the piece by Pratt that Ken used was 'A View from Deadhorse Point', which is a great climbing essay: witty, elegant, aware, stuffed with great lines – but for me it doesn't have the character, intensity, or the narrative drive of 'The South Face of Mount Watkins'.

You not only need to hear from Chuck Pratt (not personally of course – he preceded old Batso across the divide by a few months), you also need to understand why notice can be taken of his opinions, whereas those of others might safely be disregarded: 'Royal [Robbins] tells tales of Pratt's bouldering drunk, in the dark, in army boots, nobody able to come close ... He is hard to figure out and doesn't want to be figured out ... With those he loves, who see him in repose, he is gentle, affectionate and obliging. He is devoted. Others ... find him ... sombre, rebellious ... [his] imagination has taken him away from this earth and the material world into a lonely, personal flight to meditate on ultimate cause and a last climb ... he is truly modest. A cat inclined to fits of laughter, to party, or to vanish for weeks. A weird and wily storyteller ... He walks wires. He has nightmares ... As he begins the overhang, the fourth pitch of the route, I hear him say softly to himself, "Grown men."'

That's Pat Ament on Pratt. Two things here to be said: for all his oddities (you hold that against a man or a woman? Look inside ... !), Ament's the finest prose-stylist in modern climbing literature; and the man he describes here is one whose opinion, whose account, palpably is to be trusted, one of the cast in the American legend.

In Yosemite's Camp Four once, Pratt glanced at Batso the remark, 'There goes a man who's had so much pussy it's sent him right off the rails.' 'No woman I ever been with likes to think she's got a railroad engine comin' round that bend,' Harding lanced back. They were friends, the friendship furnace-forged: Chuck Pratt the natural rock-climbing genius of that generation, Warren Harding its Hephaestus, its limping blacksmith god. So there's the matter of this essay, one of the most eloquent ever written on rock-climbing, recounting an ascent on the south face of Mount Watkins. I'm not going to spoil it for you by quoting from it. Hunt it down for yourselves. Then listen as Pratt in all the clarity of his amused wonderment testifies movingly to Batso's generosity of spirit and comradely qualities, his boldness, bravery, strength and drive. On that climb, Harding sacrificed his ration of water to Pratt as they struggled up the huge, formidable wall in furnace heat that nearly killed them through dehydration. I've been on mountains with men. They steal from each other, eat rations privily, jockey for advantage more often than give or share ...

You know how he got his nickname? After a severe altercation between his car and a fast truck – shades of James Dean – had left him with a crushed leg in 1969, he adopted the *soubriquet* in reference to the Dustin Hoffman character Ratso Ritso who's Jon Voight's limping sidekick in Midnight Cowboy – not heroics, but self-mockery, self-effacement, making light of disaster rather than an epic of it. And then going out on the pinned and shattered leg the next year with his buddy Dean Caldwell, and making that incredible ascent of El Capitan's *Wall of the Early Morning Light*:

'Starting on October 23, and hauling 300lbs of equipment and supplies as they went, the pair reached the top on November 19, having spent 27 days on the face, five of them immobile and sheltering in Harding's invention, the "Bat Tent", as storms lashed the wall. The amount of time they took over the climb, and the appalling conditions they endured ("as the 15th day dragged on, still raining, in a wretched state of soggification, we realised we were in a very critical condition. We were only about halfway up ... "), caused considerable perturbation to the Yosemite park officials. A cat-and-mouse game of insistence/resistance developed around official attempts to impose a "rescue", and farcical scenes ensued – megaphones with batteries giving out, climbers feigning incomprehension, etc. – none of which were calculated to please Harding's detractors. Nor was the carnival that greeted them at the top: "I floundered up the last overhang on to the ledge at the rim ... a veritable army of newsmen, friends, would-be rescuers (and a beautiful girl, Beryl Knauth) ... batteries of camera snouts trained on us, gorging ourselves on food and champagne, ecstatic kisses and embaces ... "'

In a following year Robbins and Don Lauria made the second ascent of the wall in six days of fine weather and – having made full use of them in ascending – smashed out the bolts and rivets that Harding and Caldwell had so laboriously placed. What comment's needed on that? If any, let Batso make them himself:

' ... to the self-appointed gurus, I say: "Bugger off, baby, bugger off!"'

And again:

' ... perhaps the hope of the "Valley Christians" lies in some form of regimentation patterned after the meticulous system of climber control so magnificently conceived and employed by the Soviets.'

And then consider this: though he mocked, he was generous too with his praise, and soft-spoken, soft-demeanoured. He captured a climbing audience at a lecture once by flashing on-screen a picture of himself and Royal Robbins (in reality, stylistic disagreements apart, a good and loyal friend), with a sign over them saying 'God and The Devil', went on to comment that 'I thought Robbins was presumptuous and cocky, but he was just so much better a climber than me that I didn't really have grounds for that judgement.'

There was something about Batso that encapsulated a wild, early, adventurous aspect of the American dream. He wasn't a climbing bum, he subscribed to the American work-ethic, trained as a land surveyor, looked after and provided for his Ma; and yet by some personal alchemy he turned that base metal of assessment and containment into a Dean-Moriarty-meets-Dashiel-Hammett wild gold of unruly being, the philosophers' stone for which transmutation was his climbing. Criticism of him on the grounds of style, ethics, any of that stuff is pettifoggery and beside the point. That crack of his on Elephant Rock, *The Worst Error*, that he climbed in 1955 and that still impresses and bears comparison with the contemporary achievements of Brown and Whillans over here ... ? *The Nose*, that if it had not been done in that style at Thanksgiving 1959, would not be done in the style it is today ... ?

Batso was true to the pragmatic spirit of American pioneering. In a shrinking world, his greatest ascents were like Oregon Trails compressed in scale and tilted to the vertical. He leaves as legacy two of the most beautiful and momentous rock-climbs ever made, and a whole lot of fun, attitude and mockery too. He'll be dragging his halt leg up the steps under the eye of St Peter right now, Pratt waiting for him under a tree in the Elysian Groves, the wine uncorked, the laughter cackling out in anticipation, the scent of the Mariposa Pines hanging round them and the Merced River silvering along just the other side of the veil.

Good old boys ...

4: THE ICE CLIMBERS (1985)

There was a time, before magazine-culture and checklists of collectable experience coarsened our responses and devalued our sport, when climbing seemed capable of producing a worthwhile literature. There are signs that it may be so again, but more of this elsewhere. For the present, I offer up to the disinterested reader an extended and retrospective review of work by a group of authors who are as good as any we have in post-war mountain writing.

There is no obvious explanation as to why post-war Scottish climbing writing should be so richly diverse and excellent. It could be that the Scottish Mountaineering Club Journal, under the successive editorship of Geoffrey Dutton and Robin Campbell, has something to do with it, but in fact most of the pieces about which I intend to write do not originate from the SMCJ. Of the authors I have in mind, their backgrounds and outlooks are as different as can be, so no joint factor can be isolated there. The simple common bond lies in their subject matter – Scottish winter-climbing – a sphere of action every bit as evocative, resonant, heroic and eventful as Arctic exploration, the Alpine Golden Age, Himalayan first ascents, or any of the other great sagas of adventure and elemental hardship.

In this last is the key. It is easy enough to write gilded contemplations of sunny days on rock. But in the strange sub-Arctic of the Scottish mountains in winter, the climbers probing up in the half-light, sketchily belayed, uncertain as to route, conditions, or even possibility, the narrative takes on an intense thrust and urgency. When this is allied variously to humour, expressive skill, or a wise detachment of mind, the results can be quite magnificent. The writers I want to deal with here – Tom Patey, Robin Smith, Jimmy Marshall, Dougal Haston, and Bill Murray – are by no means the only ones in the field. There is an embarrassment of riches. I could equally well have chosen, say, Hamish MacInnes, Tom Weir, Len Lovat, or Dutton and Campbell themselves. Or I could have singled out some later outsiders writing on the same theme – Geddes and Rouse, or the sesquipedalian (in-joke between John, who's one of the great characters of the mountain world, and myself – it means an inveterate love of very long words. I once gave John the biggest dictionary I could find for his birthday, just to indulge him in this.) comedy of John Barry, for example. But the five above suit my theme, and I'll start with the man who, for many, is the favourite – Tom Patey.

One Man's Mountains, the collection of writings and verses which Patey put together shortly before his death in 1970, and which was published in 1971, is an uneven book. The section entitled 'Satire' is the weakest in the book. The hits are palpable, but they are also obvious. He has none of McNaught Davis' pungency, or the subtle lancet savagery of Robin Campbell. Something kindlier than vitriol flows from his pen. His gift is not for satire, but for comedy, and more especially comic characterisation. It is the characters we remember. If Nicol, MacInnes, Grassick, Bonington, Whillans, had never done anything other than appear in Patey's essays they would still live on in our consciousness:

'Hamish was satisfied with his "shift" and prepared now to rest on his laurels. "It's the interesting stuff that gets me, I'm afraid. I'm not much of a hand at step bashing," he said, indicating the rest of the gully with a lordly gesture.'

There you have the quintessential Patey – a delicious and warm-hearted exaggeration of character, the art of comic deflation, a delicate sense of the inherent absurdity in all our actions. This is not to suggest that Patey is limited to a single tone. He is also master of a more rumbustious, slapdash style of comedy – essentially that of situation. In 'Appointment with Scorpion' there is the delightful scene where the four climbers all become stuck 'at different points on the face between 50 and 100 feet from the ground,' which leads, later in the same essay, to the following incident:

'Grassick had been heaving himself up the fixed ropes to the accompaniment of much grunting and hoarse cackles of laughter. Now for the first time we could see his face, distorted with a horrible fixed grin, appearing over the lip of the overhang like some strange monster from the deep. At that moment, with a long-drawn-out howl he dropped from our sight. The rope to Mike went taut, and simultaneously the snow stance he was occupying disintegrated, leaving him dangling from his belay. I glanced at Nicol in dismay. 'It's all right,' he assured me. 'We're not tied on to them anyway.'

Patey's essays, the memorable ones at least, are finely honed. It seems almost at odds with his popular image as the roughcut, scrabbling and improvising individualist, but his best essays give the impression of having been worked over, polished, and brought as near to perfection as their author could manage. They begin and end well – Patey's endings are an object lesson to any young writer – and the points of characterisation are handled with a deft economy: '"Somebody's left a boot here," I shouted to Don. He pricked up his ears. "Look and see if there's a foot in it," he said.' In a conversation with Tom Weir only a few days before his death, Patey remarked that he had 'worked damn hard on these pieces.' His labour was well rewarded, and he leaves us a cast-list which shambles with comic magnificence into the legends of the sport.

Patey's better work, with a couple of exceptions (notably 'A Short Walk with

Whillans', which is his best essay) is concerned with Scotland and the Scottish winter. It's interesting to speculate on whether the colour, variety and humour of his writing drew its initial awareness from the throng of characters and individuals among whom he had his roots, and who are described so well in 'Cairngorm Commentary'. If so, why did not more good writing emanate from the school of Grassick, Nicol, Taylor, Brooker, et al? There was one other writer, naturalised in Aberdeen, who might well have developed interestingly had he lived. As far as I know, Jerry Smith wrote only one article. Entitled 'Sestogradists in Scotland', it was published in the 1958 Climbers' Club Journal, and describes the first winter ascent by Patey, Brooker and Smith of Parallel Buttress, Lochnagar, in February 1956. It's a pleasing evocation of the winter-climbing scene of the mid-1950s, and draws a mischievously affectionate portrait of Patey. Smith is particularly good – better even than Patey – at conveying the engrossing technicalities of a climb, and he does this in a style far removed from the ugly 'tools, terrors, and placements' jargon of modern ice-craft. But Smith died in an abseiling accident on the Peine a year after its publication, and apparently nothing else of his remains.

There's a little group of essays about climbs on Ben Nevis in the winter of 1959-60 which is quite unlike anything else in climbing literature. Robin Smith's 'The Old Man and the Mountains', Jimmy Marshall's 'Garde de Glace' and 'The Orion Face', and Dougal Haston's 'Nightshift in Zero' have been quoted time and again: certain passages from them appear to be the equivalent of the True Gospel to any aspiring winter climber; they have given new words to the climbing vocabulary (I lose count of the number of times subsequent writers refer to their crampons 'scarting about in crumbly holds'); they have the intrinsic gossipy interest of revealing what their respective authors thought of each other, and the routes described have inspired generations of climbers. All this conspires to make them attractive to a strictly literalist approach, but I wonder, looking at these essays again, whether their literary quality, as divorced from their content, justifies their influence? The climbs, of course, were momentous: the Orion Face, Point Five, the route on Gardyloo Buttress, the night escapade by Smith, Haston, and the novice Wightman in Zero. As a catalogue of major climbs in a brief period of time, this outdoes anything that Patey or Murray can put together. But there is perhaps not very much in these pieces, apart from their narrative content. Robin Smith's literary persona has an attractive ingenuousness, though verging at times on the arch, and there is a persuasive quality of enthusiasm and energy about his writing. Marshall's accounts are refreshingly direct, as in this passage:

'Following up was like walking on eggs, the dark pit beneath our heels sufficient warning to take care; a short step of ice above Wheech led on to the high snow slopes which form beneath the terminal towers of the Orion Face. Here the expected respite failed to materialise; knee deep and floury, they whispered evil thoughts, threatening to slide us into the black void and extinguish the winking lights of the CIC Hut.'

Haston too contributes his own sly, streetwise humour to the group. Taken together, they are a remarkable comment on state-of-the-art ice-climbing circa 1960. Taken individually, as I do not think they should be, for they gain much in the grouping, they seem pretty pale and plain journeyman accounts of the deeds which ushered in a new winter-climbing era.

To turn from Smith, Marshall and Haston to Bill Murray is like putting down a volume of Lamb and taking up one by Hazlitt. The difference in quality is as immediately obvious as if we had suddenly moved from a minor to a major key. It's become fashionable in recent years to debunk Murray's writing, about which at times there is a stiffness which gives ammunition to the attack. Robin Campbell, in a *Cold Climbs* essay, mercilessly lays into the 'Bill Murray brand of German Romanticism', and even Patey jibed gently at him in his 'Ballad of Bill Murray', though a comment earlier in the book, about routes 'so well described in Bill Murray's two books on Scottish mountaineering as to render further comment superfluous' leaves us in no doubt as to Patey's true attitude towards his mentor. To my mind, Murray's two books on Scottish climbing, *Mountaineering in Scotland* and *Undiscovered Scotland*, would alone place him among the greatest mountain writers – Tilman, Mummery, the underrated and overprolific Frank Smythe, or the doyen of them all, Leslie Stephen. They are certainly the two best books ever written about British climbs.

We have one of those curious accidents of biography to thank for the quality of Murray's work. The conditions under which he wrote his first book, *Mountaineering in Scotland*, are well known and were chronicled in a moving article (included in the anthology *Mirrors in the Cliffs*). *Mountaineering in Scotland* was written during three years spent in prison camps in Czechoslovakia and Germany, after Murray's capture in the Western Desert. I have little doubt that the qualities of impassioned wisdom, detachment, humility, and scrupulous self-honesty displayed in his writing were developed during those years.

There is an account early in *Undiscovered Scotland* of Murray's capture by a German tank commander, and it differs quite considerably from the later magazine account. I wonder at the anomalies – not from the point of view of the author's veracity, which I believe to be absolute, but from the point of view of his literary technique. The second account is both fuller and yet more restrained, more effective and dignified than the first. In the same way, *Mountaineering in Scotland* has the feel of a text which has been meticulously worked over, its events balanced and considered in their description, a fine sheen imparted to the writing. I cannot quite bring myself to accept Murray's implication that it was delivered rough-cut virtually from prison-camp to publisher, and thus let through to us the public. It seems to me probable that, in the interval between his return from Germany and delivery of the manuscript to Dent, he worked at it thoroughly, polishing, refining, increasing the dramatic effect. As a very small example, there is at one point a complex quotation, correct in every detail, from Hazlitt's 'The Indian Jugglers'. There are two possible explanations here: either that Murray's memory is extremely powerful – that he has total recall – or that on his return to Britain, as would be natural, he carefully sifted through and revised his manuscript, checking facts, dates, quotations.[1] All this is to labour a point; Murray patently not only has an extremely powerful memory, but he is manifestly also a dedicated and conscientious literary craftsman. Writing of his quality is the product of excruciating labour. In the magazine article he describes the quandary he faced when he first sat down to the task of writing the book:

'Without diary, maps, or books to refresh memory, I feared I should lack detail of the climbs, which could not be spun out to chapter length. I was right, but the daily concentration of mind in trying to remember, continued day after day for weeks, gave at last a most astonishing result. Memory began to yield up what it held more and more freely, until it came in a flood. Every detail of experience was suddenly there, and in full colour. Nothing had been forgotten. I discovered that memory safely holds all experience in minutest detail, and that what fails (from disuse) is the ability to pull the record out of its pigeonhole. The deprivation became a gain. Every climb had to be relived, which in writing terms meant re-created.'

He does re-create the scenes of his climbs with an astonishing vividness. Here he is belaying Mackenzie on the first ascent of *Deep-cut Chimney*, Stob Coire nam Beith:

'I glanced down at the sun-bright cup of the corrie. That plain view of the sweep of the snow-fields between the torn crags is stamped in my mind with peculiar intensity. I can recall it clear and sharp at will, visualise a fragile snowflake on the wall and the sinuous curve of a drift in the corrie ...

'The confined space of a gully may appear at a disadvantage, but within the

---

[1] In which I appear to be in error. Bill Murray tells me that a volume of Hazlitt's essays was among the books given by the Red Cross to one of the concentration camps in which he was prisoner.

smaller field of vision, whether the sun shine upon a filigree of frost, burnish a further crag, or flood some distant moor or river, one observes a quality in sunlight that
cannot properly be seen in the open; one sees a peculiarly rich and mellow glow,
which in open country is absorbed into the landscape and lost to the eye.'

The movement of this passage is typical of Murray's method. There is a progression from a minute and particularised description of the immediate landscape to
a quietly reflective statement upon the qualities inherent in that landscape. What
Campbell defines in Murray as 'German Romanticism' is in fact no such thing. It is
the very English quality of our Romantic Poets – a step through Blake's 'Doors of
Perception', or a surrender to the power of the Wordsworthian formula, 'emotion
recollected in tranquillity.' Throughout *Mountaineering in Scotland*, the better of the
two books, there is a sense of implicit dialogue between Murray and Wordsworth's
'Preface to the Lyrical Ballads of 1800'. It reaches clear expression in the following
passage from *Undiscovered Scotland*:

'The full action of meditation is usually made difficult or impossible on
mountains by wind and weather, time and company. But our observations can be
made for later and more effective use in privacy. We should then recall the forms of
beauty, visualising each until our love for its beauty is aroused, and end with the
greatest beauty known to us – it may be a sun rising or a sun setting, or a night sky
or mountain, the beauty for which no words can be found. Encourage unreservedly
the awe and wonder to which this last gives rise. These feelings of the heart give
nourishment and life to the will and mind, which all acting in unison raise consciousness to a new state of awareness.'

I should say that this is only the first section from Murray's plainest exposi-
tion of his philosophy. There is nothing very original about it – it derives from
Wordsworth, and before him from the empiricist Hartley – and anyone well
acquainted with 'Tintern Abbey' will already be familiar with much of the vocabulary. I don't think that matters one jot. The philosophy which underpins the work
may be borrowed, but it is nonetheless deeply felt and informed by the fine qualities
of the author's mind. And he synthesises it majestically in these two books of linked
essays on the theme of Scottish hills with the best descriptions ever written of these
particular landscapes, with exciting climbs, and with a series of character portraits
which may be slightly larger than life, but with which I would seek no quarrel. If
your theme is the potential dignity and worth of human consciousness – as it is with
Murray – then it is only right to accord dignity of motive, character, and action to
those who inhabit the expression of that theme. You could say that Murray strives
too hard at times to define the undefinable; you could say that he invests his set-

pieces too richly and too often with a roseate glow; you could say that his attempts at humour can be a little solemn and ponderous. For all that, along with Tilman, whom he knew and with whom he climbed, he is my favourite mountain writer, and the best of them all on British themes.

What, you might ask, has all this to do with mountaineering – all this stuff about Murray and Wordsworth? I can imagine the question being posed, and I think it a sad one. The answer is quite simple to give. The everyday skills of mountaineering, the techniques and mechanics, do not amount to much. Year by year they change, retaining at best only an historical interest, and are forgotten. It is for qualities beyond the mundane descriptions of events that we remember great mountain writers: Menlove Edwards at grips with the psychomachia of the mind; Patey's human comedy; Murray's lively reverence for mountains as the supreme symbols of order and beauty in Creation. It is the good fortune of post-war Scottish mountain writing that it can claim two of these writers as its own, and that the two should be so different yet so complementary: Patey the clown, whose human insights entertain us so crisply and so joyfully; and Bill Murray, the High Priest, whose prose can sing. Here's another quotation from the latter. The scenario is again a winter climb. The passage describes the aftermath of an ascent of Crowberry Gully, on the Buachaille, in February 1941, just before Murray went to join the Middle East Forces in Egypt. It was thus his last climb before internment. Whether you label it as adrenaline-induced, religious mania, or a mystical experience, I do not know, but I doubt if there are many who have not felt something towards this state, or whether there is anywhere a better description of it. It is the essence of the mountaineer's world:

'We stepped on to the open mountainside at 7:15 pm, and came face to face with a cloud-racked, starry sky. The ring of low crags under the summit, the ground beneath our feet, and all the rocks around were buried deep in fog-crystals. Although night had fallen, yet up there so close to the sky there was not true darkness. A mysterious twilight, like that of an old chapel at vespers, pervaded these highest slopes of Buachaille. We stood at the everlasting gates, and as so often happens at the close of a great climb, a profound stillness came upon my mind, and paradoxically, the silence was song and the diversity of things vanished. The mountains and the world and I were one. But that was not all: a strange and powerful feeling that something as yet unknown was almost within my grasp, was trembling into vision, stayed with me until we reached the cairn, where it passed away.

'We went down to Glen Etive for the last time, and I fear we went sadly. The moon shone fitfully through ragged brown clouds.'

5: MY LAST CLIMB WITH GEORGE HOMER (2004)

Like a dream,
Whatever I enjoy
Will become a memory;
The past is not revisited.
                    Shantideva

On the night-flight from Vancouver to Calgary, lights in the cabin dimmed and ridge upon snowy lateral ridge of the Rockies glimmery in the moonlight below, sudden-ly in this distant country I find myself thinking about George Homer. I doubt if memory of him has glanced across the surface of my mind more than a couple of times in the last ten years. I start to quantify the knowledge and cannot remember that much. Some time in the 1980s, I think, someone in a pub or café somewhere or out on a crag had come up to me, breezed out one of those bald announcements to which this community's long inured: 'You were a friend of George Homer's, weren't you? Did you know he's dead? He was piloting a helicopter and it crashed ... '

Out in Calgary I'd presumed. He'd moved there from Llanberis in the 1970s. He was a carpenter and they're always in demand in Canada, so he'd done well. The couple of times I saw him subsequently he'd acquired a prosperous air, a Canadian accent, and a copious moustache, but you sensed he was the same old George beneath it all, just a bit more slick, confident and polished on the surface. He was someone I liked a lot. I think the last time I met him was at Al Harris' wake, for which he'd flown in specially – might be wrong, though, Memory plays strange tricks, and I was out of it that night. All I know for certain is that George would have been there if he was still alive then – Harris was one of his mates, and he was a loyal friend. Also, whenever I think of him, that magical climbing epoch of the 1960s comes to mind, with Harris as the great joker, the playmaster, prankster, and the rest of us innocent enthusiasts drawn away from mode-serious into revel-wild. George was this lanky, laconic youth down from Liverpool, with big, amused brown eyes, an easy manner and a Scouse drawl. He was a good climber, too – didn't leave much to the guidebook writers to vulture over, apart from that weird, steep, creaky direct start to Hangover on Clogwyn y Grochan with Martin Jones, but he did a lot, and was relaxed about it, viewed all the magazine and newspaper hype that was just about get-ting into gear in the 1960s with laughing, ironic distaste. First time he and I got close was because of a shared experience we had within a week of each other in 1967. The obsession of that time was with South Stack's *Red Wall*, which was gathering its own *mythos*, heavily and mischievously promoted by Joe Brown and Pete Crew: rock like mud, ledges devoid of belays, Brown looking across the zawn at it for the first time, mistaking it for the main cliff of *Gogarth*, and thinking, 'Christ, I've really been left behind this time!' There was a little blue-covered cyclo-styled guidebook appeared, very minimal; and there were the experiences you had following it: I remember being on that top pitch of *Gogarth* itself with Dave Yates in 1966, laybacking up a flake in the groove above the bulge and the whole 20-ft sliver of it groaning out, me getting into a bridge and giving it a shove away, watching it bounce and shatter and spear down into the water hundreds of feet below. Or the time on *Red Wall Original Route* with Nick Gough – I was on the pedestal stance above the long, diagonal, middle pitch, leaning out from a belay of three or four angle pegs, driven into the mud of the groove behind, to watch Nick on the crucial moves when half the boss of rock I was standing on peeled away, a great red pillar of it cascading down, leaving the zawn reeking of cordite and Nick and I distinctly impressed by the adverse possibilities of our situation.

Where George comes into this narrative thread is when he and I both fixed on going for the second ascent of *Wendigo* – for the perfectly daft reason that the stance on a sloping ledge below the 15-ft crux groove was described as having no belay, which seemed ultimately cool in its day. Does the second even bother to belay? Brown smiled that toothy smile of his, Crew jeered, and we wanted to find out. Besides, the little, open groove of smooth rock with the slant platform beneath was so alluring. But neither of us wanted to approach by the descent we'd used for our previous forays. So, separately and within a few days of each other, we opted to abseil directly down the cliff to the grass ledge above the first, dirty, scrambly pitch. At that time the only *descendeurs* you could buy in this country were weird alloy things that might have been designed as Poseidon's trident, then bent out of shape a bit. They were made in France by Pierre Allain, became so hot on long descents they'd melt through nylon, and the rope could easily become detached from them. More or less everyone still used the sling-and-karabiner method, and if you want to know how much friction that gives you, take a look at the scars on my left shoulder and right forearm some time. George was lucky. He had two 150-ft ropes and had knotted them together. So when he arrived at the knot, it stopped him and he had time to cool off, but he still got burnt. I had a 300-ft rope for the abseil, and was carrying another two ropes for climbing on, as well as all the pegs, hammer, steel krabs and stuff that you had at that time. Cliff Phillips, with whom I was climbing, had picked up a figure-of-eight descendeur in Chamonix that summer – a little thing that seemed to be made of thick, bent wire. He did fine. All I could do was hold on ever more tightly to stop gathering speed – and it's a 300-ft free abseil, way out from the rock. After ten feet I was burning, and couldn't stop. I could feel my palms blistering, the skin ripping and rolling off, hanging in ragged tatters from the long thread of the rope above. By the time I was at the stance my hands were fused and weeping blobs and the grooves across my shoulder and forearm cut to the bone. We climbed off – me using my elbows – up *Red Wall Escape Route* (listen, bolloxbrain, there is *nothing* special about this, nothing remotely distinguished or heroic about saving your own skin. Do you subscribe to that *No Ordinary Joe* routine? Don't – the guy wasn't dead, so he kept on crawling. That's all there is to it ...), which is a 300-ft HVS from which you get great views of *Wendigo*, for which neither of us had much appetite by now. In the sailor's hospital on the quay in Holyhead they separated out my fingers with a scalpel, scraped out of the grooves the burnt nylon from my shirt – I've never worn a nylon shirt since – dressed me up and sent me off with a warning to keep off those cliffs from now on. And then George and I met up some time a little later and we compared notes and we laughed and the story did the rounds and gained in the re-tellings and everyone learned, as you do from mythology, and George and I had a kind of bond from then on, a sort of *brenntbruderschaft*, and that was maybe how he and I came to do our last climb together.

Of which I remember very little, and not even the name for definite. What's for certain is that it was in The Peak, it was some time towards the end of the 1970s when George was back on a visit from Canada, and that there were three of us – he and I and Henry Barber. It was a sunny day, we were climbing at Millstone – dunno what we were doing there, must have been partying in Sheffield – and getting pretty stoned as we did so, sitting among the rocks wreathed in fragrant smoke and prattling away merrily about this and that, making the odd sortie out to take in a route or two. I remember doing *Dexterity*, because it was always one of my favourite little jamming pitches, and I remember Henry, to the usual barracking, leading the two of us up something a tad more difficult – *Satan's Slit*, maybe, or maybe not, I'd remember if I saw it – but the mood of the day was all drifting and easy so our climbing was thus. And I remember too this decision to squeeze in a last pitch before the pub and leavetakings and the night miles for home.

I have this vague idea that it was called *Hacklespur*, but I'm not one of those guys who keeps a log-book or ticks and dates things in the guide so he can look them up there. Anyway, what I recall is a neat little rock-feature at some point of the route – whatever route it may have been. It was a short, semi-circular groove, it was my lead, and it all went right. Flow-moments, the levers and pivots easing on through;

same for Henry and George and all of us happy with it and each other – their elegance and composure, a sort of supportive, jokey, mellow kindness flowing between us in counterpoint to the body's momentum, the sun shining, warmth, the rock glowing ...

That's more or less all I can recall about George – a few shared experiences, a tenor of feeling, fading impressions. He feels to be worth more than that, makes me wonder how much we know or care about each other; but the past is a distant country, and I won't be going there again. Memory hold the door, let the gleams and reflections filter through for a while yet; for all the jokey boys whose smiles are dust.

6: EXPLORING ERIC SHIPTON (1985)

Early in 1930 a young planter in Kenya unexpectedly received a letter from an ex-soldier ten years his senior, who had settled in the colony after the Great War. The letter mentioned that its writer had done some climbing in the English Lake District on his last home leave, and asked advice about visiting the East African mountains. Its immediate results were a meeting between the two men, an initial jaunt up Kilimanjaro together, and the first ascent, later that year, of the West Ridge of Mount Kenya – one of the major achievements of pre-war British alpinism.

The two men were Eric Shipton and HW Tilman, and their chance meeting, out in the colonies at the very beginning of the decade, led to one of the most fruitful partnerships and entrancing sagas in the history of mountain exploration. Indeed, the centrality of their role in that history throughout one of its vital phases is unarguable. The chance of their acquaintance and magnitude of their travels aside, another aspect of these two men is perhaps even more remarkable. They were both inveterate chroniclers of their climbs and journeys, and the quality of the writings they produced places them both right in the forefront of mountaineering and travel literature.

Shipton was born in Ceylon in 1907, his father a teaplanter who died before his son was three. Thereafter, with his mother and sister, he travelled extensively between Ceylon, India, France and England before the family finally settled in the latter country for purposes of the children's schooling. Shipton's mountaineering career began in 1924 with holidays in Norway and Switzerland and was consolidated through four successive alpine seasons in 1925-1928. His first ascent of Nelion, one of the twin summits of Mount Kenya, with Wyn Harris in 1929, and of the same mountain's West Ridge with Tilman the following year, brought him to the notice of the mountaineering establishment of the day and elicited an invitation to join Frank Smythe's expedition to Kamet in 1931. Shipton distinguished himself on this trip, being in the summit party on 11 of the 12 peaks climbed by the expedition, including that of Kamet itself, which at 25,447 feet was the highest then attained. His performance in 1931 led to an invitation to join Ruttledge's 1933 Everest expedition. Thereafter the milestones slip by: the Rishi Ganga 1934; Everest Reconnaissance 1934, which he led; Everest and another sortie to Nanda Devi, 1936; the 'Blank on the Map' expedition to Shaksgam with Tilman, Auden and Spender in 1937; Everest 1938; Karakoram 1939 – virtually the whole decade was spent in Himalayan travel, and the extent of his exploratory achievement perhaps even now lacks full recognition.

He spent the Second World War in Government service in Sinkiang, Persia and Hungary, went back for a further spell in the former – accompanied this time by his wife Diana – from 1946 to 1948, and was Consul General at Kunming in southern China from 1949 to 1951. On his return to England he was asked to lead an expedition to reconnoitre the southern approaches to Everest, in the course of which he and Ed Hillary plotted out the eventual line of ascent up the Western Cwm to the South Col from a vantage point on the slopes of Pumori. The following year he led a tense and unsatisfactory training expedition to Cho Oyu. In the late summer of 1952, Shipton having been urged to lead a further expedition to Everest in 1953 and having accepted, the joint Himalayan Committee of the Alpine Club and Royal Geographical Society performed an astonishing volte-face, appointing the competent and experienced, but at that time virtually unknown, Colonel John Hunt as leader, and accepting the inevitable consequence of Shipton's resignation.

This sorry episode effectively marked a watershed in Shipton's life. After the break-up of his marriage and loss of his post as Warden of the Outward Bound School at Eskdale, which occurred shortly after the events of 1952-1953, he lived for a time in the rural seclusion of Shropshire, working as a forestry labourer. He was enticed back for a last trip to the Karakoram in 1957, and thereafter developed a new grand obsession with travel in the southernmost regions of South America, which absorbed most of the next decade of his life. Finally, in his sixties, he was a popular lecturer on cruises to such places as the Galapagos Islands, and leader of mild Himalayan treks. He died of liver cancer at the home of a friend in Wiltshire during the spring of 1977.

This, then, is the bare outline of an outstanding life. The man who lived it, through his involvement in the 1931 Kamet and 1933 Everest expeditions, had attained a degree of national celebrity by the early 1930s, yet at the time was a professionless pauper and a kind of international tramp, whose possessions amounted to little more than the clothes in which he stood. There is a passage in *Upon That Mountain* where Shipton recalls the dawning realisation that the way of life which most appealed to him perhaps presented a practical possibility. It occurs on the way back to India from the North Side of Everest in 1933. In company with the geologist Lawrence Wager, he had made his way across unexplored country and over a new pass into Sikkim. Wager was instrumental in shifting the emphasis of Shipton's interest away from the climbing of peaks to enthusiasm for a more general mode of exploration, to a fascination with geography for its own sake. Two decades later, this shift was to provide his detractors with an easy target. For the moment his mind works over the ground thus:

'Why not spend the rest of my life doing this sort of thing? There was no way of life that I liked more, the scope appeared to be unlimited, others had done it, vague plans had already begun to take shape, why not put some of them into practice? ... The most obvious snag, of course, was lack of private means; but surely such a mundane consideration could not be decisive. In the first place I was convinced that expeditions could be run for a tithe of the cost generally considered necessary. Secondly, if one could produce useful or interesting results one would surely find support ... '

When he took into account his reactions to the large expedition ('The small town of tents that sprung up each evening, the noise and racket of each fresh start, the sight of a huge army invading the peaceful valleys, it was all so far removed from the light, free spirit with which we were wont to approach our peaks.'), then the virtue to be made of necessity was obvious, and of it was born what came to be known as the Shipton/Tilman style of lightweight expedition. When he describes the result of putting his belief into practice in his first book, *Nanda Devi*, the result is a revolutionary text. I doubt if there has ever been a less formulaic account of an expedition. It has a fresh, get-through-by-the-skin-of-your-teeth spontaneity and candour, an excited commitment, a clear rationale and elation about the enterprise undertaken which previous mountaineering literature had seldom approached. From the outset the terms are made clear: five months in the Garhwal Himalaya to tackle some of its outstanding topographical problems, 'climbing peaks when opportunity occurred', on a budget of £150 each for himself and Tilman (some of Shipton's share is advanced by Tilman "against uncertain security"). The scenes throughout, from the broken-toed, frock-coated setting-out from Ranikhet to the final descent from the Sunderdhunga Col to Maiktoli, are evoked in clear and economical style. But it is the message – the simple moral that it is possible, and in terms of response to landscape and its peoples even desirable, to travel cheap and light, to move fast and live off the land – which is the book's revolutionary charge, and which was to make Shipton and Tilman, in the words of the American writer David Roberts, 'retroactive heroes of the avant-garde.'

Two major characteristics, already present in *Nanda Devi*, distinguish Shipton's writing. The first of these is an intense curiosity – which remains with him, his conclusions growing more authoritative with increasing experience – about natural landforms, whether they be mountains, valleys, rivers, volcanoes or glaciers. This curiosity acts as a stimulus, a fund of energy continually to be drawn upon and used as a basis and point of reference in his explorations: 'It was enthralling to disentangle the geography of the region ... for me, the basic reason for mountaineering'; ' ... a desire to leave the route and wander off into the labyrinth of unmapped ranges that stretch away on every side'; ' ... to follow any river throughout its course is fascinating to me.' Or perhaps clearest of all, 'Tilman and I climbed a peak of about 21,500 feet. It was an interesting ridge-climb, but the pleasure we expected, and in fact received, from it was secondary to getting the hang of the Arwa glaciers onto which we were about to descend.'

Alongside this drive to understand the physical makeup of a landscape there operates a more reflective principle, sometimes very close to traditional naturemysticism, which Shipton can carry off with great poise and delicacy, avoiding the pitfalls of bathos or inflation. As in this passage from *Blank on the Map*:

' ... we settled down on a comfortable bed of sand, and watched the approach of night transform the wild desert mountains into phantoms of soft unreality. How satisfying it was to be travelling with such simplicity. I lay awaiting the approach of sleep, watching the constellations swing across the sky. Did I sleep that night or was I caught up for a moment into the ceaseless rhythm of space?'

There is a satisfying irony in suggesting an affinity with mysticism here, for Shipton professed an agnosticism throughout his adult life, and even if only for the joy of argument – which was one of the pleasures of his social life – would probably have rejected the contention. Yet perhaps his disclaimer of religious belief was akin to that of Simone Weil, concealing and containing a sense of divine mystery within the universe. Certainly a recurrent point of interest in Shipton's writings is the tension between practical preoccupation with physical phenomena, and frequent lapsing into quietistic modes of thought. *Nanda Devi* puts me in mind of no other text so much as one of the late poems of that most ascetic of saints, John of the Cross (quoted here in the translation by Roy Campbell):

> *The generous heart upon its quest.*
> *Will never falter, nor go slow,*
> *But pushes on, and scorns to rest,*
> *Wherever it's most hard to go.*
> *It runs ahead and wearies not*
> *But upward hurls its fierce advance*
> *For it enjoys I know not what*
> *That is achieved by lucky chance.*

Those who knew Shipton well sound a recurrent note in their reminiscences concerning a quality of detachment he possessed. Invariably it fastens on a physical detail, and the following is typical:

'He had the most marvellous blue eyes, very kindly, very amused and very wise. But there was always a sense, when you talked with him, that somehow he was not with you, was looking right through you, searching out farther and farther horizons.'

It's remarkable and eventually almost comical how often that impression, almost word-for-word, is repeated. Without the evidence of the texts, it could be taken as mannerism, inattentiveness; but in his books, time and again passages recur which describe his response to landscape as one striving towards an under-standing beyond topographical grasp. In this he is very different to Tilman, his most frequent companion of the 1930s, and it is interesting to compare the two men. The ten-year difference in their ages is significant. Tilman's seniority meant that he had endured the profoundly determining influence of the Great War. It was this which made him a master of that most serious of all forms of writing, comic irony, and which caused him to veer dangerously close at times to misan-thropy. It explains the prelapsarian vitality with which he imbues his native characters, the neglectful portrayal of his compatriots, and the isolation which identifies his authorial persona. In his personal conduct, it provides the reason for his taciturnity, phlegmatism and unemotional responses to situations. The vul-nerability of youth, its lack of circumspection and eager commitment to affection or cause were in Tilman's case the victims of war, and the survivor, psychic and physical, of that particularly obscene war had need to be encased in adamantine.

Shipton's enthusiasms, on the other hand, operate under no such con-straint. He can indulge his feelings as freely as he will, and the zest and gaiety of the 1920s glitters around his early activities. He commits himself freely, and as equally to a climb as to a journey of exploration or to one of the many women who shared his life. The following comments written by Frank Smythe in 1931 capture the temperament of the man:

'No one who climbs with Shipton can remain pessimistic, for he imparts an imperturbability and confidence into a day's work which are themselves a guarantee of success.'

Or again:

'I saw Shipton's eyes light up, and next instant he went at the slope with the energy of a boxer who, after months of training, sees his opponent before him.'

The differences in their characters, by complementing each other, perhaps acted as bond between Shipton and Tilman and account in part for their sharing some of the most ambitious undertakings of their lives. For Tilman, robbed of his own youth, Shipton's enthusiasm and boundless energy must have been inspirit-ing, whilst the fatherless Shipton would surely have found in Tilman's wry, benevolent maturity a need fulfilled. In mountaineering terms, however, the roles were reversed, Shipton the obvious leader. One very telling indication of this occurs in Tilman's diary for 30 May, 1934. After reconnoitring one of the crucial – and very complex passages on the route up the Rishi Gorge, they have to hurry back to camp. The subsequent diary entry briefly states, 'Shipton's route-memory invaluable as usual, self hopeless.'

A change does occur, though, in Shipton's outlook – especially with regard to mountaineering – during the mid-1930s. It is perhaps cumulative rather than associated with specific circumstance. The influence of older companions such as Tilman and Wager must have played a part, as would the long relationship upon which he had embarked with Pamela Freston. But two related events are certainly decisive in the transition from joyful mountaineering innocence to prudent experience. These were the two avalanches that Shipton witnessed on the slopes leading to the North Col of Everest during successive expeditions in 1935 and 1936. Of the first one, he had to say 'I am sure that no one could have escaped from an avalanche such as that which broke away below us while we were lying peacefully on the North Col.'

The following year, as he and Wyn Harris were climbing up the same slope, this happened:

'We climbed quickly over a lovely hard surface in which one sharp kick produced a perfect foothold. About halfway up to the Col we started traversing to the left. Wyn anchored himself firmly on the lower lip of a crevasse while I led across the slope. I had almost reached the end of the rope and Wyn was starting to follow when there was a rending sound ... a short way above me, and the whole surface of the slope I was standing on started to move slowly down towards the brink of an ice-cliff a couple of hundred feet below ... '

Wyn Harris managed to jump back into the crevasse and re-establish the belay, the snow failed to gather momentum, and Shipton survived. It was the last attempt on the mountain that year. The point is that Shipton's faith in the material he was climbing had been undermined. Just as in personal relationships, when the trust has gone the commitment is withdrawn. Shipton's heyday as a climber is delimited by these events, and though exciting and perilous escapades happen after 1936 – the climb on the Dent Blanche-like peak above the Bostan Terek valley is a striking example – henceforwards we keep company with a much more circumspect mountaineer.

This links naturally into a consideration of what is generally regarded as one of the cruces of Shipton's life – the circumstances surrounding the choice of leader for the 1953 expedition to Everest. It is still, in the dusty rooms of the mountaineering establishment, a controversial issue, difficult to summarise in brief. Even Walt Unsworth's *Everest* book – the most authoritative history of the mountain – overlooked important material which throws a clearer light on some of its aspects. What

145

emerges, from close examination of relevant Himalayan Committee minutes and written submissions from some of its surviving members, is a bizarre tale of fudge and mudge, allegations about the falsification of official minutes, unauthorised (and not easily retractable) invitations, and opportunistic and desperate last-minute seizures of initiative by a particular faction. It is a perfect illustration of the cock-up (as opposed to the conspiracy) theory of history, and little credit redounds from it upon the British mountaineering establishment of the time.

There are two main themes to be considered here. The first is the general climate of feeling surrounding Shipton's perceived aptitude for, and interest in, the leadership of an expedition which even in its planning stage was subject to a jingoistic insistence that Everest must be climbed by a British party (that this was not to be achieved for a further 22 years after the 1953 expedition scarcely mattered or was noticed in the event). This climate of feeling willingly accepted some of Shipton's own statements at face value. In *Upon That Mountain*, for example, he had written that 'there are some, even among those who have themselves attempted to reach the summit, who nurse a secret hope that Mount Everest will never be climbed. I must confess to such feelings myself.' It also drew on more questionable evidence, particularly relating to the 1952 Cho Oyu expedition, where a combination of political circumstance and personal history undoubtedly affected Shipton's leadership.

A synthesis of these points suggested to one faction engaged in the expedition planning that Shipton lacked the urgency, thrust and killer instinct[1] which would be necessary to 'conquer' Everest. The case was immeasurably strengthened by Shipton's own submission to the Himalayan Committee meeting of 28 July, 1952, in which he expressed doubts about his suitability for the 'job' on the grounds that, being out of work with a wife and two children to support, he needed to consider his own position; that he felt new blood was needed to undertake the task; and that his preference was for smaller parties, lightly equipped.

The second theme – aside from the question of Shipton's likely attitudes and commitment – is that of the manner in which members of the Himalayan Committee conducted themselves over the matter of the leadership. The first point to be made is that the Committee was very weakly chaired. Because of this, the pro-Shipton faction carried the day at the meeting of 28 July, when Shipton – chiefly through the efforts of Laurence Kirwan – was strongly prevailed upon to accept the leadership. The contention then rested with the question of the deputy leadership.

---

[1] 'They said he lacked the killer instinct – not a bad thing to lack in my view.'
—Sir Charles Evans.

There existed a faction within the Committee and headed by Basil Goodfellow and Colonel Tobin – both of whom had been absent from the 28 July meeting – which had its own preferred candidate for this post in the person of John Hunt, who was, in Goodfellow's quaint phrase, a 'terrific thruster', and one who would bring a necessary application to the task. Tobin and Goodfellow lobbied forcefully that the deputy – or assault-leadership should fall to Hunt. Inevitably this would compromise Shipton, whose choice as deputy was Charles Evans and to whom in that role Hunt was therefore unacceptable. The crucial committee meeting took place on 11 September. The pro-Hunt faction was present in force, well-prepared, and determined to reverse the decision of the previous meeting. The more ardent Shiptonians – most notably Kirwan and Shipton's old friend Lawrence Wager – were absent. The choice of Hunt was imposed – and as joint rather than deputy leader, Shipton was effectively compromised and morally compelled to offer his resignation, which was promptly accepted. The rest of this squalid and bloody little episode is history, apart from a few later ripples spreading out from the main controversy, such as the charge of subsequent falsification of minutes levelled by Blakeney against Claude Elliott – in the words of one contemporary observer, 'as bad a chairman of committees as one could find; he was hopelessly indecisive and hesitant and was too easily swayed by anyone (like Kirwan) who held firm opinions, however wrong these might be.'

What the effect on Shipton would have been had he led the successful Everest expedition is matter for conjecture. John Hunt was patently well-equipped to cope with the ensuing celebrity, and used it tirelessly in the public domain. It could perhaps be considered doubtful that Shipton would have enjoyed, and responded so positively, to the inevitably massive acclaim. After 1953 his life went through a difficult period, but it emerged into a golden late summer of exploration in an area completely new to him. His Patagonian journeys of the 1950s and '60s were a harking-back to his great Karakoram travels of the 1930s, and would have been rendered immensely more public – and hence perhaps less satisfactory – by the burden of international fame. Instead he was able to slip quietly away to the unknown mountains and glaciers of a fresh wilderness. It was a proper consummation in the life of this explorer mystic, whose outlook and progress resonate so closely with Tennyson's 'Ulysses', from which poem he took the motto for *Blank on the Map* and the title for his magnificent second autobiography, *That Untravelled World*.

There is a phrase from this latter book which gives perfect expression to one of the great lives of the 20th century: 'a random harvest of delight', and evokes his spare, lithe figure loping off into the ranges, seeking out the undiscovered country, his distant blue eyes lingering on the form of a particular peak or the passage over to an unexplored glacier. If curiosity, appreciation, aspiration and delight are a form of praise, Shipton's stands as vivid testament of a lifetime spent in worship.

7: BIG CAT – JOHN REDHEAD (1981)

'Don't you ever train?' I ask him.

'No,' he replies.

'Then how come you're fit enough for the routes you do?'

'I'm not fit, but once you've done a few of them you can get up 6bs anyway, and 6cs with a fall or two.' He states it quite matter-of-factly. With anyone else, I wouldn't believe it, but I know with him that he doesn't climb from one month's end to the next and yet can blast straight back into the hardest things around.

'So do you just get off on the adrenaline?'

'Yeah!' A great, spreading smile, huge rolling eyes, manic laughter.

'So that's your obsession with Great Wall?'

He snickers with delight at the mention of it and starts to talk cryptically about the line.

'And it's possible. I've been down it. Looked at it. It'll go. But it's death ... there's nothing!'

A great open vowel sound for the last which leads him back to wide-eyed laughter. I just watch. Believe me, this is the strangest cat around. I have seen him poised elegant, relaxed, grinning, where there was nothing. And the moves! Pollitt is playful as a puppy: bounce, gambol, plunge, scurry back; Fawcett is the great ape, all free-swinging elasticity; but Redhead is the big cat. There is no one like him in the climbing world today.

'The painting comes first,' he tells me, and I think of his vast canvases and their tiny, intricate, detailed beauty. You could say Richard Dadd, half-imputing a fine madness, striving to identify a tone and style, but it's a faint echo and he's his own man. You could state an absolute professionalism and technical mastery of perspective, colour, form – but it's bald language, thin soil for the grasses to grow.

A warlock with a loping dog, a night-creature, sleeping in stables, yet his house glows with a gentle green.

I know Redhead. He is a master, of rock, of design. He can both represent and create. There is vast egocentricity in him and humility too, lapping oceans of unsureness; deep, rushing channels. He wanders, then suddenly bounds spring-heeled quite out of your sphere. I know and do not understand. His routes – *Margins of the Mind, the Disillusioned Screw-Machine, Demons of Bosch* – amaze. For him, they are out there on the Way of Weird. He is some sort of distant brother to our humanity, watchful, wolfish-visaged, beast-taut. If, one day, he sprang clean beyond our comprehension or just disappeared with a puff into the ether, I would not be astonished.

149

8: THE ESSENTIAL JACK LONGLAND (1988)

A photograph, taken at the old Promontoire Hut on La Meije in 1928, of three young Cambridge Fellows: one of them, Bobby Chew, is wrapped in blankets and slumbering on the *matratzenlager*; another – Lawrence Wager – back to the wall and a plate of food in his lap, looks seriously into the camera. It is the third figure which dominates. He lounges back, but even in repose the athlete's physique is obvious – the neat build, the power in chest and thigh. A book is open on the mattress and the camera catches him as he looks up from it. That passing glance from over 70 years ago gives you the measure of the man – the expression of a young falcon on a face intensely alert, strong-featured, wide-browed and quizzical. The eyes are hypnotic in their power. The whole presence of the character speaks not of arrogance – though it could be interpreted as such by a casual observer – but of rigour, honesty, effort. The men to each side – Wager and Chew – were both distinguished in their chosen professions as geology don and headmaster. The one at the centre – Jack Longland – even here at the age of 23 gives promise of being more than that.

It needs to be explained just how central to the British climbing culture Jack is. The familiar form of address is a clue. Formally, he is Sir Jack Longland – he was knighted for his services to education by Harold Wilson in 1970. But he is one of those rare people for whom the near-universal affection in which they are held is expressed by the simple forename address – to everyone he is 'Jack'. His roots in British climbing go back to the days of Geoffrey Winthrop Young (GWY), and through him perhaps even to the Golden Age of British Alpinism in Victorian times. A repository of tradition and value, those raptor's eyes – though older and less intensely focused now – still scan piercingly over the current landscape of climbing. Personally – both in his mountaineering and professional connections – Jack has not always been popular with every sector of the communities in which he's moved. He's a man of strong principles, great intelligence and devastating wit, who can stomach neither fools nor pomposity and is quite capable of savaging either when they cross his path. The idealist in him is so urgent a creature as still occasionally to become choleric. For all that, there's another side to his character which is more frequently to the fore – an impishness, a sense of fun, a relish for the robust ambiguity and the subtle pun, which made him an ideal choice as Chairman and question master to the long-running radio programme My Word. There are no emotional or intellectual monotones in conversation with Jack. He can describe human situations which will bring you close to tears, argue a precise and coherent case for their amelioration, then explode the whole tenor of the debate with a perfectly timed joke or even just a fit of giggles at the cosmic absurdity of it all. Even now, well into his eighties, his enjoyment of good-humoured and combative talk has not deserted him, nor has his ability to run ragged even the most sharp-witted of his opponents. In my life he has been one of two great mentors. What follows is neither profile nor interview, but a composite synthesised from correspondence, interviews, snatches of conversation, which have passed between us over a long period of years. They give, in his own words, the rich flavour of one of the great elder statesmen of British climbing.

His beginnings as a climber:
It was all so accidental. We had this Classics Master at King's School, Worcester, who became fond of me and my brother. He had a *gite* in the Alps and took us out there two years running to read Greek. He was a crypto-homosexual obviously, but not active at all, just the affectionate variety. I sometimes wonder if I'm just fantasising, but I think I remember that walking along level paths and being told to keep to the inside of them, and reading Homer, was not enough – that these mountains all around were made to be climbed. But I'm a bit suspicious of this – it may be a rationalisation of some kind. These times were interesting, and I did a bit of cliff-scrambling – little pinnacles and things – on family holidays down in Cornwall, but I don't know that I connected the two things up at all.

Anything in the family background to give encouragement?
I doubt it, though I think my Pa and Ma had been taken out by their relatively rich fathers and mothers to sit about in alpine resorts – there was that amount of recognition that the Alps did exist. And there's some tale of my Ma glissading down some bloody slope with a guide and shouting at him, 'Arretez, Monsieur, arretez!' But that's a pretty far cry from climbing *aiguilles*. Anyway, they knew about this sort of thing. Maybe the catalyst for me was this very quiet Alpine valley above the Rhone with the Diablerets around its head. We certainly didn't have any tradition of walking on the Derbyshire or Northumberland moors – I can't claim that's part of my background.

Jack's father was Anglican minister in Droitwich, just the other side of Worcester from the Malvern Hills.
I remember making my Papa sit on the rope while I was trying to climb the villainous bit of crag called the Ivy Scar Rock on the Malvern Hills, which I think was the most dunderheaded thing that I've done in my life, at about the time I went up to Cambridge.

He went up to Cambridge as Rustat Exhibitioner and Scholar at Jesus College in 1924.
They were very busy, my first couple of years at Cambridge. I was an athlete, played rugby for my college, and it all took a bit of time to sink in. I wish I could remember what seduced me when I went to discover where you might find the President and Honorary Secretary of the Cambridge University Mountaineering Club, but even to this day I cannot remember the particular reason that made me think it might be a nice thing to join.

It was quite funny when I did make contact. Wyn Harris had rooms in Caius and I went along and knocked at the door and a sepulchral voice bade me come in. Most Cambridge rooms have a long corridor with a very high ceiling and there were Wyn Harris and Van Noorden five feet above my head.

What were they up to?
Oh, nothing sexual, or if there was it was in an exceptionally difficult position.[1] No, they were simply practising their back-and-foot work. Van Noorden was a splendid chap and a very good climber, who was killed by Herbert Carr in North Wales on, I think, Dinas Bach below Dinas Mot – damned silly little crag. He led this thing – a Diff. or V. Diff. pitch – and Herbert Carr, who'd been following, fell off. Van Noorden, who'd been shifting about changing his belay or something, was pulled head downwards and killed.

That must have been only a few months after the first Swiss meet I'd been to involving the club, which was at Arolla. We went up the Aiguille de la Tsa and were descending the easier bit of the mountain facing Arolla. Van Noorden was going down working out the way and while he was doing that the chap above me, who was a novice also, slipped and fell and Van Noorden fielded three of us on quite a steep bit. Good job he did, because otherwise it would have been a very nasty accident. I had my revenge afterwards, though. Traversing Mont Collon, Van Noorden himself fell off on a short pitch and was extremely surprised to find that I held him.

Tl Alps after that definitely had preference, though I remember the same year camping up in Wasdale with my future brother-in-law Paul Sinker, and we climbed around quite a bit. I lost my nerve completely by falling out of *Kern Knotts*

---

[1] Jack would often manage to turn the conversation round to this topic, often in a very scurrilous way. He once told me of the *menage à trois* he'd enjoyed as a Cambridge undergraduate with both Geoffrey and 'Len' (Eleanour) Winthrop Young – extracting from me as he did so the promise that I'd tell no-one before his death, and as many as possible thereafter.

Crack and had gradually to recover it on Scafell. I was very frightened on the *Keswick Brothers Climb*, which didn't seem to have any proper finishing holds. But after that it began to come right. This was in 1928, which was the first time I climbed properly with others on a rope.

The traditional sequence went British hills, Alps and Himalayas. Did that imply a contempt for the rockclimbing this country had to offer?
I don't think the Himalayas then entered into the scheme of things, despite the three early Everest expeditions – they seemed so infinitely remote that it never struck me that one should go there at all. When I went to Cambridge I was buttoned-up and callow and shy and as soon as I met him I came very much under the influence of Geoffrey Young. For Geoffrey, the Alps were the place and he himself never bothered with the Himalayas. The doctrine of the long traversing day which you get in Geoffrey's *On High Hills* seemed to me a very good way of treating Alpine mountains, so they were obviously much more important than what I did in this country – though I enjoyed what happened here. But it was a small-scale thing, quite different for me from the Alps.

Your impetus towards the Alps stemmed in part, then, from a tradition, with a strong literary manifestation?
Oh yes, it did, and that featured quite strongly in making them attractive to us. Although we were breaking with aspects of that tradition. You see, we were just at the gap before which it was disreputable to climb without guides. It was no longer damned silly, but becoming reasonable, to do without them, and that's the point at which the Cambridge Club came in to say, 'Look, with reasonable party discipline you can do these things!' Wager put down the argument in one of the early CUMC Journals. The first time you went out you were just a piece of baggage on the end of the rope. If you were any good at all you could become a responsible second man. And if you were really good you were expected, in your third year, to be leading quite reasonable climbs. It was a progress we felt to be OK, but some of the golden oldies in The Alpine Club felt it to be ridiculous – how could you possibly learn to lead alpine climbs starting as a novice three seasons before? But to us it was both reasonable and possible, and that's how we did it. I only climbed once with a guide in my life ...

When was that?
It was with one of the Lochmatters – funny little man – good on cutting ice-steps,

153

but I had to lead him down from the Lyskamm in cloud. He was lost. He really was rather cowardly, I think. So I never felt I needed to climb with a guide again. Those of us in the university clubs couldn't afford guides anyway – that had quite a lot to do with the build-up of guideless climbing. The earlier guideless climbers – Todhunter and so on – were regarded as pretty eccentric by the Alpine Fathers. By our time it was becoming more the norm, and was more or less OK, though you had to try not to make a fool of yourself. It was an odd time to come into alpine climbing.

This integrated tradition whereby you had to pass on your accumulated expertise to an incoming generation must have acted as an inhibiting factor on your own development?
Oh probably – but in a university club of young students that was the corporate ethos. You picked up your novice generation and you tried to transmit what you'd learned, however incompetently, to them. I think that still goes on in any normal local club today ...

I think perhaps not – what you describe typified an approach founded on particular social and educational values which have given way to a more individualised drive to achievement.
I think that's quite true – in a sense, prefects and fags were part of that sort of game. There were those who wanted to learn how to climb, and those who knew only a faint degree more than the novices did thought it was their job to teach and lead them. Without being priggish, that was really quite a strong tradition with us – that's what we did. If I look at the CUMC now, that doesn't seem to exist. Anyway, the CUMC Journal now is virtually illiterate, whereas there were some quite good articles in the CUMCJs in our day, and we managed to keep a close watch on literacy.

And you managed to produce one most years?
Oh yes – and they had some classic articles in them. Now I find them virtually illiterate, not much fun at all.

Is the literary tradition on which you had to draw for the activity you pursued now defunct?
Probably, yes – when I started the person you read was Leslie Stephen, who was a considerable literary figure as well as a great mountaineer. We all felt part of a tradition and the more I got to know Geoffrey Young the more anchored that was. Climbing was very much a literary business whilst being a physical one as well ...

And neither GWY nor Leslie Stephen were writing about events hugely removed from your time,

154

and the social milieu they described was a familiar one to you.
Yes, if you think that GWY climbed with Slingsby and married his daughter, you're going quite a long way back into the 19th century. And all the people I'd read about he'd climbed with. That was a tremendous influence, and of course there was a link-up between climbing and literacy – Geoffrey in my case gave a tremendous boost to that with his personal knowledge of writers and poets.

Was that important to you, or just a pleasant adjunct to the activity?
Oh I think it was important – when you thought that GWY's grandfather had walked over the hills with Charles Kingsley, it made a real connection between literature and the mountains. The interesting thing for me is the sort of balance you tried to keep between what you did in this country and the Alps, which were then your ultimate goal. And you can see the way in Geoffrey's own writing in which he came to see that what you did in British hills and on British rock was a worthwhile thing in itself, and not just practice for doing, say, the south face of the Weisshorn.

There always had been climbers whose primary or sole interest was in British rock ...
Very few. The Abrahams went to the Alps, though they didn't make much of it. Owen Glynne Jones was killed on the Dent Blanche ...

Archer Thomson?
Yes! Well he's rather a key figure, since he virtually explored Lliwedd himself, and as far as I know he never went near the Alps – he was the beginning of the new lot – the people who didn't simply look on British rock as a training ground. But most of the rest were bisexual – partly devoted to the Alps, partly to inventing British rock-climbing, which is what they did. It took them some time to work out that there might be something worthwhile or worth doing for its own sake in British rock-climbing. If I'd been asked to choose – damned silly idea that it is – I'd have said the Alps every time, of course, and the main reason for that was that it was where GWY had made all these great climbs before the War.

That suggests that your primary search wasn't for difficulty?
No – it was for mountain tops by interesting routes.

So it was an aesthetically orientated urge – the Cambridge aesthete is an apt tag after all?
I think so – though I'm not sure I was aesthetically literate enough in those days. Still, there was the Matterhorn – I remember consciously thinking what a lovely

thing it was. When young Perren asked me if I'd like to repeat the Schmidt Route on the north face of the Matterhorn in 1931 I said 'Yes, I'd love to but I can't afford it.' It's conceivable we would have done the second ascent, but it was too much money at that time. I was also a bit frightened, I expect. It would have been rather fun. I think he was good enough and I was probably good enough too.

Climbing was only a very small part of your life in Cambridge?
Oh yes – I played around with all the usual games as well as academic work. I was a pole-vaulter, which was rather an aesthetically pleasing thing to do. Life was very compartmentalised. Cambridge term time was very far removed from what was done in the holidays. Though they did overlap occasionally, particularly where Ivan Waller was involved as he had an indulgent Mum whose car he could borrow. But there was very little interaction between aesthetic, academic and sporting life at the University.

Although GWY tried, however successfully I don't know, to embrace several of those spheres?
Yes, but again, his Sunday evenings were rather like a French Salon. And when he came to lecture to the CUMC it was rather as though he were trying out whole chapters of *On High Hills* on the dog. The salon element came in when you got to know Geoffrey through the club and went to his and Len's Sunday evenings, which were an introduction for me to intelligent conversation as well as to climbing. The Pen y Pass parties came of that. If you'd been to 5 Bene't Place half a dozen times possibly Geoffrey or Len would say 'How about PyP at Easter?' and that's how I got there. Otherwise I should never have got near PyP at all. It was a social and intellectual background which is quite foreign to what I know of climbing today.

And there operated a process of selection by which people from less privileged sectors of society were excluded?
Yes, but they'd never have been there anyway. I admit this is elitist, but they had to be at Cambridge first.

So people like the Abrahams would not have been invited to the PyP Easter parties?
Well, be fair – Geoffrey got to know and like the Abrahams, and Frank Smythe, who came from quite a different background, was welcome at Pen y Pass – but yes, I admit I do stop at this point.

(A digression in defence of a man who needs no defender: this background in climbing can now

156

seem almost unbearably privileged. Jack's academic career, too, was one of glittering accomplish-
ment. He took a First Class in the Historical Tripos in 1926 and a First Class with special
distinction in the English Tripos the following year. What matters, though, is the use to which he
put these advantages. In the 1930s he was, as he puts it, 'tempted out of the ivory tower' by John
Newsom to work for Durham Community Service Council. To this day, among older people in
the north-east of England his name is a byword for committed social concern. In his own words:
I came into educational administration at the end of the squalid and hungry 1930s,
after some years working with unemployed Durham miners and their families. I
think that those underfed children, their fathers on the scrap-heap, and the mean
rows of houses under the tip, all the casual product of a selfishly irresponsible society, have coloured my thinking ever since ... I wanted the mainline express to a new
world, and fair shares all round.

To anyone who knows Jack, the silent pain he has suffered at the undoing of his life's work in
educational administration and development by the squalid iniquities which Margaret Thatcher's
successive Conservative administrations have visited upon the community of Britain has been
devastating to witness:
I watch with appalled disgust what is happening to the education service – the sub-
stitution of a reasonably non-pompous altruism by unashamedly vulgar self-interest.
I can't remember anything nastier than the current Conservative Right in the
Commons – and I meet their like daily in pubs – since Churchill lambasted 'the
hard-faced men who'd done well out of the War' (1914-18 edition) back in the twenties.
Digression over – back to the outdoors.)

Your own technical development as a rock-climber seems to have occurred with remarkable
rapidity.
The sport was going through changes, from grouting about in these bloody gullies –
what Geoffrey Young called The Gully Epoch – to balance climbing. I'm not old
enough to have taken part in that, though I did climb a few of them and pretty repul-
sive they were. But gradually we were shedding our heavy clothes and having lighter
nailed boots, then climbing in two-and-11-pence-halfpenny plimsolls and little tricouni-nailed Hargreaves shoes. We were breaking through on to different angles and
types of rock and beginning to adapt ourselves and our equipment to that.

The new routes which established your reputation as the leading rock-climber of your day were
your climb on the West Buttress of Clogwyn Du'r Arddu, and Purgatory on Lliwedd. To a later

generation, though, your Javelin Blade, along perhaps with Kirkus' Bridge Groove, now seem to be the only pre-war climbs to merit a grade of Extremely Severe in Wales.
The *Javelin Blade* finish was a kind of comic accident. I'd thought I was doing the original route, but had clearly got lost and failed to see the not-very-difficult mantelshelves over to the right. So I was committed to something rather harder, but don't remember much except the slightly worrying athleticism of the pull-out on to the top of the Javelin itself. I hadn't done any rock-climbing in the previous six months – so much for training for climbing – being out at a German university and concentrating then on skiing and pole-vaulting. It never struck me that the climb was anywhere near as important as the West Buttress of Cloggy – which obviously has much fewer technical difficulties: though nowadays nobody can possibly realise the problems presented by hopelessly insecure grass. All my ambitions in 1930 were focused on the Alps and, just coming into view, the Himalayas. The *Javelin Blade* was so irrelevant to them that I cannot even remember ever having recorded it.

You say your ambitions were directed towards the Himalayas, yet your only expedition there was the 1933 Everest trip.
I would have gone on '36 Everest if it hadn't been for the underground rebellion among some of us who didn't think it was right that Hugh Ruttledge should be leader. So quite rightly he didn't ask me. I was very disappointed not to go on Tilman's '38 trip, though weatherwise it turned out to be a bloody awful year. But I was then in the Social Services job and the Director of the National Council for Social Services said, 'No, I see no reason at all why we should give you leave to go.'

The Ruttledge Rebellion was one of the earliest of Jack's brushes with various establishments of climbing and other spheres of life.
I wasn't heavily involved at first. It had been clear in '33 that Hugh Ruttledge didn't find it easy to make up his mind, but he was a good linguist, knew about Sherpas, and on the ride across Tibet he was a nice father figure. But when it came to mountaineering he didn't know much about it. Obviously, the crucial point was when the two soldiers, Bousted and Birnie, took it on themselves to say that conditions were too cold to establish Camp Five on May 20th. Wyn Harris, who was an infinitely more experienced mountaineer, thought this absolute nonsense. I remember I was at Camp Four at the time and Wyn Harris came down in a complete fury, saying, 'The fucking soldiery!' And he was right, because on the 20th for the next three days not only was the weather good but it was before the upper slabs were covered with new snow. There was a chance then, with that open window from 20th to 23rd May. And those funny bits beyond the couloir – they

were very much my cup of tea – I was better at that than Shipton or Smythe. Hugh Ruttledge was a nice chap, and we finished up as friends. It wasn't a personal feud, just that some of us didn't think him the right chap to be in charge of a major mountaineering expedition. His indecisiveness jeopardised our one thin chance of success.

Did your dissidence put you on the wrong side of Strutt?
Oh no – Strutt was a bastard and everyone got on the wrong side of him. He basically felt that the other ranks should keep themselves in order. But I think he was more or less on our side over Ruttledge. Longstaff certainly was – he was on the side of all our youngsters as they came up through the ranks, unlike those stuffy bastards at The Alpine Club!

There was no formal structure to climbing in your day. You were partly responsible for bringing about the present situation of representation by the British Mountaineering Council. How d'you feel your creature's developed?
I doubt the usefulness now of that particular kind of mountain bureaucracy. I'd be happier if there were just a loose assembly of all sorts of clubs at all sorts of levels in all sorts of places. The public persona of the BMC – I wouldn't say I find it repellent, but I can't say I like it very much.

You and I would agree on the usefulness and admirable nature of the club structure, but sadly it seems to have less and less bearing on the functioning of the BMC.
I'm with you on that – the strength's in the people who meet, climb, drink, marry together, with luck have a base somewhere in the mountain districts – that's what British mountaineering's about – it's not about a lot of bureaucracy and competition climbing and Christ knows what. Clubbability's better than any bureaucratic national structure. I'd be much happier with a loosely knit federal structure of jolly, solidly-based and solidly drinking local clubs who would not be inclined to apostasy on issues like competition climbing. And the anarchic tendencies and fratricidal jealousies of top rock-climbers seem divorced not only from the BMC but also from local clubs, which are regarded as being for old fuddy-duddies. The sort of neck-biting between top climbers I find totally distasteful – it doesn't agree with anything I ever regarded climbing as being, at all.

The fact that you can explain this behaviour as the inevitable result of commercial pressures on these climbers is no excuse?
None at all, though I'm sure the pressures exist. But then, who in my day could ever

make any money out of climbing?

Frank Smythe ... ?
Apart from Frank Smythe. Also, I find it intensely boring, all these chaps doing something with or without bolts to the left or right of where someone else has been.

And describing their experience in terms of a limited and repetitive set of numbers? Which is intrinsically much less interesting than the tradition of a diverse use of language in which you were brought up?
You mustn't be a snob about this but I find the magazines a frightful bore. I read a page or two and think, 'Christ, I don't want any more of this sort of stuff!' But that's what comes of being old and awkward.

You've always had that reputation!
Bloody minded, in fact – I'm all for being bloody minded!

After a conversation I had with him last year Jack wrote to me thus:
Surely a very large body of climbers would ask, 'What in the world are these silly old superannuated buggers talking about?' I can't escape a despairing feeling of alienation. And yet we were talking – not directly, because that would have been vulgar – but glancingly about a system (only that is too formulated a word) of beliefs and fantasies and escapes from *La Condition Humaine* which meant a very great deal to us, so many years ago. But we belong to the irrecoverable past, don't we?

No – where there's something to be learnt, some wisdom to be expressed, some complex continuity of human response to the wild country, the tradition lives, and within it nothing is irrecoverably lost. Let's end with a vision, bleak perhaps, but salutary, of the future, from a letter of Jack's:
It is heartening ... that not all today's climbers are oafs – and unutterably selfish to boot. I have an uncomfortable vision of climbing moving inexorably towards total irrelevance – shades of Colonel Strutt dog me here! Incomparable athleticism, plus or minus finite areas of rock, plus increasingly competitive bloody-mindedness (plus disregard for the environment and peregrines' nests) and litter and louts and the sheer disfigurement of pristine rockfaces – I remember Samivel and his three-phase picturing of unsullied rocks, followed by an agglomeration of pitons, bolts, pre-fashioned holds and ubiquitous artificiality, and (a century or two later) utterly deserted faces and overhangs, chequered by a few pieces of rusting ironmongery – and the

choughs (or 'choucas' who followed the 1924 Everest climbers above 28,000 feet) content with their uncluttered domain again. And I saw a splendid Lammergeier sailing untouched at 27,000ft above the squalid mess and shit of our camp on the North Col in '33! I wonder if we climbers have only a short life ahead – even if spared the nuclear holocaust ...

Perhaps there's a future still in which we shan't need Ken Wilsons and climbing competitions? Of course I don't know – but with Ted Hughes and the Bishop of Durham and Voltaire, there might just be a bit of a garden which our great-grandchildren might still think worth cultivating.

But pretty deeply in despair ...

Yours,

Jack

9: ' ... LIKE A FAMILY OF GHOSTS':
RECOLLECTIONS OF PETER BIVEN (1998)

We reduce our friends' lives to memories, as though the process of becoming, of departing, that they went through were a sequence of instants significant only insofar as they impinged on our own being. I have, for example, three clear recollections of Peter Biven and whenever his name surfaces from my subconscious, is encountered on the page or in the conversation of others, always they shimmer eerily across the years. Someone mentioned him to me the other day, asked why his name cropped up so frequently in the essays I write: who was he, what was he like and what had his effect been on my life?

So I faltered out a reply: he was a friend of mine; there was some curious recognition between us, instinctively, such as only the survivors who have come through will know; I was fond of him, and he of me I believe; more than that, I respected his achievements, his style, aspects of his character, wanted him remembered, protected from detractors. I wanted to ring-fence his reputation against them, wanted him kept in mind because for me he had, as Wordsworth has it of William Wallace in "The Prelude", 'left the deeds/ Of Wallace, like a family of ghosts,/ To people the steep rocks.' And then, because this suggestion had arisen, I thought to write about him, not having seen any recent account of a man influential at an influential time. By a quirk, scanning the numbers, I realised too that it is 22 years since he died, that he had then been 11 years older than me, that I am now 11 years older than he was at his death. Symmetries! The child had become father to the man. I could help him now, repay debts from a time in which, subtly or directly, he had helped me. Hence this article.

But as I thought more about it, I realised too that I didn't want to write about him in the usual way, patching together the views of others with agendas and covert discourses all their own. I didn't want the sly mendacities of supposed objectivity. Makers are always prey to detractors. I wanted his words, documentary evidence from his time, and my own knowledge and memories – that's all.

Peter Harvey Biven was born on 8 August, 1935 and died at the age of 40 after a fall from Giant's Cave Buttress in the Avon Gorge on 4 June, 1976. There is, between those dates, a childhood about which I'm aware of some facts that are neither comfortable nor appropriate to recount here; a personal and professional life with its attendant difficulties and successes, ambitions realised, small and large miseries more or less endured; and there is the beginning in a sport and his subsequent history in it, his contribution to the history of it.

As I write this, I'm looking at a diary of his from 1953. A terse note prefaces it: 'I contend that it is dangerous to own a diary, for obvious reasons.' It's a curiously occluding posture for a boy of 17 to take, but also a warning with regard to Pete's life that I'm inclined to heed. There are some areas of pain and complexity in our lives that it is not proper to put on public display, not good to have the insensitive, the sensationalist, the self-interested and the misguided gloat over. Climbing itself is so simple relative to the conduct of the rest of life, so let's stick within that sphere. The diary does – minimal entries, recording places:

'Boxing Day 1952, good snow on Carneddau'; '10 January, 1953, exploration of Buddon Quarry'; '17 January, 1953, Stiperstones and Long Mynd'; '7 February, 1953, Foel Goch Arête, 12 hours, 400 feet'; '16 May, 1953, Right Unconquerable'; '19 June, 1953, First Ascent of High Tor, Matlock'; '6 September, 1953, Gardom's, Moyer's Buttress'; '10 September, 1953, Grochan, Hangover Grooves'; '26 September, 1953, Great Slab, Froggatt Edge, Second Ascent'; '11 October, 1953, Cratcliffe, *Suicide Wall*.'

Thus the diary – occasionally there are fuller clues to his activity, as in this note written on the back of one of the plates in his copy of the 1951 guidebook, *Climbs on Gritstone, Volume 2: The Sheffield Area*:

Quietus, 50 feet, Exceptionally Severe.
Starts from the obvious ledges of the girdle traverse. A piton was inserted in the wall as a foothold. Stand on this and grasp the first of three rock flakes. Make a leap for the second and hand traverse as far as it goes, then reach for the third. Here a piton was driven in for direct aid. Pull on to a small ledge with this and by using two parallel cracks attain the top. It was climbed clean (i.e. without use of the pitons) on the fourth attempt.

First Ascent, 6 October, 1953, P. Harvey Biven.
Teasing? The historians of Peak climbing would certainly find it so. (The crux of the matter, in fact, is top-roping – more of that later.) But I need to give you some background, and one of those flickering memories I have of him is useful here. It is New Year's Eve, 1970. We'd climbed together for the first time a couple of months before on the first ascent of the Elegug Tower in Pembroke and he'd invited me down to visit him in Exeter. I went down to the South West often at that time, and would always call in on him and his wife Polly in their house on Wonford Road. It was one of the hospitable, cultured, elegant oases in the climbing desert. The weather was terrible so they dissuaded me from pressing on down to West Penwith. Their

two children were in bed. We talked. An article of mine, the second one I ever wrote, had just come out in the Climbers' Club Journal under the title 'Existential Psychochemicals'. I'd misquoted Dylan's *Mr Tambourine Man* in it, and he corrected me (the climbing world's many Dylanologists might like to know that he subscribed to *The Wicked Messenger* – ultimately esoteric Dylan info-fanzine). We talked into the night, late, late, excitedly. Polly went to bed, benignly tolerant of excited boys rehearsing their enthusiasms and unconsidering of mothers who had mornings and children to observe. At three o'clock or so, we went out for a walk around the city. It was snowing. I remember the great soft flakes waltzing and teeming down in the orange lamplight. I remember climbing mischievously with chilled fingers on the cathedral (him a magistrate and a college lecturer who would have had much to lose and some explaining to do if caught in such a venture), comparing city childhoods, seeing the white fragility of the snow extinguish itself in the dark flow of the river and turning away with a shiver for his home again, and sleep.

I recall detail from this conversation in which a kinship was established. The matter of our beginnings in our chosen sport was shared: our inner-city childhoods, his in Leicester, mine in Manchester; climbing on buildings, escapades when police-men noticed figures high on the turrets and buttresses of Victorian office-blocks, regal memorials, town halls, clock-towers, banks or department stores; whistles and scoldings, fragile carved stone snapping and rattling down into silent city streets; always new challenges, ears intent for the footfall of caretaker or police; training for stamina and arm-strength on the undersides of fire-escapes; mischief of the bold repose in a statue's lap, the extraordinary complexities of night-time urban roofs-capes, the outlaw romance of it all. I told him of the pale face of my drowned friend Geoff Watkins glimmering beneath me as he climbed out of shadow across the ledge and into the lamplight of Albert Square, pavement 90 feet below, and the puzzlement of parents as we came in grimed and excitable, high on the adrenaline of perilous play. And then there were those gritstone and Welsh beginnings, the fondness for lit-tle hills, secret quarries, tenuous moves on cool, fern-shaded rock.

For an hour or two in the city snow we shared one of those passages where, because you communicate without barriers, acknowledge shared experience, a sym-pathy based on recognition is established between you, and you become friends, and that state has a reservoir of transmitted perceptions to tap into and sustain it. These rare states in which we sing our life-songs to each other have a profound effect in a world where most human contact is etiolated, and not infrequently much worse. I recall that from the lyricism of this night where we gave each other the room to express feeling and emotion around shared enthusiasm came the first essay I ever wrote in which I began to find a voice of my own – the paean to *Right Unconquerable* in Ken Wilson's *Hard Rock*.

So you see, from one charged and intense night of conversation Peter became one of my most important mentors and I feel a need to state that debt, refer to a bond of sympathy established through recognition and memory. I was coming to my erratic peak as a climber then, he was a few years beyond his, but there was no oedipal stuff, no rivalry between us. He seems to me now, in the long retrospect, to have had an extraordinary generosity of character, an empathy and a gift for support which were enormously enabling (professionally at that time he was moving in the direction of counselling which brought him a sense of academic and personal fulfilment in the last phase of his life). And we were using the arenas we knew – the adventures by which childhood refines itself from confusion, gritstone's bold gymnasticism, sea cliffs' elementalism and their gift of exploration – to express something essential in those things which yet transcends them. I don't think the latitude climbing allows to blinkered self-assertion – particularly in these days of the great protected-adventure lie – much appealed to him. He was, in the main, one of exploration's miniaturists, and that he should have preferred the exquisite small canvases of gritstone and the South West doesn't limit his achievement.

I first climbed with him in an exploratory way too, on the occasion I've already mentioned. I don't remember exactly how the weekend came about, but I'd been talking to John Cleare about Pembroke – where Colin Mortlock and myself had had a virtual monopoly on exploration for a couple of years – some time in 1970. We'd pooled information: John had told me about the two-mile-long grand traverse from Newgale, Eldorado, that he and Peter had done in May of that year: swims, tyroleans, inescapable sections. I'd related my routes at Mother Carey's Kitchen and elsewhere and we'd both fixed on the Elegug Stacks as a crucial objective. So we arranged to go down for a spring-tides weekend at the end of October, John had a house in Broad Haven where we could stay, and on the Friday night a disparate group of us converged there: Peter, Frank Cannings, John, Ian Howell, Martin Hogge, myself and a few others. On the Saturday there was a force eight gale blowing. I remember that Peter and myself, at precise low-tide, splashed across to the big stack, I belayed, and he led a steep and appallingly loose 60-ft pitch up to a shoulder at half-height. By the time I followed, gale and wave and tide were roaring in, the others had fixed up a tyrolean to the mainland, and we beat a very prudent retreat having accomplished the most difficult section of the route.

What I remember most, though, was Peter's climbing. I'd talked to some younger and pushier climbers in the South West about him from time to time and

they'd been condescending, a little dismissive perhaps of a man whose main energies of life were applied outside climbing by 1970. So maybe I wasn't expecting that
much. I'd liked him. He was benign, rather gracious in conversation and graceful in
movement and he had a considerable physical presence – tall and Nordic and handsome. What I wasn't prepared for in climbing with him was the authority and
elegance he displayed on rock. OK, this wasn't a desperate pitch, but the conditions
were: howling wind, showers of rain and spray on a loose, birdshit-covered and
poorly-protected traverse across a vertical wall. He made it look like a staircase and
it wasn't. The rock was lethally fissile and slippery. When I followed, two flakes
snapped off simultaneously at one point. I began to swing. He held me on the rope
instantly. You could tell, watching him, that he had the rock-knowledge, the instinctive competence, the awareness of medium that the climbers of real pedigree possess.

I say maybe I wasn't expecting that much, but I'm not sure about this and to
explain that I need to go back to my own brief gritstone heyday in the mid-to-late
1960s. You'll know, of course, that gritstone is – or perhaps more properly used to be
– not so much a rock, more a religion into the mysteries of which you were not educated but initiated. I look at the pads of scar-tissue across the backs of my hands as I
work, still livid nearly four decades after their first assumption, and remember the
truth of that. And there come back to me also two events from 1967.

In the first of them I'm soloing around on Froggatt Edge on an early summer's day. I remember the exact physical feeling I was experiencing. I was 20 and
strong and good at this sport, and remember thinking at the time that it was like the
moment in learning to ride a motor-bike when you slip through from stiffness and
inhibition to a lovely, timed, relaxed fluidity where everything synchronises. I
remember rejoicing in my own strength and suppleness, the springing muscle-elas-
ticity of youth that you'll never know again and the intense joy of movement – easing
gleeful and breathless across Great Slab, dancing up and down *Brown's Eliminate* time
and again for the delight of it (no shadow of awareness then that 28 years later I'd be
giving the funeral address of another friend who was lured in to his death in just that
place, by just that impulse).

There were two men sitting at the bottom of this last route, watching. One of
them – Nat Allen – I already knew. The other was more spare in build than Nat, and
older, balding with wispy hair. He had a curiously-shaped skull that made him look
ascetic, intent, like a medieval monk, an amused, shy expression and a slightly hesitant, considered way of speaking. Nat introduced me:

'This is Trevor Peck.'

I knew about the Biven-Peck partnership. Byne and Sutton's High Peak had come out the previous year and their names were writ large in it, their picture on the cover with Peter in a wildly improbable position on the top overhang of Hearse Arête on Gardoms, the rope devoid of protection and hanging down free from him. I knew about the legendary lift given to the Biven brothers Peter and Barrie in Trevor's Rolls Royce one wet Saturday in 1952. The photographs and accounts of Peter's and Trevor's gritstone pioneering in the guidebook that was a bible to my climbing generation (*Climbs on Gritstone Volume Four: Further Developments in the Peak District*), to those who understood gritstone they were a mythos as potent to us as the Authorised Version of Brown and Whillans. Nat went off. Trevor and I climbed together, he holding the rope, encouraging, following in a sinewy, deliberate style up routes that I hope I'll still be capable of doing when I'm in my sixties, as he was then. And I heard the stories, picked up on the affection, admiration, regard for his younger climbing companion.

It was a significant meeting and I often think back on it. I remember quizzing him about *B.P. Super*, the parallel line left of *Tower Face* on Stanage that Peter and he had climbed in 1956 and on which I'd recently failed several times. 'Loose holds,' he'd told me wryly, 'used to be covered in them. I kicked most of them off.' He told me about the development of Millstone and Lawrencefield, the sieging of Malham, the time when Peter had been abseiling down Malham Cove using one of those diabolical and lethal devices called a PA Descendeur, had stopped after 100 feet on his Viking number two hawser-laid nylon rope, heard a ping and felt a slight jolt, heard another one, then realised with terror that the heat the friction had generated in the device was melting through the rope – two out of three strands gone! With a prayer, he slid on down to the ground 200 feet below! He told me of routes in the Dolomites, equipment he hoped to manufacture. He was, at the time, very much fixed in the perceptions of the 1950s and early 1960s when you spent wet days pegging your way up limestone bastions or gritstone quarries.

But climbing, that phasal thing, was at one of its periodic cusps. Within a few weeks of this meeting Ray Evans and myself had free-climbed *Troach* on Clogwyn Du'r Arddu and within a year Ray, Cliff Phillips and myself had started the process of eliminating aid-points on the classic routes of the Brown and Crew eras: *Llithwrig, White Slab, Shrike, Daurigol, Pinnacle Arête*. Times were changing, the move towards a rigorous free-climbing ethic was under way, and the reputations of those associated with an older style and outlook were inevitably thus devalued.

And yet, despite what increasing technical sophistication may have spelt as the future for limestone, for battered gritstone quarry crack-lines where aid-use created the super-routes of coming years, or Welsh rock, there was still the possibility of gaining a respectful perspective on past achievements on the edges of natural grit-stone. That was brought home to me most forcefully when, very soon after this meeting with Trevor, the second of these two events from 1967 occurred: I led two routes of which Peter had made the first ascents a dozen years before on Gardom's Edge.

They'd been on my list for a long time. I'd tried and failed on one of them already earlier in the year, when I was climbing poorly and had been driven away by a torment of midges. *Eye of Faith* and *Moyer's Buttress* are maybe the most proximous pair of outright classics that exist on British outcrops. That guidebook, Volume Four, made all the right noises about them. *Eye of Faith* was 'the most delectable route on gritstone', and 'a technical achievement for experts.' It had a few long, blind moves, a good position and some energetic sequences. The protection was pretty good for the time, its rock-architecture satisfyingly monumental (maybe the influence of those early city-climbs went deep). It deserved the three-star status it later acquired in a more numerically defined age. But it wasn't that hard a lead. Then I embarked on *Moyer's Buttress*.

There was a picture in the guide of Peter on the second crux. He was soloing. It looked a regular sort of slab climb. If you were not climbing at a high standard then, it's difficult to understand what it was like to lead in those days. Nowadays the boys out on the grit top-rope and who cares? Keep it light, man. Lead it if the gear's good, otherwise ...

The guidebook description of the time gives the other perspective: 'Moyer's Original Route, 70 feet, (Hard) Very Severe – Rubbers. A serious and dangerous expedition for a leader ... very delicate and exposed. A long reach is a valuable asset.' In the 1960s it was hardly ever led, hardly ever done. Because if you did something on grit the ethos was that if it was an established route you did not top-rope, you led it. Or if it was unprotected you soloed it. And Moyer's Buttress was a terror route. I've done it again in recent years. With Friends, hexentrics, RPs you can get a runner every five feet. It's just a magnificent, clean, characterful classic. I think the guide-book grade's around E1 or E2, the technical grade 5b, and that's about right. In 1967 it was the hardest thing I had ever led (my own Stanage route of *Censor* from the same year, which is obviously harder, I'd inspected on a top-rope because of the lack of protection, and once you've become thus acquainted with a climb – common practice on the most difficult first ascents of the time – you have the knowledge that can make its eventual first lead easier than subsequent ascents). It remains one of the very hardest and most frightening even though I managed routes graded far harder in subsequent years. There was a move at the top, 70 feet above an appalling landing and with my last runner 50 feet below, that I could not read, couldn't reach holds on, the rock lichenous and sandy from lack of traffic, every foothold and crease sloping down towards the limit of friction. Should I do it on the arête where there were small, awkward holds in a position of aching exposure above the overhanging right wall, or on the left where holds might come after a bald start? Eventually in these situations you just commit yourself convulsively to the moves, hoping better will arrive.

I've heard people for whom I have no respect as climbers question Peter's ethics, style, ability. I hear them, and I wonder: why? Maybe in these days of the decree nisi between climbing and risk, the danger-bred qualities of generosity and magnanimity have been subverted, the risk-takers who were the sport's great regulators and mediators are all dead and a meaner-minded generation who never knew has taken over. Or is this to romanticise? But the route's his and even in its modern guise, it's one of the greats. Strange, this spite that exists amongst climbers. Snipe, detract, decry goes the chorus from those who would be king, and away from their envy slips this image for me of Peter, the evening before his 20th birthday, reversing down unprotected across the crux traverse of *Suicide Wall* at Bosigran, in plimsolls and on lichen-encrusted rock, darkness gathering, the hour too late to complete the first ascent of the route that day.

Peter Biven was a great climber, and he left behind a clutch of routes that have on them the stamp of greatness: on gritstone, on Derbyshire limestone, at Bosigran, on Lundy and at Berry Head. Don't heed the mean-minded who want to level him. He rose above them. I was on *Bow Wall* at Bosigran once. It was some time in the autumn after that night walk in Exeter. On the teetery move round into balance from the overhang to the slab leading into *Doorpost* my rope jammed in the gear beneath the roof. I was on the verge of falling, had to lean back down, strength fading, to tug and flail at the rope. Peter and Al Alvarez were on the stance ten feet away watching. When my rope came free I scrabbled and fell across into them. They were shaking their heads in rueful relief. Peter hauled me in to the belay, clipped me in, and with a huge, wry grin offered me this:

'We all fuck up sometimes. It's just a matter of whether you get away with it.'

Peter, as you know, didn't. His life had run into a difficult zone. Marriage in abeyance, he'd moved on from being an Educational Adviser in Exeter to a Research Fellowship at Bristol University. He was 40, with a lot going for him and a lot paining him. A fortnight after his father's funeral in May 1976, at which he and Polly had discussed a reconciliation, he took his 14-year-old son Nick and Nick's best friend out climbing in the Avon Gorge, reached the top of the severe pitch, and then:

'I was looking up at the rope when suddenly it all came down and my father was in mid-air above me. He hit the rocks just below us.'

The reason's a mystery:

'We all fuck up sometimes. It's just a matter of whether you get away with it.'

The justification for dangerous sports? Nick's friend's father – a fit man who didn't climb – collapsed and died on holiday of a heart-attack six weeks later. Life has our number, even if the world doesn't. Peter was not only an exceptionally good climber, he was also one of the safest I ever met, and would surely have been doubly so in his son's company.

Yet the accident happened. The crassest thing I ever heard was the suggestion that it was deliberate, a suicide. Suicide's a private affair. You don't do it in front of your children. It was just an appalling accident and I wish it hadn't happened and that he were still benignly amongst us today, growing old with the rest of us, giving us his friendship still, instead of having gone on before. But at least I had the privilege of knowing him, climbing with him, enjoying that friendship. And he gave me things for which I can never now repay him, but for which I will always remember and think well of him.

The most valuable of those, I think, is a view and a perspective on this ridiculous and yet at times oddly dignified activity of ours. He searched out the play element in it, the beauty of its contexts, romanticised rather than reduced it, caught at its rhythms in his prose, his guidebook writings, his own and personal project of definition:

'The most seductive quality of sea cliffs is the extension of childhood seaside activity – hunting in rock pools, beachcombing amongst the squeezy bottles, and half expecting to find in the dank recesses of the zawns the bloated bodies of drowned sailors.'

Or again: ' ... the rising and falling of the tides and the ever-changing background of the sea, coupled with the myriad distractions of the shoreline – caverns, creeks, crystals; flotsam and the strangely-formed sea-worn and time-worn rocks, make sea cliffs delightful to be among.'

Down at sea-level there, in the crackle and hiss of the barnacles and the sluice of the small waves I've heard his voice, sensual, benign; his sea-change is into the glitter on the waves to which his experience and curiosity led us all those years ago. And on the scarps and crags of the Peakland moors as well, the colours discovered by the slant of the sun are of the places across which his exertions have passed – transmutations, alchemies, celebrations, 'like a family of Ghosts.' Thank you for the role you play in our consciousness of them.

10: PRANKSTER, MANIAC, HERO, SAINT AND FOOL: AL HARRIS (1981)

You sit down and try to write about your friend of so many years, wishing that the words would flow as freely as you wish your tears could flow, and knowing they can do no more than gesture towards the man you knew. Al Harris dead! I suppose we all thought he could keep up his clown's act on the thin edge forever, that he'd always be there playing that manic, exuberant, jestful balancing act of his; that you only had to arrive and enthuse and it would be 'I'm ready – let's go for it.' Except that latterly the troubles had been falling thick and fast and somehow he was fighting them all the time or just keeping them off, and he never did seem ever quite to get on top. So we all stood back and said, 'Harris is trying too hard these days,' and what we didn't give credit for was that he was having to. And these last few years were about fighting it off and surviving on his own path, as we all stepped aside into our little niches in the tunnel, watched fate's train go rushing by and wondered what we were doing there anyway. So that on the last late October night, when he set off on another drunken, desperate dash from haven to haven of warmth, energy and movement, only a couple of kids would get in with him and race down the dark, wet road, zapped and smashed and cutting it right down to the quick until Fortune could take it no longer, breathed out, looked away, and he crashed himself dead.

Then for a week all the philosophers dismembered his memory until his coffin sank from sight and we writhed within, knew that he'd gone and the cost of living like this.

There was nothing very original about Al, and when he curled his lip into a wintry, gratuitous sneer you sometimes felt there was nothing very good about him either. But there was something beyond any of that and compensating for all of it: liberated energy in superabundance, inspirational. He was the world's best playmate. Everything he did was noisy, gleeful competition, a restless search for the newest, the biggest, the fastest, the loudest sensation to be experienced and shared with the rest of us.

My first memory of Al is of him riding his scooter up the Llanberis Pass in the winter of 62-63, when the Pass was blocked and the road was ice-glazed and hard-packed snow. He rode like it was a speedway, digging his heel in so the snow flew. Time and again the scooter would slither away and bounce off a wall and he would be sliding down the road shrieking with laughter, would pick up the bike, rev it up, and go through it all again. He went where the play was, and wherever he went he added to it; came from Croydon, started climbing on southern sandstone, and none

171

of that matters; boasted that anything Crew could lead he could follow in win-klepickers, and proved it on *Zukator*; ended up at his cottage, Bryn Bigil, which became playshrine and focus for a generation and more; ran a Llanberis café for a few years; was as widely known and loved in America as over here. And that was it – you couldn't help but love him. He might irritate you like hell, use you, abuse you, chal-lenge you, and let you down – though never when it mattered – but you would still love him for the grace and life of it all, and you'd suffer with him too in his moments of black misery and collapse that came all too often in these latter years.

He was a good climber, frightened and emotional sometimes but very good, brilliant on boulders, enormously competitive, muscular, and all the time laughing, gibing, playing. He had enough ability to have been among the best of his genera-tion but it never meant that much to him – good to while away a sunny day, but not to get in the way of play and laughter and lightness. Modern climbing wasn't much in his way of things – all the training and the rigour and the calculated cool spelt out what he was set against – if it wasn't an instinctive, joyful outpouring of energy it wasn't really for him. It strikes me now, when I look back over all the good times I've had with Al, that what I shall miss about him most will be his spontaneity – if he did-n't like, didn't feel, didn't want to do anything, out it came straight, direct, no deceit, no hiding, no ulterior motives. And if there was something he wanted or liked or felt for, likewise he would come through with it and you would know. He was a great argumentarian with an odd and utter honesty which endeared him to most, got him hated by some, but let all and everyone know where they stood. Rude as hell, living totally by his own rules, didn't give a damn, but put yourself up alongside him and see if you come out as honest and straight as he did in the end.

There are the stories as well: the falls, the parties, the jousts, the crashes, all the texture of 20 years on the wildest shores of the climbing community, all the mad-cap come-and-go characters and bit-part players that he'd known and who'd seen him as some sort of centre and focus and special genius: all the tales that he'd told to Lucy Rees, for her to put down in their novel, *Take it to the Limit*, but that novel does-n't get near to what he was, to his freewheeling, manic, promiscuous, style, style, style – it gets Harris down as an admiring adolescent might, and he wasn't like that. He wasn't a simple sort of American super-road-hero straight out of Kerouac or *Easy Rider* – oh, he could play those parts, but that was it – they were parts to be played, roles in accord with what his needs were, outlets for all that demonic energy, or times when Al could lose himself somewhere between tight-rope artist, ringmaster and clown.

His funeral was extraordinary. It was more than just one of the climbing world's periodic closing of ranks. When the preacher of the place had rattled off his standard remarks – 'I will lift up mine eyes unto the hills. I have chosen this text especially for Alan' – I do not think any among the hundreds of people present so much as breathed an Amen. The established order of things had never seemed, even in his life, so far away from a true assessment of Al's character as it did in his death. It was oddly quiet, hushed; I think only his last mistress wept audibly. Why? Was it the tragic inevitability of it all – this cat whose nine lives must have gone 90 times over, this Icarus who flew so much higher and wilder than us before the feathers fell from the wax? Were we silent as for an elegy read over the embodiment and associate of our own youth? I don't know. I only know that a world without Harris is a little meaner, darker, poorer and more quiet than it was with him around. I only know that his is a hard act to follow and that if you go out there on the brittle edge for as long as he did your life is a charmed one, and probably a short one too. His death has aged us all.

But we have our memories. Of driving along the motorway in the dead of night, blowing a joint, changing drivers at 110, playing to the hitch-hiker we'd just picked up; of climbing through friends' windows at four in the morning and jumping gleefully into bed with them; of keeping going on speed for days on end, boozing and partying and whoring and soloing around on crags here and every-damned-where there were people to be played with, and get revved up about this or that; about sharing a bed with the same girl and sticking it out to see who would be first to leave in the morning; smoking endless joints on the stance of a climb and his voice drifting up out of the depths: 'Oh, fuck, no, he's done it!'; about tipping cars into quarries at dead of night and madly useless robberies and driving his Champ up absurd inclines and leaning into the wind of a hilltop on his scrambles bike and all the falls and all the broken limbs and the too much dope and mushrooms and joints and the too many miles for the mind to stay out and free and cold from the phantasmagoria of it all. And then the last night, when for once he couldn't get the timing quite right; the oncoming lights in the rain and a rib pierced his heart and the picture was torn apart – unpardonable, reckless, and thank God alone that no other was badly hurt.

Oh Al; it is such a fragile thing, this life, and you never gave a damn, not an ounce of compromise with it; you just kept on in there and for so long some special magic saw you through. We crouch in our retreats and know your passing. You no longer there to apply a poultice to the blister of conformity and draw the wildness from us all; us no longer able to creep back exhausted and quietened into our safe burrows, with you out there to link us to our losses. When I first heard, a couple of hours after, it was no surprise and I did not think then that the desolation would be so vast – but it is, it is worse. There is a hollow space now in all our lives, and the boundaries have moved in. At first we shrugged it off, hid from it. Now we can only grieve for the heroism and the loss, for your having stuck it out there for 20 mad years that enriched us all – prankster, maniac, hero, saint and fool ...

I sit here trying to write about my friend of so many years, and can do no more than gesture towards the man I knew. God rest and save him: with our thanks ...

11: JOHNNIE LEES – SPACE BELOW HIS FEET ... (2003)

There wouldn't, I suspect, be much argument in climbing circles against the suggestion that mountain rescue isn't really our thing – that it's more the province of centre-freaks, guides, instructors and all the rest of that crew who've turned to making a profession out of a pleasurable pastime. When Gwen Moffat – name to conjure with, there! – wrote her book about the RAF Mountain Rescue Service, *Two Star Red*, she conceded the same point in noting that climbers who were posted to RAF Valley tended not to join the rescue team there, because, as the rest of the motley crew mentioned above eventually find out, to do so would leave them less time for their own climbing. And yet, the man who founded that team was one of the most accomplished all-round mountaineers of his day. Johnnie Lees was a fascinating character, someone I knew for 40 years, and who I always rather liked, in that steely, bantering way that goes on between climbers. Johnnie remains the only man to have won the George Medal – the most distinguished of civilian awards for valour – for a cliff rescue, and he was crucially involved in the post-war development of the RAF Mountain Rescue Service. He left a few good routes behind him as well, and a solid reputation as a performer on rock.

Some biography for you – Johnnie was born in Chingford in 1927, and educated at Hexham Grammar School, to which town his family had moved. He left school at 16, enlisted in the RAF in the hope of serving as aircrew, but as opportunities for this were scaled down at the end of the war, he became instead a physical training instructor. His family moved again to Otley in the West Riding after the war, and it was on Almscliff whilst on leave that he first began rock-climbing.

This lanky, athletic youth was befriended by the likes of Arthur Dolphin, Des Birch, Joe Brown and Pete Greenwood. His cousin remembers them as visitors at his family home. In their company, Johnnie rapidly developed into a consummate outcrop climber, and when he was posted to the south of England, he continued to perfect his skill at the Wealden sandstone outcrops. Nea Morin and Menlove Edwards climbed with him down there, and Nea left eloquent testimony to the ease and style he displayed on the classic testpieces – *Slimfinger Crack, Niblick, Birchden Wall* and the like. By 1950 he had joined the Climbers' Club and the RAF Mountaineering Association, and had had several alpine seasons.

Which brings us to the point at which a developing climbing talent is turned to serve the general good. The significant moment of his career came in 1951. On the 13th of March a Lancaster bomber from RAF Kinloss on a night navigational flight to Rockall with eight men on board crashed into Beinn Eighe. Its wreckage was located a few days later on the vast triple buttresses of Coire Mhic Fhearchair. The existing rescue services in Scotland, also based at Kinloss, and the police who accompanied them were inadequately equipped – wellington boots, few ice-axes – and lacked the mountain expertise to quickly reach the fuselage of the plane where, in appalling winter conditions, it balanced precariously on 1300-ft-high cliffs. The last body was not recovered until August and rumours – certainly without substance – circulated that men had lived in the wreckage for days after the crash. The shock-waves this incident sent through the highest echelons of the RAF and MOD were profound.

In the late autumn of the same year Lees – by then a sergeant – was asked to run a mountain training course for the rescue service in Snowdonia. Early in 1952 he was posted to RAF Valley on Anglesey as Mountain Rescue Team Leader there. It would be no exaggeration to claim that the whole modern edifice of Services and civilian mountain rescue owes its sophistication and rigour to that appointment. As Team Leader, Lees was both demanding and inspirational. He insisted on the highest standards from his men in the line of duty, and he got them. The winter and summer training courses he ran were exemplary, and the *esprit de corps* he built up was formidable. One recruit, Vic Bray, recalls that in the initial pep-talk he was told that, 'if you're on an aircraft call-out, you will walk till the blood wells from the lace-holes of your boots, then stop, wash your feet in the nearest stream, put on plasters and dry socks – and walk on!'

Aside from the rescue service, another significant development in Lees' life took place in 1952. That Easter he met an extraordinary young woman who was staying with her baby daughter in a mountaineering club cottage in Snowdonia and who'd heard of his prowess on Sussex sandstone when she'd been working in a theatre in Brighton. This was Gwen Moffat, who became the first woman mountain guide in Britain, and who later embarked on a series of books that established her claim to be considered the finest-ever female mountain writer. She describes his climbing at the time: 'On the ground, with his long legs and loosely built frame, he looked as if he could scarcely move without knocking something over. Climbing, he was superlatively neat ... his movements slow and deliberate ... he never made a mistake, never advanced where he couldn't retreat ... his slow, steady caution made a deep impression on me.'

That was the climbing paradigm of those days, when to fall meant near-certain serious injury or death. Gwen expands on the point in this account of the two of them on Jack Longland's *Javelin Blade* in Cwm Idwal – maybe the first mountain pitch in Britain to broach the E-grades:

' ... Johnnie showed me another way to climb. He *thought* on rock. He planned every move before he made it, and one felt, watching, that he could reverse every inch which he had ascended. Once I saw him a little too close to his limit, but never since. We were on *Javelin Buttress* ... and Johnnie decided to lead through from the bottom and try the *Blade Finish*. It seemed devoid of holds. I didn't think about my belay until, to my astonishment, I realised that Johnnie was having some difficulty ... I had scarcely any stance; my feet were flat on the slanting rock. I was held inwards only by the belay ... He shouted that he was coming off, and my hands were wet on the rope ... I knew I wouldn't hold him. He didn't fall, but retreated delicately and rested. Then, after a long grumble, he went up again and passed the hard move without causing us any more anxiety. Following, I was very hard pressed ... '

The two married in 1955. It was a relationship that from the outside seemed both mutually respectful and fuelled by a volcanic sexual antagonism – she cat-like, volatile, utterly female; he solid, laconic, detached. Throughout their time together they addressed each other as 'Moffat' and 'Lees'. Gwen's succinct and approving description of his character is well worth quoting, and held true to the end of his days:

'Lees was often thought intolerant with people who had involved themselves or their parties in dangerous situations. His intolerance was with stupidity and incompetence, the – at times – almost criminal negligence of so-called experts taking parties of novices, often children, on the hills. It was impossible for him to hide his thoughts or hold his tongue. He made enemies easily, but these were the types who would always be enemies of frankness and expertise in the craft to which they were giving a bad name: the incompetent, those with strange or perverted motives for climbing, the notoriety-seekers, the politicians of the climbing world ... '

Lees' excellence in training rescuers was not achieved at the expense of his own climbing career. He qualified as a mountain guide in 1955, and became one of the very few to receive the guiding qualification in winter mountaineering issued by the Association of Scottish Climbing Clubs in the same year. The following year he took part in television's first featured climbing. The route chosen was *Suicide Wall* in Cwm Idwal – arguably the most difficult rock-route in North Wales at the time. The leader was Joe Brown, and a well-known Everest climber was intended to second him. In the event the Everest climber, despite wearing rock-shoes, had to retreat, and Lees, in boots intended for nothing more technical than mountain-walking (RAF standard-issue 'Boots, grooved heel' – Ray Evans wore the same boots for many of his significant first ascents in the 1960s), eased his way up the tiny holds of the vertical face on camera with complete aplomb. He went on an expedition to the Kulu. He made the first ascent of *Oxo* – that steep little V.S. classic on Clogwyn y Wenallt – at about the same time, and his best new route in Wales, the gorgeous, airy arête of *Space Below MY Feet* (E1,5b) on Craig yr Wrysgan in the Moelwynion, came in 1961, just after Gwen's autobiography of the same name had been published.

The finest achievement of Lees' rescue career, and the one for which he received the George Medal, was the winter night rescue of Major Hugh Robertson from a ledge on Craig yr Ysfa in January 1958. When Lees and his party arrived at the ledge well after dark, it was obvious that Robertson, who had severe head injuries, would not survive if the lengthy process of evacuation by stretcher was implemented. Lees therefore improvised a sit-harness out of a coiled rope, the 14-stone soldier was hoisted on to his back and the two were lowered – Robertson delirious and clawing at Lees' face – into the vertical darkness and down to safe ground. The speed and efficiency of the rescue, in bitter and savage conditions, undoubtedly saved Robertson's life. Its aftermath saw considerable technical developments in mountain rescue, notably the introduction – facilitated on his recovery by Robertson – of the continental *Tragsitz*.

Johnnie was de-mobbed in 1961, and after spells working in Outward Bound and mountain-guiding in the English Lake District, he became a Warden Service Officer and later Ranger Training Officer for the Peak District National Park until his retirement in 1985. John Beatty, who trained as a voluntary warden for the Peak Park under the Lees regime, recalls how the same rigour was applied to training his ill-assorted civilian crew as had applied to the RAF rescue team members. Lees and Moffat divorced, inevitably, in 1970, though he kept in close touch with Moffat's daughter Sheena, to whom he was an exemplary stepfather. In 1975 he re-married happily, and lived a life of quiet, ripe contentment at a cottage in Over Haddon. He'd venture out from there occasionally to the festivals of the climbing calendar – always the shrewd, appraising character in the corner, glass in hand. In his later years the worlds of mountaineering, mountain rescue, and mountain guiding bestowed their customary honours upon him. He received them with a wry grace. He was a humorous, kindly, quiet man, watchful and reserved, involved as adviser in numerous training schemes, absorbed by a growing botanical interest, bracingly reactionary, ready to engage to mischievous effect in any debate. Diagnosed with cancer of the oesophagus in April, he remained cheerful to the end, in his last days in hospital had his friends fill up his drinking bottle with Famous Grouse.

Lots else to tell – carrying the corpse up the *Terminal Arête* on Lliwedd, unroped – stuff like that that speaks of the power and competrence of the man. But

I have an endearing personal memory of him, from 1967, when I was hot-tempered, young and combative. With 'Bivouac Bill' Bowker, I was in the Cheshire Cheese in Hope after an evening's climbing on Stanage, when Moffat and Lees and a couple of clients came in and sat at our table. One of these clients was loud, boastful and arrogant, talked continually about himself and things with which he had obviously not the slightest acquaintance, climbs he'd clearly never been near. Moffat and Lees gazed pensively into their beer. After a time I got fed up with the self-celebration going on opposite and launched a savage tirade – in which the word bullshit, and a few others less printable here, figured prominently – at this guy. A silence ensued. I stood up, Bill followed, and we made for the door. I cast a quick look back. Johnnie met my eye, the corners of his mouth twitched, he gave me a broad wink that said it all. He was a martinet alright, steely, but I liked him a lot, and the standards of excellence with which he imbued rescue in this country constitute some legacy to us all.

12: STEVIE HASTON – WILD AT HEART (1996)

'He's climbed the hardest ice routes in the world, scratched up mixed desperates in Scotland and France, on-sighted 8a and redpointed 8c. Lauded by the cognoscenti as Britain's best all-round climber yet failed by the British Mountain Guides for his attitude, Stevie Haston is largely unknown by the climbing public. Martin Crook gets to know him a little better.'

That's how this next essay was prefaced when it appeared in On the Edge *magazine, and therein hangs a tale. Stevie is one of my dearest friends – intense, uncompromising, manic and utterly loyal and generous of spirit. And if he can come across as outrageously egocentric at times, when he does, the claims he makes are usually justified. When the Association of British Mountain Guides failed him, on the grounds of his attitude, in the qualification tests for the guides' carnet, I was incensed, went to the then-editor of the magazine for which I write, and suggested a profile of Stevie. The editor was not a fan, and refused. So could I write it for another magazine, since he didn't want it? Not if you want to continue writing for this one was his response. My response was to get together with Stevie's and my good friend Martin Crook – one of the enduring, unique and endearingly roguish characters of Welsh climbing – and suggest that I wrote the article, included my own view in the third person, and have Martin put his name to it. Martin, who's game for any mischief, readily agreed, and this is what went out under his by-line. Thanks, Martin ... ! And thanks also to Gill Kent, the wonderfully sassy, sexy editor of* OTE, *who gladly went along with the game.*[1]

A grey, slippery morning on Millstone the day after Paul Williams' funeral.

---

[1] Maybe she felt she owed me a favour, after having been responsible for one of the closest of my near-death experiences. When Gill was a young student in Bangor and I was some kind of fading star around the region, she used to get me to give foul-mouthed, dirty-minded lectures to the university mountaineering club from time to time, and I used to see a lot of her in an entirely innocent way – I'd turned 30, she was in her teens and in a relationship with a well-known climber who had a black belt in karate, so it didn't seem proper somehow to be other than that. One early Spring afternoon we went out climbing together, came back to Bangor, went to the pub, bought a takeaway from the Chinese in Upper Bangor and were heading back along the corridor to her room in Rathbone Hall of Residence when she turned to me and, demurely, asked how come I'd never tried to fuck her? I stammered out some kind of answer which she dismissed with a wave and told me that I'd better make up for the omission that night. We arrived at the door to her room – I think I was probably pole-vaulting to get there – she opened it, walked in with me behind her, and a very muscular naked male form rose from the bed, looked at me, looked at her, picked up an ice-axe and – clearly a man of few words – enquired 'Where the fuck 'ave you been and who the fuck's this?' Gill – I'm not sure whether with tears or laughter – screeched and fled, and I – keeping careful watch on the ice-axe and in palliative tones – asked if the unclothed one would like some takeaway? He declined tersely and I left. Life, and its sweet regrets ...

Stevie Haston, Jim Perrin and myself have just flailed up *Coventry Street*, fragile after a long night in the Porter Cottage and elsewhere. Now we're sitting on boulders beneath and Stevie's talking. Stevie's always talking – or laughing, pacing, exercising, arguing, prodding or poking everything and everyone around into some semblance of the life force that sparks out of him. But now his voice has dropped a semitone, there's a mystified underlying growl, he's relating an anecdote about his father:

'I was maybe 18 and I'd fucked off from home and was living with my girl-friend in Bradford so I was climbing a lot on Almscliff and then one day my dad arrived to visit me so I took him out there. He knew nothing about climbing but I wanted to impress him. There were some Lake District guys there – Cleasby and Matheson – and I pissed all over them, they couldn't breathe the same air as me, man, I was just so fucking good and far ahead of them, and I said to my dad, "Did you see that, Dad, did you see how much better than them I was?" And I was going to tell him that they were supposed to be the best, hoping he'd be proud, but all he said was, "They can't be much good, can they son, if you're better than them?" So anyway, I ask him if he wants to try climbing a route – maybe I'm hoping to show him that it's harder than it looks – and I uncoil the rope beneath *Western Front* and show him how to belay but he doesn't like that so he just pays it out through his hands and I don't care because I've soloed it anyway and I'm not putting runners in. Then I tie on and take the rope in and he starts to climb. He swings across the hand traverse to the foot of the crack, locks off on one hand, hanging free, and feels around in it, but he finds nothing so he calls up, "What do you do here, son?" I show him how to do a locking jam, thumb into the palm and so on, he tries it, gets the idea, and just pulls up into the crack and on to the top. He was in his mid-fifties, never done a rock-climb before, E3 5c for his first one ... '

There's a silence. I ask about the effect, whether it had depressed him. He responds by asking why should it? After all, his dad was right – if he could do *Western Front* in his fifties as his first route, it couldn't be that hard, could it?

The message was that it was an easy route and he'd have to try harder. I'm not buying into this, so I just shut up and listen to him hammering on about his dad, about his toughness, his capacity to hide pain, his being of the stuff to which moun-taineers aspire. He describes seeing his dad kicked straight in the balls in an East End fight and not flinching, just picking up his opponent and laying him out before going off to hospital himself to be operated on for a ruptured testicle:

'I tried to gain love and respect in my father's eyes, but he'd done it all already – grown up in Edinburgh – the poor part – in the 1930s (I think my dad and Dougal's dad were cousins), been a cook's boy on whaling ships, led a mutiny in World War

Two on his merchant ship and strikes in the construction industry in London. He used to tell me stories of knife fights in Zanzibar brothels and lions walking down the street. It's really sad now that he's old and paralysed, all that strength gone ... '

That's just one side of the childhood. Now he's off into scenes from Maltese – his mother's from Malta – summers, one incident after another rattling out to test your belief. I believe him. Fishing with his grandfather from the cliffs, VS climbing to be soloed across on the approaches to the ledges – oh yes, and waves and deaths – not his, but always this awareness, right through the life – Malta, East End, mountains, always the sense of life's precariousness, of the need for courage, resourcefulness, total self-reliance: 'Me and my cousin were up a tree and he fell, got impaled on a dead branch and it ripped his belly open so that his guts spilled out – yards of them, man, I couldn't believe it – and he had to walk back to my grandparents holding them in front of him and then they put him in a wheelbarrow to get him to the doctors miles away. But he lived, man, he fucking survived ... '

These strange stories, but there's something stranger still. There's been this guy in our midst for 25 years and I'll just bore you with a catalogue, with some chronological babble, about what he's done: leading extreme, and not just soft-touch but difficult stuff on bad gear like *Neb Direct* (no Friends then, remember!) when he was 15; Alpine TD and Grade V Scottish at the same age; Alpine winter season at 16, including first solo ascent of Col du Plan Direct; late-teen Yorkshire grit aficionado, with solo ascents pre-sticky-rubber of *Wall of Horrors, Slip'n'Slide, Goliath, Edge Lane, All Quiet, Small Brown,* etc; second winter ascent of 1938 Route on the Eiger, February '78; pissed up *Right Wall* a month later; moved to Wales in '79 and really got under way: on-sight flashed second ascent of *Cockblock*; first grade VII ice route in the world with *Terminator* in '80; on-sight ascent of *Obelisk* E6 6b on South Stack (one of the first routes of this grade in the country and done on-sight, completely without inspection); first of the great slate routes with *Comes the Dervish* ('82); solos of routes like *Positron*; first British solo of the north face of Les Droites, winter '83 in ridiculously fast time; first free solo of the Walker Spur in '84; stacks of routes at E6 and E7 in Wales – *Isis is Angry, Free Stonehenge, My Secret Garden*; and then he goes and wrecks himself in manic, legendary training sessions, him and Leigh McGinleigh competing; sets of 50 pull-ups with 100lbs round his waist. One night Leigh does 1000, and 2000 fingertip press-ups. Stevie does 2000 pull-ups, 3000 press-ups. What does this equal? Chronic tendonitis, crippled elbows, spasmodic climbing, but he still gets to be one of the first Brits to onsight French 7c; injury, and depression at the frequency with which his routes – *Fear of Rejection, Lost Castle of My Desires* – fall down (says something, surely, about the man who put them up!), combined with the need to work, cause his climbing to go into abeyance in the late 1980s; rejuvenation comes with a trip to Shivling in 1990 on which he met his partner of six years and now wife, Laurence Gouault with whom he went to live in much more congenial Chamonix, since which move he's on-sighted F8a, redpointed 8c (*Maginot Line, Voix*), made first ascents of two of only five grade VII ('That's Scottish grade nine,' he points out) ice-cascades in the world; first free solo of the Walker Spur in winter, in eight hours, after La Destivelle, using aid, had taken three-and-a-half days and had a helicopter meet her at the summit; the first ascent of the hardest mixed climb in Chamonix with *Scotch on the Rocks* on Mont Blanc de Tacul; repeated Jeff Lowe's *Octopussy* at Vail, Colorado – Scottish grade ten – this year in two hours without falls, and put up his own route, *After Eight*, also Scottish grade ten, in the same week that he led *Pink Flamingos*, a 5.13b finger-crack; oh yeah – and he's freeclimbed all sorts of old aid routes around Chamonix – F7c at altitude; put up the world's highest 8a, *Garhwali Porter*, at 4400m at Tapovan; 'It's basically a huge 50-ft boulder – I did it to entertain the locals, named it in their honour, and I put four protection bolts in to point out that the real defilement is what climbers do to and leave on the mountain, and to wind up no-marks who spout on when they've done fuck all and know fuck all'; ran up Shivling in nine hours, as well as climbing a sheaf of other Himalayan peaks of between 6500-7000m the names of which had better be kept quiet if he wants to go there again.

If you're of the opinion that this adds up to rather more all-round achievement than the row of beans your average Jack or Jill can trade in for endless publicity and sponsorship, then solve this puzzle: why aren't the magazines full of him? Why've you barely heard of him? How come he's not been on every major Himalayan trip in the last 15 years?

So I go round to Perrin's house, on the hill by Bus Stop Quarry. Stevie and Laurence are staying here, the old one-eyed rebel's given up his bed to them, has just crawled out of his sleeping bag and is groaning around making his first pot of coffee of the morning when I arrive.

'The deal is, Martin,' he starts off – Perrin grew up, if he grew up at all, in the 1960s, so his talk's laced with this hippyspeak – 'that the direction Stevie's going and the direction climbing's going are divergent in Britain. The stuff he does needs balls, whereas the sport in this country is mostly just for twats. So given that climbing's got this crucial metaphorical dimension around inner quest – you know, Mount Analogue and all that – what's happening is that a massive crevasse is opening up between good and bad faith in mountaineering. Which gives rise to a pretty interesting dynamic. The magazines, with all their ripped-muscle quasi-porn and training regimes, increasingly represent the wannabe stuff, with its mind-numbing conventions, assessment-by-number, and achievement reckoned by treading the paths of others. All that is essentially security-minded and defined – it's career stuff at root, but masquerading as heroism, and hence in bad faith. What Stevie does is something quite different, and pretty close to what Ortega y Gasset was talking about when he commented that "the will to be oneself is heroism." Well Stevie can't be like the rest – he's got to be himself. So he's placed in this position of being an authentic individual in a false set-up. Those who control the set-up know they're acting in bad faith, but they don't have his courage, can't step outside the structures which support them and which they hate Stevie for exposing as false. Take the debacle over his guides' certificate winter assessment. Fred Harper, who's a past president of the ABMG and generally a good, insightful guy who's unthreatened by original talent when he sees it, told me he'd seen the assessor's notes, and that Stevie had passed every single day. But they still failed him, and said it was because of his attitude. If you look a bit more into what this supposed attitude problem was, you find he disagreed with a few decisions when he had a right to do so, argued over matters of technique with some of the assessors when there was no question of Stevie's own technique being wrong, and was supposedly "difficult". That sounds to me more like their problem in not being able to cope with his lack of respect when they'd done nothing to earn it. He had no problems with Allen Fyffe, for example, whom he knows to be rock-solid and a down-the-line enthusiast. So why should he toady round these others, and be judged like the rest of the frightened little rabbits on his capacity to do so? I was talking with Joe (Brown) about this last week. We've both climbed with Stevie and we both know what he's like in tense situations, and we both agreed that when it came to Joe's grandchildren, or my son Will, the only person we'd consider using as a guide for them would be Stevie. Strikes me they cracked under the pressure of coming face to face with authentic talent. It makes me fucking angry, the way established orders do people like Stevie down, and it comes purely from envy – you know, Kleinian envy – the desire to destroy that which you can't and don't possess, and by which, in consequence, you're horribly threatened – and the realisation of their own inadequacy, and that's what Stevie suffers from all the way through. No, the mags won't give him publicity, because if they did, their pet assessors' verdicts on half of what's reported would be made to look stupid, and the system has to maintain itself, so we can't have that, can we?'

Perrin goes shuffling off into the kitchen to make more coffee, smiling beatifically at having delivered himself of his first rant of the morning. I shout upstairs at Stevie to quit his uxorious ways and come down so I can interview him, and in due course he and Laurence blearily descend and we sit down to talk.

Picking up from a point in Perrin's previous diatribe, I ask him about this guides' business. Was he pissed off about it? Of course he was, but the point is, that if an organisation is left to police itself with no independent review or appeal procedures, it will only come to one conclusion, which is that it's right. The facts, Stevie claims, vindicate him, and yet he's rejected by the authority on attitude, which comes down to suitability and Britishness. 'I feel sad,' he concludes, 'that they shamed themselves.'

What does he mean, I wonder, when he talks about Britishness? He pulls a very Latin face, explains patiently about the old boy network and if your identikit face fits. Identikit face? 'Yeah – mild-mannered, understated, self-deprecatory humour but don't you ever challenge it or take it for real or you end up like Perrin here did with that libel case because in fact it masks huge egotism.' But people, I point out, might accuse him of that, and of massive arrogance – does he think he is? He shrugs, he doesn't know, not his place to comment, so I ask Jim:

'He's not arrogant, he just comes across like that because we're unused to people demanding recognition of the effort they've put into their project instead of coming out with the usual blah about, "Oh, yah, it was nothing, you know, I'm just so naturally wonderful I don't even have to try." I think in many ways, and especially where it matters, which is towards the mountain regions of the world and the real people who live amongst them, he's very respectful, very modest. The whole thing with Stevie is not being threatened by him, but just accepting him for the noisy little mix of genius and imbecile, hero and twat that he is. I keep telling him that he should stop looking over his shoulder all the time and grieving about the publicity all these useless fuckers are getting. If he sticks to his own path, he'll get recognition for that, because in terms of all-round ability he's maybe the best Brit there's ever been, and certainly the best since Al Rouse had his very brief heyday in the 1970s.'

Stevie cuts him off. There's this incessant benign slagging-off goes on between these two, which is quite a good way to deal with Stevie, who is physically intimidating in a way that Whillans was. There are plenty of stories, like breaking a guy's leg like a rotten stick when he tried to bully him in the bar of the Padarn Lake hotel but when you analyse them, as with Whillans, there's always plenty of provocation, the violence never gratuitous. He's away again now about the British scene, compares it to the French, who are more likely to talk about the nature and style of the sport, he claims, if you can stop them talking about themselves. 'But the Brits are more conservative, climbing here is stuck in a hole. The good climber here, if he wants to get his livelihood from it, has to follow a standard formula: excel first at technical rock, proceed to the big walls, graduate to the high mountains by easy routes, so all the time you're moving away from the sphere where demands are made on the technical levels of your performance and you're losing the edge. This is why you get all the mystique and bullshit about 8000m peaks expounded by mediocre climbers. But if you think about it, they can't be any big deal. Useless women and fat old men stroll up them. Alison Hargreaves, who for all her virtues and relative fitness was hardly an elite climber, did Everest as her first and K2 as her second in a space of months.'

End of story, Britain doesn't have a Loretan, Stevie didn't burn off the cream of British alpinists when barely out of his 'teens without knowing this.

Hang on, Stevie, I demur, isn't this getting to sound a bit sexist? He's straight back at me with it being about standards and not sex. 'It's easy for women to get publicity on that account – look at Catherine Destivelle, Rebecca Stephens, Alison Hargreaves – but that's not what matters. The idea that you're somehow sanctified by possessing a fanny is just stupid.' Achievement, he suggests, is an absolute, the role model to whom women should aspire is Lynn Hill, who doesn't play the gender game, she plays the climbing game on entirely equal terms, but manipulation of the media by less gifted and committed women has the effect of concealing the reality and scale of her achievement.

I divert him on to routines of his life in France. He trains with professional dedication, huge runs, weights, the gym. Maybe he'll go out and do a hard cascade in the morning, go sport-climbing or extreme skiing in the afternoon, or go for a fast time on an alpine route. Mixing the disciplines, he explains, keeps his interest high, and then he's off into appreciation of ice – one thing not to expect from Stevie is the functionalist view – he's steeped in the aesthetic, blathers on about ice being fantastically ethereal and bizarre, glistening, beautiful, like the sets for *Alien*, and then he's away into sci-fi movies, 3D exposure, *Predators*, weird helmets, tinkling crystals, a delirium of snowflakes – OK, OK, but this is the man, remember, who brought tights to climbing. Since we're talking about ice, I ask him about Scottish ice, and he responds that he knows the Scots will hate him for saying so, but it's obvious to him that there are no hard ice-climbs in Scotland. Hard mixed, then? Without a doubt, and the hardest in the world, which is why he called his route on Mont Blanc de Tacul *Scotch on the Rocks*.

It's your pursuit of excellence, I tell him, that is part of the reason why you get people's backs up. Right, he agrees, because it exposes their weaknesses, because obsession's a dirty word in Britain. So you're obsessed, I press?

'I have psychopathic tendencies,' he laughs, 'everyone knows that. When I train, when I climb, I do it with an intensity no-one here uses. This is a country of amateurs. And that leads them to a sort of sloppiness in thinking and performing that I absolutely hate, man. There's this preoccupation with success, which Perrin here would probably tell us is spelt suck-cess, and it's all corrupt because it's concerned with nationalism, ego, gender, instead of style. They forget that it's not the destination but the journey which matters, and in that, it's style, and what you learn along it, which are crucial. Also, it's the people you climb with. Like for me, Laurence is my favourite climbing partner, and that's brought a kind of stability to my life, but it's a bit double-edged, because she doesn't like me risking it. And I never climb with people I dislike – that's why I'll even go out with this old bastard ... '

He takes a sly hack at Perrin's legs. 'So where's the project, where's the Grail, where's the path up which all this leads?' I ask. He goes quiet.

'I think about doing the eight thousanders in a year. Maybe it's possible for an obsessive, extremely fit climber, willing to take risks and with the blessing of the gods. I think about Lhotse south face, which is still unclimbed, maybe with Alain Ghersen, alpine-style, fast. On that, you'd be right in the lap of the gods. It keeps me awake at nights ... '

The hazel eyes roll, the wild, raptor-profile tilts back. He might just do either of them. This guy is, in terms of achieved standards, not arguably but undoubtedly the best all-round climber Britain's ever produced. He's world-class, the best we have. If he was any other sort of athlete than a rock/ice/mountain athlete, he wouldn't have to remind us himself how good he is – he'd be celebrated and rewarded without reservation. Why can't all these small dicks just see that and be generous? His reply to my last question sets me thinking across 16 years to when we were on the first ascent of *Obelisk* at South Stack. I'm belaying, scanning up to where he's silhouetted on the arête as it cuts through great roofs. He's struggling to get gear in, obviously shagged. When he can't get a piece to fit, he just lobs it in the sea. So much for the securities in which you invest. He gets to the stance, passes out. When he comes round he tells me not to fall off. He's belayed on two number-one stoppers in sandy shite. The belay pegs from when it was an aid route are rotted stumps. I don't fall. It still keeps me awake at nights. Whom the gods love ... !

I ask Perrin, who's stalking about with a mad expression, brandishing a pair of calipers like he intends taking Stevie's vital statistics, for a summary comment:

'The thing about climbing is that it's a sport continually reducing itself, giving the appearance of depth and shedding its reality. Climbers don't want to see this because they want to be heroes. But a hero's like a Buddhist – if you claim to be one or want to be one, then you're not. What you need to realise is that the real hero, whoever he or she may be, is out there grappling with the monsters from necessity of character, comes back humbled and changed by the conflict and bringing gifts. Who d'you want to listen to and where d'you want to be – on the Grail quest or in the Waste Land? It's your choice, and I know which one, give or take a few minor strayings of attention, Stevie has made ... '

Laurence looks wistful. The lines deepen on Parsifal's brow. He'll be praying again tonight in the icy chapel of his dreams.

13: THE CHARACTER, LIFE AND TIMES OF HW TILMAN (1988)

Tilman was one of the most extraordinary characters I ever met, and certainly one of the great explorers of the 20th century. I've written often on him – what follows is the text of a Royal Geographical Society Lecture.

I'm honoured to be asked to speak about HW Tilman tonight, and very pleased to do so in aid of the Wishing Well Fund – which is probably the only aspect of tonight's proceedings of which Tilman himself would have approved.

I'm also conscious that my acceptance of the invitation is slightly fraudulent. I knew Tilman only for a very short period right at the end of his very long life. There will be others here tonight who knew him far better and for much longer than I did. It would nonetheless be bogus to pretend that I'm anything other than delighted to be able to speak here, at the RGS, about a man who held the highest award, the Founder's Medal, of The Royal Geographical Society, and who certainly had a more profound effect upon me than any other man I've ever met.

The question is where to begin. There is, as you'll know, a 350-page biography and even that's only a more-or-less cursory narrative of the events of his life. There are his own books – 15 in number and each of them a distinguished contribution to the literature of travel, or mountaineering, or sailing, or all three because really they're impossible to categorise. And then there's Tilman's character, and it's with this, as it came through in his writings, in his conversations, and in the response of others to him, that I'd like chiefly to deal.

I'll presume that you're familiar with the simple record: with his mountaineering in the 1930s, often in company with Eric Shipton, which took in first ascents such as that of the West Ridge of Mount Kenya – as a novice – in 1930; and of Nanda Devi, the highest summit to be climbed in the pre-war period, in 1936; with his explorations in the Himalayas – up the Rishi Ganga to the Nanda Devi sanctuary in 1934; or on the 1935 Mount Everest reconnaissance expedition; or with the 1937 'Blank on the Map' trip with Shipton, Auden and Spender which contributed so much to knowledge of the Karakoram. And finally as leader of the 1938 Everest expedition – as a single decade of mountain exploration it's unsurpassed, and only equalled by his friend Shipton, with whom so much of it was shared.

Then there's his war record – on the Western Front in the Great War; in the

Western Desert – which he found boring – and behind enemy lines in Albania and the Dolomites in the Second World War, for which he was awarded the DSO, the MC and bar and made a freeman of the city of Belluno. After the last war there's brief service as a British Consul in Burma and then an extraordinary period of five years when he was continually travelling; through China, Nepal, Sinkiang, Kashmir, the Gobi Desert, Afghanistan. Finally, 23 years and 150,000 miles of sailing – in Bristol Channel pilot-cutters built at the turn of the century – to the Antarctic, Patagonia, Greenland, Spitzbergen.

It is not an ordinary life and it was not an ordinary man who lived it and you knew that from the moment you first met him. In my case that was on top of Cader Idris on a snowy day in the 1970s. I'd come up a snow gully with my dog, which was fortuitous – he liked dogs. One of his favourite quotations was the supposed maxim of Frederick the Great – 'The more I see of humanity, the more I love my dog.' I went into the summit shelter, which was banked high inside with driven snow, took out my flask and sandwiches, and then one of those meetings which are among the greatest pleasures of being in the hills took place. A short and rather shabbily-dressed old man with an old-fashioned rucksack came in. My dog barked at him, and his face, which was alive with good humour, registered an amused displeasure at finding another person there. He sat down, made friends with my dog, drank my coffee, and grumbled aloud at the intrusion on his privacy.

There is, you should understand, a sort of freemasonry about mountaineering. It doesn't consist of rolled trouser-legs, bared breasts, rubbed knuckles or any of that nonsense; it exists through mutuality and not propagation of interest; and the induction process is utterly straightforward. You have to be in the right place at the right time and that in itself is a declaration which establishes a degree of trust. So for the next few months after this winter meeting, I saw Tilman regularly and talked with him at considerable length. Initially I didn't know very much about him. I'd heard about him from a friend of mine who'd sailed with him – Ian Duckworth – who'd told me that 'he's a bastard, an absolute bastard,' and then modulated his criticism by adding 'But he's a hard old bastard!' – which to Ian was the highest praise. I'd read perhaps half-a-dozen of his books and I had the feeling that they were the best thing in mountaineering literature. I should say that at that time this point of view was heterodox. Mountain writing in the 1970s was dominated by a new style of breathless, tell-it-all solipsism and self-aggrandisement and Tilman's cultured clarity, detached irony, wit, and self-effacement were entirely unfashionable.

He lived in a house called Bodowen near Barmouth, and I began to visit him there. I was rather intimidated by him at first – not through any action of his, but through an aura of moral solidity which someone brought up as I was, in the 1960s on sex-and-drugs-and-rock'n'roll, would inevitably find rather bracing.

We did, however, have two great loves in common – one for the mountains and one for 18th-century literature, and it was the latter which for those few months brought us together.

You'll be aware of the language and the ideas of 18th-century literature – its ironies, its moral questioning, the vein of misanthropy which runs through much of it. Tilman to me was an embodiment of these, and to him I was a partner in an extended conversation which could be conducted in those terms.

When I met him he was 78, and within the year he would be dead. Our conversations were retrospective over the matter of his life. He was old and lonely. He felt isolated and anachronistic. His last boat, *Baroque*, had been left in Iceland because of crew trouble. He needed someone in those last few months to whom he could talk and to whom he could vindicate himself. Don't take from this the impression that these conversations were solemn – they were far from it. If Tilman ever caught himself out in the act of being po-faced, you could be sure that a joke directed against himself would result. The most celebrated instance of this is the famous line about himself and Odell reaching the top of Nanda Devi:

'I believe we so far forgot ourselves as to shake hands on it.'

Where he obviously feels that the solemnity of the preceding climbing account now needs to be punctured. It's a curious comment on the critical acumen of readers of mountain writing that for many years this was taken literally as an example of how pukka sahibs behaved on reaching the top of their mountains.

There was a quality in Tilman's humour which, both when you read it and when you talked to him personally, was somehow disturbing. A lot of it's concerned with making a joke about misanthropy, but the joke is ambivalent, has a sub-text. You laugh, yet you sense the laughter's really a way of accommodating yourself to the fact of a very deep-seated dislike of the human race. As an example of this, I once asked him how many of the stories told about himself were apocryphal and his response was this:

'By far the greater number, but there is one which is substantially true. It was on an expedition in the 1930s. We embarked at Tilbury, and I am said to have stayed on deck until we rounded the North Foreland, whereupon I was heard to mutter the words, "H'm, sea!"

'After this I went below decks and was not seen again until we hove in sight of Bombay. I then came on deck once more and was duly heard to utter the words, "H'm, land!"

'It is asserted that these were the only words I uttered on the entire voyage, which is more or less the truth of the matter, and the reason, quite simply, is that I could not stand the other chaps on that trip.'

He looked at me long and hard to study the effect, then burst into an alcoholic chuckle. (The drinking of beer in Tilman's house began at 12 o'clock sharp – it being decadent to drink in the morning – which meant that by one o'clock I was general-ly drunk, which explains why my pictures of him are often out of focus. He remained unaffected.) I've never heard anything like this story from any other source, and I'm fairly sure that it was a piece of extemporisation on Tilman's part. Of course, it's not a joke, not really – it's a parable, in which, if you like, he's setting forth his moral relationship with the world: the voyage; being below decks; seeing sea; see-ing land; but above all shunning the company of his fellow men.

Why?

Consider these images from his life: Berkhamsted School, 1914; the military academy at Woolwich, 1915; his 18th birthday, on February 14th, 1916, which he spent in a dugout on the Somme: 'We lost our best sergeant the other day, up at the Observation Post. A whizz-bang came through the window as he was looking out. It's always the way – the best fellows get done in, the rotters escape.'

Nobody as sensitively intelligent as Tilman could have hoped to have survived this experience at this time of his life unscathed. I asked him about it once:

'What about the Great War?'

He looked at me very sharply, shook his head, and in the heaviest silence turned away. This was 60 years after it. To my knowledge, the only thing he wrote about it was this:

'After the first war, when one took stock, shame mingled with satisfaction at finding oneself still alive. One felt a bit like the Ancient Mariner: so many better men, a few of them friends, were dead:

'And a thousand thousand slimy things lived on; and so did I.'

A part of the fascination of Tilman's life is that it has about it an almost mythical resonance. Little more than a month after his 18th birthday, this Valentine's-Day Child misanthropist is wounded for the first time – a flesh wound in the thigh. It's King Pellinor. It's Philoctetes. You see the start of the process by which the man ultimately seeks to understand this incomprehensible world through myth, and indeed the mythopoeic tendency in writers who endured and survived the Great War is startling: Robert Graves in pursuit of the White Goddess;

192

the Celtic Synthesis of David Jones. With Tilman it's the modern Odyssey, which takes him far away from what we presume to call civilisation – his attitude towards which, particularly after the Second World War, had hardened into an almost Swiftian rage and rancour:

'There is a good case for dropping bombs on civilians because so very few of them can be described as inoffensive ... '

It's interesting to observe in Tilman's language that he frequently uses the inflated vocabulary of Great War reportage and non-participation – gallant, ardent, warriors, vanquished, radiant and so on – when his ironies are biting most deeply. I don't know how many of you have been reading the Falklands war memoir of Captain Robert Lawrence which has been serialised in the *Observer* over the last couple of weeks? In that memoir you have the same process at work, this splitting off of private from public perception in the mind of the highly intelligent young officer. The image with which Lawrence presents us, of a man rejected and humiliated by those on whose account he has had half his brain shot away, and who can yet see more clearly and sensitively than those who have used him thus, is startling, shaming, and obscene:

'In the country of the blind, the one-eyed man is king.'

It is something like this, in my view, which caused Tilman in 1919 to shake the dust of Europe off his shoes and set out for a new Eden, wherever it could be found. Once he'd found it, years later among the Sherpas and hill people of the Himalayas, he was concerned to keep it undespoiled. Here's what he has to say in *Nepal Himalaya*: 'Like Tibet, Nepal has always sought isolation and has secured it by excluding foreigners, of whom the most undesirable were white men.

'A man fortunate enough to have been admitted into Nepal is expected to be able to explain on general grounds the motives behind this invidious policy and, on personal grounds, the reason for such an unaccountable exception. But now that the advantages of the western way of life are becoming every day less obvious no explanation should be needed. Wise men traditionally come from the East, and it is probable that to them the West and its ways were suspect long before we ourselves began to have doubts.'

It's very notable in his writing that the only period in which he indulges himself in celebration of his fellow men is that of his Himalayan travels, and even then it's only one faction among them about whom he writes with attentiveness and affection – the Sherpas and native porters – Pasang Kikuli, Naiad Shah, Nukku, Norbu, Mir Hamza, Da Namgyal, Tenzing, Angtharkay. And the affection was reciprocated. Here's Norbu, 40 years on:

'Tilman was always first away in the morning, carrying a load in excess of the standard Sherpa load. He always arrived first at the day's destination. Sometimes he would run along parts of the route. He would have tea brewing by the time the rest caught up with him and then he would praise those who had made good time and yell and scream at those he thought had been lazy or lacking in some way. On at least one rest day he made all his Sherpas a cake. Tashi, the Sherpa who was translating what Norbu said, was made to repeat this fact several times.'

It was an idyll, and it couldn't last. By the early 1950s those Europeans whom he sought to avoid had begun to catch him up:

'The Himalaya are extensive, no less than 1,500 miles in length, but a quiet man might well shrink from going, say, to Katmandu if he thought he was likely to meet there 11 other parties with their 5,000 porters.'

So he took to the sea and he did so, appropriately enough because there is a mischievous, subversive or even seditious element in his writing, in a Bristol Channel pilot-cutter built in 1906 and called *Mischief*:

'In the years between 1954 when I bought her, and 1968 when I lost her, the possession of an old pilot-cutter called *Mischief* enabled me to visit some remote regions north and south. In those 15 years she sailed some 110,000 miles. She was not that big, 45ft long overall, but she was an able sea boat, kind on her gear and kind on her crew.'

The problem with boats is that if they're of a certain type and above a certain size, you have to sail them with other people, and you'll know Dr Johnson's thoughts on that:

'No man will be a sailor who has contrivance enough to get himself into a jail; for being in a ship is being in a jail, with the chance of being drowned.'

And at another time:

'A man in jail has more room, better food, and commonly better company.'

Post-war sailing carries with it, of course, a set of social attitudes ranging from the Neanderthal to the palaeolithic. It's a true-blue sport where pride of possession takes pride of place. So again, we have what this time is a very amusing distancing effect between Tilman and the society of his time. On the one hand he was making phenomenal voyages in ancient wooden boats to some of the world's most inhospitable waters, and being recognised and honoured for doing so – he was given the Fellowship of the Royal Institute of Navigation, the CBE, the Blue Water Medal of the Cruising Club of America and the Goldsmith Award of the Royal Cruising Club. On the other hand, his style of voyaging and the reports of his more disaffected crew members were drawing the wrath of the yacht-polishing fraternity. In the trade journals which masquerade as their magazines, members of the latter were earnestly seeking to polish off his reputation. There were scurrilous representations of him as 'a desperate old man, repeatedly wrecking his unseaworthy old boats and maltreating his crews.' Andrew Craig-Bennett's reply to one of those attacks in the correspondence columns of *Yachting Monthly* for January 1982, gives in passing a very clear picture of what it was like to sail with Tilman:

'Mr Beavis' article raises a rather important question. What does constitute safety in yachting? We have grown accustomed to long voyages made in sponsored boats with every possible facility and for years past the safety industry and the RYA have been trying to persuade us to buy expensive safety equipment, and to obtain expensive pieces of paper called Yachtmasters' Certificates. Accidents have continued to happen – the possessor of an RYA ticket is just as likely to do something daft as the next man. I am appalled by the attitude of those numerous yachtsmen who seem to imagine that because they carry liferafts, radio-telephone, lifejackets and so forth they are thereby safer. Safety is an attitude of mind, and Tilman was a very safe man to sail with. He never sought publicity or sponsorship. He sailed to the places he wanted to visit without fuss and in doing so enabled a number of young men who would never have been able to do so in their own boat to share the experience. No-one was compelled to sail with him. All he asked in return for providing the boat and the provisions was that one should muck in and get on with the job in hand. His irritation with those who, having eaten his food and perhaps deprived others of a place, decided to tell him how to sail his own boat is quite understandable. His safety record compares rather well with that of certain competitors in recent offshore races, despite all their safety equipment. Sailing in high latitudes is bound to be more dangerous than crossing The Solent, but he always took care to minimise the risks and act prudently. His achievements speak for themselves.'

It was a teasing irony that the annual Fastnet Race of 1978 to which Craig-Bennett is referring and which ended so tragically, took place on the weekend of Tilman's memorial service. Tilman's own view of the matter was succinct:

'In my view every herring should hang by its own tail. Anyone venturing into unfrequented and possibly dangerous waters does so with his eyes open, should be willing to depend on his own exertions, and should neither expect nor ask for help. The confidence that is placed, and successfully placed, in being rescued fosters carelessness or even foolishness, and condones ignorance.'

Be careful how far you give your assent to that judgement, because it's more astringent than most of us here can stomach. Interpret it in socio-political terms and you have one of the operative levels of Mrs Thatcher's dream society.

It's a stance which reads us, which exposes our fears and inadequacies, but which also reflects our longing for that strength and independence of spirit. You see in it the sustaining power of myth, but to live out that myth is beyond the spiritual resources of most of us.

I last saw Tilman in the summer of 1977. His last boat *Baroque* – third and last of his pilot-cutters – was back from Iceland. He was calm and a little morbid, curiously resigned and prepared for his own death. I spent a morning with him. He talked about Christianity, the deaths of friends and particularly that of Eric Shipton, with whom he'd shared much of his mountain exploration in the great decade of the 1930s. He told a few jokey stories, but was otherwise quiet and subdued.

A week or two later the house was shut up, the dogs kenneled, and he was on his way from Southampton to the Antarctic as a crew member of the 24-year-old Simon Richardson's boat, *En Avant* – a steel-hulled tug converted to a gaff-rigged cutter. They arrived in Rio de Janeiro on 25th October 1977, and left for Port Stanley on 1st November.

Thereafter, no sign, no signal, no trace. If you believe in extra-sensory perception, there's the dream of Simon Frazer – a young explorer in the Tilman mould. He woke from it on an early November night in the Himalayas – a dream of a hull upturned and keelless, rolling in heavy seas, which he somehow knew to be connected with Tilman. The myth ends in Avalonian uncertainty, but its pattern holds:

> *Come, my friends,*
> *'Tis not too late to seek a newer world.*
> *Push off, and sitting well in order smite*
> *The sounding furrows; for my purpose holds*
> *To sail beyond the sunset, and the baths*
> *Of all the western stars, until I die.*

14: THE ONLY GENUINE JOE: A TRIBUTE (1998)

Mountaineering is such an odd sport. Maybe it's the range of environments in which it takes place having an effect on those participants who remain unblinded by their own egos, or maybe it's just a by-product of the clash of those egos, but it has a levelling tendency. Self-promotion is met with mockery. Few of its would-be heroes escape reductive scrutiny. A corollary to this is that accident and failure are often accorded greater respect than organisation or success. The disaster-prone, the over-reachers, the never-quite men become more celebrated than the quiet achievers. Yet even from this mess of reduction and distortion there are few, when reminded, who would refuse to accord heroic status and prime historical significance to one figure above all others.

I should say at the outset that I probably shouldn't be writing about Joe Brown because he's been my hero since I first began to climb, and in the province of climbing, as far as I'm able to retain one, he remains so. Heroism, and all the attachment and projection stuff that goes with it, is suspect these days, and rightly so. And I like Joe enormously. I've known him since I was a little, scrawny kid first setting out in climbing nearly 40 years ago, and he was good to me then. You never should forget early kindnesses. The mark of a person is the way they are to those who have nothing to offer. So don't expect this piece to be a critical overview. I'll leave people who think they're bigger than Joe is to do the knocking.

Biography first and the background's legendary. Joe was born in a tiny terraced house under a railway viaduct in the Manchester inner-city slum of Ardwick in the autumn of 1930, seventh and last child of a poor Catholic family. His father, sporadically both builder and sailor, died of gangrene after a shipboard accident when Joe was eight months old. Thereafter, his mother was left to provide through cleaning work and taking in laundry. In a rough, poor environment, the arts of self-sufficiency root strongly: 'A fatherless upbringing and a hard but happy home life encouraged me to fend for myself,' he noted laconically in his 1967 autobiography, *The Hard Years* (which was ghosted from taped conversations with Pete Crew, and doesn't really capture Joe's playfulness or wit). His early experiences of school were unsympathetic. In the 1940 blitz of Manchester even the buildings themselves were bombed, the children seldom able to attend for more than half a day a week at improvised venues with whatever teachers were available. Joe left at 14, without qualifications, to work for a jobbing builder.

There was a post-war, northern, street-kid tradition, in which I had the good fortune also to be reared, which offset these deprivations. The Pennine moors whose profiles were visible from any open space in Manchester were a cheap bus-ride away, and the ragamuffin hordes straggled into them every weekend in quest of any game with an element of danger in it: 'By my twelfth birthday I knew that going into the country was more satisfying to me than anything else.' At first it was child's play – rope swings across gorges and the like. It gravitated to pot-holing and perilous explorations of the old mineshafts at Alderley Edge with ropes taken from road-menders' huts. Inevitably, the progression was to climbing, and for Joe this began in the arctic conditions of early 1947 on Kinder Downfall: 'In hobnailed boots and with cumbersome rucksacks on our backs the ascent was distinctly awkward. I climbed the rocks beside the waterfall with a heavy brewer's rope coiled round my shoulders. On reaching the top I threw it down for my companions to follow with its protection.'

The rapidity with which Joe went on from that early encounter to become the most significant figure in British climbing's post-war epoch, and perhaps the major character in the entire history of the sport, is astounding. Within weeks this short, slight, impoverished 16-year-old who was almost totally ignorant of the traditions, venues and techniques of the sport had begun, seconded by others who were equal-ly uninformed, to lead mountain rock-climbs at the highest contemporary standard. His native talent needed an educated and organisational ability to lead it on to fame and achievement. He found it through a chance meeting at Kinder Downfall in the spring of 1947 with Merrick 'Slim' Sorrell.

Sorrell was three years older than Brown, and a pipe-fitter from Stockport whose solid and knowledgeable company underpinned the first phase of Brown's pioneering on rock. That their ability was notably higher than the prevailing stan-dards of the day was established on a visit to North Wales. They'd looked at *Lot's Groove* on Glyder Fach – one of the harder contemporary climbs in Wales. Two well-known climbers to whom they talked informed them that it was only to be tried after an initial ascent on a top-rope and the consumption of a bar of chocolate: 'Having no bar of chocolate we dispensed with a top-rope inspection and climbed the route on sight. We couldn't understand what all the fuss was about.' On the same holiday Joe made an ascent of *Suicide Wall* in Cwm Idwal – undoubtedly the hardest climb of its time in Britain. 'I didn't find it too bad,' he told me many years later, 'people had a mental block then about "hard" climbs.' For Joe, this was certainly not the case, and by the summer of 1948, having mastered the most difficult of the existing climbs, he began turning out his own repertoire. Initially these climbs were on dif-ficulty's traditional forcing ground of the gritstone edges, and his ability was now bolstered by being at the centre of a group of climbers from the Manchester and

Derby areas who had formed themselves into the Valkyrie Club.

On Stanage and Froggatt, Wimberry, Dovestones and The Roaches, the routes that marked British rock-climbing's post-war revolution and brought its achievement in line with pre-war continental standards were forged. Long-standing problems feared and revered by the sport's elders were vanquished beneath the insouciant plimsolls of a ragged and humorous 17-year-old youth. There were rumours of fearless attempts and fearful falls on lines deemed impossible by the pre-war greats. The famous episode on Clogwyn Du'r Arddu's *Vember* was one of them; whilst climbing in wet conditions, Joe fell and two strands of his hemp rope sawed through as it rubbed down a vertical edge, a further potentially fatal fall only averted by friends pouncing on him before he plunged from the ledge above the Drainpipe Crack. In a sport where the channels of information were hearsay and partial witness, a myth was born, and soon augmented by its enactor's disappearance for two years on National Service. When he returned, from Singapore in 1950, the greatest decade in the exploration of Britain's rock outcrops and mountain crags began.

It derived much of its impetus from two factors: the formation in September 1951 of the Rock & Ice Climbing Club by a group of climbers living for the most part near to Joe's home in south Manchester; and the growing association throughout 1951 between Joe and Don Whillans. This partnership between the two men, whilst never exclusive or even particularly amicable, was to become the most significant in modern climbing history. Much later, after the collapse both of their climbing partnership and indeed their friendship, Brown could still write the following of Whillans: 'The plain fact about climbing with Don was that if you got into difficulties, or couldn't manage to get up at a particular point on a climb, the chances were that he could pull something out of the bag. It followed that climbing with Don was that much safer than with anyone else. He is the best rock-climber I have ever known ... '

Given the fact that Joe didn't like Don and was never wholly at ease in his company off the rock, the generosity of that assessment is a telling reflection on Joe's character. As a team, the two men were formidable, their abilities complementing each other to an extraordinary degree, Whillans' boldness and physical strength balancing Brown's inspired improvisations and innate rock-sense. Their first significant climb together came at August bank holiday, 1951, when they joined forces in an attempt on a tenuous line of cracks up the right wall of *Cenotaph Corner*. It ended in retreat as a cloudburst soaked the rock. A month later they were back, and this time succeeded on a route that may not have marked any technical advance, but was a psychological breakthrough in that it followed a line of unremitting steepness and exposure on loose rock and with poor protection: 'All the way up little flakes of rock broke off when we pulled or stood on them.' They called it *Cemetery Gates*, after a name Brown saw on the destination board of a bus as he returned through Chester that night. John Allen's quip that it's E5,1b sums up the modern view. Thereafter the routes came thick and fast, and until the last golden summer of the 1950s, when a younger generation of climbers began to question and probe at the aura of supreme difficulty that grew up around climbs of the Brown/Whillans era, the Rock & Ice and all its activities were held in awe. Nor were the activities of this group – and Joe in particular – solely confined to British rock. In the French Alps, where British climbing had scarcely advanced in 50 years, in 1954 the Brown-Whillans team made the third ascent in a very fast time of the recent Magnone route on the west face of the Petit Dru (then deemed the hardest alpine rock-climb), and went on to climb an even harder line of their own on the west face of the Aiguille de Blaitiere that very soon gained a reputation for extreme difficulty.

This activity resulted in an invitation for Joe – though not for the younger and more truculent Whillans – to accompany Charles Evans' reconnaissance expedition in 1955 to Kanchenjunga, the world's third-highest peak, and the highest unclimbed one at that time. (Joe's acceptance, and apparent refusal to press for Whillans' inclusion, was seen by the latter as a betrayal, and the two men climbed less frequently together thereafter.) The climb was in many ways more difficult, arduous and committing than that of Everest, accomplished two years before by a far larger and higher-profile team. Joe led the final pitch to the top (minus four feet, as an undertaking had been given to the King of Nepal not to tread the actual summit of this holy mountain). His fame thereafter was assured. He followed this in 1956 with the first ascent of the Mustagh Tower, which had rejoiced for over 60 years in the reputation of 'Nature's last stronghold – the most inaccessible of all great peaks.' It was a climb of extreme difficulty, one of the most serious to have been undertaken in the Himalaya up to that time, and like the one on Kanchenjunga, accomplished in poor conditions by an expedition tiny by the conventions of the day.

So by 1956, in a career of nine years Joe had established himself as the most considerable all-round mountaineer in the history of the sport in Britain. His first ascents on Pennine, Welsh, Cumbrian and Scottish rock had significantly advanced the concept of the climbable; in the Alps and the Himalayas his record was no less impressive. If you want to get a sense of the meteoric scale and breadth of that achievement look around and see if there's anyone now who came into the sport at the end of the 1980s and dominates its achievements across the board. And if you think it was easier then, think equipment, sponsorship, knowledge, money, travel, time – and think again!

Consider too that Joe's career doesn't finish in 1956. He's continued to climb right through to the margins of old age. Whilst contemporaries have dropped away, died, or became flaccid with years and inactivity, he's carried on. But after those two great Himalayan ascents of the mid-1950s, he's done so in a more relaxed fashion. 'Sometimes I liked to forget that I was a climber,' he wrote in his autobiography, and maybe in that lies a key to his longevity in the sport. Success and recognition didn't lessen his enjoyment of mountaineering, but perhaps wrought those genial changes in character that enabled him to engage with it in a less driven way as the years went on. The horizons of his activity broadened. In the early 1960s he combed the secretive valleys of southern Snowdonia for small, steep crags on which he sketched out the early masterpeces of climbing's modern age: *Vector, Pellagra, Dwm, Hardd, Ferdinand*. He loves to fish quiet rivers, alone or with close friends. He began to be in demand for television work, where his flinty, humorous commentary, phlegmatic even when *in extremis*, acted as anchor to films and outside broadcasts from places as far apart as Iran's Valley of the Assassins, Welsh sea and mountain cliffs, Alpine aiguilles, Scottish seastacks and a wintry Ben Nevis. He even made those television shorts about fishing in inaccessible places, and acted as Jeremy Iron's double in the waterfall sequences of *The Mission* (the fact that Irons towered over him by almost a foot was concealed by careful camerawork). There's a measured wit and gravity and a light mocking touch about his screen *persona* that holds true in all the relationships of his life.

He had significant climbing partnerships with men of younger generations. With Peter Crew and others he developed Gogarth and South Stack, producing an extraordinary series of routes: *Mousetrap, Winking Crack, Red Wall, Doppelganger, Wendigo*. He continued to probe the cliff's intimacies to produce classic and teasing climbs long after Crew had failed to keep pace with his continued zeal. In the Himalayas he forged an alliance with Mo Anthoine and enjoyed trip after lighthearted trip – many of them unsuccessful in reaching their objectives, and that didn't matter to him one iota – to difficult peaks in Garhwal and elsewhere. Even in his sixties he took part in an expedition dogged by bad weather to Everest's then-unclimbed North-north-east Ridge.

That's the outline of his involvement in climbing. There's also the legend and the character. As a young climber in Manchester at the start of the 1960s, I was intensely aware of his presence. His gritstone and Welsh routes were the A-level syllabus of my climbing youth. Scratches left a few years previously by his nailed boots on the likes of *Blue Lights Crack* at Wimberry, or on *Brown's Eliminate* at Froggatt were pointed out with reverence. I met him frequently there or in Wales, and always he – *the* legend of the sport – was approachable, helpful, unpatronising. When at the age of 15 I took my first big fall from one of his climbs in the rain, he was on a more sensible route alongside, and immediately roped down, checked to see if I was unhurt, then put his arm round me and with a huge grin said, 'Never mind, lad – it 'appens to the best of us.'

I think at his peak he probably was the best I ever saw, too. He could climb in any conditions and in any footwear. I remember him and a very chastened John Cheesmond coming in, their black Gannex anoraks dripping wet, to the Cromlech hut in Nant Peris one day of lashing rain in 1965 when no-one else had ventured beyond the door. They'd been up to Clogwyn Du'r Arddu to make a second ascent of *East Gully Grooves Direct Start*, which then had the reputation, albeit undeserved, of being the most technically difficult pitch on the cliff: 'It was alright,' he told me, 'you mustn't be put off by what people tell you about these things.' I looked across to Cheesmond, whose eyes were still contra-rotating, and who just shook his head.

With all the other greats of my time, I could understand how they climbed: fitness, physique, supple gymnasticism or sheer application explained it all quite clearly. With Joe, there was something else at work. He's quite short, not heavily built, his muscles corded rather than developed, his movement smooth and deliber-ate. When I climbed with him, sometimes I would watch the way he made a move, replicate it when I came to that point, and his way, that he'd seen instantly, would often be the least obvious and most immediately right. Even Stevie Haston, no mean all-round performer himself, speaks of this ability – and Stevie saw it when it was well in decline – with a sort of rueful awe. Joe was climbing's supreme craftsman, unerringly aware of the medium. That instinctual rock-sense has served him right through and has never entirely left him. I witnessed it in his prime and saw grainy black-and-white television clips from the mid-1950s where the silken economy of movement on steep rock was a revelation. And I've seen too in the meticulousness of his preparation, the rigour he brings to the task, that his long survival in this dead-ly arena is not down to mere chance. When I came to make a television series on the Welsh mountains in 1991,[1] I intercut 1950s footage of him on *Suicide Wall* with

---

[1] I called in to see Joe the other day, at his home in Llanberis. He'd just got a new video – a very old one actually – of himself climbing in the 1950s. Jack Longland was narrating it. There was a sequence of Joe climbing a route on Curbar – a black-haired youth of 20 or so drifting

sequences of him doing the same climb as a 60-year-old. The effect was breathtaking. I've written before that it reminded me of nothing so much as an account I'd once read of Maria Callas taking a master class towards the end of her life, the sustained glories of her voice gone as she coaxed her students through – except that here and there, briefly, a ghost-echo of such rich splendour arose as to make every other sound seem utterly mundane. Thus with Joe, and with him it comes too with this generous, playful and straightforward character. He's bright, informed, argumentative. He loves the contest, loves to wrestle. Once, after a first ascent of near-suicidal looseness on Mowing Word into which I'd inveigled him, and got him soaked by waves into the bargain, he had led the marginally safer top pitch and I followed to find him sitting with nothing more than his feet down two rabbit holes for a belay, smiling dangerously. He pulled me to the ground and belaboured me for risking his life and limb, scolding me the while for what he called the loosest route he'd ever done. But he was laughing, laughing, and we ran back in perfect humour across the unmarked beach, the cliff crumbling slowly

---

with the most graceful and fluid economy up VS rock. It was breathtakingly beautiful, and the silver-haired 60-year-old grandfather on my right was regarding the image with a soft smile and an almost imperceptible shake of the head. We chatted away, then looked back at the screen. There was the picture from the old Idwal guide, but animated now, the rope moving as the relaxed figure eased upwards on the grainy, grey film. I'd come to talk with Joe about his appearing in a series I was presenting for HTV. The frames edited themselves into my television state of mind. I had to do the route with him. We made the arrangements. I heard on the grapevine that he'd been out practising the route. I was glued to my desk, so muttered imprecations about what a competitive little bugger he still is and tried not to worry too much. The likelihood was that in that subtle way of his Joe would jockey for the lead, so all I needed to do was play the inept straight-man role. Therefore the less competent I was, the better for television it would be, I argued.
'When did you first do *Suicide Wall*, Joe?'
We were walking up the Idwal path, Joe exulting in the tactic of a short-cut which had put us ahead of the producer and the film crew.
'I think it was in 1948 ... '
(Joe claims to have a very bad memory, and always introduces an element of vagueness into his accounts. When I accuse him of having a selectively bad memory, it's a charge he vigorously denies.)
' ... it was the same time as that early attempt on *Cenotaph Corner* when I dropped the peg-hammer on Wilf White's head. I'd been climbing for about a year at the time but I didn't find it too bad. I did it again after I came out of the army, which would be in about 1951. We'd been climbing in the Carnedds but were rained off – it was a terrible day – so we came back to the chapel where we were staying, brewed up, and I remember making some little slings out of line, cutting them up. They all blew off in the gale, and the only protection I had was when I clipped a downward-pointing peg. When Pete White, who was seconding, came up he fell off, swung across, and just the lateral tension pulled the peg out.'
'What sort of status did the route have for you then?'
'It was the route to do. It was the hardest thing in Wales at the time.'

behind us in the western light, the waves rolling against it. He needs that conflict – it's his brand of creative masochism – and the character that emerges from it is one of the most engaging I've ever known.

15: Cathy Powell: A Character Rewritten (1988)

Ever read One Green Bottle ... ?

We each of us have gaps in our education, and *The Grooved Arête* was just that for me. You know how it is – inexplicably, there are some routes you've never done. Perhaps you've resisted the urge to collect them. Perhaps some memory of accident or things said warns you away. Or perhaps it's just that, on that part of the mountain, your plans always stick in a different groove – the *Terrace Wall*, the *Belle Vue Bastion*, but never the soaring rib away on the right. You'll come round to it eventually – that much you know. It's just a question of when.

This is how it happened (things start in prosaic ways, so don't scoff). I was listening to the five-to-nine weather forecast on Radio Four. It was October the 11th. The weatherman was promising rain, gales, flood for perhaps days on end and I had one of those thirsts for physical activity on me which have to be satisfied. Besides, the sun was still shining – fitfully, yes, and the massed clouds were rolling in over the sea. But there was a golden light that morning, and if I was to cower behind rain-dimmed windows for the rest of the week, the need was to get out now. So off I went to Tryfan. There was, of course, the minor inconvenience of not having anyone to climb with, but that turned out to be an advantage. If I'd been with a partner I'd have been thinking of the old favourites – *Munich Climb*, or the *Belle Vue Bastion* again. As it was, I was unapologetically alone and glad to be so – why should you not take your mountains undiluted once in a while, instead of cooling the heat of the experience on the rocks of company? And even the moderation of ambition which solitude entails can be turned to advantage. What was it Moulam said – 'As good as anything of the kind in Wales'? And Tom Leppert has it down as a three-star route, 'the most inspiring on Tryfan.' That gap in my education was about to be filled. It had to be *The Grooved Arête*.

Half an hour later I was round in Ogwen, pulling the Honda on to its stand, stowing helmet and leathers away in the box and jumping up and down to get warm. A fierce easterly was gusting even at this level. Tryfan, its fine crown hidden, sat in lumpen judgement on my plans under a black cap of cloud. There was fine weather to the west and I flogged up the squelch and gravel to the Heather Terrace hoping it might push a salient through. One by one the gullies ticked by: Bastow, Nor'Nor', Green, and then I was there, with not even the route's initials scratched on the rock marring the good mood which exercise builds up.

Not only that, but as I sat down to tighten my boots there in front of me, right between my feet, was a silver sixpence: 'That's strange,' I thought, as I picked it up and rubbed it on my sleeve. 'What on earth is that doing here.' But there it was – the king's head, 1951, and a gleam upon it as though it was new minted, the milled edge sharp as a file. I put it in the pocket of my shirt along with the bike keys, fastened the waist-strap of my rucksack, and turned to the rock.

Tryfan rock was made for climbing. There are the textures, from marble through to pumice. There are the holds, often quite subtle, hidden, but absolutely reliable, and all of them buffed to a pale ochre sheen by the grinding of nailed boots through decades. The thought brought me up short. In that first slightly awkward crack which commands you from the outset to summon your forces and concentrate, there beneath the flat hold at half-height out on the right were nailscratches – quite unmistakeable – number 6 Tricounis, a fine grey dust of gouged rock on each side showing how fresh the marks were. I laughed aloud. In this world of Lycra tights, butyl rubber and climbing competitions, here on Tryfan, somewhere up above me at this moment, someone was climbing in Tricouni-nailed boots.

People complain about *The Grooved Arête*. They say that after the first two pitches you have to walk across to the left, and after the next two pitches you need to amble over to the right. So you do, but that's the nature of Tryfan and what you're making for in both cases is the next obvious continuation of the line. And why complain when the climbing is as good as it is. Take the rib of the middle section, for example. There's not a dull move on it, and you have to think it out all the way. The guidebook gives it as 100ft, but it feels more than that. You climb a slender, tall riffle of edges and grooves, often with delicate moves on rounded edges, and you're so totally absorbed that you scarcely notice how much height you're gaining, how steeply the ground is dropping away beneath. Or at least, you don't notice it until – high up on the rib and with a fall-factor now which would bounce you way beyond the Heather Terrace – it gets hard. 'What's this climb supposed to be,' you mutter to yourself, 'V. Diff?' You wonder where the holds are. After all, your rule of thumb for grading is that on a V. Diff. there is always a good, positive hold to hand. Not here, though – there's a greasy finger-jam in the groove, a toe-scrape at thigh-height on the right, and a hold of unknown worth four feet out of reach. And there in the toe-scrape were those tricouni imprints again! 'If someone can do this in nails, I should be ashamed of myself,' I thought, and hoisted on up.

At the top of the rib is a last steep little tier before the grass ledge which leads off beneath the Terrace Wall. You step out and bridge up a shallow groove near the gully edge, pull over a bulge at its top, and the true glory of *The Grooved Arête* confronts you. The most elegant of curved ribs runs up into a blocky maze of roofs and black grooves, and keeps its continuity throughout. I wandered off to the side to sit down and study it at leisure, and it was then that I saw the figure – fleetingly, high up, improbably stepping round the edge of a slab into a groove.

A lull in the blustery wind let the precise click of boot nails drop down to me, and then she was gone – just a suggestion of movement left in the shadows. I was left pondering the route.

It quite scared me. I blew on my fingers to warm them up and found myself chewing the nails. Cloud-dapple and sunshine played across the ribs above. The line enthralled me. *The Knight's Move* – the crux – it was right up there under the roofs. The exposure must be tremendous, and the moves – if they're harder than those down below then the issue's in some doubt. The wind was fierce up here, blowing me across to the foot of the rib where I cast about among the alternatives to start. Cracked leaves of rock, hollow to tap, curved up, the holds fractured into them comforting and large. At first I was out on the edge above Green Gully, then forced more and more into the corners on the left. At each large foothold, between each burst of activity, I stopped and worked out the moves ahead, climbing slowly and deliberately, learning the moves in case I had to reverse them, enjoying the precision of boot-climbing. The rock steepened. Given a second, runners, rock-boots, you could have climbed straight on at any point but the need was to balance expectation of difficulty against likely line. The figure ahead was nowhere to be seen. I found myself stepping out on to a foothold slippery with damp, with the way ahead concealed out left. Just above was a ledge – The Haven. There are times when you know how features gain their name.

This time there was no stopping. I didn't want to get caught on the crux in the threatened rain. The ledge swelled up into broken rocks, above which a wide, shallow crack with jammed holds ran up the left side of a slab. From a standing position in the crack, the slab looked like a friendly interval. There were holds. A single delicate move, with good finger-edges and a sloping foothold, took me into its middle. Up and across, up and across and I was near the edge. The position was terrific, the gully-bed 300ft below. The wind nagged me on. Beneath the capping bulge at full stretch was a hidden fingerhold, sharp and untrodden. I explored it, relinquished it, stepped up and used it, sidled round the arête into the base of a black groove – the second of two, for the first was bald and unfriendly. It was anticlimactic. Or was it? To look down the slab was to glance back on those expectations of difficulty confounded. This traditional crux had been the easiest pitch on the route. But it had also been the best. I scampered up the rest – the groove, the airy black lava-edge above, in thrilled relief, and felt as happy about it as perhaps I had about any route for years. And there was still the summit to come.

Which is where I met Cathy. I popped up directly between Adam and Eve and there she was with her back to a rock, out of the wind in the flat area down from the top. 'Good,' I thought, 'the perfect let-out! If I go through the Adam-and-Eve ritual now she'll think I'm showing off.' I went down and sat on a rock beside her. She was dressed in thick corduroy breeches and a fading anorak. On her feet were a dinky little pair of hand-made, tricouni-nailed Robert Lawrie boots of the sort that I hadn't seen for years.

'Where on earth did you get those boots?' I asked, realising I'd met with the presence who'd preceded me up the mountain.

She'd been watching as I came down. She could have been in her early fifties, hair the colour of a bracken slope in late October and wrinkles gathering round her sharp features, enlivening the texture of a skin with a curiously translucent gleam of grey about it. And the question, too, had brought a little warmth to her cheeks.

'I got them from a travelling salesman, actually – a long time ago.'

'Did he give away a free alpenstock with every pair?'

'Who?'

'The salesman.'

'Oh, him – I've not seen him for years.'

She sat back and looked at me. She had the strong Liverpool undercurrent to her accent and the Irishness you often get in people from that city, a mane of red hair, eyes a greeny moonstone grey and the cheekbones high. She was volunteering nothing and I was feeling chatty, so I got an orange out of my sack, peeled it, offered her some – she refused – and asked if it had been her on *The Grooved Arête*:

'Yes – and you came that way too?'

'I was following you.'

'It's fantastic, isn't it. I love that slab. Of all the routes I've ever done that's the one sticks in my mind.'

'Best route on the mountain!' I enthused. 'I'd been saving it up for my old age – hadn't done it before today.'

The atmosphere between us had changed, as though the warmth of shared enthusiasm had thawed her reserve, and the shared experience had made us joint parties to a conspiracy.

'Why not?' she asked, 'How long have you been climbing for?'

Top: Blaven from Sgurr Alasdair, sunrise
Below: Flake Crack, Helsby – Derek Walker climbing

Top left: Comrade Cook – the late, great Dave Cook climbing at High Rocks
Top right: Jill Lawrence on Left Unconquerable, Stanage
Bottom left: Joe Brown and Jim Perrin on Suicide Wall, Cwm Idwal
Bottom right: The Riparian, Craig Rhiw Goch – Martin Crook and Rob Collister climbing

Will Perrin on Patellalectomy

The Atlantic Ocean Wall, Land's End
Mark Edwards and the author

Top left: Stevie Haston at Tapovan, Shivling behind
Top right: Laurence Gouault, Martin Crook and Stevie Haston
Bottom left: The author on Pedlar's Slab, Stanage – frictional aficionado's gem
Bottom right: Joe Brown prepares to climb

The Strait Gate, Mother Carey's Kitchen – Will Perrin climbing (Ray Wood)

Top left: Martin Crook, Will and Jim Perrin at Mother Carey's Kitchen (Ray Wood)
Top right: Will Perrin and Mark Katz bouldering at Porth Ysgo (Ray Wood)
Below: Heart of Darkness, Mowing Word – Will finishing the traverse (Ray Wood)

Top left: New Morning, Mowing Word – Will on the top crack (Ray Wood)
Bottom left: Will Perrin (Ray Wood)
Right: Jim with Jacquetta at Bretton Hall Mountain Literature Festival, three weeks before she died (Derek Walker)

'Oh, years – I'd just never got round to it. What about you?'

'I started in 1949.'

'There weren't many women climbing then, I suppose.'

'I don't see many up here now. I used to stay down there, you see, at Cae Capel ... '

She pointed to the youth hostel among the trees. I wondered at the strange name she used. Then she went on:

'There were a few women used to come there at weekends. There was a girl called Doreen ... ' She gave a long scouse snarl to the name. 'The warden was a woman, Dorothy Elliott she was called, then there was my author. The reason I like *The Grooved Arête* is that she never sent me up it.'

Over by Llyn y Cwn there was a bright patch of sunlight beneath the bales of heavy cloud. I watched it intently, turning away from my companion in confusion. She'd been talking so heatedly, so incomprehensibly – the whole tenor of the conversation had changed. I was sitting up here on top of Tryfan with a woman who talked in riddles, and feeling that strange response, where embarrassment mixes with mild fear, which you encounter when you start to suspect that the person you're with is mentally ill. Perhaps there was an explanation for what she said. I faltered out the question which asked for it.

'Who was your author, then?'

'Elizabeth, of course – you know! You must have read her book. I'm Cathy – Cathy Powell she wanted me to be. I call myself that as a sop to her for not doing what she wanted.'

'Oh,' I replied, non-committal and uncomprehending, 'So how d'you get on with her now?'

'Badly, considering what she wanted me to do.'

'What was that?'

'Look, I'll give it to Elizabeth – she made the effort to understand, but she couldn't really. In the end she sent me back there and I couldn't understand it. And she posted Dorothy at a window to make sure that I went. Mind you, I was never that happy about Dorothy being in the book – it always struck me that she was a bit too close to Elizabeth, with all this dutiful streak she had. And all the time Elizabeth was taking out her – what would she call it? – her sociology and her libido on me. She got me to jump into bed with the chaps for her – maybe she did it herself, I don't know, or maybe she was afraid of it – and then she sent me back to Tooley Street to marry Borstal Billy. But you see, it couldn't have worked. Because I'd been out here. It's not just that I'd been climbing, and got the confidence from that. It's that I'd been brought alive to show how alive you can be through all this ... '

Palm up, she followed the horizon slowly round with her index finger, and turned to me, smiling mischievously. I was fascinated, enthralled.

'Want to know what I did instead?'

'Go on!'

'I re-wrote the ending. You see, she didn't know enough to realise that it could never have worked the way she wanted it. She thought that, full of strength through joy, I could go back to Birkenhead and reform everybody with my new-found sense of duty. What happened after her ending was that Billy got fat, drank too much, smoked 50 a day, beat the hell out of me when I told him about Len and Chris, gave me six kids he couldn't support and died in Clatterbridge of cancer at the age of 38. I didn't want that.'

'So what did you do?'

'I just told you. I re-wrote the ending.'

'What happened in your version?'

'Simple – as I was walking along by the lake, with Dorothy's eyes drilling holes in my back from that window, I realised that Elizabeth had never let me do *The Grooved Arête*, and I was buggered if I was going to stand for that. As soon as I was out of sight of the hostel, I stuffed my rucksack under a boulder and came up here to do it.'

'Oh!'

I was lost for words.

'So you've been doing it ever since?'

'Well – there's not much else a character can do when she runs away from the plan laid out for her. But I'll say this – when she had me lead *Great Slab*, she thought anything after that would be an anti-climax. But that's not how it is – I knew that much, for all her First in French and so on. It's not a battle. It's not some examination ... '

She put a marvellous drawling sneer into her delivery of the word.

' ... where once you get top marks you're through with it. It gets into your blood. If they give us any, that is. So I came up here and did something I wanted to do, and d'you know, it was wonderful. That's why I turned up for you today. Because I know what it's like, the first time.'

I was convinced now that she was one of those people you meet who are no longer in touch, friendly-crazy, but there was such a sincerity about her and a chuckling humour running through her speech, I could have sat and listened for hours. But she rose to go, boot-nails clicking across the rocks.

'I'm going down *North Buttress* – how about you?'

'*Pinnacle Rib* for me.'

We set off in our opposite directions. As I went down towards the flaky sheaves leading to the *Yellow Slab* I caught sight of her on the long traverse over the *Terrace Wall* – a flicker of neat movement across the rock. I took out my camera to photograph the scene – the wall plunging below, a lovely misty light over Pen yr Oleu Wen behind, sun gleaming on the slabs of Little Tryfan and the traffic so infinitely distant on the Holyhead Road. Then she was gone, and I hurried on down. The weather had closed in by the time I reached the Heather Terrace, her nail scratches barely visible now on the first crack of *The Grooved Arête*. There was no sound from the mist above. I rode back in the rain over the Crimea Pass to drop off a film for developing in Blaenau, and arrived home in a downpour.

'Did you have a good climb?' my son asked, helping me out of the waterproofs.

'Wonderful!' I said. 'Any messages this morning?'

'No – except Anthony called. He left a book for you. I told him where you'd gone and he said if you'd never done *The Grooved Arête* perhaps you'd never read *One Green Bottle* either.'

'Oh good – I've wanted to get hold of a copy of that for ages.'

I put it to one side. Next day the film came back. I put the strips on the light table and looked at them under a glass. No figure on the North Buttress traverse! Just an empty mountainside. I fished in my shirt-pocket for the sixpence. There was the king's head, the date of 1951, milling tangible as rock. And then there was the book. I read it. But you can't meet a character out of a novel. And one who rewrites her own ending. Can you ... ?

16: WILL (2004)

What follows is the funeral address I gave for my son Will. His death in July 2004 was the culmination of what seemed an inexorable sequence of events. He'd been working out in India over the winter, had become very depressed about the conditions of his Indian fellow-workers and the lack of provision for them and their families when they were killed or maimed. He came back at Easter, talked all that through with me, got back into his climbing – he was pretty widely acknowledged as the best young adventure climber in the country, utterly beautiful to watch on rock – went up to Hoy to try to free the old Haston-Crew aid route on the Old Man, pulled a big block off, knocked himself out and gashed his head badly, went to the local GP to get stitched but didn't have an x-ray, came to Jacquetta and myself to have the stitches taken out because he didn't trust doctors, said to me then, 'It's not good to be frightened all the time, is it Dad ... ?' He'd also broken a tooth in the fall. He went to have it capped, got an infection that developed rapidly into Ludwig's Angina, was rushed to hospital unable to breathe, had to have an emergency tracheotomy, massive doses of antibiotics and then the tracheotomy reversed, again under general anaesthetic. Shortly after he came out of hospital he was due to go out with an expedition to the big rock walls in the Cape Farewell region of Greenland, clearly wasn't fit enough, but his self-image was so bound up with his climbing that he was determined on going. His bags had gone out, he packed his rucksack, drove three of his mates down to Heathrow, dropped them off at departures and told them he was going to park the car, texted them from round the corner to tell them he wasn't coming, threw the mobile out of the car, drove home and hanged himself.

Two things first of all: the exquisite portrait of Will in the order of service – which is the favourite one I have of him apart from one in which he's wearing a nappy, and I know he would have been mightily displeased had we used that – is by our dear friend Ray Wood, and has somehow slipped through unacknowledged. So I'm sorry for that, Ray, and thank you for the use of the photograph.

Secondly, Will was anything but conventional in his outlook on life – had he spotted any black ties here today one of his sly comments, one of his wry grins, would have been heading in its direction. So if any of you are wearing one, thank you for the respectful intention, which he would have appreciated, because he had the gentlest of hearts; but you can personalise that respect now by taking them off, shoving them in your pockets, and breathing more easily ...

Will is my first-born son, and his presence in my life for the last 24 years has been something so precious it's beyond my capacity with words to express it. From the moment I first saw him, I thought him the most perfectly beautiful being I had ever set eyes upon. A sense of that remained with me throughout that phase of life when sleep is a memory and the sustenance of your sanity depends on substances that go under names like *Milton* and *Sudocrem*, *Bonjela* and *Gripe Water*. Us old people look at you younger people with a kind of fond, distant understanding of the changes that soon you'll be coming to. And the crucial word there is 'soon', and you would not believe how rapidly time passes ...

It seems to me not as though it were yesterday but as though somehow it were happening now that I see Will in his papoose and his fleecy baby-gro in the snow on top of Clogwyn Mawr above Capel Curig at eight months old, waving his arms at the ravens; another second and he's sturdy, four years old, his mane of blond hair flying as he speeds though the bracken on Llanbedr Hill and leaps at me, clinging on like a koala bear, making me wade into the middle of the mawn pool there and then getting me to put him down waist-deep in the water so he can soak me with his splashing and his laughter; or we're cooking sausages quietly and harmlessly over an open fire on a beach and some countryside policeman comes up to us and starts brusquely to recite the book of rules, offences and misdemeanours; and when I rather more politely invite him to make particular use of the handle of the frying pan, and he's flounced off in a huff to get reinforcements, Will appropriates the phrase, and stomps around in glee, kicking sand, chanting it to himself; and I have to instruct him in all the hypocrisies of appropriateness ...

Will had already nearly been expelled from school at the age of eight – strange, the things in which a father takes pride. He'd flashed a V-sign at the headmaster of Cricieth school one afternoon, and the phonecalls and the vocabulary of moral outrage that poured forth upon him was Calvinistic-comical at its most extreme. What's disgusting about a child registering contempt for puffed-up authority? Will did that by instinct, and I aided and abetted him in it, and tried to bring his bewilderment round to laughter, and instructed him as best I could in the slippery arts of social self-preservation.

He was so mischievous, and so beautiful, and so innocent, and however thick a carapace he grew as the years passed, none of those qualities ever deserted him. He had to *learn* to be streetwise. Eventually I called in a private tutor, Martin Crook, to give him special tuition in the arts of wiliness, to teach him that 'Do what you will' is not quite the whole law, and needs the addition of that terse phrase, 'but don't get caught!'

Before that, there was the occasion when he made a hoax phone call to the Fire Brigade to report that a house down the road was on fire. He liked fire engines and things like that – first word he learnt was 'digger'. The operator asked him for his number. He gave her our number. Within half an hour the local policeman arrived to give him a bollocking and leave me to explain again the means subversion must employ to escape detection.

The other time he was nearly expelled, from his secondary school, absolutely confirmed his instinctive and accurate view that society rests on a foundation of quivering and hypocritical bullshit. Will was born – necessarily I'd think in view of his parentage – with the most acute bullshit-detectors I've ever come across. On this second close shave with expulsion, some mate of his had been caught at school with the merest sliver of cannabis on him, and immediately blabbed that Will had given it to him – which was probably true, because he was always very generous with anything he had. Naturally this aroused a shock-horror response with the powers-that-be, since enough blow to make a single spliff was obviously going to rot the brains of a generation, and after Will had been suspended for three weeks he and I were both summoned to appear before a special meeting of the board of governors called for the end of the spring term.

There was a long table, grave faces along either side. Will and I and the headmaster were seated at one end, the chairman of the board of governors in all the gravity of his authority at the other. The headmaster opened the case for the prosecution – terrible, pernicious, social evil, serious view, necessity to stamp it out and make an example – and all the grave faces along either side nodded him along like toy dogs on the back shelf of a car, and it was clear that Will, who'd gone very pale, was on his way out and I was calculating how I could afford private school fees.

At which point I looked up, and my eyes just for an instant met those of the chairman of the board of governors and he, startled, dropped them to his note-pad and began scribbling away furiously. Then it was his turn to speak. He rose to his feet; in measured speech agreed with all the headmaster had spoken; and began to talk of how, despite the gravity of the offence, to blight a young man's education for one slip was too harsh, and leniency was better than over-reaction, and the poodles ranged along either side nodded him along, and suspension until the beginning of next term was suggested and they agreed and it was the headmaster's turn to go pale with anger and thwarted bloodlust; and with the illest grace and much rehearsal of his own words he was forced to accept and Will and I exchanged a surreptitious glance, and I kicked him under the table lest he should smile, and we walked through the playground and out of the gate, shaking with laughter, and he asked me, 'What was all that about, dad? I was going to be expelled, wasn't I?' And I said, 'Well, that guy at the far end of the table who spoke for you ... ' Will looked at me quizzically. 'In the sixties we all used to buy our dope from him. I think his conscience prompted him. He used to be a policeman ... '

It's maybe as well that Will started climbing – God knows where all that subversive energy, all that innocent challenge of his would have gone otherwise. I never thrust climbing upon him, and in my heart, back then, I never really wanted him to start. Too many times I've been in this place or others like it for my friends. I think it began because he had a thing about Katie Haston. Whenever I mentioned her name – and you know fathers like to bait their sons a bit around these things – he'd go bright red and profess to hate her, and then he'd be off down the climbing wall at *The Heights* and I'd ask innocently, 'Was Katie there, Will ... ?' and he'd glower at me and mutter rude things about 'stupid-old-bastards-what-do-they-know,' and carry on doing pull-ups on the door-frames and it was obvious that he'd gone down with the bug. Or maybe two bugs ...

So for about a year – and it was such a magical year – because I wanted him to know how to be safe, we went out climbing together whenever we could. I was way past my sell-by date at this time, and as Will would rightly and frequently point out, an idle old bastard in whom motion was only ever discernible once caffeine levels were sufficiently high. This meant that, as often as not, we finished routes in the dark, so it always felt like an adventure. We did a lot of the classic routes of Snowdonia together: *White Slab* on a day when we were the only people on the crag and he was bubbling with excitement all the way back down with the setting sun streaming through the *bwlch*; *Vector* after school one day, me hanging out of the cave and yelling at him to get back on the rock and do it properly, using his feet, when he'd just hurled himself at the groove coming out of the Ochre Slab and swung off. He used to believe that momentum was all the technique you needed. We finished the top crack in the pitch black.

His ability soon sailed way past the remnants of mine, and I was fortunate enough to get a shoulder injury that stopped my climbing, so I didn't hold him back. He became very, very good. I've seen many people climb over the decades who've impressed me. Will had the special gift, the rock-knowledge. The dancing god had visited him. He had such grace. But there was more to it than that. The grace was in his spirit, his attitudes were sound. Climbers are awful for bullshit. Will didn't bullshit, he just did the thing for the sharp, sweet thrill of it. He climbed with the best, and they respected him, and they liked him, because he was funny and warm and a bit mysterious. The humour of climbers can be quite savage. With Will, it was a kind of gentle, sidelong poking of fun that – for those who were listening – opened out perspectives. I think he was very wise. By the time he was about 17, he treated me, with great good humour and tolerance, as one might an errant adolescent.

He started travelling. He went off to America at 18, made many friends worldwide, did hard things in Yosemite, wandered all round Europe easing himself into scenes and enjoying the company and the climbs. He talked lyrically about the textures of rock, the atmospheres of place. More recently, I climbed with him a little again, but the gap between his ease and my age had grown vast, so I always felt what he never showed – that it was a condescension on his part.

Two occasions stick in my mind: he took me up some of my own routes from over 30 years ago in Pembroke a couple of years ago, drifting up them effortlessly, and when I came to follow, enthusing, helping me in every subtle way that he could. Generosity of spirit again ...

Another time, we were driving to a Dylan concert in Manchester on an early summer day and it transpired he'd never been to Frodsham. I was spared climbing because I had a suit on – he nicked that from me as well as the Dylan records, has probably appeared at most of your weddings in it. Anyway, we flogged up through the woods to Hoop-la Buttress and there were a couple of sweet young lads from Ellesmere Port with a mat beneath them bouldering out the roof of *Hoop-La* itself. Will was in his jeans and trainers and watched awhile, then the lads saw he was itching to take a look, so they stepped aside. He did each of the routes on that overhanging rock, one after the other, with total ease and elastic elegance, and the two lads looked at me with their mouths open, and shaking heads and bemused smiles, and they all sat down and smoked a roll-up and Will was friendly and open with them, and you could see they felt they'd met someone special.

Later on that night, outside the concert, we were waiting for a friend to go for a Rusholme curry. Will was wiling away the time walking along one of those swinging chains – his balance was amazing. A large policewoman waddled across with intent. I interposed myself, explained it was one of his recreations, and harmless. Will stood on one leg on the gently swinging chain, hands behind his back, looking with a kind of mild interest elsewhere as this downbeat altercation went on. She got into the regulations and all that, and he carried on ignoring her, and at length, baffled, she turned and grumbled away.

Will looked over his shoulder and down at me, his grin was pure, impish, provocative delight, he did a quick back-flip, stepped down, touched his finger to his tongue and marked one up against authority. And I glowed with pride ...

I cannot begin to do justice to Will in this short space. There cannot be a greater privilege in this life than to have someone like him as your child. I was asked three or so years ago if I'd choose a favourite piece from my own writing for an American anthology Pat Ament was editing. There was absolutely no difficulty in deciding. It was an essay about doing a climb on Anglesey with Will one winter's day when he was 15. In a brief foreword to it, I wrote, 'He is a supremely talented climber now, and a funny, lovely, endearing young man whose soundness of approach to the sport educates me as surely as the sport itself has educated him.'

Pat Ament ran into Will in Bishop, when he was out in California over that winter, and got him to write his response to the essay. I'll read part of it:

'Wow! This is a pretty scary place,' I thought as I left the vaguely solid ground I'd been belaying from and stepped around on to the huge white slab. I looked down at the void between my frozen feet and saw a piece of driftwood being tossed around in the frothy swell that crashed between boulders and the sides of the zawn. My body warmed a little, and the climbing became interesting and enjoyable.

'I was not finding it all that bad. It was quite peaceful really, listening to the wind whistle through the huge arch, watching the birds, with nature slowly taking its course. We were soon at the top, wrapped up warm, and I scrambled down to the end of the promontory to see where we'd been. It was beautiful. A patch of sun broke through the blanket of grey and lit up the speckled walls. My dad came down to look with me. I felt close to him. Those special moments with special people in special places are what it's all about. Isn't it?'

You, his friends gathered here today, were Will's 'special people'. And he, to me, was utterly so throughout his life. There is nothing with which I could ever wish to reproach him, no decision of his I could ever gainsay. Keep him safe and precious now in your hearts. I want you to take a little time here, in silence, to think of him, to think of his humour, the sly magic of his presence, his modesty, his awareness, and to fix that in your memories where it can live forever.

PART THREE: ON CLIMBING

What do we find in – or through – our climbing? It's a question that's exercised me throughout the decades in which I've been involved in the activity. At a simple level the appeal is obvious – the frequent beauty of the environments in which it takes place, the sensuality and satisfaction of physical exertion, the companionship, the body-chess of hard rock. Yet always for me there has been a sense of something beyond, of something here which is metonymically complex, and which the intense simplicities of climbing can enable us better to comprehend: 'This ship, the ship we sail, is the moral symbol of our life.' Maybe all I've been doing all these years is climbing Mount Analogue. The views are good but – if it matters – when do we ever get to the top ... ?

1: EATING BEAR MEAT (1992)

There is an afterword to the paperback edition of Primo Levi's two attempts – *If This is a Man* and *The Truce* – factually to record the experience of Auschwitz and its aftermath. It's entitled 'The Author's Answers to his Reader's Questions'. In it, Levi asks himself the question, 'To what factors do you attribute your survival?' Part of his response runs thus:

'The fact that I survived and returned unharmed is due, in my opinion, chiefly to good luck. Pre-existing factors played only a small part: for instance, my training as a mountaineer ... '

I like that invocation of chance, that proper perspective on the hubristic self-belief of the mountaineer. 'A small part'! That's all, I think, that mountaineering has to play in the sagas of human adventure. Yet continually, increasingly, it's referred to as an 'adventure sport'. The point to be made about this unthinking collocation concerns its inherent contradiction. Sport and Adventure are not the same thing at all, at some level may well be mutually irreconcileable. Their active principles are poles apart: sport and adventure – rules and chance.

But then, what do we mean by adventure anyway? It seems to me one of those debased words, like freedom or God – originally coined to *comprehend* an area of human experience – which have become loose tags ever more divergent from the concept they once bodied forth. I have on my shelves at least two books by mountaineers on the subject of adventure. One concludes that adventurers have big hands and a faraway look in their eyes. The other ends with the ultimate – and ultimately farcical – willy-waving fable about a man who grew and grew until finally he surpassed so hugely the mountain he'd initially stood beneath that he burst, and out of him came another man who also grows and explodes and then another, and the author 'knew somehow that, after the next explosion, my man would be just that much bigger again. And again.'

Between all this veiled tumescence and parturition-envy there's a good deal about crops, onions, cabbages, gardening and the like. My response to the whole idea as an adequate image by which to understand adventure is derision. Beyond that, it's to ask why there is this failure of imagination on the part of mountaineers to understand what adventure is about?

I suspect that the answer to what the non-mountaineering public would consider an absurd conundrum lies in the depths of that vast gulf which stretches between adventure and achievement. Can a successful mountaineer truly be called an adventurer? Perhaps that depends on what it took for him to become a successful mountaineer. If the answer is a solar-powered lap-top computer (if you think that's some notional red herring introduced to prop up my argument, I recommend an attentive reading of Chris Bonington's *The Everest Years*), then for a very simple reason the answer has to be 'No!'

That reason is the fundamental one of calculation, for once that quality intrudes, adventure goes out the window. Human resourcefulness, not material or technological resources, is what's called forth by adventure. Spontaneous adequacy, not planning and conquest, is its linch-pin. The word earns two columns of definition in the Oxford English Dictionary. The keynotes are 'that which happens without design ... chance ... hap ... luck ... a chance occurrence ... a trial of one's chance ... chance of danger or loss ... risk ... jeopardy.'

All the things, in fact, that so much of modern climbing has set its face against. Which is not to stigmatise modern climbing. To watch Ben Moon on *Hubble* is to witness exquisite gymnastic complexity. But it's not adventure, and climbing once gravitated to that. Which brings me back to Primo Levi and the title of this piece.

Levi's best book is the enthralling mix of memoir, fact and fiction called *The Periodic Table*. Its chapters are all given names of elements, and treat of characters who, for Levi, possess like qualities. The one on Iron focuses on Sandro Delmastro:
'He spoke grudgingly about his exploits. He did not belong to that species of

persons who do things in order to talk about them ... It appeared that in speaking, as in mountain climbing, he had never received lessons; he spoke as no-one speaks, saying only the core of things ... To see Sandro in the mountains reconciled you to the world and made you forget the nightmare weighing on Europe ... We would come out at dawn, rubbing our eyes, through the small door of the Martinotti bivouac, and there, all around us, barely touched by the sun, stood the white and brown mountains, new as if created during the night that had just ended and at the same time innumerably ancient. They were an island, an elsewhere.'

One February day (the period described in the book is the early 1940s), Levi and Sandro set out 'for the winter climb of the Tooth of M, which for some weeks had been one of our projects.' Here's Levi's account: 'We slept in an inn and left the next day, not too early, at some undetermined hour (Sandro did not like watches: he felt their quiet continuous admonishment to be an arbitrary intrusion). We plunged boldly into the mist and came out of it at one o'clock, in gleaming sunlight and on the big crest of a peak which was not the right one.'

They discuss the matter. Levi suggests that they carry on and 'be satisfied with the wrong peak, which in any case was only 40 metres lower than the right one.'

'Sandro, with splendid bad faith, said in a few dense syllables that my last proposal was fine, but from there "by way of the easy north-west ridge" (this was a sarcastic quotation from the Alpine Club guidebook) we could also reach the Tooth of M in half an hour; and what was the point of being 20 if you couldn't permit yourself the luxury of taking the wrong route.'

The ridge turns out to be disconcertingly difficult, covered on the one side with melting snow, on the other with verglas:

'We reached the top at five; I dragged myself along so pitifully that it was painful, while Sandro was seized by a sinister hilarity that I found very annoying.

'"And how do we get down?"

'"As for getting down, we shall see," he replied, and added mysteriously, "The worst that can happen is to have to taste bear-meat."'

They survive the night, in the morning return to the inn:

'This was it, the bear meat; and now that many years have passed, I regret that I ate so little of it, for nothing has had, even distantly, the taste of that meat, which is the taste of being strong and free, free also to make mistakes and be the master of one's own destiny. That is why I am grateful to Sandro for having led me consciously into trouble, on that trip and other undertakings *which were only apparently foolish ...* '

Sandro's end runs thus: a resistance fighter, in trying to escape from captivity with the *Fascisti* he 'was killed by a tommy-gun burst to the back of the neck by a monstrous child-executioner, one of those wretched murderers of 15 ... recruited in the reformatories. His body was abandoned in the road for a long time, because the *Fascisti* had forbidden the population to bury him.'

I wonder if there's an image of the degradation of mountaineering in his fate? I know that unless you understand *viscerally* what it is to 'eat bear meat', you contribute to its death.

2: TRAINS, CAFÉS, CONVERSATIONS (1981)

(This next piece was written during the early years of that pernicious era of government headed by Margaret Thatcher, not long after her infamous pronouncement that 'there is no such thing as society.')

An hour or two ago I was sitting on the back step of a new house in Heaton Mersey, wondering if it would rain, whether I would get out to Pex Hill for some climbing tomorrow night, and what these streets would be like a century from now. Gazing vacantly across a neatly mown and boundaried square of lawn at the disused and trackless railway embankment beyond, it occurred to me that this same embankment must have carried the railway from Manchester's Central Station along which the ramblers' specials to Chinley, Miller's Dale and Matlock rattled most Sundays in a period over 20 years ago when I first took to going out into the Peak District at weekends.

This train of thought once invoked, the most vivid memories came flooding back: of eager crowds waiting on gas-lit platforms in the dusk of a wet Sunday, and the comforting, warm, misty-windowed atmosphere of a carriage full of people come in from the rain, their flannels and cotton anoraks steaming, light patches spreading across the darkened fabric as the conversation, the incessant, friendly conversation flowed. And then the streaming out from Central or Victoria Stations into the city night and the buses for home.

I'm not basing this railway idyll on the celebration of such delights of a pre-Beeching era as might appeal to the Steam Buff – the blackened architecture, hissing and polished pistons, gusts of smoke swirling across platform ends, the dusty smell of third-class carriages, names of long-forgotten stations and the like. I feel no particular sadness at their passing, but what has gone, along with all these, and what had a special meaning for lovers of the outdoors, is the subtle sense of community which this mode of transport brought about.

It wasn't, of course, confined to railways or transport. I wonder how many readers remember Ma Thomas' Hathersage café in the days of her prime? When Ma Thomas died, a year or so ago, there were no notices or obituaries in the outdoor press, yet her influence on my generation of Peak District climbers was momentous. We all of us have scintillating memories of this ferocious little South-Walian woman. Her tongue was razor-fine, her politics sturdily Labour, her wit was fast yet kind, and her food ... Well, I dare not say, perhaps less out of respect for her memory than from a sort of residual fear of ever daring to complain to her face. I remember Martin

Boysen did so once, about an egg afloat in a sea of grease littered with the flotsam of white and sodden chips. The Prussian hauteur of Martin in his youth was speedily discomfited by Ma's summary rejoinder that if her food was not good enough for him, his custom was certainly not required by her.

I could write a great deal on the subject of Ma Thomas – the way, for example, she ejected Major Something-or-other, canvassing for the Conservative candidate, from her premises one weekday, when I was playing truant from school to go climbing on Stanage: 'If my 'usband was alive you wouldn't 'ave dared set foot in this 'ouse, and you buggers needn't think I'm any different from 'im.' All this as she chased him down the hall with a frying pan. And there was her partisanship for Richard McHardy, thrusting her daughter upon him, or him upon her daughter, I can't remember which, in preference to another suitor who, in her frequently-voiced opinion, 'hadn't got the brains of a rat.' The slapstick and the bias aside, there was something more about the place. Obviously you went to Ma's to eat and drink, but not just for that. She was a catalyst to good conversation, would listen in when she was not too harassed, and drop a cutting phrase across what, to her, was an inflated argument, or a commonsensical anecdote into a sympathetic theme. It was her personality which drew us there each Sunday to sit around the big tables after a day on Stanage or Burbage in a second-family atmosphere, the talk fizzing along, tea leaves floating idly and an hour to go before the train.

Things that have gone! Sitting here now, I wonder if I actually do remember, or only dream I remember, being in Bala Station in about 1960 and seeing a train pull out on its way to Trawsfynydd? I certainly remember the stations at Bala, Corwen, Llanberis, and Bethesda, and they are now all long gone. And with them the facility to transport the walking population of a city *en masse* to some particular outdoor venue. You might think that this was not much used – maybe these days it would not be – but you would be wrong. One such excursion comes back to me with great clarity. Again, it would be 1960 and I was 13 at the time.

There was a ramblers' special to the Dee Valley from Manchester Exchange. I remember city streets deserted in the early Sunday morning except for groups of ramblers resolutely converging on the station. The train was packed, 12 or more to a compartment. We went to Bala and the fare for me was, I think, two-and-sixpence. At that time I used to go out walking with a group of people from Oldham who called themselves the Kindred Spirits – there must have been hundreds of such walking clubs in the Northern cities. From Bala we raced up the Milltir Gerrig road at a steady four miles per hour before trailing along the Berwyn ridge in Len Chadwick's wake, to end up running along the last two miles of road between

Cynwyd and Corwen to catch the train on its way back.

But most of all I remember the journey home, the carriage packed full and every other one likewise and all of them ringing with animated conversations, between people white-haired and ruddy, young and fresh-faced, friends and strangers, all clad in regulation garb of old flannels tucked into socks, cotton or gaberdine anoraks, heavy skirts for the women, Timpson's boots. Once the details of the day's activity had been recounted, discussed, and consigned to the vaults of memory, the talk started. There was a great, brown, jovial fellow, eccentrically clad in leather shorts, called Lees Shaw and he held forth in grisly detail about industrial accidents and the need for legislation on safety at work as the stations – Llangollen, Rhiwabon, Wrexham and Chester – clacked past. You could take that as the type of these conversations – a drift from the particular to the general – the telling of a tale and then its taking apart, its being held up to all sorts of differing viewpoints, from that of a jejune 13-year-old with no life-experience whatsoever to those of 50 or 60-year-olds who had spent their lives working in cotton mills, taking WEA classes in the evenings, and walking at weekends and holidays. The tone was universally helpful, amiable, interested, courteous. In that train on that day there was a mood of light-heartedness, friendship, exultation, attentive consideration and community such as it is one of the greatest joys of humanity to achieve. And like the stations to which we were bound that day, it seems largely to have gone. We are no longer entrained together in humour, good fellowship, and joint purpose. Our television age and newspeak have undermined the capacity to talk. We no longer have the presiding spirit of a Ma Thomas in our cafés. Our clubs are not the same. The barrackers and the comics, the apprentices, the orators, the wise men and singers of songs have all been swept before the grey tide of personal, individual ambition at all cost, battered on the rocks of cynicism, or frozen out by the wintry sneer. We go out in our cars and strict couples, enjoined to secrecy, to lick the lists and climb the status ladders and the sense of community is gone.

Or has it? Have I grown older and gone beyond and forgotten, lost touch with all the good of it, or have my roots truly gone? I cannot see them, but perhaps I cannot see them for looking. There are still times, on the outcrops, say – perhaps on Pex Hill tomorrow if it stays fine – when an easy camaraderie will exist. But the times are rarer, surely, now? We are all intent on self-realisation rather than the sharing and comparing and learning from the wider experience. Our new modes of education from the earliest age accent it thus. I cannot but think that in all this the last two decades have wrought another of those subtle and grievous losses in which our rich and progressive age abounds. And I cannot but wish I was wrong.

3: Contumely of the Conquistadors (1993)

Re-reading *The Ascent of Everest* 40 years after its first publication, I'm struck on the one hand by how decent and worthy, indeed gracious a book it is, and on the other by how entirely alien it now appears to the consciousness and mores of the last decade of the 20th Century. Its very first sentence sets the tone: 'This is the story of how, on 29th May, 1953, two men, both endowed with outstanding stamina and skill, inspired by an unflinching resolve, reached the top of Everest and came back unscathed to rejoin their comrades.'

My post-modernist perception struggles to set that language in context. As Yeats wrote, 'We traffic in mockery.' There is a problem in those words' register that haunts and strives to undermine them. They no longer conjure up images of joyful achievement and aspiring, of innocent mountain ambition, but darker ones, satirical shades. It's the speech of Newbolt and Kitchener; it frames the poster from which the recruiting sergeant's finger points out to underline the message that 'your country needs you'; it's the imperial afflatus that Wilfred Owen undercuts with the grim reality of 'sacrifice' ('What passing bells for these who died as cattle?'); it's the same nightmare or farcical rhetoric spoken by the court martial in Joseph Losey's *King and Country* or the General underneath whom the boards burn in the closing sequences of Lindsay Anderson's *If ...* We can no longer take it seriously, mutter to ourselves in sardonic accompaniment a chorus of 'Play up, play up, and play the game!', view it from a cosmically different perspective where martial celebration is beyond the pale. The standpoint of 1953 – that Everest had to be climbed – has become the philosophical scapegoat to an era where what's chosen for celebration is mountaineering bad faith.

But this, without substantiation, is perhaps to assert too much: 'martial celebration'? 'Everest had to be climbed'? Our current bad faith? Are those charges true?

The first is easy enough. If you read through the whole history of human involvement with Everest, it interlinks inextricably with that of the Great Game, is riddled with militarism. Consider only the ranks of those centrally involved in its exploration: Colonel Younghusband, Captain Noel, General Bruce, Major Tilman, Brigadier John Hunt – the list goes on. The military presence throughout sets up a fascinating tension with a more individualistic parallel tradition that reaches its most succinct expression in an anecdote recounted to me by Jack Longland to explain the failure, 20 years before the successful expedition, of Ruttledge's trip in 1933:

' ... the crucial point was when the two soldiers, Bousted and Birnie, took it on themselves to say that conditions were too cold to establish Camp Five on May 20th. Wyn Harris, who was an infinitely more experienced mountaineer, thought this an absolute nonsense. I remember I was at Camp Four at the time and Wyn Harris came down in a complete fury, saying 'The fucking soldiery!' And he was right, because on the 20th for the next three days not only was the weather good but it was before the upper slabs were covered with new snow.'[1]

It's a tantalising prospect, that had it not been for the inexperienced autocracy of 'the fucking soldiery', with a fit, capable and competitive team of Shipton and Smythe, Longland and Wyn Harris well positioned on the mountain, Everest might have been climbed during the dark years of the depression instead of synchronously with the 'glad confident morn' of the Coronation. The military, after that fiasco, needed to redeem itself and how *gloriously*, in 1953, it did so – with knighthoods and honours all round as just and due reward.

All of which tends to obscure the fact that the 1953 venture was less expedition than expeditionary force. Its planning was meticulous, disciplined, exemplary; the terrain was studied from every angle (one of the most telling passages has Hunt poring over aerial photographs of the South Peak and summit ridge); lines of supply and command are firmly drawn up. There are ways in which *The Ascent of Everest* reads like a text-book of classic warfare. I open it at random and read thus:

'First we must stock our Camp IV with stores sufficient to enable us to await an opportunity offered by the weather; we were already planning to besiege Everest for a fortnight. If the mountain held out for longer than this, then we should be forced to replenish from Base Camp. At the same time we must place the stores required for the Assault – all those to be carried above the head of the Cwm – at Camp V, which would thus, in effect, be a depot of the Assault stores. The exact amounts and their weights were already known, and consequently the number of High Altitude Sherpas required ...'

The message is relentlessly hammered home: Everest had to be climbed. This was why Eric Shipton, the original choice of leader, was removed by – in the deputy leader Charles Evans' phrase – 'an unworthy device.' Shipton was compromised and forced into resignation by the Himalayan Committee's designation, against Shipton's will, of John Hunt in increasingly senior roles on the expedition. If I have one criticism of Hunt's book, it is that in it this saga was glossed over in a single, and possibly disingenuous, sentence: 'Eric Shipton himself had already started to lay down the foundations for planning and was available to give advice from his immense fund of Himalayan experience.'[2]

---

[1] For more context to this, see 'The Essential Jack Longland' in Section Two ...

[2] ... and for more background to this sorry chapter of British mountaineering politics, see 'Exploring Eric Shipton' in the same section.

Nearly 40 years after this was written, when I interviewed John Hunt, I had a feeling that this omission still rankled in his conscience, urging him 'wherever possible to pass much of the credit back where it belonged, with Eric Shipton.' I don't wish to delve into psychological theorising, but there seems to me an element here of an honourable man (and forget MacNaught Davis' cheap sneers about 'Sir Isaac Hoont' that Ken Wilson chose to publish in *Mountain* some years ago, for as his record of public service alone shows, Hunt is exceptionally principled and altruistic) having been placed in an invidious position by the perceived necessity for Everest to be climbed. With Shipton, they were taking too much of a chance; with Hunt, as far as it ever can be in the mountains, chance was to be eliminated. The Good Soldier had been put in charge. His team was hand-picked and assembled round its leader, every member vetted: 'There was the need to be sure that each one of the party really wanted to get to the top.' The thing was becoming competitive, the Swiss had already 'entered the lists', Everest had to be climbed.

And climbed it was, through exemplary planning and magnificent teamwork and no small personal example on Hunt's part. Everyone under his care came back alive. The success was celebrated in appropriate style: 'In our light-hearted mood, we remembered our two-inch mortar. It had not been called upon to clear a path up the mountain for us, but it would carry out a no less appropriate function now. A salute should be fired, a *feu de joie*. We had 12 bombs, a gift from the Indian Army. With each of us taking turns, these were duly loosed off, to the delight both of ourselves and of the whole of our numerous retinue. This was followed by some practice with our equally neglected .22 rifles, the targets being some spare mortar-bomb detonators ... '

Yet however much John Hunt's book strives for magnanimity of gesture and stately appropriateness of language, there is a sub-text to all this that cannot entirely be concealed. It's the same one picked up by Tilman after his ascent of Nanda Devi in 1936: 'after the first joy in victory came a feeling of sadness that the mountain had succumbed, that the proud head of the goddess had been bowed.' Victory necessarily implies defeat, and conquest subjection, and invasion loss, and the treading of peaks can be the crossing of watersheds of the spirit. I believe John Hunt recognised this in his concluding chapter:

'Ultimately, the justification for climbing Everest, if any justification is needed, will lie in the seeking of their "Everests" by others, stimulated by this event as we were inspired by others before us.'

The words (witness that qualifying 'if any justification is needed') are uneasy. Hunt is too intelligent a man not to be aware subliminally of the implicit problem they raise.

Which is this: there are other 'Everests', but there is no other Everest. The mountain climbed 'because it was there' has done a disappearing act, is no longer there. History has absorbed it, feet have trodden it, words have described it. We do not know what it is like to stand on the actual summits of Kangchenjunga or Machapuchare,[1] but we do know – personally in increasing numbers and vicariously by the tens of thousands – how it feels to raise the flags over Everest. The ultimate has become the everyday.

We're made the more aware of how momentous was the ascent of Everest by studying the directions taken by mountaineering thereafter: emulation or regression – you could take your pick but one or other it had to be. In a spirit of emulation, there was for a time the increasingly desolate and dispiriting movable caravanserai of Second Lieutenant Christian Bonington, camping out under the latest last great problem with its corporate sponsorship, contracts, career structure and increasing death toll.[2] There were the crack regiments of the army moving in to clean up on the conquests he'd not made. And thankfully, apart from that tradition-robbed-of-its-focus, there were the regressives, those who looked back to Shipton, Tilman and Longstaff for their examples and from whom, for the last 15 or 20 years, mountaineering has derived its stimulus and drive. They cut in early, their banner raised by Charles Evans' brilliant and reverent reconnaissance expedition to Kangchenjunga in 1955, when Joe Brown and George Band climbed up to, but not on to, the summit. The 'more individualistic parallel tradition' I mentioned later reasserted itself under the banner of 'alpine-style': not pulling together but personal responsibility, not management but living-on-your-wits inspiration and self-sufficiency, not emblems but the unknown, not the world's acclaim but authentic experience.

Which is how – reactively – mountaineering came to be embroiled in issues of authenticity and bad faith. Take that sentence I quoted at the outset and our ironic mockery of it. There is no doubt about its authenticity. This, without false modesty, is what John Hunt believes, and is perhaps what we still aspire – robbed of our ultimate symbol and aspiration – to believe about ourselves. But our characteristic mode now, post-modernists all, is irony, wherein, according to Sartre, 'a man annihilates what he posits within one and the same act: he leads us to believe in order

---

[1] Holy mountains to indigenous peoples in the surrounding regions – expeditioners gave pledges, formerly honoured, not to tread the actual tops but stop a few feet short when they were clearly achievable.

[2] He eventually, to his credit and greater personal relish, deserted the project and joined the guerilla faction.

not to be believed; he affirms to deny and denies to affirm.' Belief requires a focus, and the focus has gone, the ultimate despatched. Experience alone, keynote of the regressive tradition, is left: 'If man is what he is, bad faith is forever impossible and candour ceases to be his ideal and becomes instead his being.' But man is defined by his aspiring, which in Nietzsche's phrase is 'a bridge and a going across.' Once over the abyss, astride the peak, it is no longer emblem but commodity, attainable, measured, and the style in which we record our response to it modulates inevitably into bad faith. I look back on the innocence of that opening sentence of John Hunt's and realise with shocked clarity that in the success of that climb was the Fall. Whither, or wither, mountaineering now ... ?

4: AFTER THE FUNERAL (1995)

In 1995 Paul Williams – one of the most notable and endearing characters in British climbing – died in a fall from Brown's Eliminate on Froggatt Edge. I gave the eulogy at his funeral in Hathersage Parish Church, and afterwards, as what felt like a necessary gesture, with Martin Crook I went up to Froggatt to climb the route.

The edge – it is broken and granular, livid yellow against the weathered ochres. I touch it delicately, caressingly as a nurse cleansing a raw wound:

'Not the rock's fault, not Paul's. It is just accident,' I tell myself, and look down at the flat, good landing 25 or 30 feet below where Martin stands holding the rope, meet his eye. In this tenuous position of balance I dare not shrug, but my imagination shrugs:

'He shouldn't have died, Martin, not from here. Nine times out of ten you'd be talking maybe a broken ankle ... '

It's changed so much since I last did it, and hugely so in the 33 years since I first did it, this route. I pull on to the sloping ledge above, apprehensive now about the flat knob my right hand cranks on, body off-balance to the left, conscious of pained joints and strength declined from its prime. Nine days ago it was the next move in Paul's life, the move he did not complete. On top I sit on the edge to bring up Martin. There is a drift of fine rain in the breeze, a musky, sweet smell of rowan blossom threads up to us from the woods below, new leaves on the birch trees are tinged with scarlet and as the air ripples across them they turn their pale undersides towards us, dappling and rustling.

He follows in the considered and powerfully graceful style which makes his climbing a joy to watch. We sit together, who were both close to Paul, an arm around each other's shoulders for comfort, and tell wicked stories in celebration of his full life. The air's cool and fragrant, the landscape subdued, its outlines merging into grey mist:

'Oh, Martin, life's so sweet in these moments.'

We, having lost him, are thinking of what he has lost: the glad contact with friends; the occasional magic of intimacy and union with his woman; the wholeness and sensuality of body and mind in the experience of rock; blood-pride in his son, who saw him fall. Ripple of a wave through the silt of millions of years ago, imprinting a weakness even into metamorphosed form, has ended all that. After the funeral, in what seems to us a proper way, we have come to bid him goodbye.

The community which gathered in the church is the one I have lived among, been supported and checked by, celebrated, analysed, criticised and known since I was 12 years old. It's my honour to speak to, and to speak as well as I can for it, today – to give some account of, accord rightful praise to, Paul's life. To these 400 people, among whom are most of my friends, I do my best to express what I hope are common feelings, shared responses, joint gratitudes for the way he was and the way in which even his weaknesses helped our understanding. I try to tell of how to come to terms – as we all must, if our humanity is to flourish – with anger and fear, of the dark mirror through which we could, but need not, view the bright, blameless, redeeming rock across which our characters flicker and play, are revealed and perhaps even enhanced.

These gatherings are extraordinarily moving, expressions of great love and generosity of spirit, times when the factionalism and spite – to which any sphere where the ego holds too much sway are inevitably prone – are put aside. When I was young and my friends began dying – Brian Ripley, Arthur de Kusel, John Brazinton, Hugh Gair, Danny Murphy, Lawrie Holliwell, with all of whom I climbed, all of them and others too gone within a year or two either side of the turn of the 1970s – I raged against the rock, but the rock is just rock, and at some level, for pure accident is a rare thing, the flaw is often our own.

What other community is as ours is, coming together with such frequency to honour the dead? And coming together across the generations – Peter Harding and Joe Brown sitting just a few feet away from Ron Fawcett and Johnny Dawes? We are disputatious, factional, even vicious, yet at times like these, reconciliation and decency of impulse alone hold the floor. In some subtle, and I think *essentially* religious way, their deaths and our celebrations of their lives offer us the opportunity for redemption of our own faults. That strange process perhaps has something to do with a collective recognition of the true nature of our activity, something to do with being jolted back into an innate sense of our own smallness, presumption and impermanence by contrast with the indifferent grandeur and impersonal beauty of the mountains among which our games takes place.

But I would hate to become solemn on this. It is just a thought, and there was an incident back at Longland's, the Hathersage restaurant to which we went for the wake, which put it into perspective. John from Huddersfield – I don't know his other name,[1] just that he phones me from time to time introducing himself thus, that we maybe knew each other years ago through Richard McHardy when he lived in Glossop, and that he's a little fellow with long grey hair who's been around a long

---

[1] I do now – it's John Lumb. Thanks for the book, John ...

time – came up to me, gave me a book shyly and walked away. It was called *Cold Mountain: 100 Poems by the T'ang Poet Han-shan*. So I went into a corner and opened it and the first lines I read were these:

> *Living in the mountains, mind ill at ease,*
> *All I do is grieve at the passing years.*
> *At great labour I gathered the herbs of long life,*
> *But has all my striving made me an immortal?*

My grandmother believed implicitly in divination by The Book, and maybe I keep a vestige of that belief, so I laughed quietly to myself, reminded myself of the 'lonely impulse of delight' that underlies our motives, however cloudy they can become, stood up, and walked straight into Nat Allen, into recognition of the closeness of death and the proper strength of character which hopes beyond hope and refuses easily to submit. He looked tired and grey, but still cracked jokes and talked futures.

Ten days later Nat died – his heart, after long illness, unable to cope with a blood transfusion. So the day after I went back to Froggatt again, to the place which is, I suppose, most associated with Nat.

Nothing had changed. The wet mist was still on the wind, the slender birch branches hung heavy with leaf. There were people around, but surprisingly few for a Sunday. I sat at the foot of *Brown's Eliminate*, where Paul had landed – the flowers his friends had placed were still there, only a little wilted – and recalled maybe the first time I ever led the route. I was so young, in my early teens, wandering along beneath the edge on a Sunday, and I came across Nat sitting here. He was a hero of mine. I wanted to impress him, so my motives were impure. I led the route. Nat held my rope, joked and calmed and talked me through the moves, and he then followed up in his neat and unhurried style. This was half Nat's lifetime ago, and three-quarters of mine. Afterwards we sat on top, dangling our legs over the drop, and what Nat conveyed, through attitude and anecdote, was wisdom, humour, joy – was as sound a basis as anyone could be given for a life in climbing.

I'll not mourn for any of them, good men that they were – not for Nat, nor Paul Nunn, with whom I climbed on Stanage on the day of Nat's funeral and who's gone now too – avalanched on Haramosh, nor for any of those who've gone down the long slide before us. I could have wished them longer lives, but immortality's not our lot. They, who added to the richness of life, through their deaths remind us how good life is. So on this new morning my companion and I do Nat's route, *Green Gut*, which she leads with great enjoyment and application, and then *Brown's Eliminate*, which I lead and in which she revels. I'm a little nervous again on the big ledge before the crux sequence, but Nat's voice calls up from old memory, and anyway I will not be frightened off by potential consequence. A dog comes across to the flowers at its foot, sniffs, cocks a leg and pisses on them. I think about how Paul would have laughed, would have enjoyed the irreverence. The sun comes out. We go to Stanage and lie in it in the Plantation, talking.

Some time later, in sweltering June heat on top of *Goliath's Groove*, the woman I'm climbing with draws me to her and kisses me. The larches below are very green and stir gently their fronded branches. On the flat top of a boulder a boy and girl dance with exuberant elegance to the faint beat of a radio. The valleys are filling with dusty mauve shadow, the moorland ridges clarifying out towards evening. Form takes precedence over texture, colour and atmosphere intensify, the sun is heading down. It is all so utterly beautiful. We must love one another and die.

5: IN PRAISE OF COMPETENCE (2002)

Glancing up for a moment from examining the shattered red block where I've found a crack that just might take a peg – though whether or not it will be one I'd like to put my weight on remains to be seen – I catch sight of Bonington slinging 150 feet (and no, I don't mean 45 metres – we're talking 1968 here) of nine millimetre rope over his shoulder and slipping over the edge. Puzzled, I wander over, peer down that complex and outrageous stretch of steep, broken rock, crumbling ribs, vegetated and undercut slabs that runs round from Lighthouse Arête into *Red Wall* Zawn at South Stack. Chris is already 50 feet beneath me, the sea another 250 feet beneath him, and he's picking his way methodically, smoothly, through ground it hadn't occurred to me to treat as anything other than an abseil route. He looks up, gives me a quick affirmative nod and a smile – he's enjoying life down there, it seems – and carries on. So I grab my gear – a bundle of tapes and krabs round my neck, a bunch of pegs, a hammer stuffed in the back pocket of my jeans, a rope round my shoulder – tighten my P.A.'s and follow him.

Actually, it's not so bad. There are these little gravelly runnels your feet skid around in, and everything you touch has a temporary feel to it. Also there are small matters of the angle, and of the sea 300 feet beneath. If you start to slide on this stuff, nothing much will stop you – there'll be a few bounces, a couple of rag-doll whirls, and then it's splashdown time. In 30 years my old climbing mate Dave Pearce will die here. But that's consequence, and to guard against it, you creep on down in a kind of ecstasy, a concentration on weight-and-balance transference, and in my case keeping up a muttered, giggling, crazed commentary on the absurdity of it all as I go. In fact, I've a perverse liking for this kind of terrain.

Halfway down to the sea on this rib alongside *Red Wall* there's a platform. Brown and Crew came this way on the first ascent in 1966, and so did I a year or so later, abseiling, and from the platform another long diagonal abseil across vegetated, gravelly slabs and down a slimy overhanging wall takes you to the pebble beach in the zawn – or at least, if it was low tide that's where you'd end up, and otherwise you took your chance with the waves. Anyway, Chris was already wandering off across the slabs by the time I got to the platform so I followed him. You couldn't exactly say the line of descent was well-marked in those days, and these more sensible days it's never used at all, but Chris was scuttling around and peering over the lip of the last steep wall. He found a way down it, soloed up the vertical grass on the opposite side to the stance at the foot of the route, and by the time I'd joined him he had a peg belay in, had tied on, took the rope I was carrying from my shoulder as he handed me an end, had it uncoiled without a moment's fuss, gave me that end as well, and with a wipe of my boots I was getting to grips with the first pitch of the climb.

I've had my differences with Chris over the years – climbing is so small and factional a business in this country that perhaps that's inevitable – but I've never forgotten this, nor very often encountered much to compare with it: for efficiency, boldness, a kind of battle-joy. Also competence, and most particularly, I think, this last. I was brooding about it again recently when I was in Spain with Ed Douglas. There was a sea cliff we went down by bizarre means, and it was in my mind then how Bonington would have relished, have been entirely engrossed in, that terrain. I'd had the same thought a day or two earlier in the 'gorge of hell' – the Barranc de l'Infern – up in the Marina Alta behind Xabea. The 1000-ft rock walls are so close they occlude even the high Spanish sun. Light filters down, a pale blue cast to the shade that the pale grey of the gorge wall absorbs. Every stone we step upon clacks into a sharp reiteration of echoes, our labouring breath amplifies, lizards scamper into crevices impossibly tiny, etching their greens and browns into the grey. Across the rocks, from one to another we skip – Ed, Jose Garcia and myself, through depths as impressive as any natural place I've been. We slip from rock-vat to rock-vat where the flood-waters are boiled, bolts here and there, chains, frayed lengths of knotted rope down awkward short slabs, or stretched across traverses high over pots. Into some we abseil, and must climb the scoured and polished rock out again. Above me on one 30-ft wall with a hard move for the top, Ed slaps for the rim, his groping hand dipping into a pool, sluicing water down the slab. I curse him playfully, move tentatively up, trainers angling on buffed, small edges, to slip from which would mean a broken ankle maybe, and a lengthy, embarrassing, difficult evacuation. It's like open-air caving, and I've always found that one of the most satisfying and exploratory of activities. Fig trees that will never fruit lodge in unreachable niches high above. Flood debris is jammed into cracks far above our heads. In pale imitation of the water itself, its ghost-absence inviting us to dance, we race through, speed of the essence here.

Two descents over 30 years apart, but there's some sense of connection in my mind between the two of them. In the same way that Bonington was on *Red Wall*, Ed and Jose have the competence, the ability to move fast and safely through dangerous terrain, that I've always considered to be one of the crucial qualities needed for the fullest enjoyment of the environments we, as climbers, seek out.

Yet as I think about it, a paradox takes shape. You see, the quality I'm talking about here has absolutely nothing to do with technical virtuosity. I'll leave Jose out of this equation because I've never seen him climb, but neither Chris nor Ed – good, bold, committed and enthusiastic climbers though they both are – would lay claim to having been among the hyper-technical hot-shot rock-jocks of their respective generations. And yet, they have this ability to move quickly and safely across testing ground. You could argue that nowadays in rock-climbing it's not something that's often called upon or needed – stuff the descents, man, clip the chain and let it run! Pity Rachel Farmer didn't have that option when she started her last descent at Buoux. The crags are (and please heaven, will always be) a dangerous environment, where mere technical skill won't always see you through. Also, you can have as many M.I.C. or M.I.A.C. or A.B.M.G. or S.P.S.A. awards and certificates and qualifications as you like, you can have studied all the worthy technical manuals and have the appropriate protection procedures at your fingertips for any given situation, but how long will it take you by the book to get down the gorge of hell, to get down to the foot of *Red Wall*, and do you want 6/8 time or something slower than the slowest of waltzes? As The Queen reputedly said, 'there are forces at work in this country', and it looks like they'd rather see you standing around queening it in your ball-gowns than out there on the dance floor.

I tell you what. There is absolutely no necessary overlap between technical virtuosity and competence in climbing. I remember Alex MacIntyre, of that great early-1970s generation of Leeds University climbers and quite possibly the universal-all-time-rascal-party-animal. Now it may be for this reason; that the only times I climbed with him were after some major debauch when he was hung over, reeking of vomit, wrecked – and I loved him like a brother and would never wish to do him down; but in all conscience he was a crap rock-climber, weak-armed, flailing, irresolute. Yet there were things he did all over the World's mountains that I'd think once, think twice, think a dozen times about and then decide very firmly against. And so would you. But Alex was safe as anyone upon them, and his death by some little whirring tragic stone on the south face of Annapurna one of the worst jokes ever played on joyful mountain innocence.

Sometimes I wonder if what we're doing to the whole experience on offer in the mountains, in the hills, with our alphabetico-numerical obsessions, our superfluity-excisions (no descents other than by rope from crags; no vegetatious crap to be climbed – purely for ecological protection reasons, of course; no long approach marches or scrambles to the foot of crags to be countenanced), our career-structure-punditries, doesn't amount to something akin to those ghastly snippets you get on Classic FM or 'Easy Listening Classics for Pleasure', or some other such filleted stuff. What I do know is that when it comes down to the long perspectives, what sticks most clearly in my memory are not the small, clear, neat movements, but the longer, complex approaches, the expository bits, the places where all the major themes are introduced, the descents, the discords, the dangers, the inspiration of the players who take risks, who have the competence and confidence and appreciation to join in the whole symphony, and not just practice and fiddle away at the odd nice tune. What d'you say? Want to dance ...

6: GRADE DRIFT (2005)

The first time this concept registered on my consciousness was in the course of a conversation with the ineffable Ken Wilson. He had been telling me about the activities of some mutual acquaintance who, way back in our youth, was the kind of climber you might expect to meet on Clogwyn y Bustach (Ogwen version) more frequently than on Craig Gogarth – which is a roundabout way of saying that in those days he was not particularly bold, competent, venturesome, or whatever other adjectives you can use to avoid saying 'good'. I had expressed some mild degree of surprise at Ken's account – 'Him get up that!' or some such – and Ken, with his usual clarity, had brushed this aside with the brusque explanation, 'Grade drift, of course,' which raised all sorts of odd images in my mind of individuals like tectonic plates, grating against the cliffs and rising up to their crests by dint of some remorseless power within them.

Being rather dim and slow on the up-take, and having some vague notion that it could be turned to my own advantage as the ageing process hit home, I'd naturally questioned Ken further on all this. In his explanation it appeared to me logically that if, as he insisted, increasing equipmental sophistication, normative behaviour around issues like training, habituation to situational demands and a kind of general osmotic imbibing from the community-ether led inexorably to vastly-raised levels of performance, then all I needed to do was sit back, go with the flow – perfectly acceptable mode, of course, to a sixties-survivor like me – and by the time I was 93 I would be able to solo *Hubble* with untroubled ease. Form and ambition were as nothing. Wait, keep buying the gear, and it would simply come to me.

This troubled me to an extent, seemed to me more likely to engender complacency than energetic enjoyment, so I called round at my local medium's to check it out with my dear late comrade, Dave Cook. Wiping away the ectoplasm, he crinkled his eyes in that old, amused way of his, and in his great, booming, ghostly voice directed my attention to the flaws in Ken's argument, the ways in which it placed the climber in a subservient and vulnerable position in relation to a consumerist ethos, put her or him (he did stumble for a moment or two around trying to find a way of speaking 's/he', but since he'd never managed that in the flesh, it was unfair to expect him to achieve it in the ectoplasmic state) in thrall to the appetitive stimulation on which, as I would know from my Marcuse, capitalism depended for its own continuing existence. So with my dialectical materialism thus finely honed, I went back to consider again this idea of grade drift.

It seems, from Ken's account, that there is a host of climbers out there – all of them in their forties, fifties or sixties – who are climbing better now than ever they could in their teens or twenties, and that fact, if true, rather beguiles me. Those who once struggled on *Great Western* can now cruise *Western Front*? I have a suspicion that if I were to put that point to the arbiters, some special pleading might take place, and gritstone, to a degree, be allowed to retain former status. But aside from this, the point seems an interesting one, and to hang upon what we actually mean by climbing well. I can remember what that felt like very clearly – the strength and bodily ease, the instinctual slipping into the right positions, the silken speed of it all. And I can remember too in the years when, if I am brutally honest with myself, I was way past my time as a good rock-climber, that there were occasions when I found myself leading routes well up in the E-grades and harder than I might have dreamed possible when I was at my supposed peak as a climber. Which is, I suppose, exactly what Ken means by 'grade drift'. But I have a certain inward knowledge that, however competent the performances on the harder climbs may at times have been, I was not then climbing as well, was not as good a climber, as I had been, and that what in fact was taking place was a kind of disinhibiting process – an expansion of the margins of safety which allowed me greater freedom but did not actually confer greater ability in terms of those imponderables of climbing action which I always found most satisying: rock-knowledge, grace, the magical sense of interlocking sequence. Actually to achieve some externally-assessed gradation of performance is as nothing, surely, compared to the exercise of those? Which is maybe where I feel a sense of unease around this notion of grade drift – because its focus is so clearly on grade and not on experience, and grade, as we should all know, is something of a farce, and maybe you find yourself in the middle of the big pitch on *Jaywalk* on the Trilleachan slabs and you are 50 feet above your last runner which is a frayed and tatty little thread and a single black squally cloud drifts in from the direction of Skye, where they are bred, and drenches its burden down upon you and are you then any longer on an E1, or something altogether different? This climbing, with all its anomalies ...

It seems to me that if, on an individual level, we are dealing here with something that is clearly possessed of a dimension of illusion or even self-deception, then we can apply the term with equal validity to the grades themselves, which quantifiably drift – and do so both up and down. Which introduces an interesting degree of complexity into this discussion, and a certain interplay now between grade drift as applicable to individual levels of performance, and grade drift as seen in changes to defined levels of difficulty of particular climbs.

Take *Great Western* on Almscliff as an example of this in a minor key. It may or may not be the only four-star climb in Yorkshire, depending on your individual taste, but one thing which is more certain is that it has drifted up a grade in the last quarter-century. It used to be V.S., and now it is H.V.S. I have no argument with either of those assessments. All I wish to comment on is the observable fact of change, which has taken place despite the fact that the route remains – give or take a little polish and accretion of chalk under the roof – exactly and entirely the same. So in terms of the perception of it, it is not to a current generation as it was to a previous one. The difference may be slight – a matter of a single grade – but it is telling. It has drifted up. Which is not to suggest that grade drift for the individual is wholly predicated on grade drift by guidebook committee *diktat*. But there might be an element of that to add to Ken's list of ingredients. And the examples in that direction, particularly from gritstone, are legion – most of them, interestingly, devolving upon the matter of style and breaking down further into two modes. The first is brutal mode – jamming, for example, which is no longer popular but which is perceived as a skill that can be acquired. Modern protection ensures that what can be jammed can also be protected, and so the drift of grade is pegged to reasonable levels. I loved that story of Ian Parnell's about the guidebook committee meeting at which the grade of Whillans' masterpiece, *Sentinel Crack* on Chatsworth, was discussed.

A vote was taken. There were only two people who wanted its grade raised from the current E2, so that's the grade at which it remained. There were only two people in that vote who had actually done the climb. You've got it ... ! So what happened there – the triumph of the conceptual over the actual? What right did those guys have to insist on applying their definition to a climb of which they had no personal experience? Weird ... !

Anyway, to leave *Sentinel Crack* aside for the moment, the other style-mode is the unprotectable, and this is an area that has seen the most intense drift-activity. To stick with gritstone for the moment, I have in mind three favourite climbs of my long-past youth, all of which I've done again in the relatively recent past, and all three of which, to me, seem to have been possessed of the right grades 40 years ago and to have been savagely inflated for subsequent climbing generations. *Namenlos* on Stanage, *Sunset Slab* and *Brown's Eliminate* on Froggatt, all used to be V.S. If Ken's explanation of individual grade drift is right, then all three of them ought to be even easier these days with habituation and the advantage of sticky rubber footwear. And yet, their current grades are, respectively, E1, H.V.S. and E3. It is actually quite difficult for someone of my generation, to whom these were the standard easy solos, to get their head round the supposed fact – quantifiably defined – that *Brown's*

Eliminate is a grade harder than *Sentinel Crack*, and I don't think this anomaly is entirely explained by the fact that none of the committee that graded the latter had actually done it (if you've done it, you will have a particular scar on one of your thumbs, but I won't tell you whereabouts or on which hand in case you go bullshitting about it).

Is it the case, then, that we can only drift where perfect safety is assured, and that grade-inflation is the direct result of that abomination in modern climbing, absence of protection? And since grade-drift is something to do with getting up harder routes, even though they may or may not be actually harder, but not performing on them so well, would it not be more fitting then to call it grade-struggle? I'd better get back to Ken on that one. And also, check it out with Cookie to see if what I'm saying is politically correct ...

7: ON THREE HISTORICAL IMAGES (1996)

i) The Great Wall

To what extent can a single photograph define the age it reflects? The reason I ask the question is because recently I was leafing through John Cleare's and Tony Smythe's *Rock-climbers in Action in Snowdonia*, published by Secker & Warburg in 1966, and to my mind still one of the most satisfying statements about a given period of climbing ever to have been contained within hard covers. To my generation of climbers, its route-choices became the desired objectives, its captions – 'Crew lay-backing on undercut hand-jams below an overhang on *Pellagra*', 'I had this dream, see, and I was falling upwards in a shaft of light', 'You go, you commit yourself, and it's the big effort that counts' – assumed for us the significance of mantras, chanted before our own comparable or more feeble efforts.

Among the book's many atmospheric and characterful studies, for me one stood out and remains to my mind one of the greatest images ever produced of our sport. It reaches out in subtle and mysterious ways after some essential quality it possessed and was practised for then, and which perhaps still appeals now. It's captioned, quite simply, 'Alone on the Great Wall of the East Buttress of Clogwyn Du'r Arddu.' The 'Descriptions of Plates' section expands on this as follows:

'More widely known as "Master's Wall", on account of Joe Brown's exploration and attempts to climb it. When Crew succeeded, he decided in accordance with privilege to change the name. The climb is just about the ultimate in difficulty and entails a 200-ft run-out using only three pitons for aid. A great controversy was waged over Pete Crew's ascent. He abseiled down the wall, cleaned out the crack and inserted all the chockstones, thus preparing the route beforehand. But this technique is accepted and had been used before on the cliff. The only other ascent to date was made by Dave Yates using a similar technique. The photograph is of Crew taking another "look" in 1965.'

The activist, blind to historical perspective, will no doubt sneer at the facts in that, whilst the historian, conversely, will ponder on its implicit statements about practice and value. For my purposes, what matters are that at the time of writing it was still considered the ultimate in difficulty, and the climber portrayed was the original ascensionist.

Consider, by way of contrast, how the first ascensionist of a modern 'ultimate' might be portrayed in a posed photograph. The accent there would be on the physical and the literal. The photographer would be close in, the subject's muscles ripped, each tiny sequential limestone pinch and undercut would be chalk-marked for our attention, the inevitable bolt would be within two or three feet of his or her midriff, unobtrusive but confirmedly present. As too, no doubt, would makers' names on gleaming gear and stylish garb – this is not to disparage, or to suggest that these pictorial tactics are necessarily cliches, but it is to point up the differences, the original qualities, in John Cleare's picture.

There used to be – may still be, for all I know – a lively debate within photography as to whether takers of colour transparencies can be considered photographers at all. 'All they do,' went the argument against, 'is press the shutter release button of their automatic cameras. The results are down to chance, not art. What do they know of the craft of the darkroom, the arcane processes of holding back and dodging in whereby the literal image is given expressive form?'

When you look at Cleare's masterpiece – and it is that – it is hard not to grant substance to the argument. This is not the Great Wall as anyone has ever in clear and objective focus seen Great Wall. If you believe that, compare it with the picture on the rear cover of the current guide to the cliff, or better still and more comparable, with Ken Wilson's admirable and more literal treatment of the route in his famous sequence from *The Black Cliff*. Wilson's images – and this is one of his strengths as a photographer, and derives no doubt from his architectural training – are informative. Yes, he has a sound grasp of the intimate and the physical, in the same way as Cleare does in the weirdly claustrophobic study of 'Crew committed on the *Direct Finish to Erosion Groove*', but essentially, these pictures are matters of record, studies of actual situation and predicament. And John Cleare's is anything but those.

If it's not record – and we might question here whether a climber merely 'taking a look' at his own route from the relatively less difficult first 25 feet is an event worthy of record – what, then, is it? How does this fit? Is it, if you like, a stage set designed and lit by an expressionist for a performance of what he sees as the psychodrama of climbing?

Let's look at the photograph itself more closely to substantiate that view. There is a tiny and predominantly white-clad figure dead centre at a quarter height. A thread-like arc of rope loops down from where he leans, awkward and spreadeagled, into an overhung groove. The rope ends without apparent connection to another human being. The rock around the figure is burnt in to give the comfort of detail. Above him, converging diagonals of dark cracks on the one side, a highlighted water-streak on the other, lead the eye up through an area of vague, streaked detail to an astonishing upreared spire beneath which every vestige of graspable promise has been held back in darkness.

If you were to go to the cliff and look for this spire, you would in fact be very

243

hard pressed to find it. It's a blunt pinnacle on the rim of the Eastern Terrace above the top groove of Jelly Roll, and its rearing presence in the picture is entirely a function of the angle of view. One of the sequence taken by Wilson is from almost exactly the same point, but in Ken's picture the spire is cropped out, detail of the top wall burnt in. What becomes obvious from all this is Cleare's deliberately seeking after a particular effect which expresses something of what he feels climbing to be – that his picture is typological rather than realist in its intent.

So what is its symbolism, what is Cleare's view of the essential nature of climbing as expressed by this crucial picture in his portfolio? Scan its elements again: the cut cord of connection, the tiny white figure's awkward, urgent lean to its task, the forbidding dark mystery above through which his journey lies – this is a pilgrim's progress, a transmutation through silver nitrate alchemy of the base metal of sport into an heroic ideal. Maybe climbing was like that in the 1960s, or maybe it was just one man's vision of it. Either way, the symbol, in all its beauty, power and artistic intent, resonates and satisfies still.

ii) Strapadictomy

He didn't, contrary to bad-mouthing rumour, choose the picture of himself for the cover of his own guide. Dave Gregory, Series Editor for the gritstone guides at the time, did, and the choice – by a man who knows more than most about time, grit and the climber, was inspired and inspirational, encapsulating its time. *Recent Developments* was the title, it came out in 1977, covered all the routes – *Nectar, Silent Spring, Coventry Street, London Wall, Hairless Heart, Moonwalk, Profit of Doom, Fern Hill, Five Finger Exercise, Requiem, Reticent Mass Murderer* – of gritstone's 1970s revolution, the author was Steve Bancroft, and there he was on the cover, on the Froggatt route *Strapadictomy* that John Allen and he had climbed the previous year.

The photographer was Bernard Newman, the picture was a revelation. It was black & white, horizontal format, wrapped round the cover, and the roof on the lip of which Bancroft was so extraordinarily poised jagged out nearly three-quarters of the way across the frame. If you knew grit, it hit you instantly – your reaction was, 'Oh, God! What are they capable of getting up now?' Half the shot was blank texture scarred by a useless crack. Bancroft's position was ludicrous, the fall he'd be contemplating if he came off looked vicious, slamming back in beneath the overhang. What got to you was his waif-like elegance, the apparently casual rightness of posture, his insouciance – the rolled-up Levi's, the scrawny limbs, the lank mop of hair and that gaunt, intense face, 'Hollow of cheek, as though he drank the wind/ And took a mess of shadows for his meat.'

And how he was focused, how he was beamed in to some ludicrous ripple of nothing at the top of the frame. Yet at the same time he looked languid, effortless. That move to come – surely it wasn't even *possible* (you didn't discover until much later that from that angle, from that position, no it wasn't possible and that wasn't how you did it, but that was wisdom after the event and we're talking immediate impact, and all you could do at the time was gasp!)

Looking at it now – now that it's become history – it still keeps its perfection and its shock, its stunning compositional rightness, but other things register about it now for memory and record: the Whillans harness (cruellest and most sardonic joke ever played on the male sex); the way we rolled our jeans to get freedom of movement, the thick socks in the EB's to assert that comfort was paramount. (You would laugh now if you knew what a debate had once centred on that issue – should you buy them a size too small for the tightest fit and suffer the agonies – ingrowing toenails, corns, callouses, hot-day agonies – in consequence? We all did, till we got wise or the choice and availability of options increased. We all used to climb in PAs – EBs as they became – and would barely consider the alternatives – Masters, RDs, ugh!)

Other details spring out too. Where's his chalk bag? How come the edge of that crack's not bleached out with chalk? And mentioning the crack – brief, unfinished, taunting feature that it is – see how delicately it's been brushed. That's a new departure, a technique that only came in during the 1970s. I'd hesitate to be dogmatic on this, but I don't recall seeing evidence of the wire brush being used on gritstone before that time. I remember an occasion in the late 1960s when I was climbing at my best on gritstone. It was on Stanage. I tried the line taken now by *Wuthering*, got round on to the front face way beyond the present crux, and ground to a halt terrified at moving up on sloping pockets in which your hands and feet skated on granular lichen. I called for a top-rope and forgot about it.

When I went back a year or two later, the face was scrubbed to a gleaming silver, the moves up the pockets were entirely straightforward. And so with this picture of *Strapadictomy* – the photograph records the advent of a technique – economically applied here – which previously had not been considered. It reveals a shift in ethical practise which contributed to the leap in standards of achievement.

All this is just the detail, though, and what matters most about this picture is the overall impression – of this young, gaunt, manic (no-one else until Stevie Haston burst into prominence ever managed to look so convincingly manic as Bancroft) figure casually posed on the edge of seeming impossibility. It spelt something out about the sport's future: anything goes, nothing's off-limits, we can succeed. It was riveting in its laid-back assurance. You knew, seeing it, that climbing was moving on.

And move on it did in the 1970s, in just the way this picture predicates. 'OK, so it looks hard – let's take a look, see what there is, how it pieces together.' Remember that young student from Leeds, friend of Bancroft's, newcomer to climbing, who went out on a windy autumn day to Almscliff and made a faultless sight lead, his rope streaming out behind him in the blast, of *Wall of Horrors*, which had the reputation then of being the hardest and most serious route on British rock? John Syrett he was called. Posterity might judge that he didn't do enough to be numbered amongst the greats of the sport, and posterity, for once, would be wrong. He had all the gifts: grace, skill, radical approach, and his use of them flagged up the new possibilities. He generated excitement, optimism, competition, a way of looking. He had coal-black eyes that shot you sidelong glances and seemed to say, 'I'll believe it when I see it – until I've tried it, there's nothing you can tell me about it.' He had more influence on the sport, through what was possibly the crucial generation in climbing's development in this country – Livesey, Fawcett, Bancroft, Allen – than many of the most major pioneers from other periods.

There's another aspect of this picture which cries out to be taken account of, and yet which is so obvious it could easily be ignored, so immersed do we become in the climber's predicament and style.

The route is on gritstone.

All the great climbers prove themselves on grit. Limestone's nothing. It's rock for athletes, bolt-heads or thugs. All you need is power, and it's better if you leave your technique at home – you'll lose it soon enough anyway as you slap and lurch up a bulge on The Cornice, where it would only slow you down. But grit's the mysterious rock, balanced, abrasive, puzzling, calling on all the inventive wiles. Whilst the jockstrapped muscle-shoals sweat it out in the dales, once or twice in every generation, up on the edges some young genius, some punk with attitude, whether his name is Harding or Elliott, Whillans or Brown, Bancroft, Allen or Dawes is reinventing in the forge of his own spirit with the hammer of his need the sport of climbing, and Bernard Newman's picture captures the moment.

iii) Cave Route Right-hand

Keep in your mind the two previous photographs featured in this series – John Cleare's of Crew on Great Wall and Bernard Newman's of Bancroft on *Strapadictomy* – as you consider John Beatty's extraordinary picture of Ron Fawcett on *Cave Route Right Hand* at Gordale Scar. Remember the dialectic embodied in Cleare's and Newman's – the opposition of puny marionette and profoundly impressive rock architecture, out of which proceeds a sense of the engaged human spirit. In both of them atmosphere, rock texture, the placing of figure in context, are of paramount importance. They are studies in connection, statements on the nature of the sport as it then was.

This picture of John Beatty's is certainly the latter, an absolute denial of the former. The nature – the priorities, perceptions, significance and values – all these have changed.

Look at the picture closely and ask yourself where is the rock?

There are a few small excrescences nearly in focus in the region of Fawcett's right knee. The rest is an amorphous greeny-grey mass into which the yellow ropes disappear. It has ceased to be rock and become matter with which the climber's contact is entirely marginal. Consider fingers and toes, which are the means by which we climb rock. The famous Fawcett digits – or at least those of his right hand – are on view, scooped as they emerge from his chalk bag, contorted away from the rock which they do not touch. The rest are hidden, not the slightest suggestion of what configuration they may be exploring or gaining purchase from.

Even the intense focus of Ron's eyes is beyond the confines of the frame, and so remains inexplicit. The effect is one of internalisation. The whole thrust of the picture is towards a statement on attitude – on a new attitude adequate and necessary for the new routes of climbing's 1980s limestone revolution – on the attitude caught here in the moment when rock-climber metamorphoses into rock-athlete; to which the medium through which the figure moves ceases to signify and becomes intangible, absorbed into the abstraction of number; by which mind, contact, context are sloughed off and the butterfly body emerges from the chrysalis of the old head-game and mind-sport.

For this picture is entirely about body – body in a vacuum, its limbs arranged to display only themselves, each muscle-group defined to perfection. And it signifies new skin for the new ceremony. It sets a style which is followed to this day, points the way to a future at which we have now arrived – gymnastic muscularity and athletic commitment – and defines it also in the instant it hung on the cusp of modernity.

If we were to move on from this picture of Fawcett and the mid-1980s, maybe it would be to Heinz Zak's masterful study of the late Rachel Farmer in the act of stretching for the lower-off bolt on her first F8a (E7,6b) – note the necessary prefacing abstractions – lead by a British woman of *Rain Dogs* at Malham, in which her *pièta* face is intensely concentrated, registering anxiety, directing the viewer's attention at personal struggle rather than at the Everyman impersonality of Cleare's image in particular. And note too the bolt. Modern pictures flaunt their bolts, they're badges of pride, points of focus. The politics of the climbing photograph, its signifiers, have changed along with the changing mores of the sport. The human eye and the metal eye connect in anticipatory gleam. The old shadowy sub-texts of involvement, environment and risk have gone, to be replaced by effort, security and release. The sport has become rarefied, removed curiously from the arena in which it takes place. And perhaps, along with this detachment, goes the diminution of respect for the rock, go the picked-over bones of Chee Dale and Malham, and the exclusion zone of Craig y Forwyn.

Which introduces a crowning irony; for the committed exemplars – the Ron Fawcetts and Rachel Farmers – who are used by the photographers to make these implicit statements of new values are often the ones whose subscription to them is the most hesitant, the least current.

Out there on the gritstone edges, for example, daily in the sunshine or in the wind, Ron still climbs, loving the feel of the rock under his fingers and the movement of his body across it, revelling in the exercise of a craft at which for perhaps ten years or more he was the supreme practitioner in Britain and in which he can still perform at levels capable of surprising the most ardent and aspiring of pretenders half his age.

Uncelebrated, though. He came just too early to capitalise on the cults of personality of which this picture is so clear and early an expression, was too rooted in an earlier age to have generated much enthusiasm for the competitions by which wealth and celebrity accrue and to which the British Mountaineering Council, in what increasingly appears as a short-sighted, wrong-headed and obtuse policy, gave official endorsement and financial support from the 1980s onwards.

So when I look at this picture, register the lean, taut body and the intense, handsome face, I reflect that not only was Ron used by those who wished to represent a direction in which his heart didn't lie (I'm not referring to the photographer, but rather the commercial interests which preyed on Fawcett), and lost out when his currency was no longer current, but that perhaps it represents a moment (from which its present ills proceed) when the sport began to lose out too, in the recognition of its essential nature, in its proper remove from the safe shallows of society?

But perhaps that's to view a coloured image in terms too black and white for it to bear ...

8: WHAT'S GOOD IS BAD, WHAT'S BAD IS GOOD ... (2004)

Such a tyranny, the star system – how come we even begin to take it seriously? I was rapping on to Ray Wood this afternoon about Millstone Edge and that phalanx of three-star ratings strung out along it. They're all crap. There isn't a good route at Millstone apart from Green Death and no-one in their right mind has gone near that since Keith Myhill smashed himself up on it back in the 1970s. For the rest of them, not a subtle or interesting move between them, just cramming your fingers into nasty, reamed-out, battered cracks, cranking like fury and doing what you can with whatever bit of smooth your feet come to rest on. Take Coventry Street – E4, 6b, three stars, one of the essential ticks, and what do you get? A crackline totally devoid of any technical interest or textural pleasure until you arrive at one of those grue-some tippy little cranks that lands you more or less in a horrible sandy cave where you're faced with the alternatives of either lowering off some frayed tat looped round arbitrary ancient ironmongery or doing an equally unpleasant, slightly easier but rather dirtier, flakier and more exposed top pitch. Three stars? Who says ... ?

If you're looking for joy of climbing movement and not star-balances in your climbing account, how does this apotheosis of climbing dullness compare to, say, *The Press* on Ramshaw Rocks, which for all I know, not having the relevant guide-book, probably gets no stars at all but is rock in its very best free-ecstatic mode? You swim up this floundery crack, swing out on a hand-traverse across a leaning wall, heel-hook back left, crank on your right arm, right leg trailing free, reach for locking jams in the hanging crack above, pull into a standing position and step up and out on to the arête above, soloing high above the turf – best ten feet of climbing in the world, out there on the pure and hanging grit. I first did it close behind John Syrett on one of his esoterica-solothons, still remember that wild, beautiful face of his with the raven curls and the sharp and darting eyes, gleaming as he stretched out of the hand-traverse into the jams. Bless ... ! He knew that what counts is quality of move-ment, quality of move, and not all this quasi-capitalistic and avaricious nonsense that the nepotistic apparatchiks on the guidebook committees foist upon us. Never trust appraisal by committee. When I think of my own new routes, the one of which I'm most fond, by which I'm most pleased, is an insignificant little thing along from *Mississippi Buttress* on Stanage that's called *Pedlar's Rib* and is HVS, 5c, which tells you straight away that it's the perfect gritstone solo grade. I called it that because of the two routes on its right – *Pedlar's Arête* and *Pedlar's Slab*, the latter of which is one of the great and glorious gems of gritstone folklore, peddled like a shibboleth among aficionadoes, dream-frictional and stretchy-tenuous – thinking at the time that a

pedlar was just a variant peddler and something to do with that packhorse trail nearby; but then Geoff Birtles told me that it couldn't be my route, *Pedlar's Rib*, because
the routes were called after some Sheffield climber from the 1950s called Barry
Pedlar. So there you go – if you're still out there, Barry, have a route from me to make
up the trinity, and it's a good little route too, different to your mini-masterpiece but
satisfying, a bit anxiety-inducing high up, considered and elegant and exquisitely textural in the way of natural grit and the way you never get on all that quarried blah.
Not a star in sight for any of them, of course (or at least not in the last guidebook I
ever saw to Stanage), and pray heaven it stays that way. Who wants climbing bankers
when our little world's full enough of their rhyming slangsters as it is. Anyway,
enough of all that downright abuse. Having made a few more enemies in Sheffield
– never an easy task, of course, that city's climbing community being so entirely
non-factional – let's tread on a few Welsh toes.

Now this is the place where you really get the star-and-adjectival inflation.
Take, for example, the case of that little trip round some of the crumblier recesses of
Wen Zawn that goes under the whimsical title ('a masterpiece of climbing nomen-
clature' or the merest twaddling sentimentality?) of *A Dream of White Horses*. Three
stars of course, and the guide-writers would probably give it six if they were allowed.
They queue up to drip sticky adjectives on to it – you know, all that 'great', 'classic',
'magnificent', 'stupendous' tosh. But what does it amount to as a route? OK there
was that thrilling Leo Dickinson first-ascent photo of a big wave breaking, but so
what? It's only worth doing in the piss-wet with a raging sea. Gives it some atmosphere then. In anything like normal conditions it's abject ledge-shuffling across
dreary rubble without a single memorable move in 400 feet. Classic? By what standards? Listen, *Concrete Chimney* is about a million times better as a route on any
count: quality of line, position, interest of climbing, weirdness of rock. It's a bit like
the aristocracy, isn't it – none of them had three brain-cells to rub together, yet they
always regarded themselves as the *creme de la creme*. Go for the plebeian every time, if
you ask me. I can think of route after uncelebrated route that sticks in the mind far
more than its stratospherically-renowned near-neighbours. Maybe those star-ratings
are actually no more than an index to committee-approved universally acceptable
and supposedly desirable qualities. Wanna know what the best route on Clogwyn
Du'r Arddu – the best cliff in Wales – is, in terms of line, sustained interest of climbing, position, the indefinable element of character, aesthetic appeal etc., etc.? It's
Black Cleft, and no-one ever does it except in winter because they don't like to get
dirty and wet and you have to put your hands in tickly, slimy places and it smells of
vegetation. When dear old Paul Williams was doing the guidebook I pestered and

badgered him for months, sang of its joys, because of course he, like every other 'sensible' climber had never been near its cool and summery delights – only thrashed, sweated and hacked up it in the rare and frozen seasons. We used to do it with socks over our rock boots – can you imagine? does it come more traditional than that? – and your hands would be bloated at the end after all that sodden jamming. Eventually Paul relented from his dismissive mode, decided I was serious and mine the ravings of a true enthusiast, so he called it 'compellingly uncompelling' and gave it three stars anyway, which kind of defeats my argument and maybe I should have been happier with it having none and me with the knowledge in my heart that it was of the pantheon.

What are they really about, these stars, I wonder? They're supposed to be guarantors of absolute quality, yet are forever comparing like with unlike – absolutism with built-in relativism. Is Millstone's *Jermyn Street* really of the same order of excellence as *Shibboleth* on Slime Wall on the Buachaille? Excuse me if I think not. So in a situation so shot through with anomalies as this, surely the realistic option is to disregard the application of stars entirely? Go for the unsung and see what happens on the experiential front. I was thinking just now of a couple of routes from years ago that I did around Lydstep – not in the popular areas like Mother Carey's, but at Lydstep Point and in Prow Bay. Over 30 years on I can recall the exact detail of both of them, the feelings and sensations they induced with aching clarity. I did them both with my brilliant old mate Colin Mortlock, who is one of the great and necessary philosophers of the climbing world – read his book, *Beyond Adventure*, and you'll learn more about the true nature of climbing than from all the feted – or should that be fetid? – annals of self-promotional derring-do. The route at Lydstep Point was called *Poseidon*. It gets HVS, 5a and no stars in the guide, which is fine by me because how do you quantify experience? I remember old Murky traversing into the back of a sucky, slurpy, green zawn on the first pitch and doing this immense stride across it – he had ridiculously long legs – and sitting there on the other side, belayed and laughing and expecting me to fall in, and me scrabbling across somehow on slimey little lancet edges and then my pitch was a huge, stretched, wandering affair that ended up high on the point on this belt of slab between two sets of overhangs. For 20 feet there was beautiful rough untouched limestone with a fret of orange lichen across it, jewel-like; there were small, square holds, phenomenal rope-drag; there was struggling up the opposite rib and emerging on to a pinnacled crest of ridge, sitting in silk-like grass under an opalescent sky at the fullest stretch of the ropes and Colin joining me. Stars? There was a galaxy of them in my head, the glitter of which the paper versions could never match. Then this other route – I bet it's never been done from the day of its first ascent to this. I couldn't even remember what it was called until I looked it up in the guidebook just now to find that it's down as *Absalom* (HVS, 4c). What does all that mean, that weird little appendix of letter and number? How does it come to stand for spending two hours on a 120-ft pitch, and every move a tottering block to be prised off and thrown down, a grass sod to be lifted and the dirt swept away, a fissile edge to be snapped and consigned to the depths and pathetic protection and the tide creeping in and the detritus floating on it, the rocks plummeting into water, Colin dodging the fusillades, creeping up on to higher and higher ledges, complaining with tense amusement at my sculpting and gardening, me laughing like an imbecile high above, revelling in fingertip exploration. *Dream of White Horses* would have been like this on its first ascent, and maybe an element of that still adheres in each revisiting experience. Shouldn't we leave it in that realm of the experiential and stop pretending through some daft system to these absolute endorsements? Like everything else in life, it's less the object than the perception you bring to it that counts, and that can be as valid and excellent when there isn't a single star in sight.

9: WHY DO TREKKIES LIKE TO VISIT BASE CAMPS? (1999)

Look, I'm not putting to you one of those weird 'Do Androids dream of electric sheep?'-type questions. I'm just genuinely puzzled. I'd go out of my way to avoid spending unnecessarily time at a mountaineering base camp, yet from Annapurna to Everest, from Tapovan to Concordia, the trekkers arrive at them in their droves, realising thus what at first they deem to be the height of their ambitions and dreams. Why do they do it? Why do trekkies so love to visit base camps? Would you?

I've just been out in the Tien Shan, and some of the time I was on a trek. As it happened, the climax of this was a helicopter trip in a Soviet-built helicopter (bought back by the Kazakhstan trekking agency we were with from Air Burundi) up to the South Inylchek Glacier, where this agency has a permanent base camp. If you want to try your luck on Khan Tengri or Pik Pobeda, that's where you have to go – mess-tents, toilets, regimentation, visas – you know the sketch. I didn't go. I'd been plotting to get out of this bit since the itinerary arrived. I have this recurrent nightmare about air-crashes, you see, and all my mangled body-bits mixed up with those of people I might not like. It's deeply pathological, no doubt, but there you go. Anyway, my woman put her foot down:

'You are not flying in a Russian helicopter and that's that.'

These days the protocol is that men have to do what women tell them, but under no circumstances must women do what men tell them. I read that in Susan Faludi's new book. It suited my purposes in this instance, though getting out of it was more difficult than you might imagine.

'I'll just walk back to the valley base in Karkara,' I thought, but when Kazbek – the square, squat Godfather to this operation, hands like dinner-plates *and* he'd been up Chomolungma – was told of what I planned, down came the guillotine: scheme vetoed on account of bandits, robbers, avalanches, crevasses, bears, snow-leopards, the dangers of being alone in the hills – all that bollocks. Also, the disbelief that registered on his face when it became clear to him that I intended to keep a promise made to a woman who was not there to check up on me expressed a great deal about cultural values and sexual politics in the region, and I have to say made me considerably more determined to keep that promise. So what I did was borrow a fast, sturdy, flying-maned little horse and with a couple of nomads we had a phenomenal, wild, gusting 60-mile ride over ridges and down valleys, galloping through riverside meadows brilliant with flowers, trotting across passes, ending up in the nomads' yurt amidst dirty, angelic children and lovely daughters and wives, on cushions at a low table spread with great wheels of fresh bread, with rich jams and buttery tea and yogurt, and little, tinking glasses of vodka too that sent a glow through every aching muscle. Oh, that was a trip. That was a heaven-sent and truly adventurous day. All it cost me was a fleece, some overtrousers and a pair of sun-glasses that the horsemen pointed at and made clear that they wanted. That wasn't robbery. It was a fair day's fee for the hire of the horse and anyway, Erik gave me a flea-infested Kirghiz jumper in exchange, as token that I was his friend and given 20 years' practice he might make some kind of an inferior horseman out of me.

Meanwhile, up at the base camp on the Inylchek Glacier, the trekkies were eating noodles and drinking thin tea and having the time of their lives talking trademarks with climbers from a Korean expedition that had been on Khan Tengri (which I have to say looks rather a desirable peak, though maybe not in the Machapuchare or Shivling or Dhaulagiri league of mountain beauty).

Have you ever had a conversation with a Korean climber? Once you've got the subject of whether or not they know Dennis Gray out of the way ('Ho, Mister DennisGray, yes – British climber!'), it's conducted in a strange modern label-esperanto that's always accompanied by a good deal of dollar-bill-and-object-brandishing:

'Ho, yes, Spraywayjacketverygood, Goretex, one-hunnerfifty-dollar-maybe, betterthanNorthFace, yesno?? Hnnn! DMM, verytechnicalaxe, Predator, two-hunna-dolla-yes? LoweAlpinesalopetteshitflapmostuseful, me give you hunnadollano? Youwantnotnowanymore? Knife is Epinel yes? Here ten dollar, mehaveyougive, cutropemaybesometimeSimonYates.'

There was the time Ed Douglas nearly lost a Lowe Mountain Cap this way. We were sitting outside the Hotel Ganga Niketan in Gangotri on the way up to Tapovan where the boulderers go these days even though Almscliff's still better, and a group of Korean mountaineers became very excited about it, offered him 20 dollars, were getting the scissors and tape-measure out there and then to dismantle it, measure it up and set the production line going. Odd lot, but I rather liked them. Ed didn't much, but then it was his hat. He snatched it back and got quite huffy for a while, which is not like him.

These are, of course, chance observations and beside the point of the main question. The more I think about it, the more completely bewildered I become about this focus the trekking companies have on getting their clients up to climbers' base camps. The climbers don't object. After all, when a group of trekkies arrive it's a great excuse for smoking dope and getting pissed and copping off and not having to talk to those you've been up and down the hill with for the last five weeks.

But what do the trekkies get out of it? I suppose if they're female or the climbers are gay, or if they're male and the climbers are women, they might get shagged, but at that altitude and after the inevitable lengthy spell of opposite-gender-deprivation on the climbers' part it's unlikely that it will be either good or protracted. Anyway, I think it's more subtle than that. I think it's comparable to the public turn-out at whatever huge venue he happens to be speaking for the annual Sir Christian Bonington multi-media, web-site-authenticated, satellite-linked apologia (ever see that piece about the Bonington website by John Naughton in the *Observer*? You should visit it. Naughton was spot-on) for only getting within 2,000/200/three * (*delete as applicable) feet of the summit of whatever marvellous/ dramatic/unknown/sooper* (*delete as applicable) peak in the back of the Himalayan beyond. (Wow! I like that sentence – it's messier than the surrounds of your average base camp. Substitute toilet paper for parentheses and you've got a mirror image.)

It's vicarious living. It's what Chris is so good at giving his public. Stroke them, flatter them, convince them that you could have been there and what have you got? You've got a following. Take your trekkies to the foot of Everest, Annapurna, K2, and you've got a bunch of people who in their own subsequent versions have been on Everest, Annapurna, K2. Good luck to them, and to the companies that make money from them. They've rubbed shoulders with that death-defying band of exalted beings, the mountaineers. If they're especially lucky, like the tourists in their cars beneath Clogwyn y Grochan, peering up through binoculars for hour after hour, they might even see a bit of death-succumbing. That's probably why televised climbing never caught on. It didn't give the viewing public – those latter-day descendants of the Coliseum's baying mob – what it really wanted, which was the plummeting body, the battered flesh. The highlights were all too subtle. Like that bit where the camera cuts to Joe Brown, who's pissing himself laughing as Chris gibbers and whimpers across the traverse pitch of *Big Top* in the wet. You couldn't get a TV sports commentator bringing that out. Too sly. And when climbing went indoors and became a sport, I remember that awful soundtrack to the World Championship:

'Uh, uh, uh – yes! Go for it, Jerry, oh yes! Oh yes! Oh YES!'

That was either post-modernist allusion to Molly Bloom, or the guy was coming in his pants. I prefer not to think about it.

You see what I'm getting at here? Guilt by association. We play to this instinct, like to be thought the heroes, dress and strike our poses accordingly. And it's bullshit. We're no heroes. base camps aren't nice places to be. They're hornets' nests full of jockeying, buzzing little egos all busy manoeuvering for personal advantage and pole position. But the trekkies – well, they're kind of innocent. They've been sold a line of the mountaineer as exalted one, physical embodiment of striving and noble humanity. Ain't true. We shit on the fluted purity of the ridges, we leave tat everywhere, we use the mountains to bolster our egos and at minimal expense the native peoples from around their foot to get us up them, because they're better at that than we are. I love it – the triumph of the west!

But I do think that maybe if these trekkies were taken instead to some quiet place apart from the camps, away from those who trample, use and abuse – some place where they could look on at the incandescent purity of the peaks unaware of the corruption infecting their flanks, summits and literature, away from the crowds and the environmental carelessness, then maybe that long cultural power of the mountain to thrill and inspire might in some degree root and flourish in them. Pity that in the main these innocents will continue to be sold a version that must inevitably disappoint ...

10: A VALEDICTION (1973)

I suppose you might ask, 33 years after this piece was written, how come I'm still climbing? Hey ho ...

School ends; there are more phases to a man's life than just one, though each phase as it progresses brings a clearer realisation of its own nature, or a firmer grasp on the security it seems to offer. I have been climbing intensively now for 12 years, and I have more or less had enough. I have come to see the nature of the sport; it is not a creative act and it has little left to give me. I expect to give offence or be criticized for what I have to say, and would thus like to define the conditions which lead me to say it. I am not referring to the mountain environment or to the quiet pleasures of days in the hills, not referring to the huge range of interest encompassed in this scene, not referring to the sheer bodily and sensual pleasure of movement on rock, although all these things impinge upon the central experience about which I write. The experience to which I am referring is the intense, neurotic urge to seek out the limits of subjective possibility on rock, the desire to push oneself to the extremes of endurance, adhesion, physical and mental control. I shall be making value judgements upon this experience; whether or not the reader feels intuitions of sympathy towards these is of little account. I have searched myself and found them valid to my situation.

I have heard people claim that climbing is an art form, a creative act, and read the same statement in essays such as Harold Drasdo's 'Education and the Mountain Centres'; the people who make these statements have neither sufficiently considered the nature of a creative act, nor the nature of climbing. They are talking inflated nonsense; there is an element of the mystical about climbing, yet the climbers are lost not in God but in themselves. This is valid enough at a certain stage in life, but it is a lesson which must not be allowed to harden into a habit. In a sense it represents a shaking off of the last egocentricities of childhood, and a coming-to-terms at last with the external world. The act revokes its own motivation. Commitment to a series of extreme moves on rock is a tenuous expression of belief in one's personal omnipotence; by its very nature it is an illusion, and one bolstered so often by the mean little tricks and dishonesties of the climbing world as to lose the integrity upon which its validity must rest. No one is omnipotent and on rock we all strive to be so. The ego and the will are the driving forces in climbing, the philosophy behind it is one of despair. Consider us and what we are: we are not well-balanced individuals, as long as we climb, because we have committed ourselves to a pure sphere of self-

257

assertion and will. We turn from a world of which we cannot be the centre, to an experience so intense that we cannot but see ourselves at the centre of it. Every new trip up Sisyphus' Hill hardens the ego a little by proving to us that we can do it. Ego and will by no means lead to happiness; the times when I have been best at my climbing have been the least happy times of my life. Yes, there have been moments of desperate laughter and utter relief, even some warmth of companionship from time to time from an experience shared. But this continual focusing inwards of the climber's mind, this sifting and weighing of every fine weakness of response, this endless preparation for mental masturbation, these sudden explosions of the assertive will, are a path to restraint, and not freedom, of response. They are lessons to be learnt, not ones always to be lived by, and their repetition becomes not only absurd, for this element was present in its nature from the beginning, but also negative and destructive, and a denial of the potentialities of life. Obsessive climbing is a reprisal against nature for making self so small within it. The toying with death (any arguments that this is not so are utterly spurious) that represents so strong a part of the attraction of climbing adds yet another facet to the basic negativity of the sport. Each new death is a reiteration of the question, 'Is it worth it?' from the answering of which we always shy away. At Lawrie Holliwell's funeral every face was haunted by the realisation of a death that could as easily have been theirs. Is it worth it? Yes, for those who are weak, aimless, discontent, strong and directionless, childless, unhappily married, unresolved or in despair. For all who fit these categories the activity is eminently worthwhile in that it brings them close to ridding themselves of an existence that could so easily become a burden to them, and by the proximity of that negation increases the attractiveness of life.

> I balanced all, brought all to mind,
> The years to come seemed waste of breath,
> A waste of breath the years behind;
> In balance with this life, this death.
>
> WB Yeats, *An Irish Airman Foresees His Death*

Well; all cannot be brought to mind; there is body and soul, there are feelings, intuitions of beauty and wholeness, softness, fullness, warmth. These things climbing alone cannot fulfil; the hard, cold world of intellect and will seeks to destroy the whole man.

I have learnt things from climbing: that the seemingly impossible can be achieved by precise, co-ordinated movement, by direction of energy and conserva-

258

tion and timed application of resources. That things are easier than they seem to be; that falling off is not the thing to do until every last possible scrap of resource has failed you; that a sufficiency of commitment will usually see you through; that a real and authentic desire is the only worthwhile spring to action. But these are lessons to be applied now to the creative act of living, in conjunction with the more warm, full and human values of love, feeling, knowledge, compassion. They are no longer ones to be squandered in the negative sphere of rock. We pass from one lesson to another armed with a new strength of knowledge, and should be glad that it is so.

11: Confidence Moves (2001)

'Every song I ever sung was a folk song. I never heard no horses sing none o' them.'

Leadbelly

Every move I ever made on rock – apart from a few involuntary downward plummets – was a confidence move; but it's all a question of degree. I was thinking about this the other day out on Stanage. It was one of those bright, cold winter afternoons, perfect for butyl, terrible for fingertips. And I was pratting about ...

More specifically, I was in one of those 'move up, move down, move up again, shiver a bit, dip in your chalk bag, feel timorously at the holds, swear at yourself, let the inner voice talk of cafés and graceful retreats' moods that still holds a faint possibility of two outcomes, but makes one of them on balance the more likely. I was on a route I knew, as well – one that used to be a regular in the soloing repertoire when youth and spring were mine. Even then I could get a bit nervous of it on occasion – *Wall End Slab Direct*, Frank Elliott's route from 1930, that still gets E2, 5c or some such in the new guides. You reach a break about 12 feet up, I suppose, and stand in it. It's one of those lateral breaks that you have to extricate your toes from cleanly before moving up, otherwise the whole succeeding sequence gets unbalanced and lacking in momentum. Above you there's a sparse trail of weird little pinchy, knobby undercuts and smears and rounded layaway pockets and when you're flowing you just ease over the rough texture of the rock and don't even notice a certain lack of definition to what assists your upward progress. It's gritstone, and gritstone's like that. Nor do you notice either all those wicked, ankle-wrecking, leg-snapping, rib-crushing boulders beneath, among which you're certainly not going to end up so why worry?

On the other hand, when you're in a state of funk and your mind's pleading with you not to be so daft, and that toe you must kick clean and arch out resolutely if you're to do the thing at all well (or even at all) refuses to clear the lip and your weight's never going to project itself upwards to the point at which the undercut you're so tentatively exploring is going to hold you in balance and push your feet down into friction and let you sail across left and up and complete the sequence, and the toothed maw of the savage rocks beneath yawns ever more nastily-smiling-wide – well, when you're like that you might as well go home, or at least find something more in keeping with your ability on the day; which is exactly what I did in reverse order, wandering along ruefully to *Heaven Crack*, which is V. Diff. and the shortest three-star route in creation if you believe in that stuff and always makes me feel bold and competent because it has holds into which your arms disappear, and after that I tramped off briskly over Higgar Tor and down Padley Gorge, happily, because walking has that effect, to the Grindleford café and vast mugs of tea and fond, soft memories of sprightlier days.

If ever a route exemplified the notion of a confidence move, it's *Wall End Slab Direct*, and what you must do to launch out into the crucial sequence, with nothing to pull on, nothing by which upward movement can be defined, nothing but hope and a complex, co-ordinated muscular spasm to set you on the track to the top. But I don't even know if the term is still current, except among wimpish old fogeys like me, and others of my generation whom I won't name and shame but who may, despite grade-drift and its self-deceivings, just possess the self-honesty to recognise their condition. Maybe it's a term on the brink of extinction, soon to join all those other lost concepts like 'festering' (what people used to do before 'working on routes' was invented) or 'the coroner's belay' (putting the rope round a pebble on a ledge where there was nothing else to tie on to, so that when you and your climbing partner were dead and the plonkers from PyB or the rescue team reported back to the coroner's court, at least they'd presume from evidence of the knots that there'd been a belay, even though it had failed. I remember using one of these on the sloping ledge between the little low-down pitches of *Wendigo* at South Stack, where you can now get a Rock 7, six RPs, a Tricam and a flexible Friend – if they haven't taken the latter off you for buying all this stuff, that is).

I digress. What I was wondering was – for anyone other than me, does the confidence move still exist? After all, it's a notion predicated on fear of falling, and no-one under the age of 40 has any hang-ups whatsoever about that these days. 'Fear of Flying' wrote Erica Jong. 'What ... ?' came the bemused response. A confidence move is a move you make without knowing exactly what's to come, what's round the corner, whether your feet will stay on the rock, whether or not at no very great distance above you the rock and yourself will part company and you'll be consigned to the regions of the air. What would that matter to the sports climbers, protection experts, bolt-freaks, indoor-wallers and top-ropers who are no doubt responsible for a very considerable proportion of the activity that goes under the general banner of rock-climbing in the first decade of the 21st Century? 'Yo ... ! We like to fly! Where's the problem and what's the big deal?'

Well, it was rooted in psychology, and that was the domain in which the main attraction of climbing lay before it was travestied by the narcissistic sub-discipline of 'sports science and psychology', with its endless stress on goals, focusing, motivation, physiology, and all that guff that so neatly tabulates and homogenises individual impulse and human variety of response. Climbing's greatest-ever prose-writer, Menlove Edwards (no-one else has come close to the wry intelligence and visceral clarity he brings to recording the climbing experience – the rest of us are two-dimensional by comparison), was a psychiatrist. Imagine if he'd had to couch his comic-ironic, mock-heroic masterpiece, 'A Great Effort', in jargon, in fatuous egocentricities like these. He did have something to say about 'confidence moves', which had a clear reality in his time:

'Have you ever watched a beginner on the Slabs? A most instructive little psychological study. He puts his foot on a hold which he doesn't like and then does his very best to prove to himself that he's right in not liking it. He fidgets about but he doesn't succeed in getting the foot to slip off. So he develops a tremor and tries to shake it off. Still it stays firm, so in desperation he gets on to it, lies down flat against the rock and with a yell of triumph pushes. With the right direction of effort the mind of man can accomplish almost anything.'

I wonder how many instructors at Plas y Brenin or any of the other centres throughout the country use that little parable, which tells you directly and by implication everything you need to know about climbing rock, in the course of their daily pedagogic routines? Time they did. It's a perfect anatomy of the confidence move, just as 'A Great Effort' is the definitive rumination on its stages and thought-processes.

But I was speculating on whether this concept could possess a modern reality, and however amusing and satisfying I might find it, harking back to situations the term used to comprehend doesn't answer that at all. OK, so I could spend the rest of this essay on a prolonged contemplation of the agonies endured, the torments of an imagination fastening on to how I'd whack against the far wall of *Gardom's Unconquerable* if the unseen holds beyond the corner were greasy or crap or I was too weak to use them, before launching round the arête on the strenuous and imposing sequence that's *Whillans' Blind Variant* (E1, 5b), and that's Whillans through and through. Nowadays the gear's above you when you make the move, and in it your confidence is placed. Friends have been with us for a quarter of a century now. On grit in particular, place one of those and your confidence goes in with it.

So as I search around for somewhere, some venue or style of climbing, in which the confidence move might still have a relevance, I come up with something very anomalous. I start thinking of names like *Scarlet Runner* and *Poetry Pink* on the Dinorwig slate – both of them technically straightforward, both of them feeling overgraded when the moves are flowing for you, both of them involving thin steps on little, fissile holds to clip dubious bolts, both of them involving potentially damaging consequences in the event of – what? Panic? Technical inadequacy? Rock or rubber failure? Misjudgement? But none of that's going to happen to you. You're going to cruise it. Mission statement endlessly rehearsed, you're going to reach your goal. Aren't you? You've been inwardly chanting the sports-psychology mantras for months. The great, tuned and acquisitive ego that's now yours is going to pull another one in.

Hey, I'm feeling nostalgic for the feeble, the indecisive, the worried, the tentative. Was I always this unconvinced (rightly so now!) about my own ability? Or do I just like to give the opposition a fair and sporting chance ...

12: FEAR IS THE SPUR (1998)

There was a different fear in crossing to the island. I'd met the boatmen earlier in the day. They were peering into the engine hatches of a boat they'd just bought, a force eight gale blowing in the bay. That trip was wild, but the fear passive: an 'Oh well – it's out of my hands' shrug, a deterministic acceptance of whatever might come. Besides, you could tell these boatmen were something else. They needed to be, where they lived.

I'd not come to this island for the climbing and on first impressions it didn't look as though it would have provided much if I had. Sure, there were plenty of little boiler-plate glaciated slate slabs so that the whole place looked like a crouching armadillo. An outdoor centre might have squeezed some interest out of them for elementary rock-craft. That was the size of it. On my second afternoon I walked from the village to the far side. The whole of the back of the island had been ripped off by the ice. It had left cliffs like I'd not considered in years – serious, big cliffs with great folds and striations in the darkest, most forbidding black rock; quartz-spattered Ordovician slate, smooth-looking treacherous stuff.

I'd passed the one I'm chiefly talking about before I saw it. I'd been dawdling along an old trackway towards the island's high point and when I looked back there was this suggestion of rock slipping from sight behind a ridge. I wasn't sure if I could be bothered to make the detour back to it, but somehow it looked intriguing, so I did.

The gale was still blowing. Down in the depths of this zawn the rollers were surging and boiling and the spume was being whipped up on the wind, the air full of white sea-blossom. I walked to the edge, looked down and gasped. It was huge, a great black diamond of rock with stark lines etched and creased into it and it plunged 400 feet and I was terrified yet it drew me in. I couldn't look across without wanting to climb it. And I remembered that feeling as I pulled out my camera, braced myself against the judder of the wind, shielded the lens from rain and spray to take a few shots before the weather hustled me away.

Oh yes, I remembered that feeling.

Joe Brown had it when he first looked across from the promontory by Castell Helen and saw *Red Wall* at South Stack, thought 'Oh God, what are they getting up these days?' and slouched off feeling like his time had passed. The terror of the place and that thrilling ache of curiosity it induces in our psyche drew him back in, and within a few months *Red Wall, Wendigo, Doppelganger* were its expression. All right, so this fearsome place I'd found, this Black Diamond Bay, is half as high again, steeper,

264

harder to get at, harder full stop, and I'm an old, wrecked climber who might just not be capable of anything on it and will probably have to enlist the crazy services of Big George Smith. But it's working its magic nonetheless. I'm training, planning, scanning the shots like Kirkus slipping open his shipping-clerk's drawer and the lines tracing and crawling all over. I'll be back.

What is it about climbers that makes us so unable or unwilling to resist fear's weirder blandishments? It's like one of those relationships you encounter rarely in your life where the other taps into some deep and vulnerable level, senses how to control you and you're disempowered, drawn in unwittingly, unwillingly, unable to escape, and you have to go on and on until the Jocastan face of the erstwhile lover becomes a hollow-eyed mask of tragedy and the only options are repetition, destruction or retreat. Dark as the rock I gazed upon. Eternal circles. Keep on, die or get out. I think our relationship with fear is thus, a desperation at its root. Did you see the wild in her eyes, her hands full of the cold fruit? Yes, it brings us the most exquisite pleasure in the afterglow, the adrenaline-breakdown-times when the colours of the world coruscate and flare, become physical sensation, ache, splendour, in so near a way to that in which the most intense expressions of sensuality often come in the worst relationships, and mundanity rests in the solid domain.

I saw *Red Wall* too and ran away. You couldn't comprehend it then. Too big, too rotten, too weird. No use asking Brown or Crew either. Pete would put you down because that's what Pete did, brusquely in that throwaway dismissive mumble of his. And Joe just grinned his enigmatic grin, told you in a slow drawl that it was all right, and how much did you then know? That the routes had been done, that's all, by heroes maybe but not yet by you so you make your own movie and flash it on the wall: 'I am curious – Red.'

Because I am afraid I will be unafraid. Know what I did? I had a boot-lace, literally a boot-lace, and I abseiled down into the zawn beneath *Red Wall* from that. Fuck you. It was early summer and the year after it had been done. We did the third ascent, me and Nick Gough and we're both working at Plas y Brenin and have been up all night shagging (no, not each other – that's the macho man's ultimate fear!), because that's what you do when you're 20 and work there. And when you're on with it, engaged in the intricacies, focusing down, this move, this move, of course the fear goes. Even when I'm on that top stance, that boss of rock with the pegs driven into mud, four, five of them and who cares and half the stance peels off and rushes into the zawn, 300 feet and the cordite smell drifting up and us laughing. You think I care?

I care, but I want to go back. Like that time when I went to do *Wendigo* with

Cliff, 300 feet down the wall to the first stance, abseiling sling-and-karabiner style, those bent-wire figure-of-eights maybe just on the market and I didn't have one though Cliff did and I'd been there before and he was scared so I carried the ropes, the gear – pegs, hammer, heavy stuff, so much weight that ten feet down, free already, I know I'm in trouble and the skin on my palms blisters and tears, the rope cuts into my forearm and shoulder, deep grooves and there's this voice saying you could die here, Jimmy, you could die and I'm giving it fuck you no way and cling on because I know what to do where there's pain, get out of there man, dissociate, because it won't last, it will be over, always was, kids know, so I grip tighter to keep the same speed and not accelerate into free-fall and when we've climbed out up the escape route they cut my fused fingers apart with a lancet in the sailors' hospital and I don't care I've had a good trip and yes it's over it's only scars hereonin fuck you man with your good sense and scaredy-cat judgmental eyes I've survived and I know.

Facing up to our fear – is it really any such thing? Or is it escape from the comforting whirr of Penelope's wheel, her spinning web, to a world born anew in every instant of thrill? In a rush of blood I slipped from between her thighs. They cut the cord, I drew my breath and howled, deep, deep, apart. 'Tis not too late to seek a better world', but is it just a brighter, a more garish one in the shock of electricity transmitted along each dark and unknown flake, each aching void beneath?

Oh God! Not again ...

13: ... THE LOST AND PERFECT HOLD (2002)

There was this sketch last week where Will and I were on our way over to the Dylan concert in Manchester (me being a sad old Bobcat and Will a surreptitious one who took every last piece of Dylanalia I'd accrued with him when he finally left home, in the way that sons rightly and usefully do because we're better off without this stuff). We passed under Helsby, thought better of it, then diverted on impulse for a look at Frodsham. You don't even get a glimpse of Frodsham from the road – not even in the winter when the trees are bare, and this was in the great green rush of May. So the look turned into a closer look, and I'd forgotten quite where, because these are little red buttresses hidden in a big wood. Which is how come these two bouldering cats looked up from sunning themselves in the dappled light that was falling on their bouldering mats, and saw with some surprise a balding old guy in a suit stumbling up the slope towards them, with a cool young dude more appropriately clad coasting up behind him.

So a conversation ensued in which the old guy in the suit peers up questioningly, myopically, at this gorgeous clean sandstone roof all dabby with chalk and enquires vaguely of the bouldering cat with big muscles, 'Isn't this Hoop-La ... ?' and the muscular cat says, 'Yeah, that's right ... ' and I suggest '5b ... ?' and he looks at me appropriately and says pretty tricky 6a and he's just had a struggle and backed off, not being really in the mood today, so with a touch of the Paxman eyebrow I convey this to Will, who's just arrived, and intimate that it's okay if you can jam (which Will can) and you get them in the right way (which is always important with jams), or at least it was in my day when it had great classic easy jamming roof problem status so Will drifts up in his trainers and he is so elegant, my boy, and he does it all with a kind of studied smooth precision that makes it look effortless and being his dad I feel proud and the cats on the mats drop their jaws in admiration and then Will, who does this 'I'm a bit gormless but really nice' act that Ron Fawcett had to perfection and that conceals the fact that they're both sharp and sly as foxes, ambles over to them and begs a dip in their chalk bag before – with the same consummate and unhurried ease of movement – easing his way across a much harder problem the name of which I definitely don't remember that slants out right into a slappy kind of sequence that he does statically and in total control over the neb on that side. This time the sun-cats just grin, shake their heads, and start up an animated, friendly conversation, sharing information like the decent guys they turn out to be. Then Will sets off rock-wandering again. There's a pocket on the lip of the roof out left of *Hoop-La* and I've a distant recollection that this may be the crucial hold on something called *Pearce's*

Route that was a party-piece of Dave Pearce's (who died on the wicked descent to the side of Castell Helen a couple of years ago) back in the 1970s when the Altrincham All-stars used to come here regularly on summer Tuesday evenings. Dave used to do it by a fearsome cranky dyno from this pocket to some good sandstone horns way up above, and I've done it that way too in the distant past when the green sap was springy in my limbs. These days I wouldn't recommend anyone to treat sandstone with that degree of disrespect, but in those days we were all scrawny and elastic and not much older than Will is now, so if the edges did snap, as was their wont here-abouts, you'd bounce down among the leaves and then bounce back up again. Looks like it's happened to that pocket – a bit paler round the lower lip than it used to be, a bit less deep. Anyway, Will, who's not looking seriously, fingers it and I say 'Long way – watch the rock – don't want to miss Dylan do you?' and he leaves it and we make our farewells and skip off down. But I remember – and this is the point – that pocket on the lip so exactly, the way you feed your fingers in, distribute, weight all the tendons equally as you can, the bite of it, the body positioning beneath, the surging moment before you leave it behind.

It's the weirdest thing about rock-climbing, this exact memory of fingertip sensation. I was on the phone to my mate David Thomas the other night and he was running through what he'd done lately: 'That route of yours,' he said, 'on that little crag down in the Lledr Valley by the river. Beautiful place – *The Riparian* it's called. That top wall ... !'

'Oh yeah ... ' I responded, 'the pockets ... !'

That was what came to my mind – those pockets. Sitting here thinking about it now, about a summer's afternoon in 1972, there's all sorts of overlay. No-one went there in those days. There was the pool in the river beneath where you could swim, and I was with this girl from Liverpool and there was all the lovely dimension of flesh warming in the sun together after cold immersion. But the memory of that's a mood, undefined, lacking in clarity. Those pockets I can feel now in every detail. There are two of them and the top one's like an elongated figure of eight slightly on its side. Good wires haven't yet come in so my last one's about ten feet below as I start the moves, and they're big moves that take you away from it fast. With the first pocket I rock up and over on to my left foot on a sloper at the top of the gangway, straighten and – slightly off-balance – reach for the pocket. It's plugged with moss so I gouge that out, flick the mud away, and cram three fingers of my right hand into it. It's constricting and full of razor flakes, slimey still from the cleaning but I ram my fingers into the back of it, run my feet up and crank for the top. I swear as I sit here now the nerves in the third finger of my right hand are remembering the experience, twinging, aching ...

Holds so imprint themselves on our memory. Even where I can't remember the moves around them, or at times even the routes they were on, they materialise there in my mind, detached, individual and perfect as sculptures. I think about those epoxy bolt-ons that people make, or the ones built in by climbing wall manufacturers – all the strange phallic and vulval shapes that their imaginations devise – and none are so sharp and crisp as those of the stilled matrix that have left their impressions on my flesh down the years: on Cratcliffe when you've raced up the blind flake layback of *Five Finger Exercise*, re-adjust yourself, reach and there over the top the solid rough grit that your palm moulds around, crystals against skin; a time on Scorpio – the best of all the little wall routes on Du'r Arddu – and I'm with Tom Hurley who was a motor-bike racer, died in the Alps somewhere, years ago. Tom has this sidelong Scouse enthusiasm and wit, is bubbling about it because he's done it before and I haven't and all I know is that the crux is right at the top and it has a reputation in those days for trickiness and long lobs on to crap gear but I've seen this photograph in *The Black Cliff* of Jack Soper on it at the crux with his hand round a big jug but Tom says it isn't and the key's a good pocket high up right and I think it good to be with guys who know the code and when I get up there to the top of this Welsh and slick blind flake Tom's right and the big hold isn't – in fact is barely a hold at all – and Hippy Phil Bagnall is sitting on top of *The Shadow* peering down all goggle-eyed and I see the pocket of promised excellence and get my left foot up, semi-mantelshelf, and span way up right to reach it and two fingers go straight in and guess-what-no-edge, nothing to pull on. 'It's an undercut,' yells Tom so I rotate my fingers and keep moving through, leaning out now and the sweet finger-jugs above just slip to hand but that twist and grip of the knuckles are there as bright feeling memory still (you know how it is); and times when we were callow and laddish and the routes easier, that top pitch of *Bovine* that's sublime and only has the one difficult move and in those days we called it the obstretician's move – I'm not going to go into that now though your finger did with a kind of wrist-aching awkwardness, instead I'm going to tell you about a route on Mowing Word's Hidden Wall that Little Sid Siddiqui and I did and we called it *The Good Soldier* for no good reason except that routes have to have names the same as books have to have titles and some of them are plain silly or pompous (one day I'm going to write an academic treatise on 'Pat Littlejohn, Joe Simpson and the assertion of significance'), but it was pretty good as a route and had this weird, brief, leaning and overhanging fist-jam crack quite high up on it and I remember getting bunched up with a good left fist jam and a toe jam in just beneath it at the top of this thing and reaching up right into the groove above and my palm nestling onto this clot of stuff that has the texture and solidity of a stale rock-bun on which I instantly begin to pull and it instantly parts company with what I instantly realise was not its parent body, leaving a clean white scar and I have not relinquished the security yet of that glorious fist-jam on to which I whang back down causing considerable abrasion to the skin (and subsequently a clean white scar) and surprise to Little Sid who's holding the ropes on the ledge below and looking up with some concern and what I'm thinking is how sad because of the perfection of the fit of that rock-cake-rock into the hollow of my palm and yes, that was the perfect hold but transient, transient ... I wonder if memory of all these imprints into your DNA, and if so, will Will spend his life wandering in search of the lost and perfect hold? Hope not – it's gone like the swifts in September, but another time, another place ... ? Who knows what might last.

14: THAT OLD THING ABOUT GRACE (2001)

What set me thinking about this theme was nothing to do with it really. Or maybe it was. Perhaps there's a connection that will become apparent as we go along. But I warn you, it's tenuous, and it stemmed from a throwaway comment in a book of Edmund White's, about how people like Jean Genet and Isadora Duncan 'turned their own lives into myths and had a creative approach to the truth.'

The last bit had me laughing. I know plenty of people like that in climbing and so do you, but I'm sure as hell not going to list them here because you know who I mean anyway and you never know – they might get litigious? So let's leave it be, since as I told you it's got nothing, or at least not much, to do with what I'm writing about, and let's duck in to that miniature climbing wall through the door in the back bar of The Heights in Llanberis about five years ago.

There are all these kids in there – 13, 14 years old, second-generation North Wales ghetto climbers: Katie Haston, Matthew Toms, my son Will, plenty of others too – and they're all doing the nailed-to-the-wall dance. Which goes like this. You invent a sequence of moves that goes nowhere (that wall is so small anyway that this is a perfectly logical proposition), and you work on it so that the movements of which it comprises become as balanced, effortless, elegant as yourself or your harshest critic – and the two ought to be the same person – could desire.

'Ah,' go the old cynics, 'triumph of style over substance!' And they turn back to gut-enhancement and the slurping of beer. Stuff them.

This scene stuck in my mind and came back to me like a vision – time and again over the intervening years, and I was impressed. You'd go to the big walls – Rope Race, The Beacon, wherever – and all the acquisitive honchos would be thrashing up their particular line, stuck and fixated on objective, and there were these kids floating in my memory with the unconscious, instinctual deep subjectivity of truth upon them. You can tell everything you want to know about a person by the style they bring to a project – more, even, than by the project itself. I remember this bridge carrying the road over the River Bollin in Hale one wet evening in an early spring maybe 30 years ago. There's a little corner, shadowy, green light filtered through leaves and the dirty stream down below. The corner's slick with a green algal growth that's a slimy black beneath when you break its surface. The stonework of the bridge is Cheshire's old red sandstone, pebbly, like those little quarries at Alderley Edge where we used to go as kids from Manchester, and this feature, this corner, well, it's shallow and there's a bulge, pockets and everything slopes. There is no achievement in the having done this thing, only in the how of doing it. I'm out for a walk with Martin Boysen after he's finished teaching for the day, he's got shoes on, a green jacket, and I look back down at his face in the shadowy light. He's some kind of Sufi mystic with a soft smile, entranced by a way of doing. Oh, ease and poise, and the long reach that's the way out, so fine and tenuous in its taking. Do you see what I'm getting at here…?

So five years on from the scene on The Heights wall there's this group of youths (how old is a youth, and what gender, or is it all a function of mind?) who hang out in 'beris. There's Leo Houlding and Patch Hammond and Simon Panton and my kid Will and Big George Smith who's weird and old and funny but definitely still a youth, and I'm gleaning from word and hint and output and preoccupation and report that what they're into is something other where style and play are, you know, central. I was reading an essay on nationalism in the west by Rabindranath Tagore the other day. He talked disparagingly in it of 'the cult of the self-worship of the nation.' You can apply that in climbing too, and it's as misplaced there as in any other sphere of human activity. Ethnic cleansing, eh? Bollocks to that. Once you're into style, you're not into support groups and ends justifying means and all that bull, you're into the real creative criticism and what Coleridge calls 'the shaping spirit of the imagination' and that's the real adventure. It's within.

Maybe there was always a sense of this in climbing, but I think culturally it was colonised, annexed, grasped – you know, old Geoffrey Winthrop Young gushing on about handsome giants striding forth and leonine profiles and all that homo-erotic aesthetic of his. He wanted to believe in some aristocracy of the hills so he invented it from his own sexual appetency. He was pretty odd. Jack Longland told me once to ask Peggy about that cloak of his in the famous photograph:

'Oh yes,' she said, 'the cloak! He'd come into the wash-house at Pen-y-Pass during those Easter parties and we'd be bathing – the women, you know – we bathed separately indoors. Not as much fun, of course, and you had to watch out for the ones with moustaches. Anyway, I'm sure you know what I'm driving at – nothing on underneath, as he'd let us know. Yes! Really not much to be proud about, mind – little thing like that wasn't going to scare a girl off marriage … ' Then she and Jack smiled fondly at each other with all that glowing, gathered intimacy of age about them, and he made her blush by threatening to show me his favourite photograph that had been with him on Everest, of her doing the backstroke whilst bathing in the lake. This is taking us away from the point, if there ever was one. But it reminds me of another photograph.

This one's of a man called Gilbert Peaker – you couldn't invent a name like that – on Grey Slab on Glyder Fawr – good route, best soloed at the end of one of those long and wandering Idwal days when you drift around, chatting, no serious intent other than maybe watching the sun set at the back of Snowdon from the top of Glyder Fach and then a race down the scree at the side of the Bristly Ridge and back down the Miners' Track to Ogwen in the dark. I saw this photograph in the old Cwm Idwal guide and told Ken Wilson about it. I think he put it into *Classic Rock* but who knows? I don't have a copy any more. It's having a son who's a climber, see. First of all your books disappear into their bedroom, then they get swapped for a Rock 1 or a flexible Friend. Who cares? Shedding's good for the soul. In this picture Gilbert Peaker is so self-consciously stylish according to the perception of good style prevalent in his day that, frankly, it makes me laugh. Hands down, heels low, consider your next move. His knuckles rest lightly against the slab to reinforce the point and he's got this pipe sticking out of his gob like some great dummy to give that masculine air of authority that we all so loved to hate. He even had a moustache. I don't want to labour this point, and yes, it's to air a prejudice and maybe some people will be offended, but really, to have a moustache without some cultural imperative like you're Polish or gay or one of the feds, what does it say about you? It's like those crop-haired psychos with trim beards trying to look like Action Man. Enough said. This picture was the kind you'd stick on your wall and throw darts at. Really, it's that bad – have a look. Style as pose, and that's no style for any sheep to emulate: 'She knows there's no success like failure, and failure's no success at all.' You know that first sequence in *Don't Look Back*, which is the greatest-ever rock documentary, Dylan with his placards mouthing it to *Subterranean Homesick Blues* and success is spelt suck-cess? Yes?

What comes from style is grace. You take the belief that style is crucial into yourself and it expresses itself. Simple as that. All the great ones I've known, they've been great because of that. And others, you know, the machines accumulating away so that their names go down in history. You call that worthwhile? What are they possessed of in themselves?

I remember once, down at The Roaches with Syrett. We did *Crack of Gloom* which is one of my favourite gritstone routes: roofs, wide jamming, cutting loose, all green and leaning and mysterious with the strangest little exit from it. This was mid-1970s. I was supposed to have done the first free ascent of it maybe ten years before and maybe I did but who knows or cares? I think it was Tony Nicholls, anyway, and for the sake of those to whom these things matter, he should be credited with the first ascent of *Wall of Horrors*, too, and not dear old Tubby Austin who top-roped it into memory and oblivion. All so long ago. Whatever I did, it wasn't in the same league as John. He drifted. This is overhanging slimy exhaustion and he eased and ghosted through, pale face gleaming in the shadow. Jesus, I loved that guy. It's the quality of the inner life expressing itself. Like those kids, essentially uncorrupted as yet. With our lot, it's like Lou Reed sings, 'Stick a fork in their ass and turn them over, they're done.'

Trust the young. They'll show you. They ain't got mortgages on their souls just yet.

15: 'DENN BLEIBEN IST NIRGENDS.' (1976)

Remember Whitman's 'Song of Myself': Do I contradict myself?/ Very well then I contradict myself ... There's an essay above entitled 'A Valediction', which my good friend Pat Ament labelled a 'psychological retreat'. Quite soon I had to recant, and this is the result. The title is from Rilke's Duino Elegies, and means 'for staying is nowhere.'

They say the male menopause occurs in about one's 30th year; and thus I feel worried, for here I am, entering my 30th year in a hot flush of new-found enthusiasm for climbing. I seem to have spent years in a fruitless attempt to give it up – for as long as I've been climbing almost I've been trying to give it up – yet here I am at the supposed changing point of a man's life, and the old symptoms back with me more strongly than ever. I sit by my fire in the evenings and visions of pieces of rock float past my mind; or I'll leaf idly through old copies of *Wilson's Wonderful World*, and a picture, even just a name, will cause my palms to sweat, my fingers to flex and unflex at the touch of each tiny imagined flake.

Yet, believe me, I've tried very hard to give it up. Oh yes, so very, very hard. And this stern moral overseer, whom I call my malefactor, implanted in me during a Catholic childhood, whispers to me continually, 'you must choose not to climb, it is mere hedonism, wilful, the self-destructive portion of man, the sin of Lucifer, Godless, and too much on a Sunday.' And if it's not him it's soft-spoken Belial whispering, counselling, tempting with visions of Sunday mornings spent in slothful ease, toast and marmalade, the Sunday papers, a warm bed and a voluptuous woman, and believe me, that is a style of life which I would not affect to despise.

But still I want to climb these rocks.

Now as my best friends will tell you, I have little consistency, and for this reason I try to give my slightest inference the weight of a moral pronouncement – as with a certain heaviness one learns to spell, so it is on one's Odyssey, I think almost that I do not trust consistency; we look for life's essence in its fix or flow, and I would rather, in my own self, live in the flow, I love movement, especially movement on rock; not only my own, though this especially, but also that of others. Have you noticed to what degree you can tell a man's character from the way he moves on rock? Study it, and there it is in essence, Boysen for example: a languorous aesthete possessed of the most devastating polish of phrase – a sort of climbing Oscar Wilde, beauty for its own sake in his every move, and effortless as glass. Or Crew, so quick to grasp the essentials of a situation, yet with such a tenuous hold on them, such an infinite capacity for falling off. And then there's Wilson, muscle-bound and galumphing, the rock shuddering to his touch and a Rock-Ola jukebox on every stance. You could make a speculative science of it, like palmistry but more liberal. But this is to digress: I wanted to tell you how it came about that I couldn't give climbing up.

You see there are bad Catholics, like Joe Brown, Paul Nunn, and myself, and ours is the climb up to Hell; and there are good Catholics like Achille Ratti – theirs the kingdom of Heaven. So much is self-obvious; our solemn devils say to us 'you must suffer' and therefore suffer we must, and devilish hard we find it. Joe Brown explained to me once that the routes you did were directly proportional to the size of your rat – the bigger the rat, the harder the route. I said to him 'in my church there were no rats, only an Irish priest.' I must tell you here that both he and I come from the poor areas of Manchester, he from Ancoats and I from Hulme; it's a moot point between us which area was the worse, but either way both were bad. Paul Nunn comes from Macclesfield, and Cheshire rats are relatively tame; to eat cheese makes one melancholy is a likely explanation, but to come back to rats, Joe began to explain:

'The rat is in your belly and it gnaws you into doing the routes.'

'Is it like a wife?' I asked him, but he replied:

'No, because you're the rat who fills her belly and then she nags you not to do the routes.'

I knew what he meant, but it wouldn't do for me; you see Joe's always been rather bellicose, and I've always had this secret desire for the soft and sensual life, peppered by the cerebral. Now this is where we tread the path to Heaven, strait is the gate and all that. One of my new climbs in Pembroke I called *The Strait Gate*, and a very good climb it is too, but of course they began to call it *The Straight Gate*, which made me irate, so that I had no reply but a string of witless puns, *The Strait Gate? Oh* yes; well one day it occurred to this implanted adviser, this malefactor of mine, that climbing was something I actually enjoyed. As soon as he knew this he took pains to conceal it from me, and would have it that I was a scared and jaded noncombatant, which like all unfair criticism contained the germ of truth. So he would have me give it up, and he deprived me of that sensuous touch of rock, that gross bodily awareness, that awful surrender to movement.

I had to creep back undercover.

On a winter's day I took myself down to Cader Idris and found myself, by chance as it were, beneath the *Cyfrwy Arête*. Oh shades of Arnold Lunn, the Pearly Gates on ski – package tours to Heaven; there's no getting away from the malefactor. If you're cursed with a memory like mine it will open up to you its files and memoranda at the most awkward possible moments: 'You and the rock both in body are unsound' it told me, and proceeded to recount to me in loving detail the fall of that good Catholic, until finally it tailed off into incoherent ramblings about states of grace.

And I, I wanted the heights and the naked edges and the steep plunge of rib and groove, the splintered rock, wind-whistled and myself upon it. So up I went on that shattered hillside in company with a certain fear. It was so beautiful, I was lost. There were pinnacles and great drops; there were moves to be made and lakes far below, mauve horizons and I was unutterably alone; and the mountain did not shake me off, for I am not hubristic. It led me on like the eyes of a woman moving to her recline, and I could not but follow to the green slopes and grey-bouldered crown where I ate my sandwiches and drank my coffee, for I had come well-prepared, and watched ravens in the cold air above me. And do you know, those dark birds delighted in their flight! How they revelled on the wind, upturned and playing, and I thought, it is not a rat has brought me here but a joy, and I shall no longer listen to you, malefactor.

And so I began to climb again, though my muscles ached and it was hard, I called it an epiphany and I was very happy, though climbs that had once seemed easy now seemed hard. There is nothing hard about these new extremes, I told myself, doubtful at the moment of speech, and committed myself to one. I had not remembered that holds could be so exiguous, nor that overhangs could loom so; I struggled, and muscles twanged across the frets of my bones in the music of pain, but I did not mind, for afterwards I was alive and surely practice will make it easy once more. Where strength has been, strength shall be again. Very good. What man has done, men will try to do; we live up to examples, their peaks fire our imagination, and the upward trek goes on ...

16: FICTIONS (1981)

My theme is the complex interdependence between the imaginary and the real. However much we may structure our approaches to experience, from individual to individual the approaches will vary. Likewise, the moment when the apprehended is projected into reality will vary in the degree to which we commit ourselves as vehicles of its expression. There is a vital dimension of approach. Augustine of Hippo defines it thus:

> *'Who can deny that things to come are not yet? Yet already there is in the mind an expectation of things to come.'*

What happens within this dimension is unique in every person, though curious patterns will recur. Allow me to take one such pattern and ally it to my theme.

It is a matter for very considerable doubt whether Cesare Maestri and Toni Egger climbed Cerro Torre. There is scarcely any doubt that Keith McCallum did not climb many of the routes he reported in 1967. More recently, the account of the route *Big Bug* at Tremadog was almost certainly false. The people concerned have each been pilloried for their claims, but the issue at point is not so simple as that of telling lies. Each of these men researched their stories more or less exhaustively, studied their putative ascents from greater or lesser distances and, we must presume – otherwise it would be simple lying – believed more or less in their own accounts. In Maestri's case, the fiction was even re-written and physically enacted at a later date.

In all these instances, the primary stage of the ascent, the imaginative apprehension of the climb, was not at fault. Where the faults occurred, and faults they undoubtedly were, was in the dimension of approach. The 'expectation of things to come' worked upon their minds perhaps in such a way as to inhibit commitment to creating in actuality the ascents of their imagination. Their fictions thus did not, through their own actions, comprehend reality. In this they came quite close to the collective fictions of inadequacy which each generation of climbing creates in order to sustain the sport's momentum.

Clogwyn Du'r Arddu alone has seen at least three such: the *Master's Wall* was beyond the reach of Joe Brown, though he probed at it. Peter Crew, of the next generation, climbed it after the fashion of the times, and then created his own mischievous fiction of inadequacy in *The Final Judgement*, the name of which alone strives after apocalypse. Recently this has been climbed, as *Psychokiller*, by Ron Fawcett, and Fawcett's generation has its own fiction of inadequacy in the right-hand route on Great Wall attempted by John Redhead.[1]

Each of these in a sense is a measuring of ourselves against the 'expectation of things to come.' Each poses questions: can a climb exist, fictively, before it is co-erced into some kind of reality? Or indeed, can it ever exist in any sense beyond that of individual fictive consummation? St Augustine again:

'True then it is that man is purged by none but the "beginning", but this "beginning" is by them too variably taken.'

The process is interesting. We are continually affronted by the exigence of reality. Against isolation, we set partnership; against time, regeneration; against our own inconsequentiality, we set the fiction of heroism. Fictive heroes each of us, asserting our adequacy, our consequence, in the face of loss and decay. Climbing provides an opportunity, a hollow marvel, for this. Let me take an example from my own experience; not a deeply significant or a traumatic one, but more in the way of everyday process. When I first saw South Stack's *Red Wall*, in the mid-1960s, I did not think at first ever to climb upon it. It filled me with terror when I projected myself imaginatively upon it. But very soon, within weeks or months, I had created for myself the fiction of climbing it. This fiction was, more or less, my way of apprehending the contingencies of a sustained steepness, looseness, difficulty of access, intricacy and exposure beyond my experience in climbing at that time. As the mere fiction it was insufficient, its role being no more than one of imaginative acclimatisation. But it was a transitional phase, a step leading across to its own transmutation into a moment of time – something close to Wallace Stevens' concept of a Supreme Fiction – something which I would call a consummate fiction. Which is what I want to consider – the climb as consummate fiction – a fiction made perfect by each one of us in its enactment. And a compulsion to experience, as I was compelled, within months of first seeing it, to climb on *Red Wall*.

Time is important in the argument that a climb cannot exist except as a type of fiction. The poetic metaphor's meaning expands in the resonance set up between object and context. For the climber, he makes himself the object, the climb is his context, and memory supplies the resonance. The perspective opens out, the con-

---

[1] This line was climbed, as The Indian Face, in 1985 by Johnny Dawes

texts recede, memory drives the point home:

Truly, though our element is time,
We are not suited to the long perspectives
Open at each instant of our lives.
They link us to our losses.

Philip Larkin

This is to jump from prologue to conclusion. The fiction, the first stage, is so constructed as to apprehend experience and allow us to engage with it, the process of which engagement is "too variably taken", or even not taken at all. With some of us, perhaps even the majority, the fictionalising element continues beyond the moments of engagement. We conceptualise about the events which have taken place, we fine them down into more perfect versions than the records would allow. (The practice is widespread, and even where it is not blatantly pursued, we still create the conditions for our own fictions – we garden, rehearse, rig, bolt.)

And then, we climb. It is so brief, this experience of climbing. When we have primed ourselves with imagination, in which process our imagined ultimate victory is concomitant, when we have waited and plotted, created or happened upon the conditions for a successful engagement, when we have stalked through the dimension of approach and arrived at the central experience, then, in all probability, it distils down to a few crucial moves before the assurance of conquest.

And afterwards, what? Ecstasy? Increased self-assurance? Gratified desire? Or something more nearly allied to post-coital melancholy? Thus Tilman, on top of Nanda Devi:

'After the first joy in victory came a feeling of sadness that the mountain had succumbed, that the proud head of the goddess was bowed.'

The proud head, of course, is not bowed. All that has happened is that, for once, imagination, action, and context have conjoined and we have nowhere left to go. So we start afresh, of necessity. We create new fictions, for their enactment, all too briefly, takes us out of time to fix us in time. Though they compel us, we are to some extent their masters. We sketch out their lineaments, we tailor them to our muscle, we abate their power as our own faculties fail. Ultimately, perhaps, we allow them to move completely beyond ourselves and bequeath them, as fictions of inadequacy, to coming generations. To whom, also, the record of our consummate fictions is there

280

to be read. Spots of time, peculiar to ourselves, yet catalogued, accessible to others' re-enactments. Climbs, stories, lies, aspirations, hallucinations, heroic acts:

'The generations of men run on in the tide of Time, But leave their destin'd lineaments permanent for ever and ever.'

William Blake

Out there, in the night, in the rain, the cliffs drip and lour. Their climbs are graffiti on the walls of our minds; attempts to apprehend, to define, to control, to bring solace. Shall the sun shine tomorrow, or shall it be colder? Shall I be strong tomorrow, or shall I be older? Fictions, friends, creations, transmutations – gold or base metal, let the experiences at least have been real, etched sharp in every detail, expected, created, lived through, and not forgotten. Each one of them an act of good faith, a memory, almost a prayer.

17: RAINED UP, RAINED OFF (1998)

It's not that I dislike rain. It's just that I've long since passed that age of discretion where perception of it changes, from viewing it as added challenge to seeing its wicked and persistent slant and dribble down the panes of my window as oppression and frustration. The problem is, I've never quite acquired the taste for indoor walls. Sure, I can appreciate their value as fitness aids, but for me they exclude too much of the essential experience of climbing. And – particularly in wet weather – they're so crowded. The wall's replaced the club as the place to meet, and I never did much like clubs either. So when it rains these days, for me it spells inactivity. I stay indoors, or go out walking maybe. It was not always thus, though looking back I'm sure that I was more often caught out by rain than caught in the act of deliberately seeking it out.

I'm looking out of my window just now at the grey clouds of this sodden season scudding past, the stippled puddles in the roadway, the pearl intensity of moisture wind-gathered before the field walls, the hunched misery of the grazing sheep. Countrywide the rain spreads. Before day broke it was lashing against the Atlantic cliffs of Aillidie, darkening into a frown the Burren limestone's alabaster complexion, turning the little outcrops of Black Head into scowls furrowing the brow of the hill, sweeping on over bog and plain to eddy round the bays of Dalkey Quarry, glistening their granite before it leapt across the Irish Sea to lash against the cracks and walls of Gogarth, muddying the bright, dry efflorescence of their summer lichens; Clogwyn Du'r Arddu it conceals in a pall of cloud behind which it drenches wall and gully, sheets of water rippling down *Llithwrig* and *Troach*, falls and torrents coursing down the corners of the West Buttress, and still the columns of rain march on – a sheen of swirling drops hurled into Pothole Quarry, a lashing deluge washing the sand down the sombre front of Helsby Crag, wave upon spumey wave of wind wuthering against the scarp of gritstone edges east of the Derwent, and for once not a climber in sight along the whole length of them. All this invasive tyranny of weather, from which we cower away indoors, shudder at an imagined reality of drip and slip and cold, and look at pictures of sunwarmed Thailand and Spain. I open my e-mail and there's one from my son in California:

' ... back to the land of milk and honey! We've just got back to Bishop after a little trip away. We went to a place called Castle Rock near Santa Cruz, which was really nice – Fontainebleau sandstone in lush green forests, and only half an hour from the beach. Back to Yosemite after that and days spent throwing myself at one of the best problems/routes you'll ever see – a ten-foot jump from one boulder to a six-finger edge 12 feet up another, then 25 feet of balancy slate-style wall to the top. I didn't do it though – only managed the jump three times out of maybe 60, and then only to fall off on to a huge pile of crashpads.'

Youth and sunny days ... ! This weather's making me so gloomy all the sunny days I can think of now are ones that ended in rain. There was a gorgeous morning, maybe it was in 1972. You know, one of those days that begins in so intense a way you think the whole of the rest of your life might be like this. I'd been sleeping in a hay-loft up the Capel Coch road out of Llanberis, somewhere near the youth hostel – there's a whole history to be written about this hay-loft, but maybe this isn't the place. Audrey was serving in Wendy's Café that Al Harris ran that morning – she had red hair, was so friendly and pretty, gave you such a sexual buzz just talking to her and piled your plate high on the days that she liked you and Harris wasn't looking too closely. I don't remember who I met now – maybe it was Timothy Ifor Morgan Lewis (I always thought that was a wonderful set of names), or maybe it was Terrick Clare. It was early. We ran up to Cloggy and did *Leech*. I led that first pitch up the scoop and found it weird and hard – insecure moves leading the same way that all the little holds sloped, just to unnerve you. The top pitch across into *Serth* – one of the best and most underrated routes on the cliff, incidentally – felt much easier. We did *Taurus* to finish, which is flakey and mucky and a bit ferocious too, and clattered back down the Western Terrace feeling we'd done enough. The sun was high, we loafed across to the far side of the lake and lazed in the boulders. It was a weekend. By now the cliff was crawling with people – Cloggy was popular in those days, the place to go – a bit like the Gerlan boulders nowadays. We rolled up a joint (must have been Tim I was with) just to mediate all the decomposing adrenalin, and sat back to watch.

A great black cloud rolled in from behind the ridge, tore itself open like a wet bag and the rain deluged down. Those grooves above *Great Wall* became waterfalls in an instant. Lightning sheeted and flickered around. I've never seen such chaos ensue. Maybe there were 200 people on the cliff, and on Cloggy you can guarantee they'll be distributed over not more than 20 routes out of the 100 or more that are available. There was someone just arriving at the foot of the ragged crack on Great Wall. Another leader was way out on the last long pitch of *White Slab*. Up beneath the overhangs of the West Buttress some stalwart was involved with the unprotected intricacies of *Bloody Slab*. As if of one mind, the whole congregation turned to balletic retreat.

So imagine the scene. Suddenly everything grinds to a halt, takes stock for anguished seconds, then turns from upward crawl to downward motion inexorable.

All over the cliff, suddenly, frantic activity – leaders lower off from the sketchiest protection, parties huddle on tiny stances, clip themselves in to belays, hurl out coils of rope to snake down and interweave, shouts and bellows and angry remonstrances echo through the hiss of the rain. The thunder roars. There's a great jumping and abseiling and regrouping and grabbing of sacks and running. The path's turned in an instant to Oxford Street at Christmas as the whole gabbling caravanserai departs. In 20 minutes the crag's silent and deserted, abandoned runners gleaming and dripping on dark walls, the odd jammed rope left to sway and writhe as the climbers drain away to dampen all the valley cafés with steam and condensation and thwarted ambitions. We crouch under our rock and smoke on, vastly entertained. From some cranny Ken Wilson appears, bellowing at us of the human grandeur of the scene, the exemplary display of competence on all sides. We smile agreement and wave him on his way as he follows the flood of humanity down. Clogwyn Du'r Arddu gathers itself into majestic seclusion once more. Days like these ...

Don't imagine I think myself immune. I've been caught out like this too. There was a time when I was living in Cwm Pennant. Doc O'Brien and myself had been working on a racing Triumph 650 I used to have in the back kitchen of my house there. I'd made this piston ring compressor, but when it came to getting the barrels in place I'd nearly cut off the end of my little finger. There was blood everywhere, the top was flapping around and I'd nearly fainted, so Doc wrapped it up and said we should go climbing because fear was good if you felt queasy.

Up at the top of Pennant, by Bwlch y Ddwy Elor, I'd cleaned the grass off a beautiful, diamond-shaped 200-ft dolerite slab, round on the left-hand-facet of Craig Cwm Trwsgl where the peregrines nest. We walked up there, the bike being non-functional (it died completely a bit later on that year, on the way to Darlington, but we won't go into that).

Doc was – probably still is – a great man to be climbing with. First there was the continual stream of anecdotes from down the long years of Bangor student climbing – even then Doc was the oldest student ever, and he went on for a few more years yet – all delivered in this sly Scouse drawl. Didn't matter if his stories were true or not – their verve and invention got them past the critical apparatus anyway. Then there was his physical solidity – whatever the weather, he wore impeccably white and pectoral-displaying tee-shirts and you felt with that development of musculature, if you fell off anywhere he'd just stick out a hand and catch you, throw you back up there till you finally did it. I loved climbing with him.

So I set off up this cleaned project I had. There was a little fluted pillar of rock to begin with, bulging. I flailed up, found a lateral break, jammed in a hexentric – no

Friends then, and manteled on to the break. It was one of those awkward ones where you have to extract your toes and keep them well clear when you step up. By now I was 20 feet up and it felt like 50 – steep ground beneath, jagged boulders – that sketch. I had a set off Chouinard stoppers, which had just come in, and I got a decent-sized one in a tailor-made slot just above. There was a perfect two-finger pocket, a little scooped groove, it was all slipping in to place.

A rising toe-traverse, no handholds on it and the footholds not brilliant and sloping, led out left. I balanced up, palming the rock, Doc lancing up encouragement from below. At its end I was wrong-footed, facing out left, perched on the outside of my right foot and needing to move right, nothing to hold on to, no way to reverse it, and what was obviously the crux in front of me. The slab was set at about 70 degrees. There was a sloping foothold of the sort that even friction rubber hasn't made that friendly behind me at hip height. If I dared stand on it, at full stretch above was a vertical fingertip sidepull rib. Run your feet up on friction using that and you'd reach the thinnest sliver of fragile dolerite I'd ever seen jammed in horizontally below a little overlap. I was examining that distantly and apprehensively, brooding on the possibility of retreat to the last runner that was over half the distance to the ground below, when the first large drop of rain splashed straight between my eyes. More fell, blotching the rock darkly, and the blotches were beginning to join up. I jumped for the sidepull ...

This is over a distance of 24 years and it's clear as day, that memory – jiggling a tape on to the flake, flowing up the rest of the pitch like rain. We called it *The Exterminating Angel* because I'd just seen that Bunuel film where the doors lock, the guests can't leave, and one by one they start dying. It was one of the first 6a pitches in Wales. I always think I was rained up it. Doc followed grinning and screaming. We roped off from the stance above and came back to do the top pitch on another day.

18: WORKING ON THE NIGHT MOVES (1998)

We were in the tent at advanced base camp on Shivling. It was on a snow shoulder at 16,000 feet, a long slope curving up from it to the foot of the ridge we were climbing. I was cooking and Tom was grumpy. He ended up so grumpy and hypercritical that a couple of days later I went down and left him to it. It was nothing to worry about. You get like that on expeditions. Especially when you have to share minuscule tents in dangerous, uncomfortable places and you get some inept geriatric like me as companion rather than the fine, voluptuous and capable woman you've been dreaming about for weeks. It's manageable if you're good friends. If you're not, the tensions build. Anyway, it was dark, I was cooking some preposterously vile noodle concoction that the research had shown was an ideal combination of energy-giving carbohydrates and all that blah – quite inedible of course, tasted like six-day-old camel droppings, but there you go. The tent at advanced base camp was stocked with enough of these things to last anyone who could eat them a year at least. God knows what would have happened then, though – Gluten Man staggering down the glacier, turning ice to goo at a glance.

Above the roar of the stove, out of the darkness, vaguely I thought I could hear a shout. I told Tom. We stuck our heads out of the tent door. Nothing. Wind and mist. A few wraiths of snow wisping past. We wriggled back half into sleeping bags, carried on with cooking this noodle mess. Another sound, clearer this time. Heads out again, torch beam slicing the dark, a definite shout in response. We called back. I shugged on boots and duvet, climbed up on a knoll, shouted. Vague shape moving across a slope in the mist, alone. In minutes he was with us. It was Haresh Thakur. He'd been the liaison officer with a Czech expedition attempting one of the routes on Shivling but they'd treated him abominably. He was a devout Hindu and they'd fed him meat, told him it was cow, things like that. Mountaineers can be such shits. Sometimes they make football hooligans look like decent human beings. Put them in a gang, an expedition, a club and they turn savage. I don't like them, mostly. Bonners is okay and so's Ed Douglas. Then there's Stevie, of course, but he's as deranged as I am. I did like Haresh. We all did, racists apart. He was about 30, had a sort of calm and a wisdom about him, came from a hill village in Himachal Pradesh and was full of fun and vitality. He ended up moving in with us, and he'd borrowed gear, recruited our 18-year-old liaison officer, Chander Mohan, and together they'd set off up the hill. He didn't even have a windproof jacket. And now here he was, alone, in a fleece and shirt and thin trousers, outside our tent in the mountain night. So we took him in and fed him and he told us his story. Chander, our liaison officer, was up in the camp on the ridge. He was fine, just tired and grateful to be alive. They'd climbed Shivling. Chander had had a fall on the summit snow slope coming down, had lost his axe but stopped before the seracs. It had been an adventure. Haresh was heading down to base camp in case the military came up to check on things. They can get difficult. We gave him some new head-torch batteries – his had given out somewhere on the descent – and waved him off into the dark. Away he went down the snow slope, across the hanging glacier snout, through the boulder-field, along the interminable moraine to drop finally to Tapovan. That's working on the night moves good style, with the peaks all glimmery and the silence of the frozen hours upon them, the wind soughing, ice creaking into its rigidity that only the sun disturbs. That's the magic of being alone, on the mountain, in the dark.

I was thinking about this again yesterday. Will and I were sitting in the sun and he was relating all his latest climbing exploits to me. He was telling me about finishing *Pagan* on *Left-hand Red Wall* in the dark, about his leader grinding up the last pitch, 'behaving like a real mincer' whatever that means, about the beam of the South Stack lighthouse swinging round all ghostly, a brilliant bar of silver traversing the dark, briefly illuminating holds, imposing its rhythm on the ascent, imprinting the position of holds in memory that will be used in a quick rush, in a flash before the dark floods in again behind. We talked a bit about the route, but mostly what held me was the memory of that magical, thrilling stuff when you get caught out there on the rock in the interstices of the darkness and the light. Will's no stranger to this. He used to get really pissed off with me when he was younger and I'd hang around and make any excuse – another pot of coffee, have to find my gear, must make a phone call – to delay departure so that we'd get benighted. I don't know why I used to do this. Except that I'd always done it, and it used to guarantee, you know, urgency, tension, all that adrenaline stuff. Time and again looking back. There was that occasion in the Cheddar Gorge, a bleak, raw December day and Sue Whaling and I had slept in her Morris Minor at the bottom of *Coronation Street* and then just messed around all day like you do, started on the route at three o'clock and that was such pressure so you just motor. I love that – the cutting loose, the not thinking, the insistence of the failing light. Out beyond the Shield hand-traverse the gorge was already losing detail, you had to peer at the rock to make out any feature and I could see in those days. Pitch-dark by the time we'd finished, black, and then the getting down. Make the rules, create the situations, so that you're at maximum disadvantage. Isn't that the real game?

Maybe you don't think so but I did, often. There was a time with The Newt, who was a slow, methodical climber, ponderous, ruminative, when we went to do

Fantan B on the Lleyn Peninsula – December again, and cold, and not getting on to the rock until the afternoon and who knows where in Christ's name this route goes and it is huge – what, 700 feet of it? And wandering, complex, unlikely? And no options. I like that. Options I can't cope with. You know, you decide for me or put me in a situation where you just have to get on with it, cut loose, no choice. It's the aspect of the climbing experience that Jim Madsen so gloriously defined as he slipped from the end of his abseil ropes at the top of El Cap back in 1968: 'Ah what the fuck ... ' he said – said! – to the guys he'd been rappelling down to rescue, and them open-mouthed witnesses to his last flight. On *Fantan B* The Newt was sly. He had two head-torches in his rucksack. He was a boy scout. But to play fair, he didn't pull them out till the thing was done. That was decent thinking. It would have been sacreligious on the route. Because you went into that darkness knowing, and thereafter it is the instinct, do you see? It is the desire, and the wild in you on which you must learn to draw.

Sometimes, though, I have been baffled. Once on *Vector*, not long ago. I was 50 then, already, I think, and Will and I had gone out after school, after dinner, in early summer, to do *Vector* at Tremadog where he says no-one now goes because it is just punters and besides the hard routes there are very hard, unbelievably hard. This is the thinking, he tells me, nowadays. If Vector Buttress were to fall down, good! Pete Crew used to say the reverse of this years ago. If all Tremadog apart from Vector Buttress were to fall down, good! It didn't happen, but it will. Geology necessitates. There are buttresses here that are the scars of rock-falls from a geological second ago. I like the intimacy of dark-and-light rhythms. It mediates that immensity. So there we were on *Vector* and Will's feet slipped off on the moves out beyond the ring peg on the Ochre Slab – weird that that's still there. So I gnarled at him and told him ditch the sloppy, think precision, go down and do again – all that paternalistic stuff that some old fart had drilled into me millennia ago. It was Paul Nunn and Richard McHardy actually, on *Fag End Slab Direct* at Brimham in our boots in the snow after an Alpha Club dinner in the early 1960s. Jeez! Snowballs and soloing! So this day on *Vector*, me now very old with my son, we changed over belays in that horrid so-called cave that makes your back ache and how come that's not fallen down and it was getting dark. By the time I was out there at the foot of the final crack it was quite dark and I had not brought my glasses, without which these days I cannot see and anyway they are tinted to protect me from the light and I was climbing the crack's left wall instead of the crack itself which is just daft and there was a voice of someone I maybe knew calling up from the road saying, Jim, how're you doing, do you want a rope? So I was kind of irritated and said no, firmly but politely, and eventually somehow flailed up with no style which is not as it should be because when you draw on this instinctual force it should be good, strong, precise, like I had just told the whipper-snapper always to be, but you know, life always turns it round to the joke's being on you, which is a cosmic joke, and that's proper, that's the way it should be.

19: No More Heroes Any More (2001)

It's a big responsibility, being a hero – especially being your own hero, having a project you yourself deem heroic. Because if you hold to that, you'll have a sense of the ever-widening gap between aspiration and reality, you'll be living externally, becoming ever more confounded internally, and there's no squaring that circle. So steer clear of heroes – they're a confused lot. I was doing a gig down at the Adventure Travel Show in London a couple of weeks ago, and all around me there were hordes and hordes of people who believed in heroes and were out looking for them, wanting to touch them, even become them. And, you know, nature abhors a vacuum so heroes were there on display. Weird bunch ... ! There was an old guy had driven from south to north through the Americas way-back-when in a 1920s Austin Seven. I thought he was pretty cool. He told me he'd been re-tracing Anton Tschiffely's ride and I had a dim recollection of reading that book – *Tschiffely's Ride* – in my school library a few light years ago; this old guy was the best, with his bag of tools and his battered car and his puzzled look. Apart from him, there were a couple of people who could have passed for New Labour spin-doctors talking about how they'd got up Everest in the usual way for these days. This strikes me as dead boring, but in London they love it because Everest has slightly more digits to its height than a commodity broker's weekly bonus and sometimes leaves those who climb it with one or two less than their natural quota. Actually I'd have quite liked to have gone to one of these talks, because it was by Rebecca Stephens, who tells the dirtiest jokes I've ever heard in an impeccably and dissonantly plummy accent. I went to dinner with her once and she rolled out this story that involved the Queen saying 'cunt', Fergie (a red-haired duchess, not The Manager), and a Range Rover. I don't quite remember how it went, but you know, details like that, mix and match. She wouldn't have told it at the *Daily Telegraph* Adventure Travel Show – rest assured of that. The old *Rabid Bellylaugh* likes its smut, but knows when to draw the line. I sent a commissioned travel piece in once about an American city and it opened with a description of walking inadvertently into a gay bar, standing next to this guy as I waited to be served, and him politely enquiring whether I took it up the ass (vernacular American, that – nothing so perverse as donkeys in this piece). My editor came back with the usual nice supportive stuff and a polite enquiry as to whether we might slightly re-phrase the opening, since it constituted what Bill Deedes apparently used to term 'a marmalade-dropper'. Wonderful term – a whole social milieu summed up in three words.

    To come back to heroes, 20 or so years ago I took Ken Wilson (an endearing figure from climbing's distant past) – for the sake of his immortal soul along to a production, very rare, of Sophocles' least-known, strangest, and perhaps best play, the *Philoctetes*. It provoked in him one of those benignly baffled rants that were his most appealing form of self-expression. I thought that, as Dave Cook's best mate, Ken would have understood the subversive dialectic of the play. Sure, The Stranglers expressed it more succinctly with 'No more heroes any more', but Sophocles' was the subtler analysis. I'll give you the great American critic Edmund Wilson's précis of it, from the title essay of his collection, *The Wound and the Bow*:

'*The victim of a malodorous disease which renders him abhorrent to society and periodically degrades him and makes him helpless is also the master of a superhuman art which everybody has to respect and which the normal man finds he needs. A practical man like Odyseus, at the same time coarse-grained and clever, imagines that he can somehow get the bow without having Philoctetes on his hands or that he can kidnap Philoctetes the bowman without having regard for Philoctetes the invalid. But [Neoptolemus] the young son of Achilles knows better. It is at the moment when his sympathy for Philoctetes would naturally inhibit his cheating him – so the supernatural influences in Sophocles are often made with infinite delicacy to shade into subjective motivations – it is at this moment of his natural shrinking that it becomes clear to him ... that the bow would be useless without Philoctetes himself. It is of the nature of things – of this world where the divine and the human fuse – that they cannot have the irresistible weapon without its loathsome owner, who upsets the processes of normal life by his curses and his cries, and who in any case refuses to work for men who have exiled him from their fellowship.*'

Get the picture...? There's this guy on a desert island with a stinking wound. He's got something you want. But you can't have it – because the desert island and the stinking wound go with the deal.

Heroes ... ! I blame the Americans for lowering the tone of the debate. You could always tell the hero in all the westerns I used to watch when I was a kid (and still do when I get the chance). It was obvious. The hero was the one who looked like a hero. Same deal still applies, of course, in our culture. Look at the rough deal, the exacting scrutiny, that John Dunne gets compared to style-icons like Ben-and-Jerry (hydra-headed monster rumoured to have cloned itself infinitely and have become endemic in Sheffield basements). I heard this great story about John Dunne the other night – at the Warrington Wall stuffing himself on four hamburgers in a row; then he walks outside and there are four scallies nicking car stereos. He gives chase and they drive off. Down the road a way they look back at old fatty Dunne trailing along, chest heaving, and say to themselves, 'Hey, one of him, four of us ... '

291

Car stops, scallies pile out. Unwise move!

Someone's phoned the feds, and by the time they arrive it's JD who's miffed and the scallies who are glad to see them. I like heroes who don't look like heroes, or at least bring a bit of complexity and subtlety, a bit of fragility and imperfection even to the role. Who are they trying to fool, the perfect ones? Are they from heaven descended ... ? I think not. All those guys who round on the miscreants and the fantasists and the ones who fall short – I've seen them on their bad days, bending the rules they claim always and so righteously to uphold. And there's another point to get across here – perfection gives no latitude to the creation of myth. Not that you always have to create myth – with some people a little tasteful embroidery around their more outrageous actions should suffice. Think of people like Whillans, Stevie Haston (distant cousin to the more fallible Dougal) and John Barry. These guys shouldn't be thought of as exemplars but as entertainers, lightening the heavy moral texture of all that insistent pressure to focus and excel. Their actions are in the nature of decisive, brave steps to the rhythm of fortune's dance. One of my great and truly exemplary heroes died a couple of weeks ago at the age of 90. He was Benny Rothman, who stood up on a platform in 1932, ballsed it out in front of a police presence of 200 and then led 500 ramblers up on to the forbidden land of Kinder Scout. Give thanks to Benny next time you're wrestling with the innards of *Extinguisher Chimney*. Joe Brown would never have done what was his first climb if it hadn't been for him. Benny told me once about being at one of Oswald Mosley's fascist meetings in Manchester's Belle Vue Hall in the 1930s (Benny, like Dave Cook, was a lifelong communist). The stewards threw him off the balcony into the crowd below for distributing leaflets and then more of them set about him down below. Benny was about four-feet-eight but built like a brick shithouse and giving as good as he got until escorted out to safety.

... oh Jesus! Pressure of uniformity, need to conform, scales of achievement, absence of real risk, programmed athleticism replacing random instinctual response. Where's the daring and the acceptance of difference? I don't think climbing throws up many heroes, and when it does they're the odd ones who are irritants to society's digestive tract (or were – the conventionality of what was on display at that Olympia event brought home how grave the shift may be). Here's my theory – sport for the most part just isn't a milieu to produce heroes. Very occasionally (in boxing bouts most notably – Ali against Foreman, say, or that brutal contest where Nigel Benn was battered through the ropes by Gerald McLellan and yet was so bloodily obdurate that he came through to win), sport produces something where the individual refusal to give in before apparently insuperable odds becomes tinged with the heroic. But it's still a kind of heroic self-belief, and it's the self bit that troubles me. When the Greeks were getting it on, their heroes were champions for a nation and a cause and I can respect that (I'm enough of an old hippy to have had 'Che' Guevara as one of my heroes, and he stayed that way even after I'd been to Cuba, which he'd left long before he died). But those acclaimed as heroes through actions predicated on ambition or self-preservation, on the ego or on the survival instinct – well, come on, what's heroic about that? It's not a fireman rushing up the stairs into the smoke of the twin towers, is it ... ? Crawling down The Ogre or Siula Grande (they do a lot of crawling, our climbing heroes, don't they?) – what's heroic about that? If they hadn't, they'd have died, and that's a terminally limiting choice – no more company of women with their mysteries and sweet talk and soft, musky bodies? No more bluebells? No more Irish whiskey and walking down from Cloggy in the sunset and autumn days on the grit? No more lying in bed with your beloved in your arms, puzzling over a remembered quatrain of Rumi's? Forget it! And that's the other point to be made. These disaster-stricken players had chosen to be there. Whatever the guys jutting their jaws at the Adventure Travel Show might think, you don't choose to be a hero. Some find themselves on rare occasions in a situation where you have to make a moral choice that leads into the pantheon – Tony Streather on Haramosh, for example – but you sure as hell don't posture your way in. Or as Neoptolemus spiked at Philoctetes when the latter was trying to crawl out of his situation, 'The fortunes that the Gods give to us/ We must bear under necessity,/ But men that cling wilfully to their sufferings ... / No one may forgive or pity.' I've just been reading one of those glitzy cosmopolitan thrillers by the two *Observer* journalists who call themselves Nicci French. Its villain's a climbing hero, won his glory through astounding selflessness and resilience on a Himalayan peak called Fanirat or some such, and he turns out to be a real psychopath with big agendas around rejection ... knock off the peak, knock off the woman! Now I wouldn't go that far, but they might have the glimmer of a point ...

20: WAYS OF SEEING (2002)

My friend Al Bevan gave me this little stack of guidebooks that currrently sits on my desk. He picked them up from the second-hand bookshop down in a cellar on Mosley Street in Manchester, and thought I'd like them. He's always been generous like that. I love him dearly. He's been one of the solid influences in my life for 40 years, more or less. I first met him at Philomena O'Rourke's 18th birthday party, at the Mynydd Club's cottage up at the head of Crafnant in the early 1960s. Everyone was after Philomena in those days. I was too young to be taken seriously, so because I was no threat I got to spend more time with her than most. It used to drive me demented, all this unconsummated proximity. She was a convent schoolgirl, from Abbeyfeale down in County Kerry originally, and had a kind of glistening, sassy, easy beauty on her then that was irresistible. And unattainable. She married a millionaire, and I've gone weak at the knees in the company of Irish women ever since. They're a breed apart.

Phil and a mate of hers at this time had fallen in with a very amiable and mis- chievous version of bad company called Brian Royle, with whom I used to climb sometimes. He was muscular and funny and dependable. I was climbing with him the day after Phil's party, which is where I met Al Bevan for the first time. I wanted to do Bovine on Clogwyn y Wenallt, because I'd seen this picture of Brian Wright on the top pitch and it looked amazing – Jug City, stretching into the sky. Everything looked so much bigger in those days: 'one of the best pitches in Wales,' said the guidebook. Maybe it was. There weren't so many of them then. We went over there, jouncing down the old road into the Gwynant in Brian's A35 van.

Al came too. He'd not climbed before and fancied doing some, thinking it might cure his hangover. I'd arrived at the phase in a young climber's life where the realisation dawns that climbing is actually very simple – reach up, find a hold, pull on it. But it's a sollipsistic time. You're so enchanted by your own grace and strength, by your body's habituation to the message that first pull on a hold sends shimmer- ing through it, that almost inevitably you lack empathy. Al was a big, strong guy, and there wasn't much he was afraid of. I remember being in a city-centre Manchester pub once as a scrawny kid, and this fellow started picking on me, prodding me in the chest and all that. Al took a swing at him from behind me and he went down like a felled tree. I suppose it didn't much occur to me that I needed to look after Al too. What I could do he could surely do just as well, I thought. But there's a trickery of the body in climbing and it comes so instinctively after a while that you're not con- sciously aware of it. You come to believe it actually is as simple as the way Peter Biven described Menlove Edwards' climbing: 'hand on hold – move up.'

So there was Al at the bottom of *Bovine*'s top pitch, and I was belayed to some little spike on the grass slope at the top, out of sight and earshot. There's a move at 15 feet on this pitch, before you hit Jug City, that Brian told me was called the Obstetrician's Move. He was a rude boy.

Al fell off and swung round to the right to hang in mid-air. My feet shot from under me on the wet grass. The loop of No.1 nylon stayed on its tiny nubbin. I was hanging grimly on, head down the slope with the rope running through my armpits. Al weighed 16 stone, I weighed about seven. I had to lower him. It took the skin right off my hands. Something like this happened to the Holliwells once on *Red Wall*. Les was following a top pitch and pulled off a big block. Lawrie's belay was too long and he shot head first over the edge. He was using a shoulder belay and, upside down with 300 feet of cliff beneath, the rope had come over his head and was running through his hands. His and Les' eyes met, 20 feet apart. Les still had his arms round the block. 'For fuck's sake, get rid of it,' Lawrie croaked. He did. They survived that one.

I like to remember these topsy-turvy episodes, these clear moments beyond the swift onset of panic. You see things so differently in them, the world having been turned upside down. Something of that sense comes home to me as I keep finding my gaze drawn to this little stack of guidebooks that appeared on my desk when I moved house recently. They're different. They express ways of seeing that can only exist for us now beyond a barrier, and one that is crossed adventitiously, if it is crossed at all. They're the first series of *Climbing Guides to the English Lake District*, edited by HM Kelly, volumes one to four – beige cloth with rounded corners and red lettering on the covers, the 'new' series published in the 1930s and still on sale and more or less current when I started climbing at the very end of the 1950s. 'Scafell Group. This edition 1936.' Imagine the outcry if the current guide to Malham, say, dated from 1975? And contained passages like this, from the prefatory historical essay:

'1898 may fairly claim to be a vintage year through OG Jones' magnificent performance in ascending directly from *Lord's Rake* to the *Waiting Room*, and so by way of the *Mantelshelf* to the Crevasse ... '

I love the certainty of those thudding, capitalised epithets applied to each feature of the rock. The writer – CF Holland of *Holly Tree Wall* fame – goes on:

'It would be intensely interesting if one could become clairvoyant and see the route taken by Jones, crawling up those slabs in his stockinged feet as the evening shadows gathered; the exact line taken can never be known, but the climb was an epic ... [in 1903] a great set-back was suffered in the accident on the Pinnacle face during the attempt to reach Hopkinson's Cairn from *Lord's Rake*, and for some years the spot was avoided by climbers. Jones' route by the Mantelshelf was taken to be a phenomenal effort by a phenomenal climber, and this section of the cliff was set down as unjustifiably dangerous.'

John Beatty and myself were talking about this self-same route last week. 'There's nothing there!' he stated, his eyes widening. 'You wander out on to that face, and it's like when you pull over the bulge on *Pellagra*. It's blank.'

That's maybe to exaggerate (or to state the paradoxical truth that the hardest climbs of every era in some strange way are all the same grade), but I remember being brought up short by the unexpected difficulty of antiquated climbs – this one among them – on many occasions. I remember soloing the *Mermaid Climb* – an Archer Thomson special on Llechog from before the Great War – in bendy old walking boots and coming across a groove like *First Slip*; or being 40 feet above the thread that was my last runner on Javelin Blade – in the old grey cloth-bound Cwm Idwal guide it was graded a lowly V.S. and is now E1, 5b – one damp day in the late 1960s. Nick Estcourt was seconding me, was huffing and puffing away on the belay about it being an ancient and therefore piss-easy route, and why didn't I get a move on because he was getting cold and damp. So was I, and I was scared too. And when I stopped dithering and procrastinating and launched into the sequence, I was well impressed – friction bridging up a slabby but holdless groove, reaching out for a fingertip flake before swinging up on to the Javelin itself, and all that long 80 feet of bouncing fall beckoning beneath. Done in 1930 by Jack Longland: 'I think I had pretty strong fingers in those days from pole-vaulting,' he told me, when I had one of those 'What-were-you-thinking-of?' conversations with him, 50 or more years on from his ascent, 20 from mine, 'and you know, maybe something's come off,' he added, to make me feel better about notions of progress.

Flicking through these old guides brings so many memories like that back to mind. There was a time on Dow Crag with Al Bevan, for example. I remember it was winter, and the waterfall into Torver Quarry at the start of the walk up was entirely frozen. We decided – well, you know, it was decided – that we'd do *Eliminate 'C'*, because that was supposed to be the easiest of the crag's VSs, and I'd got into the frame of mind that, whatever the conditions, anything less than VS was unworthy of a climber's attention – same way that nowadays any climber worth his or her salt wouldn't be seen dead working on anything less than F8a+. *Eliminate 'C'* started out of some icy gully. I recall a lovely, delicate pitch on perfect, rough, sound rock, that led out on to the arête:

' ... leader needs 70 feet of rope. One of the finest climbs on the crag ... (1) 45 feet. Enter a shallow recess in the left wall and from a doubtfully wedged flake climb the narrowing slab for a few feet, then step out on to the wall itself and follow it to a rock ledge. An awkward traverse across and down to a small grass ledge on the arête is then taken. The next section lies up the arête itself, the first movement being delicate ... '

I doubt if a modern guidebook editor would allow that degree of expansive description for so few feet of rock. Terseness is our rule, along with hero-worship of course. And even this liberality with words doesn't capture the experience of that winter's day: no gear, unable to feel my fingers for the cold, everything becoming a bit tenuous round the arête with having to protect Al across the pitch – he'd done a few more routes by this time, but not that many; the pale blue sky and Goats' Water crisped and fretted with ice. Still, we had a good time, and we survived.

The style of those guides doesn't, though. All their emphasis on the features of a cliff, their restraint, the descriptive attention of them, the simple designating proprieties of their route-naming, their mountain-centred vision so beautifully underlined by those moody and luminous painted Heaton Cooper frontispieces where people were entirely excluded (none of your statuesquely-posed-foreground-figures-in-red-socks or your forearms-and-lycra photographs for these guides) – all this reticence argued an appreciation and mildly fearful respect for the mountain environment that no longer has much currency. Maybe attitudes like those that I describe as having brought myself to the hills so long ago are part of the explanation for the change. I wouldn't even assert any superiority for the old approaches, perceptions, ways of seeing. But I pick up these little books one by one – *Pillar Rock & Neighbourhood, Dow Crag, Great Langdale & Outlying Crags* ('Bracket & Slab Climb. 295 feet. Severe. Rubbers. One of the longest climbs on Gimmer.') – with a curious, fond pleasure now, much in the way that you might pick up some curio in a folk museum, feel the wear hands have imparted to it, and ponder on its lost use.

21: KALEIDOSCOPE OF THE SENSES (1995)

Shale – the word's only the hovering of rationality around the dip and slip of rock beneath my fingertips. There's an illusory friction in its patina of lichen that I rub away, a fine, grey-green dust adhering in the whorls of each finger. I cloud it with chalk, cough away the inhaled dryness, press on the shelving hold again and ease unwilling joints across to where, for balance, body must stay in a tensile arch. My runners in that shattered crack are 15 feet away, the terrace 25 feet below. Looking down for footholds I catch Martin's eye, shake my head ruefully, he raises an eyebrow and smiles:

'I could make it to that streak of birdshit 20 feet up, but there's no gear, I'm pressed enough just hanging on here, it steepens above that and God knows how I'd get down.'

The raven swoops, air hissing through its pinions. There is metal in its blackness and sardonic cry. Giggling laughter and retreat. Later, above Martin's belay, just momentarily the instinct choreographs a dancing step or two; bridged across a strange groove with loose block at chest height, there comes the visual rush. A layered terracotta pillar leaps into vivid life, its grainy pastels imprinting into memory. On top, on a terrace of deep heather with the cuckoo's call drifting muted from the valley woods, we give best to Clogwyn Pot, name our exploratory route '*Ravens on Speed*' and run away.

Of that action, I recall the stone I stepped on in the ragged wall coming down the scree – a slivery ochre piece which twisted under my foot. For a moment the rocks above it slid grudgingly, then a roaring and crashing and bounding, a sulphurous smell, I was gasping for breath 20 yards back, clinging to Martin, shrieking with laughter, stones pouring like lava down the slope.

Iwan's across the valley, a white dot endlessly moving up and down a slab on a buttress the name of which I don't know. From beneath the crack of *Spectre*, on the road below I see a mini-van with flower transfer pull in to the lay-by. Two figures emerge – a man's red hair, liquidity of a girl's movement accentuated by swirl of hair and skirt. By the wall they kiss. My son comes across the slab to join me. I fret at the belays, flay a shin as I struggle and flop into the crack above, and from its prickling soreness comes distant laughter of dead friends with whom I've shared this climb – Tim Lewis, Al Harris – dearest I ever had, and how different things might have been had they lived, who were a part of our collective sanity: the screams in the hospital night, the wet road on an autumn night – oblivions for graced lives.

His pale face below me – at 15 – was I his age when I first did this climb? With

Bill Birch, more than 30 years ago. The feel of that afternoon. There was strength and ease in our bodies that day, an accord between us who'd never climbed together till then. I remember how elegantly you climbed, the good humour and the friends around us; also, the configuration of crystal in a particular hold, the way it cut off sensation and numbed a finger joint. It's here's again to bring it back. When the planes shift, this other Will, my son, with his anxious face as I ease past the stacked blocks into the groove on *The Grasper* and him secured only to two pegs on that perch of a stance. What detail will cause him to recall? I did so little with my own father. Lightness and protruding bones as I carried him from bed to chair in his last illness, when I was Will's age, in exorcising which waste I rage to record.

Weirdwood with the knotted branches and bearded rocks, my sly-sweet inquisitive friend after his forms of knowledge again. Ah, Martin, with your women and your rocks, I share your bent again today, recognise the thrill of curiosity, jostle with you even a little to be on with it, but it's properly your climb, your fingers probe the passage, your limbs comfort themselves along its curving ridge. We sit astride this jokey pinnacle your imagination searched out among the trees and on its quivering top conspire together in the appropriate symbol of release, leaping across the void to mainland mother earth. 'Priapic Worship' we call it, in order to mock. The Doric Column, Old Pan at play in the sacred groves, yet they passed by, all of them, on the road, bound for the heights against which to measure themselves, the numbers by which to assess, whilst it waited across the water, secret, discreet. Dust blew in our eyes and the husks of dry grass seeded our hair.

Twenty-four hours in another place, the sunset coastal road heading south speeds past, needle flicking time and again over the 100 pricks at every sense whilst Andy and Martin sleep. Irish friends in the Bosherston pub, good-humoured jockeying games played out around the table or in the clifftop car park, waves hushing under a sailing moon, sleep lacey with aspiration and good memory, morning sun on the dewy gorse, its nut scent mingling with the new-biscuit smell of morning piss, figures groaning from sleeping bags into clothes, ordering of strewn chaos, Mrs Weston's rolling South-Walian tones warming you with promise of coffee and eggs and toast that comes starred with yellow butter dripping clarified between your fingers where your lazy, delicate tongue reminds you you're alive and across on the ranges the death-dealers crump and crash and roar.

South face of Mowing Word. We're here because military activity and the bird bans have occluded other possibilities, and now we're glad of it. Andy and Martin are on the ledge below *Charenton Crack*. When I first climbed it, 23 years ago, I named it after the Paris lunatic asylum in which the Marquis de Sade was incarcerated. It seemed appropriate. There was fear and the strength beyond panic as runners flicked out and made their stuttering descents of the rope. My fingers were lacerated from the calcite edge of the crack, smeared with clay dug from it, blood oozing from cuts and splashing in crimson drops on to the grey block around which I belayed. Out among the sculpturesque bosses at the edge of the tidal platform today I trail those same fingers in a salt pool as Martin fights his way up, know that this time it will be easy, I will be safe, and strong enough, and know what to do, and so I turn away and look down into the crystal pool.

The life that's here starts out and astounds me. Mussel shells lie open, showing a gentian blue; there are dusty pink corals and all manner of draining and crackling and popping shells of the names of all of which I am entirely ignorant, all manner of forms of which I want to sing in praise – encrustations and labia and fronds, threads and ribbons, castles, curves, with texture and colour glimmering across the spectrum. In and out between the closed anemones there are green worms winding, and they are so mossy and delicate I sit wide-eyed and stilled, and when I look up the waves are surging against the cliffs and time has ceased, I'm become a part of it all and there is only the urge all around of process, of which you on the sand over there were a part when you stepped so delicately from your orange bikini to run naked into the foam and hiss of the waves, and you too, dear late lover, were also a part, telling of your pleasure as we listened to these waves, of your release into delight, your blood shadowy in the moonlight across my hand, its metallic taste between our lips, so intimately were our sensations shared, and everything we have known through the full life of the senses is still present in this moment. How much of this do we all know? I solo up to the ledge and ask about the worms:

'Maybe they're six inches long, velvety, mossy, dark green and so lovely ... '

You who decry or ignore have the dead albatross about your necks. You find peace when you bless the worms.

22: FOR ARNOLD PINES
BROADCAST VERSION (1979/1993)

I may never have met Arnold Pines, but even about this I am not quite sure. Certainly, I've met people who knew him, even knew him closely. And I may have met the man himself. But this is not the point. Arnold Pines is dead. I read as much in an obituary column, and certain details set me wondering if I knew him. But I'll come back to this. On the day that I read Arnold Pines' obituary, a letter came in the post from Kevin FitzGerald:

'What with ... a fresh fall of snow last night, and a general feeling developing that it can't be long now, and that I shall in consequence miss your novel, I am not in the best of moods ... '

Well, I sit here today in my study, the novel unwritten, the Carneddau mist-shrouded beyond the window, rain dinning on the roof, washing away the last of the snow, and I'm beset with thoughts of death. If this sounds morbid or melodramatic to you, let me confess straight away that, like Montaigne, 'ever since I can remember, nothing has occupied my imagination more than death, yea, even in the most licentious season of my life.' As a climber, in fact, it doesn't seem to me proper to think about the mountains and our activities amongst them without considering the element of risk and consequent death they body forth. Acceptance of the possibility, even proximity, of death is at some level concomitant with the pleasures and rewards of mountaineering. You might not subscribe to Hazlitt's view that 'a life of action and danger moderates the dread of death.' But do you find no measure of agreement with him as he continues: 'It not only gives us fortitude to bear pain, but teaches us at every step the precarious tenure on which we hold our present being'?

You can scarcely disagree that the risk of death is indissociable from the thrill of climbing. The coward's 1000 pre-deaths are all known to the climber upon the rock, as he or she weighs up the consequences and guards against the contingencies of a fall; and as for vicarious deaths, those too, and by the hundred.

I'm sometimes tempted to suggest to the British Mountaineering Council, since it purports to represent this strange and so-called sport, that it should erect a roll of honour. Just such a one as you find in schools, in village halls, on roadsides, in town centres or chapel yards throughout the land, always inscribed with the old, insidious lie about the men of these names having died for God, King and Country, that rightly would read, 'Betrayed by Mammon, obligation, the egoism and cupidity of politicians.' Only the mountaineering one would properly be inscribed to error, accident, insouciance.

The names come readily to the tongue. In the 30 and more years I've been climbing, the people I've met, known, been friendly with, who are now dead are many. No theory explains away all their deaths. What connection is there between the death of Lawrie Holliwell, whose abseil belay gave way on Craig yr Ysfa up there in the mist beyond my window – and that of Nick Estcourt, killed thousands of miles away in the Karakoram by a slab-avalanche as he crossed a snow-slope on K2? Or between Dave Sales, who died of a ruptured spleen after falling from the over-hang of Quietus on Stanage, and Arthur de Kusel – Liverpool Arthur, a mop-haired manic ragamuffin of filthy personal habits and irrepressible laughter, who was struck repeatedly, jolted, screaming against the thunderous night. In the bright morning after the storm he was silent, charred by lightning where he crouched, foetal, burnt, in his bivouac on the Grand Capucin above Chamonix.

No explanations, no statistics encompass or suffice, no theories would have prevented these deaths. Yet the theories, of safety, of causation, are touted abroad. Consider for example the Cairngorm tragedy of November 1971 in which six teenagers died. An enquiry quite stunning in its assemblage of a cast almost totally unwilling or unable to answer the questions put to it, failed to reach even the sim-ple and unavoidable conclusion that if you place a party of young people on a high, bare mountain summit in a blizzard, then no matter how well-equipped they are, in the course of a day or two most of them will die. It is in the nature of things. The mountains in winter are inimical to life. Even brute creation shuns a storm-swept mountain and cowers in its lair. Why then expect young, untrained human beings to survive? Why put them to the test? Which latter is really the crux of the matter. If they choose the test of their own volition, all to the good. But to persuade, instruct, inveigle them into following models of apparent competence – is that fair, or wise?

People die in the mountains because the risks of mountaineering can usually be minimised or abated, but they can never be excluded. There will always be occa-sions when the human animal, with all its aspirations to dignity, power and control, is reduced to a limp bundle of crushed flesh and rags. How then should we react to it, when any death could as easily be our own? Lawrie Holliwell was killed on a summer's day on that mist-shrouded cliff up there. His tape belay for an abseil pulled off a rounded spike. Yet I can remember more than a few occasions when I've used unsuitable, unsafe belays for abseiling. There was the time on the West Wing of Dinas Mot, retreating late in the day from the midway terrace rather than com-plete the scrappy upper pitches of a route. At the bottom, after a 150-ft abseil, only the slightest flick was needed to bring down the rope. Once, on Anglesey's sea cliffs,

I fished out from my rucksack a length of frayed bootlace and – in a spirit of devil-may-care brinksmanship – used it as an abseil loop. I shudder to think of it now.

Then there's the death-toll from soloing: John Taylor, Tony Wilmott, Jim Jewell – the two last killed on easy routes. My most frightening solo exploit was not the notorious drug-propped escapade when I came down from a cocktail of speed and cocaine 300 feet up Coronation Street in the Cheddar Gorge, but ten years earlier, in 1967, 120 feet above bouldery ground at the top of a route on Millstone Edge in the Peak District. With my hands on a detached dinner-plate of rock, both my footholds snapped off at the same moment. To this day, I have no idea why I didn't fall, what quirk of fate saved me.

What of accidents on dangerous ground above and around cliffs? I remember too well Hugh Gair – sweet-tempered, grey-bearded Hugh, starting out staid and sensible late in life on his first extreme climbs – I remember him falling from the dangerous, broken ground between the top of Llithrig and the foot of Octo on Clogwyn Du'r Arddu in 1968 – 300 feet through the air before landing terribly injured, his grey flesh misshapen, marbled with blood and the life-breath guttering out, on the path under the crag. A day or so before, I'd climbed *Red Wall* on South Stack with Bonington. Instead of abseiling in we had blithely scrambled down the usual abseil ridge and traversed across into the back of the zawn, unroped, on loose and slimy dreadful rock throughout the 300-ft descent. After Hugh's death I had wondered then, as so many times before and since, why Hugh, why not me? I am no more careful. I had no more reason to want to stay alive. Why him? Why not me?

Of course the question is pointless, too compounded with our emotions, too simple, too wistful. We indulge ourselves in imagining our own deaths: the things it would excuse us; the certitude at last of our friends' caring; the judgmental finality of it all by which we might come to know where we stood, the crushing irony being that we would not know. I recall the curious sensation Ken Wilson, then editor of *Mountain* magazine, produced in me through a chance aside in a conversation about obituaries that he and I had some time in the 1960s: 'Oh, I suppose I'd give you three or four column inches in *Mountain*.'

Francis Bacon wrote that: 'Death hath this also, that it openeth the gate to good fame, and extinguisheth envy.' I don't suppose many would be too envious of 'three or four column inches in *Mountain*.'

These are private considerations, secret imaginings. We cannot easily joke about death and yet it has a jokey aspect. I remember Tilman – the century's greatest mountaineer-explorer – talking about it coolly, sardonically, treating the whole thing as a huge jest, not much to be feared, rather even to be welcomed, in a conversation I had with him in 1977 before he sailed – in his 80th year and as an ordinary crew-member – for the Antarctic on his last voyage. At the time there were thoughts racing round my mind of what others who had sailed with him had said about what their reactions had been to his imperturbable manner in the face of peril. Ian Duckworth was a friend of mine who died in an accident in Scotland in the 1980s. As a young Marine lieutenant he'd sailed to Jan Mayen Island with Tilman in 1968, on the voyage on which Tilman's boat 'Mischief' was lost. 'He's a bastard,' Ian told me, 'an absolute bastard. But my God, he's a hard old bastard!' From Ian there was no higher praise. Tilman is the only man I've known who was undeniably prepared for his death. The source of his serenity, good 18th-century man that he was, lay in his Christian faith. What of others who've not shared that faith? What of Jim Madsen's gloriously acerbic resignation as he slipped from his abseil rope at the top of Yosemite Valley's 3,000ft cliff El Capitan in '68? Falling past the climbers he was on his way to rescue, he calmly called to them, 'Ah, what the fuck ... '

What does it matter? Of what account is our ceasing to be, our cutting apart the Gordian knots of life, our accepting future designs as by us forever unfulfilled, our transposition from the morass of experience to the flux of history? With all those questions goes the resounding affirmative response we can give to whether or not this activity of ours, that risks life and limb, is worth its occasional cost. Dr Johnson had it that 'the known shortness of life, as it ought to moderate our passions, may likewise, with equal propriety, contract our designs.'

Why should it? Why make of life such a thing as an examination question, where due, balanced, and just consideration be given to certain elements before reaching a well-balanced and judicious conclusion? Is that a better way than to allow your mental and physical capacities a passionate engagement with the contingencies of life? Should we, in mountaineering terms, keep well within ourselves, opting in considered fashion for what's been called a 'risk-free role', or should we explore our limits? Faced with that choice, the obvious rejoinder is that it is based on the curious idea that we may avoid death. Yet accident, by its very nature, is adventitious. There is no such thing, in mountaineering or anything much besides, as a 'risk-free role.' Death, at some unknown point along the way, is inescapable.

To those who do not bear that in mind, what can you say? 'Beware, the Struldbrugs are coming!' Who would want to be like Swift's terrible, anguished, ageing immortals? In mountaineering terms, they are the mountain rescuers, who gravely pontificate on the dangers of the hills, and all the while are unacquainted with them, only with their sometime consequences. In great danger, there is great joy. Life is then very light; it weighs upon us hardly at all and could so easily be blown away: such a delicate, tenuous hold in this short span between laughter and oblivion.

The rescuers, in their great beards and heavy boots, who stump along the roads with a dull emphaticalness, bearing stretcher and winch, bound down with heavy coils of rope and the weight of saving lives, will never know this joy of toying with death. All their pronouncements are virtuous and merciful rehearsals to place on a pedestal and praise that which we should treat with detachment, levity, disdain. Nothing so very dreadful about death, in the natural order of things. Sorrow in part-ing, yes. Unfulfilment, yes. A certain selfish grief at the loss of the company of friends. (How dearly I have loved, and would wish still to be able to enjoy the com-pany of, Biven, Tilman, Estcourt, Harris). But nothing about it that's so very dreadful. A shocking moment beyond recognition of accident and then release, res-ignation, and for a time, grief. To attempt to avoid the possibility of which is to follow the example of Aeschylus, of whom it was prophesied that he would be killed by the fall of a house. So he kept out of doors, only to be killed by a tortoise which escaped from the talons of an eagle flying above. Prudence, as the Greeks knew, is no guard against cosmic jokery.

And so to Arnold Pines. A month or two ago I went out one afternoon for a walk. Pen yr Oleu Wen first, that great down-bound escalator of scree above the Ogwen tea shack. I limped along the exquisite ridge above Ysgolion Duon in hissing squalls of hail and a blustery east wind, stopped briefly on Carnedd Llywelyn to drink tea by the icy summit cairn and admire a coppery October sunset on Caernarfon Bay, then turned to descend over Craig yr Ysfa to Ffynnon Llugwy.

At the top of Craig yr Ysfa, a party of two had just finished Amphitheatre Buttress and another party was engaged on the final pitch – a couple of youngish men and one in his late 50s. There was a great deal of teasing and jocularity as the older man climbed. I sat and watched as they came up, then set off down slowly as I had torn ligaments in an ankle, cartilage trouble in a knee. The younger members of the party overtook me on the zig-zags down to Llugwy, but not their companion. Darkness was falling over the lake and only a glimmer of light remained higher up. I sat down by the path and looked for the older man; I could see him well above me, faltering down the scree, setting off little trickling falls of stone the component sounds of which were curiously sharp and amplified against the windless quiet of the cwm. I waited, and when he came up with me, offered him tea from my flask, stewed and foul though it was, thinking he might be tired. Then we set off together along the path, well suited to each other's hobbling pace.

On that walk down, I learnt several things about my companion, but not his name. I learnt that four years before he had been to Nanda Devi, that we knew some of the same people, that he was a doctor, lived in Hertfordshire. I gleaned something of the way he felt about being in the mountains, about the climbs he'd done, his family, and the times he would be back here. It was no more than a chance encounter, a half-hour's idling conversation as we walked down in the autumn darkness to the valley. At the road we parted, he a few yards left to where his friends were waiting, and I to walk along to Idwal Cottage and my car. I don't know who he was, but a few weeks later a 58-year-old doctor from Hertfordshire, who had been to Nanda Devi, died in a climbing accident on Tryfan. A hold fractured as he was soloing on easy ground, and he fell. His name was Arnold Pines, and he may or may not have been my companion of that evening. I don't know, and it doesn't matter.

The point is simply that someone died in a climbing accident on Tryfan, that his death was unexpected, its time and place unforeseen to him or to either of us as we walked towards its moment in the gathering darkness that evening. It seems best to end with another quotation from Montaigne, who would, surely, have appreciated the point:

'Did you think never to arrive at a place you were incessantly making for? Yet there is no road but has an end. And if society is any comfort to you, is not the world going the selfsame way as you?'

23: OCTOBER (1987)

It is the eighth month, the harvest month. Except that it is no longer the eighth month but the tenth, whatever it may have been to the ancient Romans (who had only ten months, of which this was the eighth). This is to play with number (Numa was the inventor of January and February), which they say holds sway over the flux. But count the days, count the lunar cycles as we will, we cannot allay loss of the green hours, or even divert the trickle of time. This is the red month, the year brittle with age and ready for the fire. The tendon snags in its sheath, the bone once broken nags its pain; but the days are so few now that we have to stumble on. The equinox is past; light gives way to the night.

You should start climbing in the spring of the year and the life – giving the impulse time to establish itself before the fingers chill and winter comes. Also, because you are set thus in the cycle your senses feel no dissonance between activity and age, attune more directly therefore to what we should notice in the environments among which we move: the jackdaw chicks which hissed at our hand in that April crack; the hyacinth fragrance of bluebells beneath those boulders in May; or purple-veined *Lloydia* around us in all its delicate rarity as we lay on that Devil's Kitchen ledge the next day – all are chiming with our green age. Memories accumulate, to enrich in the long perspective the landscapes they inhabit. Come October, comes their synthesis, and the time to gather, revisit, relive.

Let magic be encountered early. Do you know the painting by Turner, 'Norham Castle at Sunrise'? It is all yellows, mauves, ochres and almost gentian-blue shadows, utterly saturated with colour yet delicate withal and unformed, the shapes unresolved, shimmering, optimistic. There is perhaps a valley, a castle, a cow, but as yet we cannot quite tell, for behind the picture's gentian heart the sun's presence is veiled, not stated. It puts me in mind always of the October days in my first season's climbing. Do you remember what it was like to be awakened by daylight on your first outdoor mornings? You are in the Grand Hotel, say, as the carved name above Robin Hood's Balcony Cave at Stanage calls it. Your companions – having had a skinful of beer in *The Scotsman's Pack* last night which you, as a 13-year-old, could not afford and were not allowed – are still snoring. You slither in your sleeping bag across the sandy floor, out of the entrance, over to the lip of the ledge. The cold air of morning on your bare shoulders causes you to shiver a little and shrink down in your cocoon. In front of you, from the pupa and chrysalis of the night, the birth pangs of the butterfly day are being enacted. There is a sea wash and a swirl of white mist in the valley floor. It is all in motion, vaporous tongues licking at elephant peaks which laze on a white savannah: Win Hill, Lose Hill, Bleaklow stretched out, with the sun not yet risen behind you so the colours are muted – but they will come, the bracken will crackle aflame among spectrums of heather, the mist will boil and distil, suggestion will resolve into form, it will all happen before your eyes on this autumn morning of your youth with much of your life before you and the whole day in which, perhaps, to climb.

Gritstone's the rock for autumn, the rowan fronds bright-berried across its grey-green walls, the leaves gathering to rot down in the dank undercliff, the fairy toadstools in the woods beneath. Its scale is all so appropriate. The day less expansive now, the intimacy of the crags keys in to the season as if the months' passage had shape-softened them into their blunt roundness of character. Every year, Indian summer! Or so it seemed in youth. It is not the great memories necessarily which remain. They have become too token, too oppressively of their stage of life, too often relived. It is the small glimpses come at by chance which retain their capacity for surprise. On a London train, during dull discussion at a committee, or sitting on your child's bed waiting to read him a story when he comes from cleaning his teeth, suddenly you're transported to that climb, that October day so very long gone. It is here now! There is no continuity. It is a single frame, a still from the life-film, a scene you'd always cut in the editing of your own story. There is a boy, slim and dark-haired, the rock and his clothes both drab against the autumn leaves. He is looking up, holding the rope, shouting encouragement. I turn to listen, half-irritated, testily ask to be allowed to concentrate: on a scoop just above knee-height in the surface of the rock, a ripple rubbed clean by the wear of feet, a rawness, pink flesh of sandgrains showing through. It glows in the afternoon sun. The rope runs down freely into his hands, no runners. He is 30 feet below and to one side. There are boulders beneath. Grains of sand, solidified, bite into the soles of my boots. I can feel them intensely, not in their individuality but in their effect. His voice comes up again, intrudes into my enjoyment of the feel of my body, its springy relaxedness on this sloping foothold, its caress of the round edge which I must somehow use to pivot around, to impel me upwards to that hold three feet out of reach above. The mind is at work, grappling with aesthetic conviction, calculating moment and force, and all of it instinctively done. My right fingertips, wrist cocked, squeeze the edge. I palm the rock with my left hand, leaning that way, curve out my knee and lift the rim of my right boot in total enjoyment of the precise, easy movement as it places itself just so in the scoop. And then – it is happening – the electric impulse from foot to hand to hip, and their suave hoist, reciprocity and interlock. Ah! I have made of those moves an elegance! I have done them well! There is happiness, smiles, relaxation. It will sustain me tomorrow in school as I stumble through the conjugation of irregular Latin verbs which I ought at this moment to be learning. It all fades. It is all gone. I am back on my son's bed with *The Magic Paintbrush* in my hand again and the first time I ever did *Sunset Slab* on Froggatt returns to the brain cell which holds it, to delight again, perhaps, at some future time, or to die in darkness.

The companionship, the friends you've made, figure large in these memories. Good days in good company have their own rich warmth and flavour to impart. Roll the years forward from that scene on Froggatt, and more than two decades later an October day in 1982 flickers on to the screen. Stanage again, but this time with Jill Lawrence. We drive down to it from Barnsley through all the furls and rolls of purple moorland by Langsett and Ladybower. If I had been taken out of time for those 20 years and were suddenly returned to the scene, the contrast would astonish. The crowds swarm, cars are parked on either side of the road in either direction for half a mile and more. The climbers themselves are so different. All the fawns and ragged greys, the tattered jumpers, the rusting krabs, the furry grey stiffness of nylon ropes and slings, have given way to bright multiplicity of colour and a purposeful adornment of equipmental intricacies. Yet the gaiety of outward show, the harlequin pants and jingle of Rock and Friend, is balanced by a seriousness of demeanour. These climbers are intent on acquisition, on attainment of objectives. Things will not just happen, they will be made to happen. It is not a world in which the friends with whom I grew up could easily have belonged. I try to imagine characters like Arthur Nirk and Pie-can and Brian Sullivan dressed up like this and behaving like this, and laugh aloud at how they would have relished the former, rejected and ruined the composure of the latter. But our old anarchic world of outside is subsumed now into convention and formality.

Still, we have arrived and parked at Stanage and if we look along the crag, there are great gaps in the crowds. It is only by the collectable routes that the people mill and gather. We walk up along the broadening track with the hillsides around not vibrant as they are in spring or in evening sunlight after rain, but pulsing with a soft resonance of light. It is easy at times to understand those old theories of the objects of vision transmitting not reflected but their own light to the eye. It is like the miracle of sitting by a fire of coal or wood on winter evenings and feeling in its heat and flame the release of energies born of ancient sunlight.

We arrived at the crag. Geraldine Taylor had just come down after a session working on *The Dangler* and that induced more positive thoughts. If ever a route had offered gender-stereotyping, even down to the matter of its name, it was *The Dangler* – the big, butch, macho crack up which real men with real muscles forced their way, the whole scenario replete with images of sexual energy and violation. Yet I remember Barry Webb in drunken play swinging unroped across its roof on his way back from the pub. I remember the last time I did it, a year or two ago, cocksure, keyed in to memory bank with my imagination on other things, like a jaded lover going through the motions. But at the lip, my fingers on the edge, the programme went blank. I pulled up, people watching, the last runner too far back, arms weakening, unable to reach into the top crack, panic and impotence hovering, the memory-message insistently pleading the move's straightforwardness and ease and the body crying out that it was not so, this ridiculous conflict continuing until the logical mind stepped in: 'Look, old chap, you just throw your right elbow over and get in an arm lock.' Ah, so you do! Panic subsides, tension dissipates, laughter supervenes. 'Just thought I'd do a few pull-ups for exercise, Pete,' I call down, and afterwards expiate this arrogant irony by confessing to him my panic and forgetfulness.

Jill and I talk with Geraldine. She is excited, fired by a desire, insistent, working logically on mistake and weakness, psyching up for the next attempt, at which she will get it right. It is good to watch someone in this honest and painful process. We move along the crag, take the traditional entry into a day by soloing the Rusty Wall routes – up *Rugosity*, with its skip-and-cling of a 5c first move, down *Green Crack*; up *Rusty Wall* of the pinch-and-lurch, down *Via Media*; up *Via Dexter*, cautiously, and down *Oblique Crack*. The feel of the rock, the sense of its friction, the tuning of the body-pitch, is achieved. We move on. It is to be a day on the classics. *Harding's Super-direct finish* to the *Cave Innominate* comes first, a wild, swinging one-armed jugpull right at the top of the crag and surely one of the best 15ft routes in Britain.

We pass on through the crowds and fetch up at *Pedlar's Slab*, snort with disgust at the chipped hold at its base and work through its three-route repertoire – the slab, the arête, the rib, soloing again, building up an ease and support between us that relaxes into the climbing and enables us both to move better and more rhythmically. It is the desire that the other should enjoy the routes that is coming out, and not that so-often-dreadful-in-its-effect game where the other must be outdone. On *Pedlar's Rib* I step up blind-footed and ask if my boot's on the hold before moving on. She guides it there.

At her turn I stand beneath, confident and aware of what she can do and remind her of the hold not obvious from where she is. It is the brief gestures, the respectful minimalism of assistance, the arm slipped round a waist and then away again, not in sexual play but in friendship and support, which state the harmony, and thrill and thanks. The day goes on: *The Unconquerables, Goliath's Groove, Wall End Slab*

Direct, Tower Face Direct. There is a cool, gold wind blowing across the crag and a rhythm of chatter and silence between us. On *Tower Face* I watch her face on those creaking flakes which make the climb far harder than its given grade of HVS 5a and marvel at the honesty of emotion portrayed there: alertness, apprehension, the awareness of vulnerability. It is all so different to the non-expression of rock technocracy. And the bodily movements too have an effortless, rhythmical quality quite different to the thrusting economy of the best male climbers. Their characteristic is a lightness, a fluidity of movement centering around the pivot of the hips, an exquisite and almost formalised balance like that of Indian dance.

The crowds have drifted away as we work back – though work is the wrong word for this activity – along the crag. The light's going as we descend, and there are different points of the compass to which we must head. She goes north, my way's west. There is a spontaneous embrace by the cars at the recognition of how it was, a brief, warm kiss – one of the moments of contact which make endurable the deserts of solitude. All's then given over into October memories, harvested and stored away on the long drive west.

And West is the real October country. There is the low-angled light slanting into the hills and against the cliffs. There is the way the richness of texture in the rocks, the veins and foldings, the crystals and the ribs and the stippled lichens soak in the soft brilliance of the sun. There are the hillside woods like old tapestry or brocade, which seem to tell of stories set there. Wales – the text of its landscape is more resonant than that of any other country. And all the stories and histories have that autumn twilight quality, diffused and haunting and lingering down the sterile times of winter coming – for an industry, for a people, for a culture. They are so old, as old as the year in October. They rustle their suggestions among the quiet places of the hills, the soft clatter of their names like leaf-fall in a forest. In that oak-tree roosted the eagle from whose flesh the maggots fell. This split rock here was cleft by the flung spear. But it was so long ago. The barracks of the quarryman who came after that time, they are occupied now by the elder and the ash. Where the kettle hissed after the day's work, the leaf falls; where the fire flamed, the rowan flames. That wall blew down in the equinoctial gales, but who knows how long ago? It is gone, the memory, just as this year is going to join it, just as our years have added something before they rot, or are lost, or used up from the long store.

October, you are crowded with ghosts. Here, walking by my side over the road from Deiniolen with the morning sun in our faces, is John Brazinton. I am not even sure of the year – the autumn of 1969, perhaps, or 1970? We trek from Deiniolen to Llech Ddu, on foot, the wild ponies winter-coated now and watchful across the Afon Llafar, the grass bleached tawny summerlong by the sun and rain, the path squelchy with moisture. It is a return visit. Once before this same year I have come this way – to climb *The Groove* with Brian Fuller, that strange, sardonic, likeable member of the Rock and Ice and Bradford Lads generation whose nickname was Fred the Ted. We had arrived beneath the great scar of rock up which *The Groove* cleaves its way, sat down to talk and gear up, and heard a whistling in the air above us. A sheep, fallen from a ledge 400 feet up, landed 20 feet away, spattering us with blood and intestine. We joked about it, wiped ourselves clean, took out sandwiches, and were disturbed by another whistling in the air. The same again, almost the identical place. We felt nauseated. Minutes passed. We roped up, studied the first groove. A shadow hung in the air above us, whooshed past, exploded by its two former companions, predeceased. We felt hunted, crept away to a quiet VS round the corner.

But this time, with John, the mood is lighter-hearted. He, at 19 or 20, is my apprentice and I, at 22 or 23, am supposed to be the young star and we want to do the route free. Mo and Cam (neither of them ever known by anything other than these names), who did the first ascent four or five years beforehand, had given perhaps the only completely honest first ascent description written for a post-war route in Wales, mentioning every point of attachment used, whether for aid or gardening. Either through malice or uninformed gossip, thereafter the climb had been looked on as overaided, four or five aid-points in 400 feet.

It is odd how fragmented your memories become over long periods of time. Three sections only of the route come back to me. There is a wet, loose, dripping bulge somewhere near the beginning – perhaps on the second pitch – where I had to layback on a downward spike which moved out towards me as if daring me to see what would happen if I pulled harder. There is a traverse left across a steep wall, with hard, blind moves into a shallow groove where a sidepull came off in my hand and I nearly swung off with it, and turned to swear at John for no better reason than that he was the only thing around who would take any notice. And finally, there is a stance in slings in the groove itself from which *The Groove* gets its name, and the near-disappointment of just pulling from hold to hold in an easy ecstasy of strength. I remember very little, then, about the route, nothing about getting back down to the foot of the crag, only vaguely recall the peaceful trudge out along Cwm Llafar towards the evening sun and the descent in darkness into Bethesda. But it's as clear as yesterday to me, the pleasure of going into the *Douglas Arms* and finding Keith Carr there in a corner of the front room.

Keith was a member of the Wallasey Mountaineering Club, which was one of the liveliest and most anarchic organisations in Welsh climbing. It had its heyday in the late 1950s and early 1960s, and was based at a converted barn set on a hillock right in the middle of Nant Gwynant, beneath Clogwyn y Wenallt. The club had close associations with Ogwen Cottage before that place became the staid outdoor centre of a local education authority. Its members were people like Mo Anthoine, Davey Jones, Ginger Cain, Terry Vasey, all of whom were climbing at the very top standards of the time, but it wasn't as a climbing ginger-group that the Wallasey was well-known. It was the originator of the tradition of the wild party which reached its climax in the Al Harris bacchanals of 15 or 20 years later. The barn in the Gwynant was the perfect site – no fear of intrusion, objection or the giving of offence. The beer would be imported by the barrel, there would be none of the strobe-and-disco suppressions of the daemonic imagination on the crutches of which today's partygoers lean. Instead there were the evil geniuses, the out-drinking, out-phasing and out-grossing gamesmen (and women) and performers, all thrashing around in pursuit of the fiercest squeal of shock or outrage the evening could produce. Whose is that body the head belonging to which is under X's skirt? Why is Joe Brown helplessly giggling on the floor in a corner? What is the well-known warden of a mountain centre doing walking around dressed in nothing but his wife's underclothes? When will those three figures thrashing on the top bunk roll senseless to the floor?

The rhythm builds to a crescendo, noise and hilarity and confusion mount. The lords of misrule are gathering. A space clears round the stove in the centre of the barn. The men throw off their clothes and roll tightly a spill of newspaper – the older hands rolling it the more tightly for slower combustion. They light it at the stove, clench it between their buttocks and dance round in fiery, smokey display, the women cheering them on. Those who've not rolled the spill tightly enough soon howl, clasp their posteriors and mingle back among the watchers. The cunning old foxes dance on, their wives and girlfriends re-lighting the brand when it smoulders out. Smoke coils into the rafters and the flames reflect on faces whose humours are worthy of Bruegel. The hilarity pitches higher and hysterically higher until the last dancer pirouettes incombustible and supreme. And then every man who has taken part ritually gathers round to piss on the stove. *Epater les Bourgeois?* Even the Great Beast Aleister Crowley would have been proud, and this was enacted most weekends at these Wallasey parties under the title, 'dance of the flaming arsehole'. It was over times like these that Keith Carr, John Brazinton and myself squawked and joked this October evening in *The Douglas*, and continued late into the night back at his house in Mynydd Llandegai before John and myself walked back to Deiniolen over the moor in the moonlight, with the sea glinting down in Caernarfon Bay and the light on Llanddwyn Island flashing out to us.

Now the play's gone, the summer's over, the nights are drawing in. John and Keith, companions in reminiscence those many years ago, are both dead: John killed by stonefall in the Chamonix Aiguilles the season after we did our route together, having volunteered typically to go back up to the foot of a route to collect his and his partner's sack. And Keith, in his forties, of cancer or another such gratuitous disease. All along your path you lose the friends you make and only your memory keeps their names alive: John, with whom I enjoyed this day's climbing of a quality I've not often known; Keith, in whose warmth and wit I've basked and revelled many times in the pubs and convivialities of the climbing world. The months, the years draw on. The leaves fall.

Let me go to the sea to rid myself of this despondent mood! One weekend in October of 1971 springs to mind. I'm living in London. John Kingston, Rob Ford and myself are going to Pembroke and on the Friday we set off in John's Sunbeam Rapier down the M4, which ends at Cardiff. We bear on down through Morriston and Pontardawe, Carmarthen and St Clear's, rattling on all the while in one of those wonderful London weekend protracted arguments which passes away the long driving hours and covers every topic from politics and the Stock Exchange to sexual anthropology and the invertebrate life of Hemel Hempstead before bringing us after midnight to the deserted and derelict cottages (National Trust holiday lets now) at Stackpole Quay, where we creep upstairs, spread out sleeping bags on the dusty floor, and rap out our concluding comments before sleep rules all further discussion out of order.

The next morning we breakfast on cream cakes in Pembroke and walk across the untrodden, clean-washed beach of Barafundle to Mowing Word. All those miles of coast along to Stack Rocks from St Govan's, where new routes were done in their hundreds in later years, we ignore. We're not here to pioneer, don't feel like the mental strain involved in that. All we want to do is disport ourselves a little on known rock in the late-season sun. We solo down *Square Chimney*, always a good little test-piece to see how the nerves will cope with the day's climbing. On the wave-platform beneath we skip across the razor-edged scallopings and walk to the tip of the promontory. The sea's in a lovely green calm, with waving fronds of weed clearly visible deep down in the water. I point out the few existing routes. We traverse round beneath the south-west face, the sharp rock nicking and grazing at our hands, and gather beneath *Cormorant Flake*, with the water idly trickling into little coral pools. I've been thinking that a combination of the first pitch of *Heart of Darkness* and the top pitch of *New Morning* would be a perfect combination, so talk John, who's enjoying the rock and the scenery, into leading off. I psyche him up for it: 'Once you're round that arête, John, it's 100 across an overhanging wall into a bottomless corner, and then 40 feet out to a hanging stance!' What I'm omitting to tell him is that huge holds and good jams mediate the impressive situation. He launches out, disappears round the corner. After a time Rob follows, and at John's insistence, to reverse the joke, takes all the runners out. The ropes swing across a void. I reach the corner and gulp down my anxiety: 'You bastards!' I shout across. 'V Diff' John retorts. I know it's not that, and scuttle across before my arms tire. We move on up to a higher stance and I hustle for the top pitch:

'It's all jamming, this, John – you'd better let me lead!'

He does. I exult in it, a perfect thin crack running up an otherwise blank head wall for 70 feet, the rock a gorgeous bright orange colour from the sunlit lichen. The jamming's a joy – there's surely no more satisfying technique of climbing, nor any which is more elegant or relaxed. You stretch, place the jam, arch your back, run up your feet, jab in a toe, lock in one-handed, stretch and arch again in a smooth, unhurried flow. It is sensuality in movement. You ration runners – one good one every 20 feet will do – to keep the aesthetic line of that rope running down, to conserve strength and maintain the thrill. Rob and John run up and rave. We slither down *Square Chimney* again for another route or two, then give best to the incoming tide and repair to the pub. The next day we go to Mother Carey's Kitchen (which sounds like a local name but isn't), do a few routes, recover a sling left behind a month or two before, already bleached white by the sea, and as the tide comes in again we pack up and drive vociferously back home. Weekends away! What a habit and a delight they once were! But the month's ending. November looms. The clock, which goes always forwards, has gone back. Hallowe'en, All Soul's Night, Samhain, all the pagan festivals of fire and darkness concentrate in the mind.

I drive to Cwm Ystradllyn, near my home, walk up to the shoulder of Moel Hebog by way of the old, hidden and deserted quarryman's village that has no name beneath Braich y Gornel. The mist circles the hill at the level of the shoulder. It is full of presences, my mind peoples it with memory, projection and desire. With shortening breath I pant on up the slope. A stonechat chips away at silence from a rock. Where the steepness begins to relent, the cloud thins and soon there's blue sky above, and a cold wind chills across my face. I wipe the drop from my nose and leave its stain on the light green of my sleeve. Obdurately the body paces itself to the summit cairn, the rough brown rock around it solid, solid, solid to the touch. Beneath me now Nant Gwynant is fading into shadow, the brilliant golds and ochres, the yellow and orange of the trees mutely retreating out of the light, the lakes lying leadenly amongst them, the knoll where Menlove's ashes were scattered standing out like a peacock's crown in a twilight garden. Behind me, the sun is setting out at the point of the Lleyn. Ynys Enlli, the Isle of the Currents, of the Saints, hides its western Avalon or Eden behind the hump of a hill. It is getting dark now. The slope steepens in the descent. Only Bryn Banog lies before me to complete the circuit, and Moel Ddu, the black hill, which l must cross before I reach home.

24: THE WAY & THE OUTCROP (2002)

Went for a walk from Crowden the other evening – I had it in mind that I'd make that grand old circuit out by way of Hey Moss, Westend Moss and White Moss up on to White Low and Tooleyshaw Moor, across to Soldier's Lump and back by way of Red Ratcher and Laddow Rocks along the *Pennine Way*. Gritstone climbers of a certain age will have sympathy with an impulse like this. The Dark Peak is a special place. A clear, light glow of green from the young bilberry leaves was patched across the moor. Teased-out bobbing heads of bog-cotton merged across the mosses into a shimmer of pool-reflected white. I smelt the sweet, faint insistency of young heather, listened, and from nearby came a plaintive, piping alarm call of the golden plover, that, of all the sounds of nature, is one of those most perfectly of its place. I looked, and saw him 30 yards away at the edge of the heather – one of the gloriously handsome northern race, once classified as a sub-species – the intense black of his face, neck and breast set off to perfection by the white stripes on either side that curve down from the eye to the rump, and the gold-braided back glistening as it was caught by a brief foray of the sun. 'The Plover lo'es the mountain,' Burns sang. I watched him, but his eye wasn't fixed on me. That piteous note of alarm kept pleading out.

I scanned round and the reason became apparent. Gliding low, phantom-grey on the wind, a hen harrier languidly quartered the moor, pounced suddenly, wings upturned, and in a flurry of motion took to the skyway again, some small bird – a meadow-pipit maybe – held fast and limp in his talons. As he drifted away, a whirr and clatter of red grouse rose into the air, milling about clumsily before dropping back into the heather. Where I gained the curving gable of the moor – cloughs etched dark into its flanks – that encloses the secret, wide valley of Crowden Meadows, a mountain hare loped away, paused on a heather pedestal, surveyed the moor, eyes liquid-bright and ears swivelling, and bounded on. Yellow wagtails darted among the boulders and waterfalls of White Moss Slack. At the edge of Tooleyshaw Moss, suddenly, as though through a gateway, I left the enclosed groughs I'd been following, peat and heather gave way to moorland grasses and mosses, and a bare half-mile away rose the distinctive Ordnance Survey pillar on Soldier's Lump – the lonely summit of Black Hill. I hastened on, elated by the sense of space all around me, the height, the remove. With a queer, swift, slopping motion I slithered over the final, infamous surrounding pools of bare and liquid peat and arrived at – solid ground, a corbelled cairn, a flagstoned way that is the *Pennine Way* winding in from either direction, the neatness of civil engineering casting its presence and facilitation across the wilderness.

The last time I was here, on one of the Rucksack Club's annual Marsden-

Edale winter excursions six or seven years ago, the paving had only extended a little way up from the Isle of Skye road, but the peat was frozen and we skated over Black Hill's icy flats in the mist. Today I could admire the completed work in its full glory – the fine stone setts from the old mills of Lancashire and Yorkshire that were lifted up here by helicopter to be bedded and aligned across the moor. Some like them, others loathe them. Me, I'm ambivalent, think there's a pretty good image here for the way our rock-climbing's gone, about which I'm ambivalent too. I found myself musing over a passage written by the Tibetan Buddhist scholar Marco Pallis – a member of the Wayfarers' Club, and a participant, 70 years ago, in the first free ascent of Scafell's *Central Buttress*. It goes like this:

'That certain knowledge is to be picked up on the hills which elsewhere is hard to come by, under the conditions of ever-increasing sophistication that modern urban life imposes, is a commonplace for those who have sought peace of mind as well as bodily health among the mountains; for ... others, this experience extended itself to the point of opening the door, not only of unspoiled nature, but also of the traditional world in one of its most intact forms ... '

So there I sat with my back against the cairn that conceals the erstwhile concrete foundation of the Ordnance Survey pillar – and gave myself a post-modern talking-to about how I was a fortunate one, of a generation able to benefit from the resourcefulness of modern environmental management, with a nice new pavement to walk along to my next objective. I made comparisons in my mind with other constructed ways in the hills – the packhorse trails of The Peak, General Wade's military roads in Scotland, the miners' tracks in Snowdonia and the Lake District, the cotton famine roads that thread around the margins of these northern moors – remembered all the pleasure following those had given me, and the *Pennine Way Pack Animal Trail* seemed somehow not so bad after all. Rather like indoor climbing walls, or sport-routes, in fact ... a kind of fell-walking version of *Sardine*.

Forty minutes later, after a couple of miles of jarring along this upland pavement, I might have revised that opinion. I'd jolted my way over Grains Moss and Red Ratcher – more of the hidden, elementally-named places of these moors – climbed up above Crowden Great Brook, and come to the little pulpit-pinnacle that marks the northern end of Laddow Rocks.

Even now, with encroaching age, there are some things I find entirely irresistible, and snatched solos of the classic routes on the remoter gritstone outcrops – Laddow seems to have attained that status these days – is one of them. These were the places where I first came at a sense of the outdoors: there were times when, as a kid, I'd shiver away some November night propped against the wall and huddled in a blanket in the Laddow cave; the moorland night-sounds all around – grouse, fox, curlew, owl, wind; the clear morning smell of peat and bracken and heather; the roar of the primus, the first raw gulp of hot liquid, the sun probing and flooding and warming the crag. So with the shadows deepening, I slipped down the descent path, glanced up at *Cave Crack*, the revolving chockstone of which I'd wrestled with so often as a boy, made my way round to the foot of *Tower Face*, took out the rock-shoes I'd stuffed into the depths of my rucksack against just such an eventuality as this, and put them on. I packed my walking boots into my sack, strapped trekking poles on to it so I wouldn't have to come down again – always was lazy in this respect – felt at the first stiff, awkward pull through the bulge on to the slabby face above, and made it – this with sundry gruntings, scrabblings, judicious use of knee and all the other standard tricks of the ageing gritstoner. Then guiltily, joyfully, utterly alone in the cool refracted light of evening, I drifted upwards, balancing, caressing, easing cautiously and rustily into pivots and levers that I first learnt on rocks like these long decades ago, conscious of lost friends, revelling in the crystalline, rough texture of millstone grit, given to the moment in a place as familiar and attractive to me in its own way as any I know. On the other side of the valley, the bluffs of Bareholme Crag were gleaning late, pale shafts of the sun. I could see the *Bareholme Crack* and the curving wind-sculpture of *Shy Ann Arête*. I was thinking back to climbing over there with Malc Baxter and Feste Parker ten years ago when we'd looked over at Laddow and been congratulating ourselves on the unworn place we'd chosen, the lack of paths, the silken grass. But Laddow now is going back, the moor slowly reclaiming it, the lichens fretting and flowering at the edges of the polished holds.

Sitting on top, dangling my legs over 60 feet of perfect gritstone climbing, the post-adrenaline rush intensifying all perception to a kind of mystical and all-embracing beauty and calm, I felt glad that this had been my sport throughout most of my life – that I'd learnt its lessons, drawn from it and invested in it a sustaining pride, could delight in its harmless and gentle pleasures still. And there was another thing, too – difficult to express. That pavement down from Black Hill, I'd been helped and eased and directed along every foot of the way by it to get here – and yet, climbing for me has always at best had about it a kind of errant delight, an extempore surrender to the moment. Where we build the way, we lose the way, perhaps? What's your sports plan, this year? Talked with your trainer, your sports psychologist, about it … ? Still have time to look around, to see … ? Think you can spare an afternoon out from the schedules to wander up to the Crow Stones beneath Outer Edge, eat cloudberries on the way, boulder on those hidden, silvered, unvisited walls that gaze into the dark heart of Bleaklow, find time to stand atop the pinnacle and slither down the wind-worn chimney again, sleep maybe in that exquisite sandy bivouac under its capping slab and wake to the calls of the grouse and the morning scent of the earth itself, rich and musky and sharp as a woman's...?

After a little more time on the edge of rock, among the memories, I put my boots back on, poured out the remnants of my thermos flask as libation to the tutelary spirits and joined the old way that comes in by way of Wilderness from the Chew Valley, to straggle down to Crowden again, and friends' company, and all the goodness of life in this glowing, numinous world.

That we didn't build ...